Explore the Wonders of the Universe: Revealing Cosmic Secrets.

Jovan .Q Patel

All rights reserved.

Copyright © 2024 Jovan .Q Patel

Explore the Wonders of the Universe: Revealing Cosmic Secrets. : Discover the Mysteries of Outer Space: Unveiling Secrets of the Cosmos.

___Funny helpful tips:___

Avoid taking conflicts to bed; resolving issues ensures peace of mind.

Cultivate a habit of reading; it broadens perspectives and enhances knowledge.

Life advices:

Rotate between solo and group reading; shared experiences can enhance comprehension and enjoyment.

When faced with adversity, remember that the strongest trees grow in the windiest conditions.

Introduction

Welcome to this book, your gateway to the captivating wonders above. In this guide, we will explore the beauty and mysteries of the celestial realm, making stargazing accessible and enjoyable for everyone.

Discover the amazing things you can see in the night sky, from twinkling stars to dazzling constellations. We'll provide you with signposts to the stars, guiding you to locate prominent celestial bodies.

Navigate the night sky confidently with star charts and learn about the visible constellations. We'll delve into the fascinating stories behind each constellation, connecting you with the myths and legends of ancient cultures.

Embark on an astronomical journey through the constellations, starting with Andromeda, Aquarius, Aquila, Aries, and Auriga. Explore the cosmic tales of Boötes, Cancer, Canes Venatici, Canis Major, and Canis Minor.

Discover the Winter Triangle, a captivating formation in the cold months, and encounter Capricornus, Cassiopeia, and Cepheus. Dive into the captivating legends of Cetus, Coma Berenices, Corona Borealis, Corvus, and Crater.

Unravel the celestial stories of Cygnus, Delphinus, Draco, Gemini, Hercules, Leo, Lepus, Libra, Lyra, and Ophiuchus. Embrace the tales of Orion, Pegasus, Equuleus, Perseus, Pisces, Sagitta, Vulpecula, Sagittarius, Scorpius, Serpens, and Taurus.

Venture further into the night sky with Ursa Major, Ursa Minor, and Virgo, and trace the arc to Arcturus and speed on to Spica.

Finally, we'll introduce you to the awe-inspiring Summer Triangle, a prominent asterism that graces the sky during warmer months.

By the end of this guide, you'll be equipped with the knowledge and enthusiasm to explore the night sky with confidence and wonder. Get ready to embark on a celestial adventure and let the stars be your guide!

Contents

The Things You Can See 1
About the Deep Sky Objects 2
Multiple Stars 9
Variable Stars 11
Star Clusters 11
Nebulae 15
Galaxies 17
Signposts to the Stars 20
Ursa Major 21
Orion 21
Star Charts & Visible Constellations 22
Star Chart Tables 23
Chart 1 47
Chart 2 48
Chart 3 49
Chart 4 50
Chart 5 51
Chart 6 52
Chart 7 53
Chart 8 54
Chart 9 55
Chart 10 56
Chart 11 57
Chart 12 58

Chart 13 59
Chart 14 60
Chart 15 61
Chart 16 62
Chart 17 63
Chart 18 64
Chart 19 65
Chart 20 66
Chart 21 67
Chart 22 68
Chart 23 69
Chart 24 70
The Constellations 71
Andromeda 72
Aquarius 78
Aquila 84
Aries 89
Auriga 95
Boötes 100
Cancer 105
Canes Venatici 110
Canis Major 117
Canis Minor 123
The Winter Triangle 125
Capricornus 126
Cassiopeia 132
Cepheus 136

The Constellations of the Andromeda Legend 138
Cetus 141
Coma Berenices 143
Corona Borealis 148
Corvus & Crater 153
Cygnus 159
Delphinus 166
Draco 171
Gemini 177
Hercules 183
Leo 188
Lepus 195
Libra 201
Lyra 207
Ophiuchus 213
Orion 219
Pegasus & Equuleus 224
Perseus 230
Pisces 236
Sagitta and Vulpecula 238
Sagittarius 244
Scorpius 250
Serpens 256
Taurus 261
Ursa Major 267
Ursa Minor 273
Virgo 278

Arc Down to Arcturus and Speed On to Spica! 280
The Summer Triangle 283
The Greek Alphabet 287

The Things You Can See

About the Deep Sky Objects

Many of the objects mentioned in this book should be easily seen with just your eyes or binoculars – but, as stated earlier, some of the binocular objects may be a challenge and there might be a few objects that can only be observed with a small telescope. To some extent this is unavoidable; bright and easy objects are not evenly distributed throughout the sky and, consequently, some constellations and objects are easier to find and observe than others.

Wherever possible, I've tried to stick to the objects that can be seen with binoculars as many households will have a pair available. I own 8x30 and 10x50 binoculars; the first number is the magnification and the second is the width of the "objective lens" – that is, the lenses that point up toward the sky. The 10x50 binoculars provide a slightly higher magnification (10x, in this case) and with 50mm lenses the binoculars are able to gather more light, making it possible to see more as a result.

(10x50 binoculars are a good choice for astronomy, especially if you're just getting started. You can buy larger binoculars but, of course, they'll be heavier and may require a tripod for steady viewing. 10x50 binoculars are still light enough to be used over an extended period of time without your arms getting fatigued.)

My [Celestron](#) UpClose G2 10x50's are excellent for observing the night sky. Of course, there are other 10x50's by other manufacturers - [Orion](#), for example, have a binocular stargazing kit for less than a family meal at a restaurant - and a decent pair won't cost an arm and a leg. Even if your binoculars are smaller or older (as a kid, I used my step-grandfather's binoculars from World War I) or you feel your binoculars aren't the best for whatever reason, use them anyway because I always believe that *something* is better than *nothing*.

Binoculars are an excellent starting point for anyone interested in learning more about the night sky. Not only are they inexpensive, but it's often easier to find objects as they provide a wider field of view compared to a telescope. There's also something to be said for hunting down (and bagging) a target as opposed to letting a GoTo telescope find it for you. (Think of it like learning to ride a bike before learning to ride a motorcycle.)

And, unlike an astronomical telescope that will invert your view, binoculars can be used during the daytime too. (My girlfriend and I take ours to the beach for whale watching!)

Finding a highlighted object doesn't just depend upon your skill as an observer or how good your binoculars are – it will also greatly depend upon the sky conditions at your location. Assuming the skies are clear, your location may also be adversely affected by light pollution. Light from nearby towns and cities can brighten the sky and make it harder to see the fainter objects in the sky.

This is, basically, why you can't see the stars during the daytime. The light of the Sun brightens the sky and makes it impossible to see the stars, and the full Moon has a similar effect. This will prove to be important as you hunt for fainter targets, such as variable stars, star clusters, nebulae and galaxies, but bright stars will mostly be unaffected.

Before we get started, let's take a few moments to review the information to be found within this book You'll need to be aware of a few things before proceeding.

For each constellation I've provided a star chart showing the constellation and the stars surrounding it. I've also labelled the stars named in the text to make it easier to identify any objects of interest.

Besides the chart of the general area, most constellations will also further review featured stars and objects and will include three images to illustrate the objects being discussed.

Some of these images will show an *asterism* to be found within the constellation. An asterism is a pattern to be found within the larger context of the constellation itself. The best (and most famous) example is the asterism of seven bright stars in Ursa Major, the Great Bear. This asterism is famously known as the Plough in the United Kingdom and the Big Dipper in North America.

This pattern is so well known that many people think it's the constellation itself, but in reality, the constellation contains many fainter stars and is much larger than the asterism formed by these seven stars.

Besides asterisms, these images will also show you the simulated view through 10x50 binoculars of the highlighted objects. This is based upon my own Celestron binoculars and your view might vary slightly, but hopefully it'll provide you a good idea of what to expect.

There are a few other things to bear in mind when looking at these simulations.

Firstly, the other deep sky objects are drawn depicting their true size in the sky. In reality, you won't see most of the objects this large in your binoculars unless you're observing under very dark skies. As stated earlier, what you'll see depends upon your equipment, your location, the sky conditions at the time and your own eyesight. The same is true of some of the background stars depicted; how many you'll see will, again, depend upon those same factors.

Also, it's difficult to accurately depict the multiple stars because, in order to show which stars are brightest, it's necessary to make the dots representing the stars larger. So some stars may be depicted as being much closer together – or even overlapping – because at least one of the stars is bright and the pair might be quite close.

All the charts and simulations were created using the Mobile Observatory app for Wolfgang Zima. Unfortunately, it's only available for Android devices but I consider it an invaluable tool and it's still the only astronomy app I'll use on a daily basis. (You can find it on Google Play and there's more information at http://zima.co)

Of the text itself, wherever possible I discuss the mythology associated with the constellation and then I give a little information on that constellation's brightest star.

I've discussed these stars as potential objects of interest; for example, many have interesting names that tie in with the constellation itself or have features that set them apart from other stars.

The names of the stars are often Arabic in origin, but you'll notice some may have names like "Gamma Delphini." The first part of the name (gamma, in this example) is a letter of the Greek alphabet. Thousands of years ago, the Greeks assigned letters to the stars based upon their brightness. So the brightest star in the constellation would be assigned the letter Alpha – their equivalent of the letter A. The second brightest would be Beta, then Gamma, Delta and so forth. (There's a table detailing the Greek alphabet in the Appendix.)

The second part of the name refers to the constellation the star belongs to – in this example, Delphini refers to Delphinus, the Dolphin.

The system has been refined and updated since then, but it's still very widely used. After all, not every star in the sky can have a name and this is an easy, convenient alternative.

Some stars may have a number, such as 53 Cancri. Although the brighter stars have these numbers too, they're more commonly associated with the fainter stars as these weren't easily visible to the ancients. However, with binoculars or a small telescope these stars can be more easily seen and catalogued.

The number refers to their position within the constellation with the more westerly stars having a lower designation. For example, the most westerly star in the constellation of Cancer would have the designation 1 Cancri. The number of stars in the constellation will vary, as not all the constellations are the same size and each constellation will have a different number of stars.

Of the other stars, many constellations contain double or multiple stars and variable stars that can be observed with binoculars. I've provided a little more information regarding the nature of these objects on here.

Besides the stars themselves, the constellations also contain what are commonly called *deep sky objects.* These are star clusters, nebulae and galaxies and some of these objects may have their own names, such as the Andromeda Galaxy or the Owl Cluster. More often than not, they're named after whatever the object resembles (such as an owl) or sometimes the constellation it resides in (such as Andromeda.)

The book also mentions Messier objects. These are objects that were noted by the French comet hunter Charles Messier in the 18th century. Some deep sky objects can appear distinctly comet-like (especially globular star clusters) and Messier wanted to avoid confusing them with any potential discovery.

Charles Messier, public domain image.

There are 110 Messier objects in all and this book mentions 36 of them. Some are actually quite clearly not comets – for example, the Pleiades – and many astronomers have wondered why Messier went to the trouble of cataloging them. Other objects, such as the famous Double Cluster or the Owl Cluster, are easily visible and yet

Messier didn't list them at all. You will often see Messier objects with an "M" designation; for example, Messier 45 (the Pleiades) is often referred to as M45.

Whether we're talking about stars or deep sky objects, all these sights will have a *magnitude*, which is basically a measure of the object's brightness. The lower an object's magnitude, the brighter the object. For example, Sirius, the brightest star in the sky, has a magnitude of -1.4 and most suburban locations will allow you to see stars to about magnitude 4. A good rural location, far away from any light pollution, might provide skies dark enough to see stars down to around magnitude 6 or even fainter. This makes the difference between seeing a few hundred stars and a few thousand!

Obviously, again, the number of stars you see will also depend upon your eyesight and the conditions of the sky above you, but generally speaking a person with good eyesight should be able to see stars to about magnitude 5.5 under clear, dark skies. Binoculars will extend the view out to around magnitude 9 (again, depending on the quality and size of the binoculars) and a telescope will allow you to see much fainter objects still.

You'll notice there are no photos of the objects and there's two very good reasons for this. Firstly, more often than not, they don't accurately depict what you'll see with your eyes, binoculars or through a telescope. Too many new astronomers get discouraged because they see beautiful, colorful images in magazines and online and expect to see something similar. Those photographs are created by dedicated individuals who'll spend hours combining many images and fine tuning the final result until it's the best it can be.

I don't want you to be discouraged; the night sky can be stunning and awe inspiring but sometimes you have to use a little imagination and truly take into account what you're looking at, especially when it comes to binocular views. You may not see much of the object through binoculars, but when you consider what it is you're actually looking at, the view can suddenly become quite amazing!

The other reason relates to Kindle and eBooks in general. Adding images can greatly increase the file size of the eBook and this can cause problems with downloads and distribution. As it is, there are over 120 images in the book!

With both these reasons in mind, I've kept the use of images to a minimum and have tried to optimize the star chart images to provide the best view without compromising quality.

Multiple Stars

I hate the phrase "star gazing." For me, it always conjures up an image of someone standing still, staring up at the night sky. Or maybe peering through a telescope at a single bright star. Someone else might walk by. "What are you looking at?" they ask. The observer points up at the sky. "That bright star. That one, right there."

Many non-astronomers think this is what "star gazers" do. It's like when I stopped eating white and red meat during the 1990's. People thought I just ate peas and carrots instead. (Incidentally, I've since returned to the dark side.)

Nothing could be further from the truth, especially given that many stars are not single stars at all. In fact, most of them are *multiple* stars. To the unaided eye, they'll appear to be a single star, but when you observe them with binoculars or a telescope, that star is split in two. Some stars may have three or four components.

There are two kinds of multiple stars: those that are true multiple star systems, where the stars orbit one another, and those that are *optical* doubles and only appear close together due to a chance alignment. In reality, they may be light years apart.

The best thing about multiple stars (beside their abundancy and variety) is that they're largely unaffected by moonlight and light pollution. As long as both components are reasonably bright (such as Kuma), they'll still shine through the brightened sky caused by an intrusive Moon.

The double star Kuma, aka Nu Draconis. Image by the author using Slooh.

Variable Stars

On occasion I'll mention a *variable star* that can be observed in the constellation. As the name suggests, these are stars that typically appear to vary in brightness over a period of time. Some may change brightness over a matter of hours, some will take a few days while others (and more commonly) may take tens or even hundreds of days.

For example, one of the most famous variable stars is Algol in the constellation of Perseus. Its normal brightness is magnitude 2.1 but it will fade to magnitude 3.4 for about ten hours and then return to magnitude 2.1 again. In all, it takes 2 days, 20 hours and 49 minutes to complete this cycle. This is known as its *period.*

Why does this happen? Algol is the class example of an *eclipsing* variable. Unseen to our eyes is a smaller, fainter companion that regularly passes in front of the brighter star and dims its light. Hence, the magnitude appears to drop as the star fades. The faint companion takes ten hours to move across the face of the brighter star and then Algol brightens as the eclipse comes to an end.

Not all variable stars are the same. Most have much longer periods and are often red giant stars nearing the end of their lives. Their brightness changes as the star pulsates, like a heart beat, as the star expands and contracts over a regular period of time. Others are irregular and unpredictable while some are classified as recurring novae – stars that suddenly and inexplicably brighten before fading and unpredictably brightening again.

Star Clusters

Star clusters also fall into two categories: open star clusters and globular star clusters. An open star cluster contains tens or hundreds of stars, all of which literally appear clustered together in the same relatively small area of sky. This is not a chance alignment – these stars are genuinely grouped close together in space and are born from the same nebula. Consequently, they're usually quite young and are quite literally, stellar siblings.

A few clusters appear fairly large and only require binoculars with member stars scattered across the field of view. The famous Pleiades and Hyades open clusters are excellent examples. Others are small and compact and may require the higher magnification of a telescope to be properly appreciated.

The Pleiades open star cluster in the constellation of Taurus. Image by the author using Slooh.

The other type of cluster is the globular cluster. These are spherical balls of stars in space and contain thousands or even millions of stars within a tightly packed area. They lie thousands of light years away, usually close to the hub of the galaxy, and are very old in comparison to the younger open clusters. It's not unusual for a globular to be over ten billion years old – nearly as old as the universe itself.

Through binoculars or a small telescope a globular can often appear like the head of a comet without the tail. Alternatively, you might think of it as being a faint and fuzzy star. The higher magnifications provided by telescopes will reveal the individual stars around the outer edges. You may also notice chains of stars or the cluster may appear to be misshapen. Not all globulars are the same! For my money, the best globular in the northern hemisphere is the [Keystone Cluster.](#)

Whether you're observing open or globular star clusters, you'll get the best views away from the lights but you can still get some great views from the suburbs, even with light pollution.

The Keystone Cluster in the constellation of Hercules. Image by the author using Slooh.

Nebulae
There are several categories of nebulae but the most common are clouds of gas and dust in space. These are the birthplaces of stars and can cover an area light years in diameter. The Orion Nebula is

the best example of this in the winter nights of the northern hemisphere. It's easily seen with the unaided eye as a tiny, misty patch in the sword of Orion, provides an attractive view through binoculars and can be a stunning sight in a telescope.

Another type of nebula is the planetary nebula. These nebulae are small and appear disk-like when observed through a telescope, almost like a planet. The Saturn Nebula in Aquarius is one such nebula and can be observed during the autumn nights.

The last kind of nebula is a supernova remnant. There are only a few of these but one is particularly well known. The Crab Nebula is the remains of a star that exploded nearly a thousand years ago. Located in Taurus the Bull, it can be a little tricky to find for binocular observers and, consequently, I've decided to focus on the Hyades and Pleiades open clusters in that constellation instead.

The Orion Nebula in the constellation of Orion. Image by the author using Slooh.

Galaxies

Galaxies come in all different kinds of shapes and sizes but may be disappointing to the beginner. There are a lot of images around showing star-studded spirals in space, but the reality is that you're likely to only see a small, misty patch.

Also, the vast majority of galaxies are small, faint and can be difficult to locate. With experience, you'll be able to spot a number of them, but to begin with there's only one that's easily seen. The Andromeda Galaxy appears as a misty patch with the unaided eye and is conveniently located close to a number of bright stars.

(I have also mentioned a few others but you'll definitely need clear, dark skies and some experience to see them.)

The Andromeda Galaxy in the constellation of Andromeda. Image by the author using Slooh.

Signposts to the Stars

Ursa Major

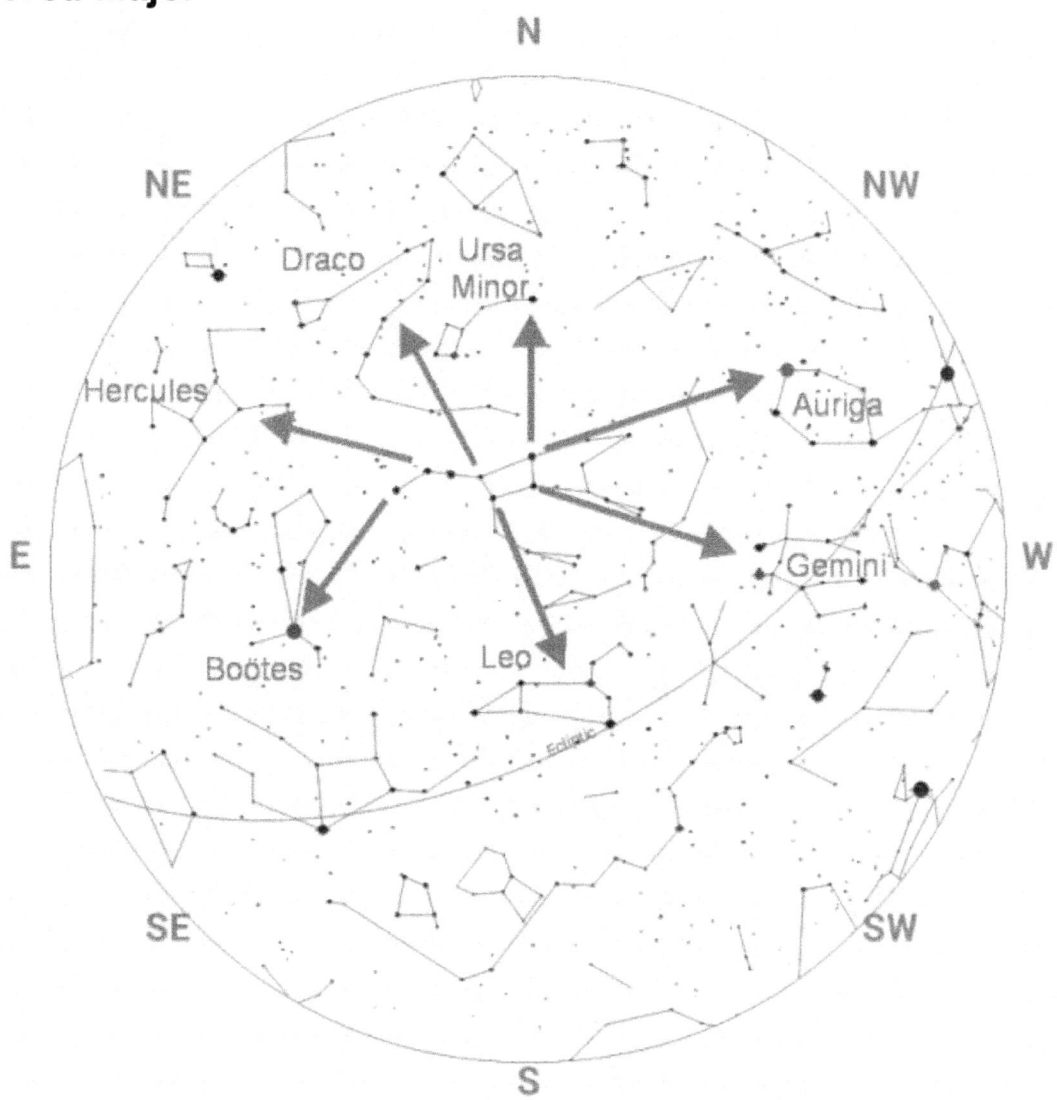

You can use the brightest stars in Ursa Major, commonly known as the Big Dipper (or the Plough in the United Kingdom) to find these constellations: Auriga, Boötes, Draco, Gemini, Leo and Ursa Minor.

Orion

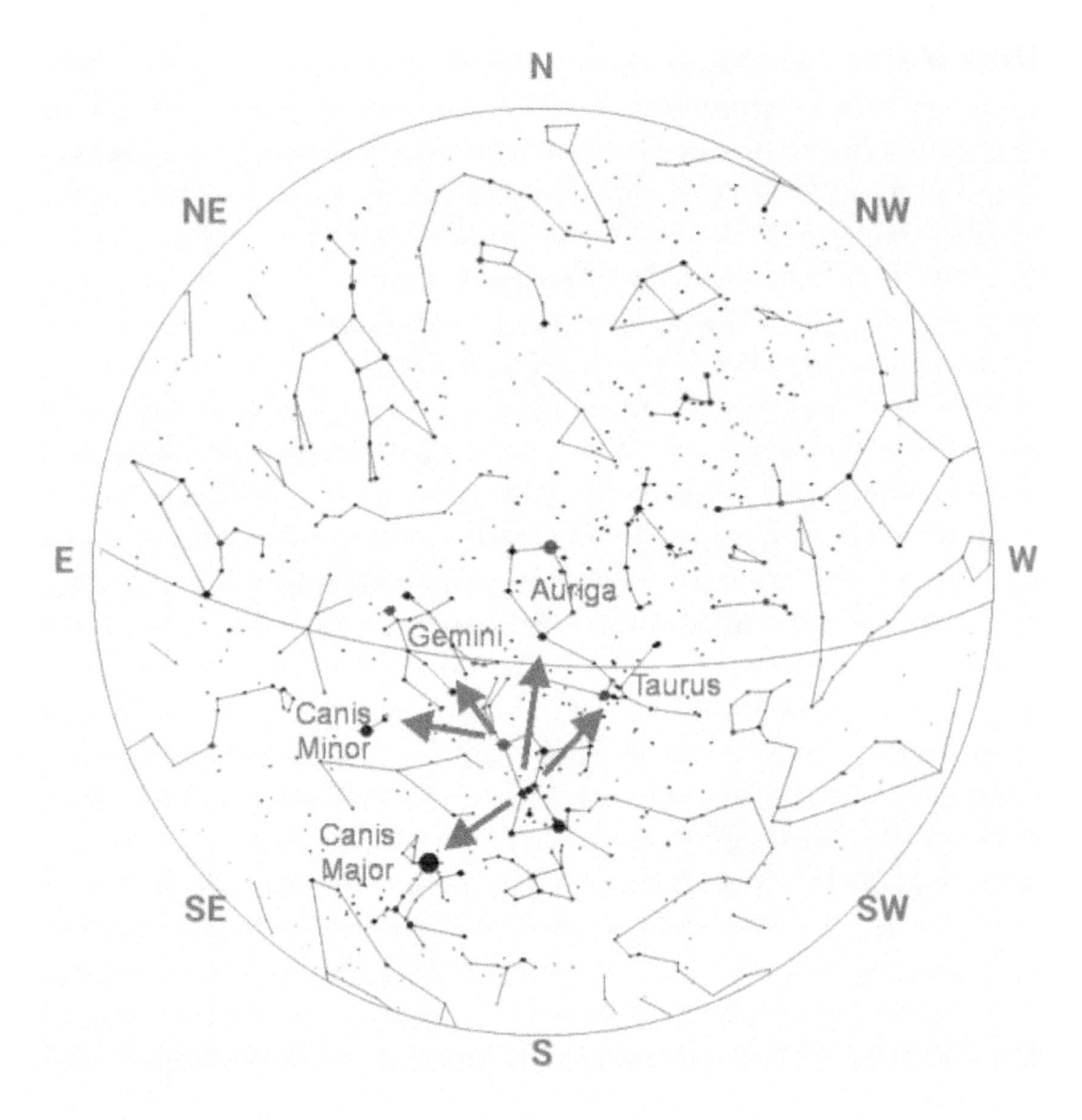

You can use Orion to find these constellations: Auriga, Canis Major, Canis Minor, Gemini and Taurus.

Star Charts & Visible Constellations

Star Chart Tables

If observing during daylight savings time, first deduct one hour and then refer to the corresponding chart number. For example, for 10pm daylight savings time in early August, use chart 18.

Early January

Time	Chart #
6pm	Chart 1
7pm	Chart 2
8pm	Chart 3
9pm	Chart 4
10pm	Chart 5
11pm	Chart 6
12am	Chart 7
1am	Chart 8
2am	Chart 9
3am	Chart 10
4am	Chart 11
5am	Chart 12
6am	Chart 13

Late January

Time	Chart #
6pm	Chart 2
7pm	Chart 3
8pm	Chart 4
9pm	Chart 5

10pm	Chart 6
11pm	Chart 7
12am	Chart 8
1am	Chart 9
2am	Chart 10
3am	Chart 11
4am	Chart 12
5am	Chart 13
6am	Chart 14

Early February

Time	Chart #
6pm	Chart 3
7pm	Chart 4
8pm	Chart 5
9pm	Chart 6
10pm	Chart 7
11pm	Chart 8
12am	Chart 9
1am	Chart 10
2am	Chart 11
3am	Chart 12
4am	Chart 13
5am	Chart 14
6am	Chart 15

Late February

Time	Chart #
6pm	Chart 4
7pm	Chart 5
8pm	Chart 6
9pm	Chart 7
10pm	Chart 8
11pm	Chart 9
12am	Chart 10
1am	Chart 11
2am	Chart 12

3am	Chart 13
4am	Chart 14
5am	Chart 15
6am	Chart 16

Early March

Time	Chart #
6pm	Chart 5
7pm	Chart 6
8pm	Chart 7
9pm	Chart 8
10pm	Chart 9
11pm	Chart 10
12am	Chart 11
1am	Chart 12
2am	Chart 13
3am	Chart 14
4am	Chart 15
5am	Chart 16
6am	Chart 17

Late March

Time	Chart #
6pm	Chart 6
7pm	Chart 7
8pm	Chart 8
9pm	Chart 9
10pm	Chart 10
11pm	Chart 11
12am	Chart 12
1am	Chart 13
2am	Chart 14

3am	Chart 15
4am	Chart 16
5am	Chart 17
6am	Chart 18

Early April

Time	Chart #
6pm	Chart 7
7pm	Chart 8
8pm	Chart 9
9pm	Chart 10
10pm	Chart 11
11pm	Chart 12
12am	Chart 13
1am	Chart 14
2am	Chart 15
3am	Chart 16
4am	Chart 17
5am	Chart 18
6am	Chart 19

Late April

Time	Chart #
6pm	Chart 8
7pm	Chart 9
8pm	Chart 10
9pm	Chart 11
10pm	Chart 12
11pm	Chart 13
12am	Chart 14
1am	Chart 15
2am	Chart 16

3am	Chart 17
4am	Chart 18
5am	Chart 19
6am	Chart 20

Early May

Time	Chart #
6pm	Chart 9
7pm	Chart 10
8pm	Chart 11
9pm	Chart 12
10pm	Chart 13
11pm	Chart 14
12am	Chart 15
1am	Chart 16
2am	Chart 17
3am	Chart 18
4am	Chart 19
5am	Chart 20
6am	Chart 21

Late May

Time	Chart #
6pm	Chart 10
7pm	Chart 11
8pm	Chart 12
9pm	Chart 13
10pm	Chart 14
11pm	Chart 15
12am	Chart 16
1am	Chart 17
2am	Chart 18

3am	Chart 19
4am	Chart 20
5am	Chart 21
6am	Chart 22

Early June

Time	Chart #
6pm	Chart 11
7pm	Chart 12
8pm	Chart 13
9pm	Chart 14
10pm	Chart 15
11pm	Chart 16
12am	Chart 17
1am	Chart 18
2am	Chart 19
3am	Chart 20
4am	Chart 21
5am	Chart 22
6am	Chart 23

Late June

Time	Chart #
6pm	Chart 12
7pm	Chart 13
8pm	Chart 14
9pm	Chart 15
10pm	Chart 16
11pm	Chart 17
12am	Chart 18
1am	Chart 19
2am	Chart 20

3am	Chart 21
4am	Chart 22
5am	Chart 23
6am	Chart 24

Early July

Time	Chart #
6pm	Chart 13
7pm	Chart 14
8pm	Chart 15
9pm	Chart 16
10pm	Chart 17
11pm	Chart 18
12am	Chart 19
1am	Chart 20
2am	Chart 21
3am	Chart 22
4am	Chart 23
5am	Chart 24
6am	Chart 1

Late July

Time	Chart #
6pm	Chart 14
7pm	Chart 15
8pm	Chart 16
9pm	Chart 17
10pm	Chart 18
11pm	Chart 19
12am	Chart 20
1am	Chart 21
2am	Chart 22

3am	Chart 23
4am	Chart 24
5am	Chart 1
6am	Chart 2

Early August

Time	Chart #
6pm	Chart 15
7pm	Chart 16
8pm	Chart 17
9pm	Chart 18
10pm	Chart 19
11pm	Chart 20
12am	Chart 21
1am	Chart 22
2am	Chart 23
3am	Chart 24
4am	Chart 1
5am	Chart 2
6am	Chart 3

Late August

Time	Chart #
6pm	Chart 16
7pm	Chart 17
8pm	Chart 18
9pm	Chart 19
10pm	Chart 20
11pm	Chart 21
12am	Chart 22
1am	Chart 23
2am	Chart 24

3am	Chart 1
4am	Chart 2
5am	Chart 3
6am	Chart 4

Early September

Time	Chart #
6pm	Chart 17
7pm	Chart 18
8pm	Chart 19
9pm	Chart 20
10pm	Chart 21
11pm	Chart 22
12am	Chart 23
1am	Chart 24
2am	Chart 1
3am	Chart 2
4am	Chart 3
5am	Chart 4
6am	Chart 5

Late September

Time	Chart #
6pm	Chart 18
7pm	Chart 19
8pm	Chart 20
9pm	Chart 21
10pm	Chart 22
11pm	Chart 23
12am	Chart 24
1am	Chart 1
2am	Chart 2

3am	Chart 3
4am	Chart 4
5am	Chart 5
6am	Chart 6

Early October

Time	Chart #
6pm	Chart 19
7pm	Chart 20
8pm	Chart 21
9pm	Chart 22
10pm	Chart 23
11pm	Chart 24
12am	Chart 1
1am	Chart 2
2am	Chart 3
3am	Chart 4
4am	Chart 5
5am	Chart 6
6am	Chart 7

Late October

Time	Chart #
6pm	Chart 20
7pm	Chart 21
8pm	Chart 22
9pm	Chart 23
10pm	Chart 24
11pm	Chart 1
12am	Chart 2
1am	Chart 3
2am	Chart 4

3am	Chart 5
4am	Chart 6
5am	Chart 7
6am	Chart 8

Early November

Time	Chart #
6pm	Chart 21
7pm	Chart 22
8pm	Chart 23
9pm	Chart 24
10pm	Chart 1
11pm	Chart 2
12am	Chart 3
1am	Chart 4
2am	Chart 5
3am	Chart 6
4am	Chart 7
5am	Chart 8
6am	Chart 9

Late November

Time	Chart #
6pm	Chart 22
7pm	Chart 23
8pm	Chart 24
9pm	Chart 1
10pm	Chart 2
11pm	Chart 3
12am	Chart 4
1am	Chart 5
2am	Chart 6

3am	Chart 7
4am	Chart 8
5am	Chart 9
6am	Chart 10

Early December

Time	Chart #
6pm	Chart 23
7pm	Chart 24
8pm	Chart 1
9pm	Chart 2
10pm	Chart 3
11pm	Chart 4
12am	Chart 5
1am	Chart 6
2am	Chart 7
3am	Chart 8
4am	Chart 9
5am	Chart 10
6am	Chart 11

Late December

Time	Chart #
6pm	Chart 24
7pm	Chart 1
8pm	Chart 2
9pm	Chart 3
10pm	Chart 4
11pm	Chart 5
12am	Chart 6
1am	Chart 7
2am	Chart 8

3am	Chart 9
4am	Chart 10
5am	Chart 11
6am	Chart 12

Chart 1

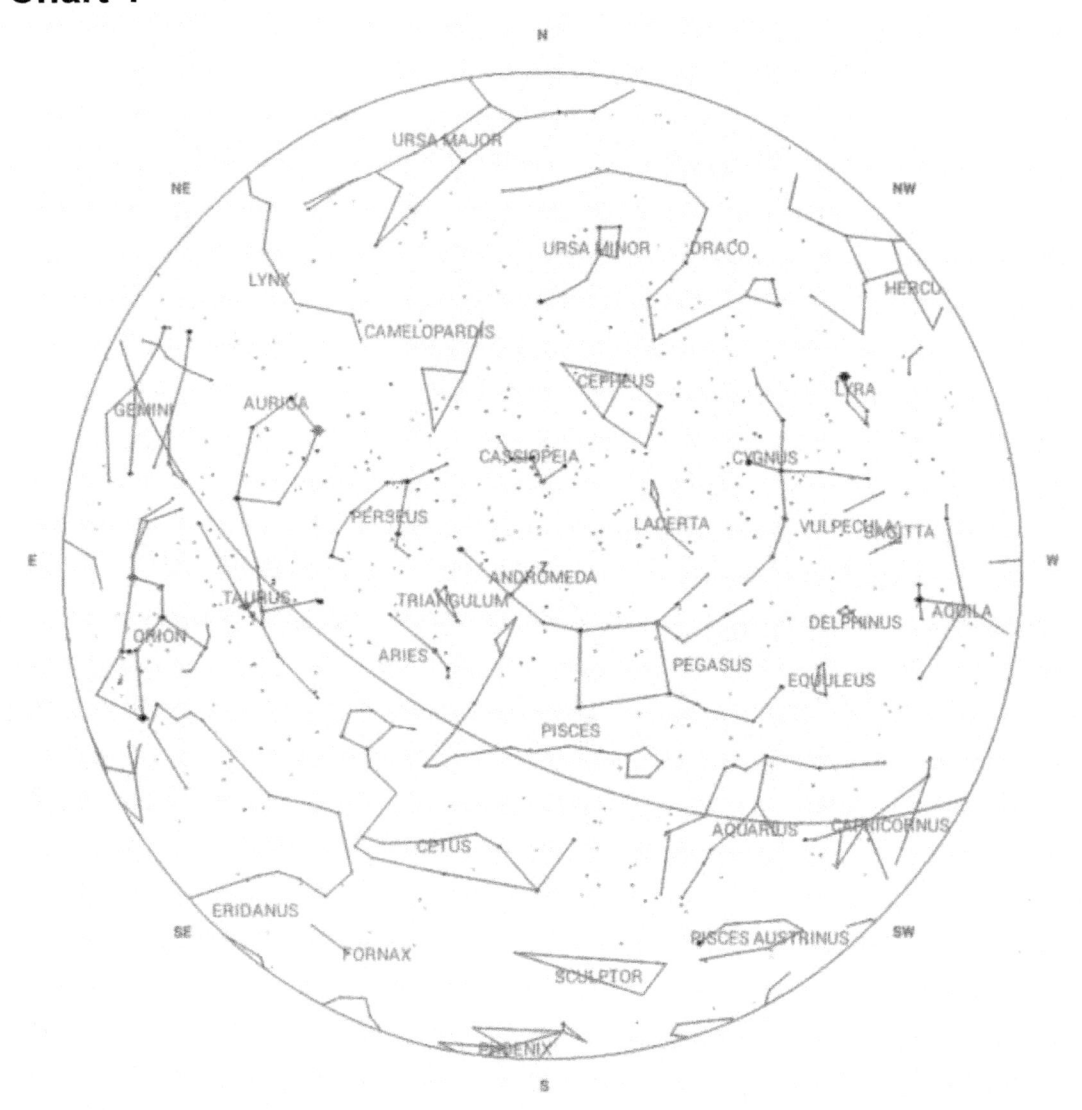

The following constellations are well-placed for observation at this time: Andromeda, Aquarius, Aries, Auriga, Cassiopeia, Cepheus, Cetus, Cygnus, Delphinus, Draco, Equuleus, Lyra, Pegasus, Perseus, Pisces, Sagitta, Taurus, Ursa Minor and Vulpecula.

Chart 2

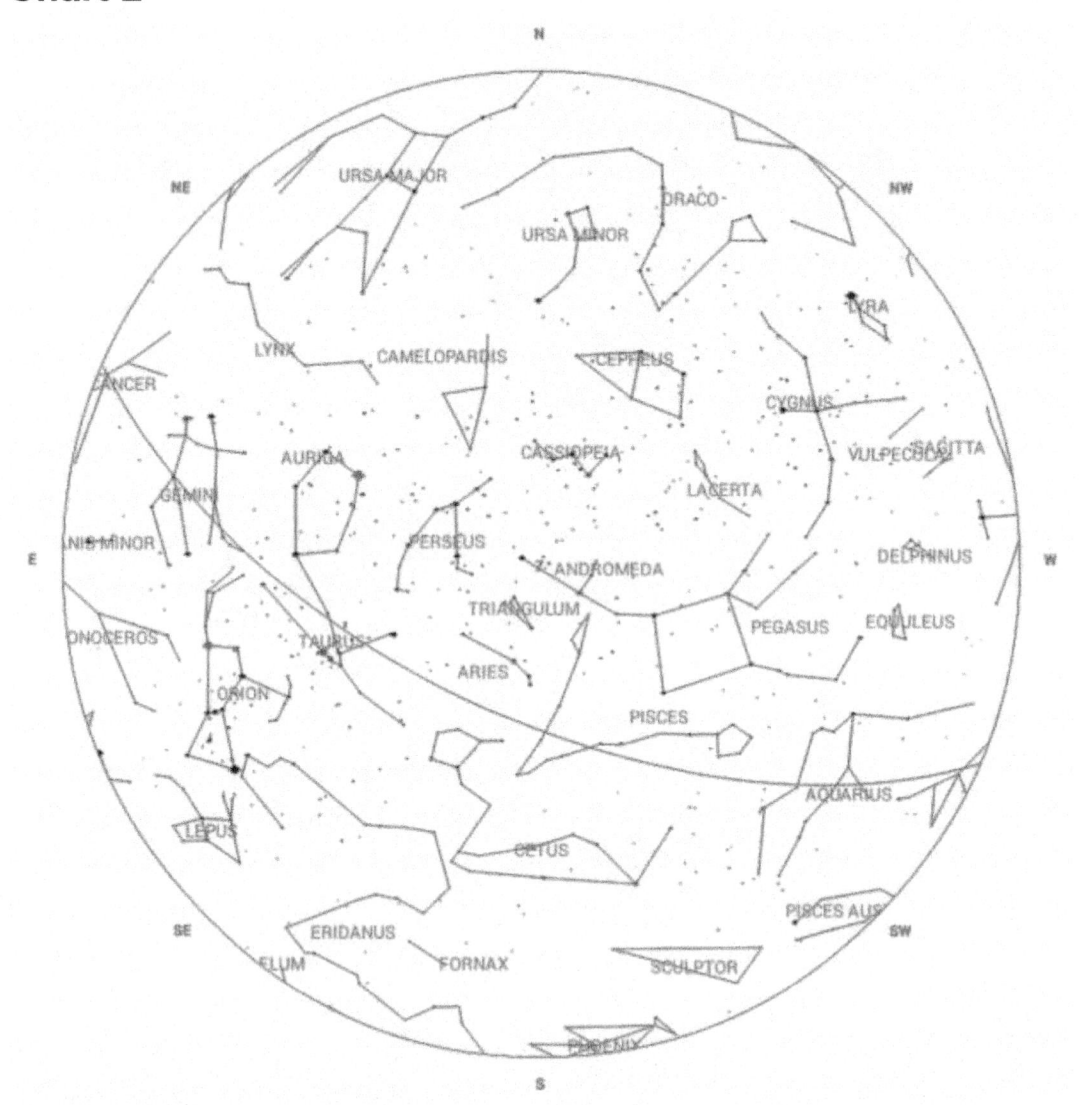

The following constellations are well-placed for observation at this time: Andromeda, Aries, Auriga, Cassiopeia, Cepheus, Cetus, Cygnus, Delphinus, Draco, Equuleus, Gemini, Orion, Pegasus, Perseus, Pisces, Taurus, and Ursa Minor.

Chart 3

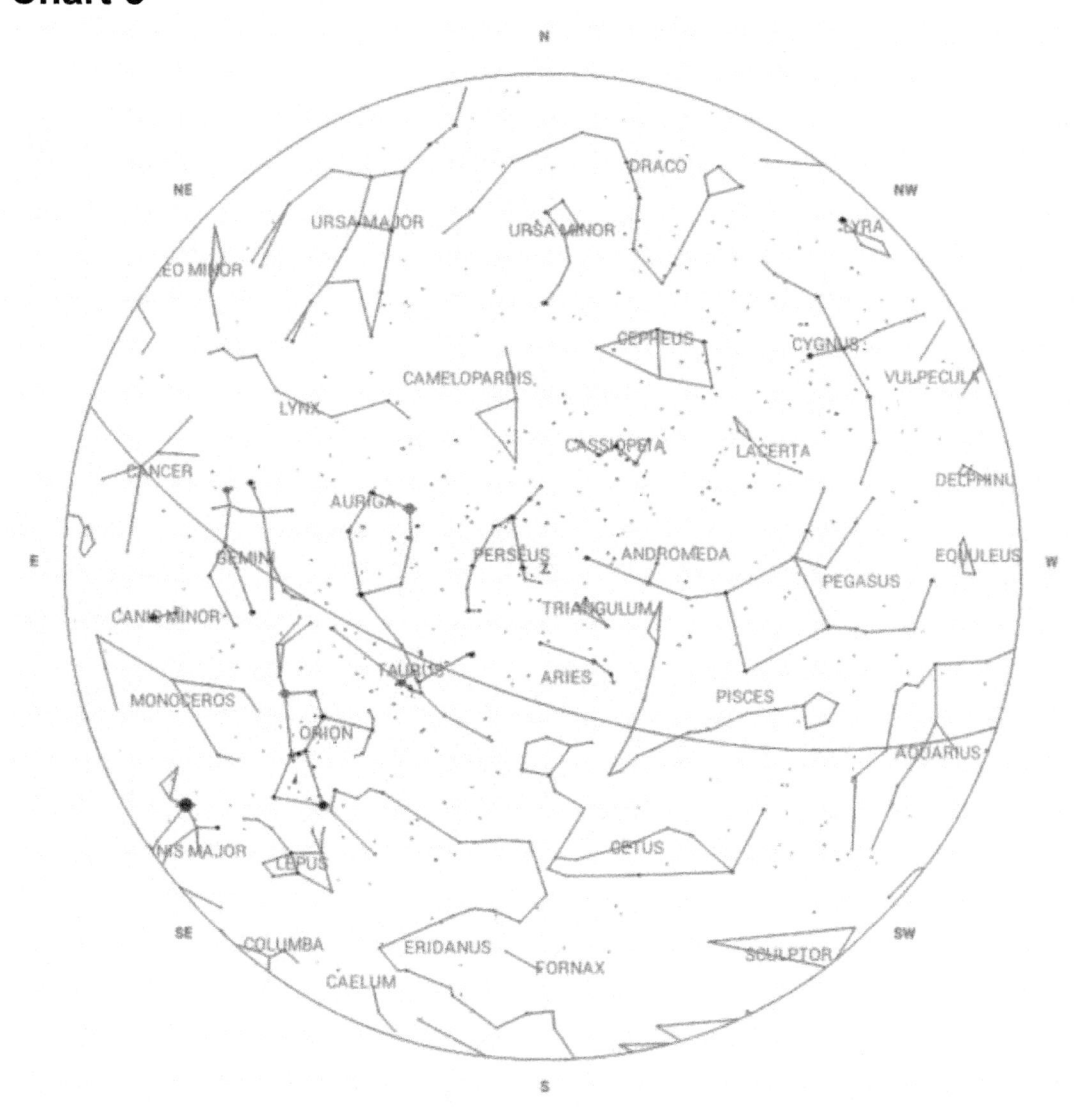

The following constellations are well-placed for observation at this time: Andromeda, Aries, Auriga, Cassiopeia, Cepheus, Cetus, Gemini, Orion, Pegasus, Perseus, Pisces, Taurus, and Ursa Minor.

Chart 4

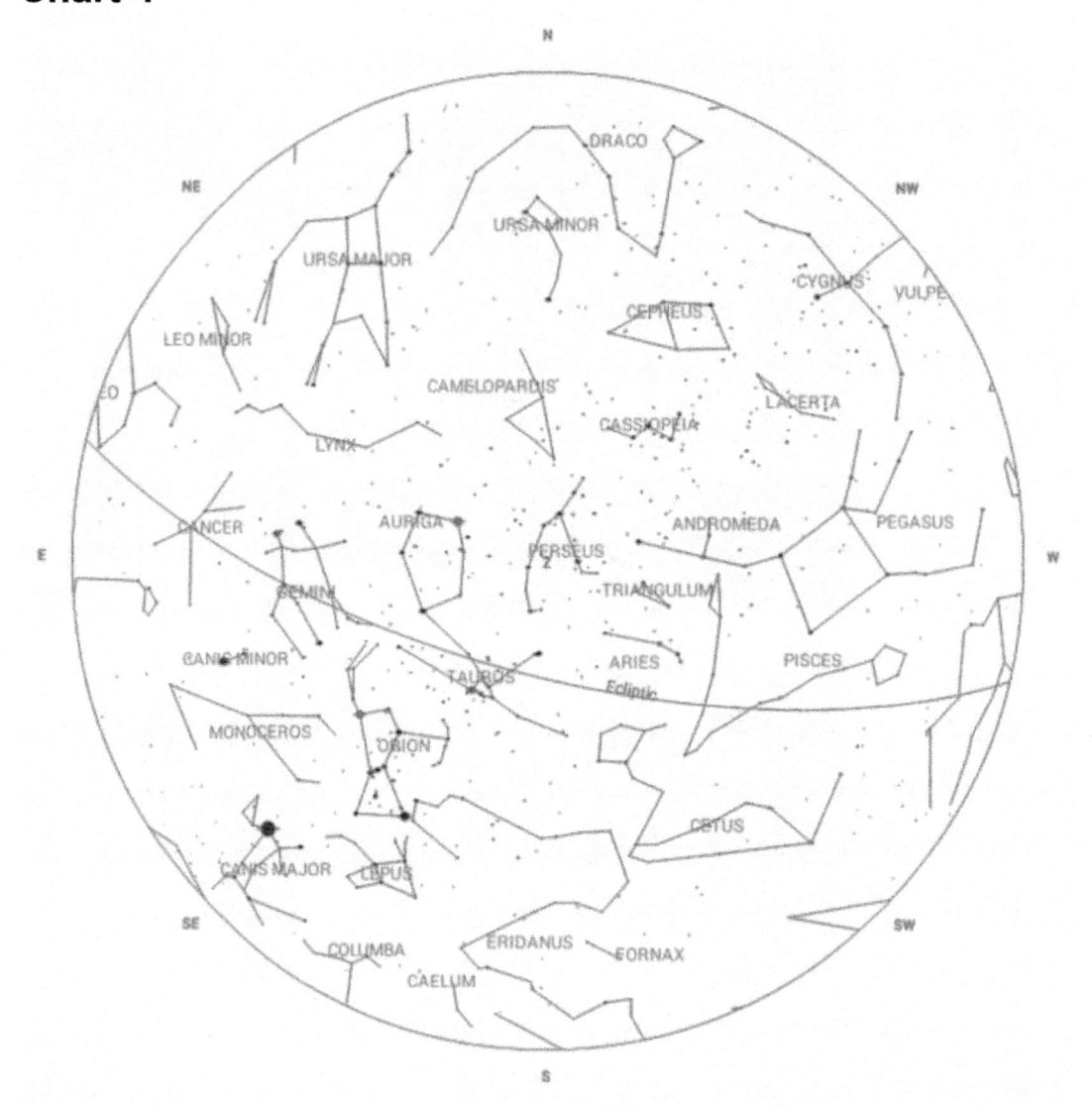

The following constellations are well-placed for observation at this time: Andromeda, Aries, Auriga, Cancer, Canis Minor, Cassiopeia, Cepheus, Cetus, Gemini, Lepus, Orion, Perseus, Pisces, Taurus, and Ursa Minor.

Chart 5

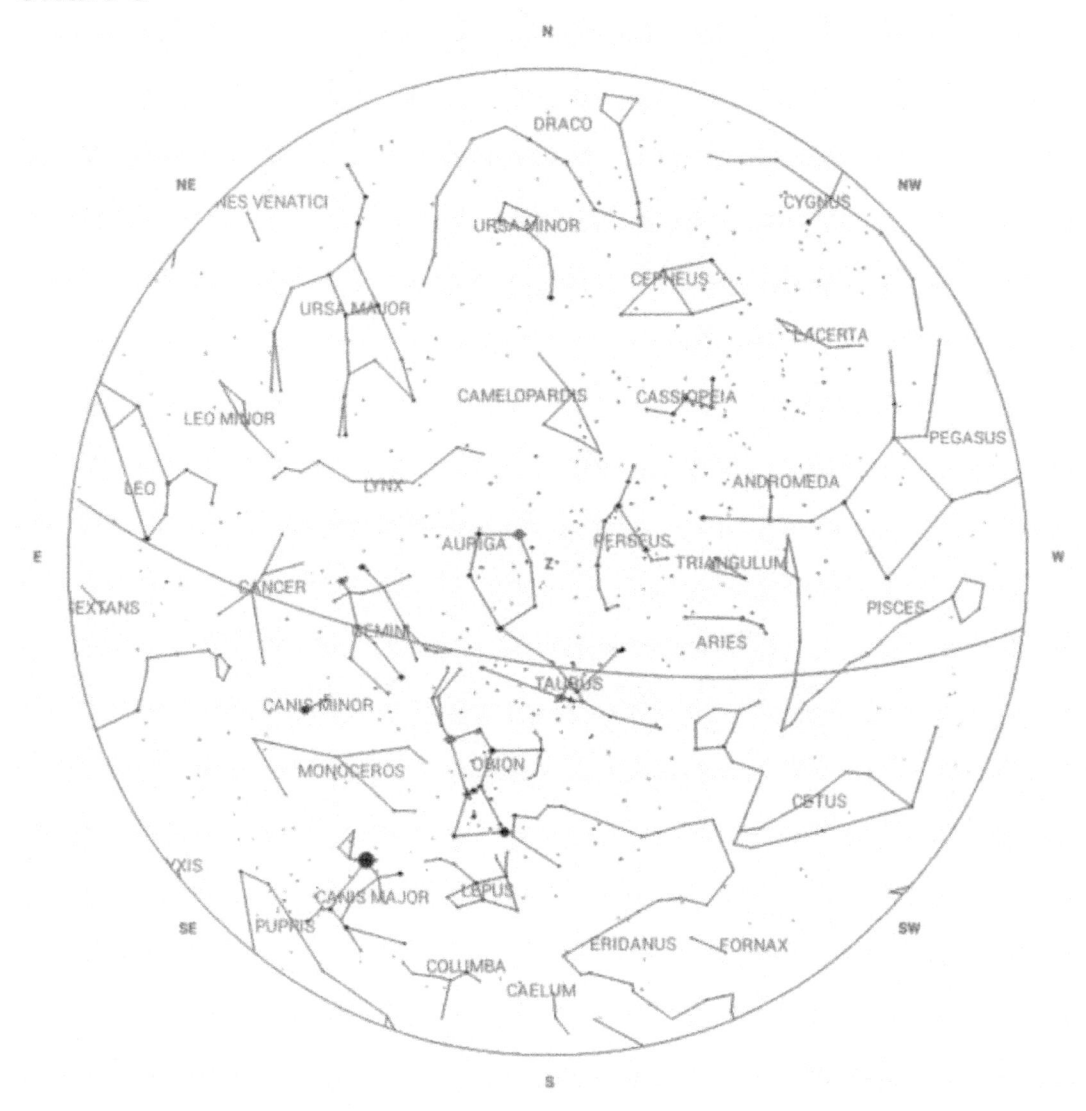

The following constellations are well-placed for observation at this time: Andromeda, Aries, Auriga, Cancer, Canis Major, Canis Minor, Cassiopeia, Cepheus, Gemini, Lepus, Orion, Perseus, Taurus, and Ursa Minor.

Chart 6

The following constellations are well-placed for observation at this time: Andromeda, Aries, Auriga, Cancer, Canis Major, Canis Minor, Cassiopeia, Cepheus, Gemini, Leo, Lepus, Orion, Perseus, Taurus, and Ursa Minor.

Chart 7

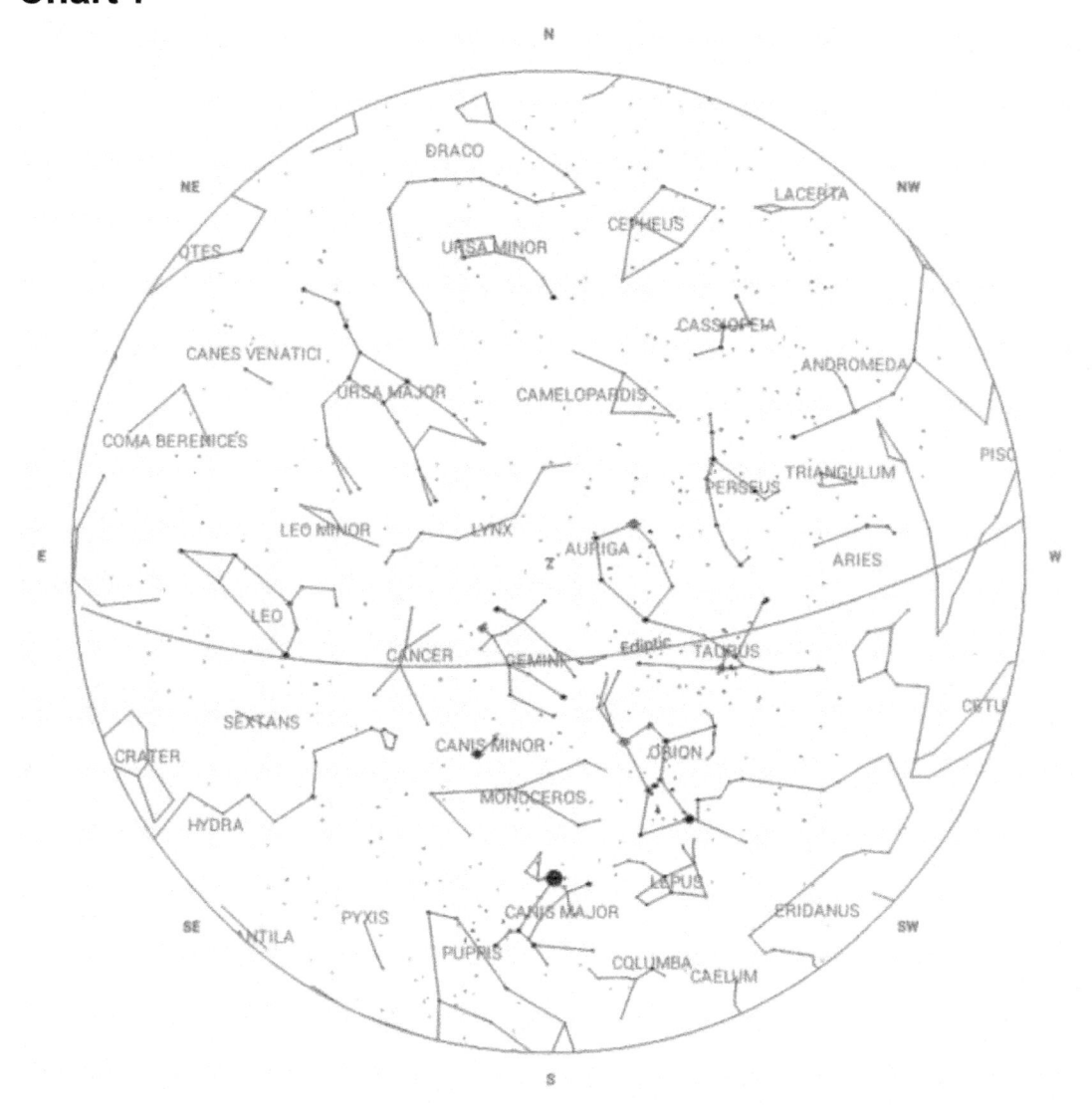

The following constellations are well-placed for observation at this time: Aries, Auriga, Cancer, Canes Venatici, Canis Major, Canis Minor, Cassiopeia, Cepheus, Gemini, Leo, Lepus, Orion, Perseus, Taurus, Ursa Major and Ursa Minor.

Chart 8

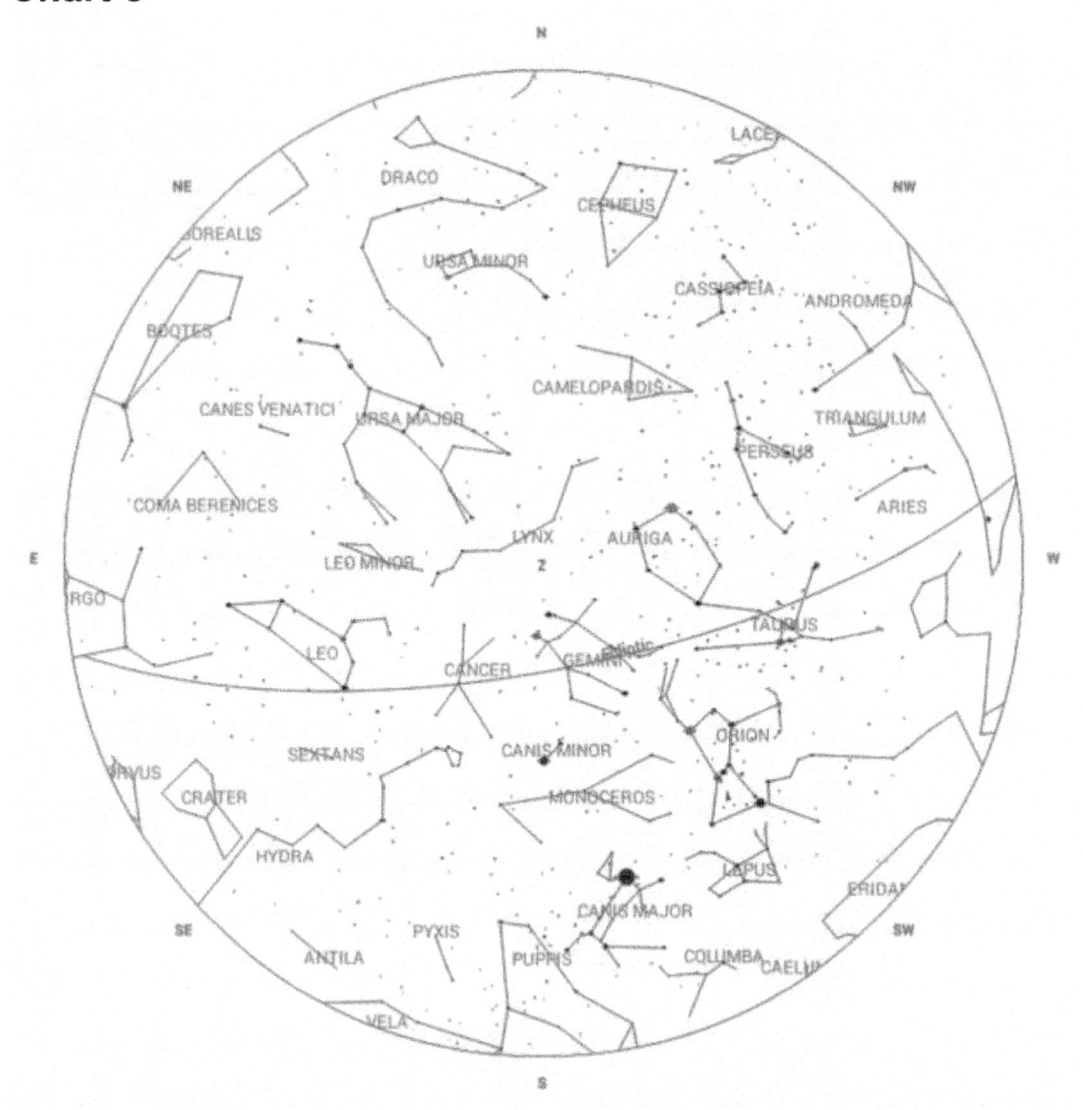

The following constellations are well-placed for observation at this time: Auriga, Cancer, Canes Venatici, Canis Major, Canis Minor, Cassiopeia, Gemini, Leo, Lepus, Orion, Perseus, Taurus, Ursa Major and Ursa Minor.

Chart 9

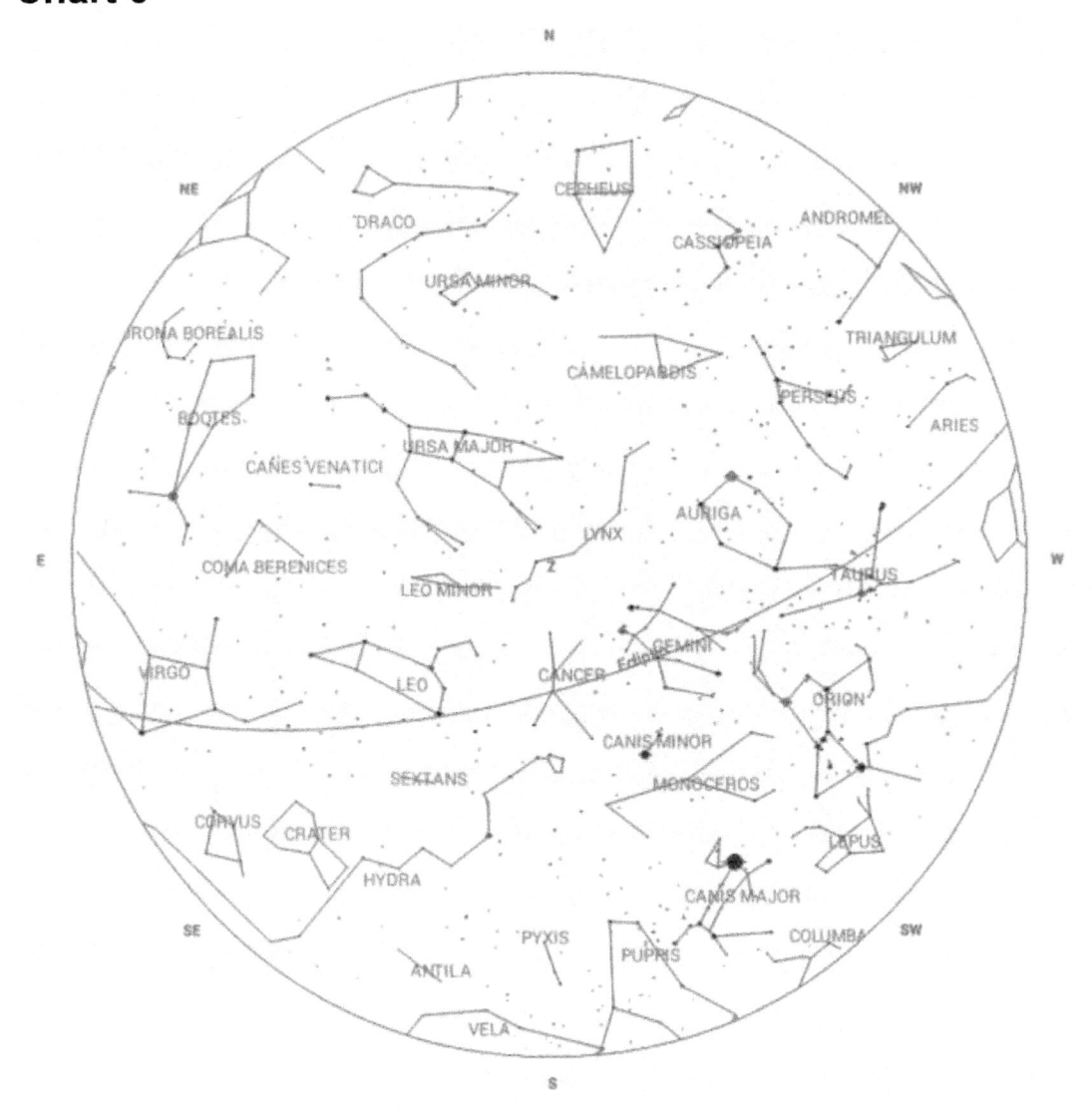

The following constellations are well-placed for observation at this time: Auriga, Boötes, Cancer, Canes Venatici, Canis Major, Canis Minor, Cassiopeia, Coma Berenices, Gemini, Leo, Orion, Perseus, Taurus, Ursa Major and Ursa Minor.

Chart 10

The following constellations are well-placed for observation at this time: Auriga, Boötes, Cancer, Canes Venatici, Canis Minor, Coma Berenices, Crater, Gemini, Leo, Ursa Major and Ursa Minor.

Chart 11

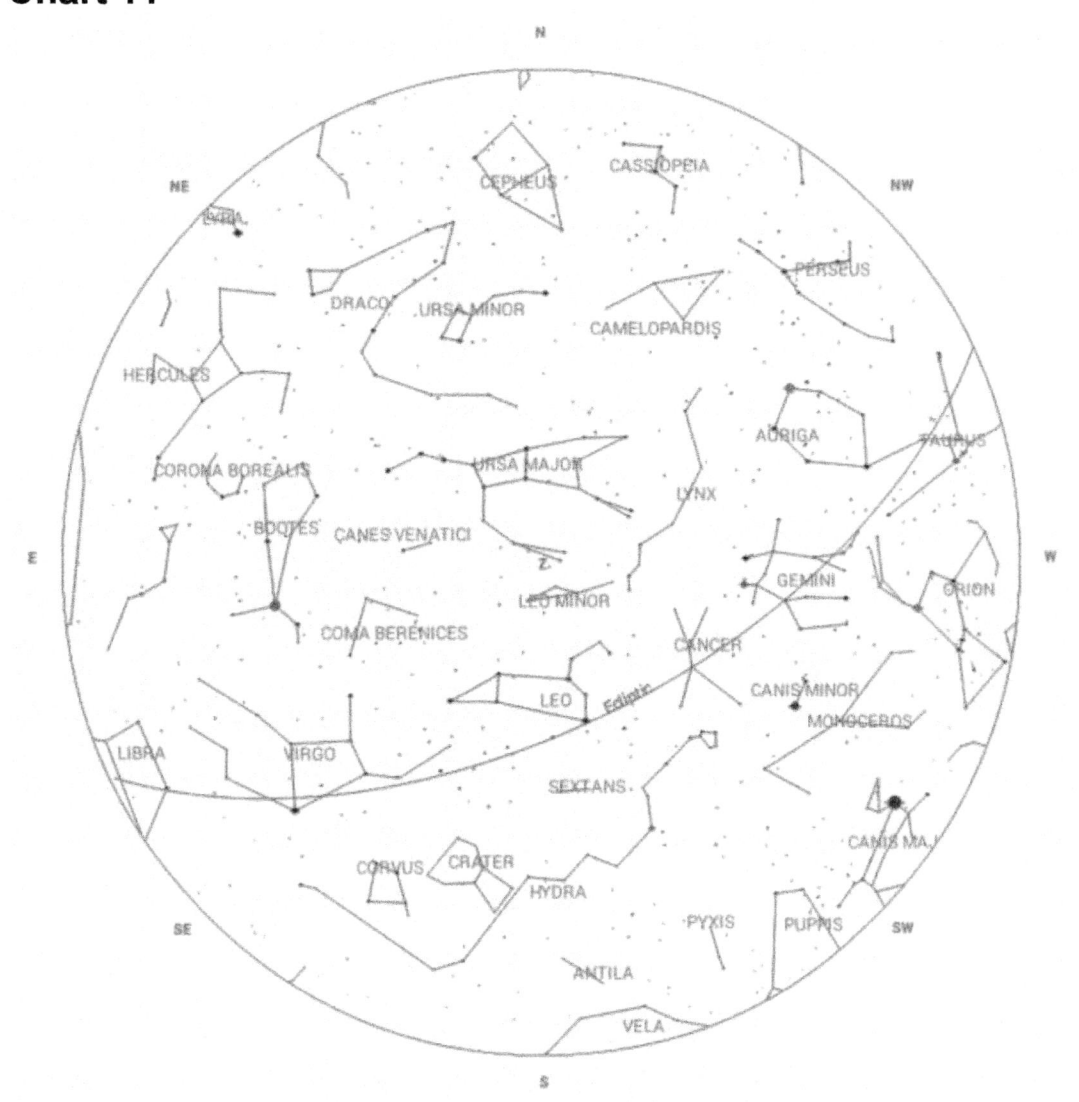

The following constellations are well-placed for observation at this time: Auriga, Boötes, Cancer, Canes Venatici, Canis Minor, Coma Berenices, Corvus, Crater, Draco, Gemini, Leo, Ursa Major, Ursa Minor and Virgo.

Chart 12

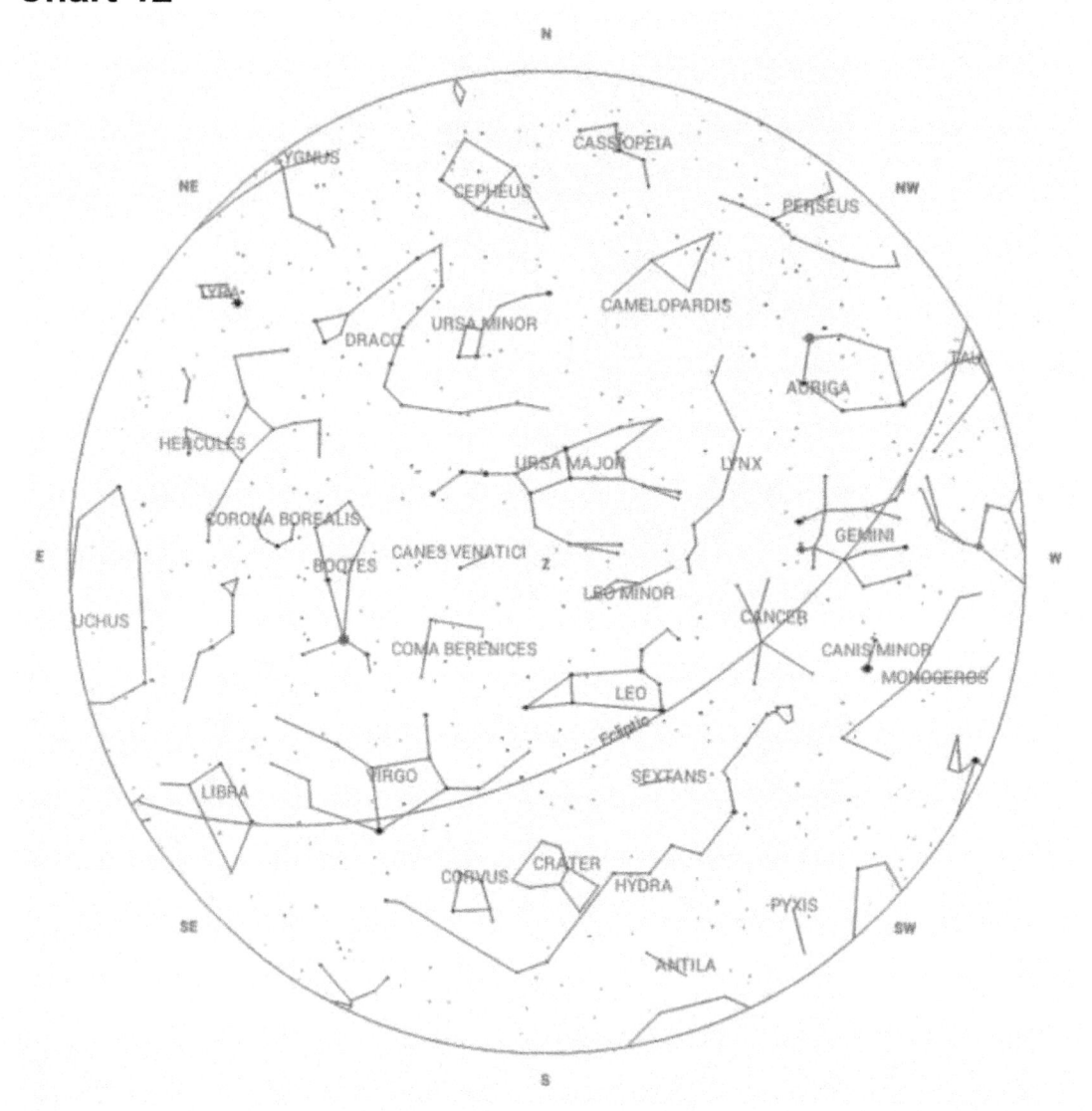

The following constellations are well-placed for observation at this time: Auriga, Boötes, Cancer, Canes Venatici, Canis Minor, Coma Berenices, Corona Borealis, Corvus, Crater, Draco, Gemini, Hercules, Leo, Ursa Major, Ursa Minor and Virgo.

Chart 13

The following constellations are well-placed for observation at this time: Boötes, Cancer, Canes Venatici, Coma Berenices, Corona Borealis, Corvus, Crater, Draco, Hercules, Leo, Lyra, Ursa Major, Ursa Minor and Virgo.

Chart 14

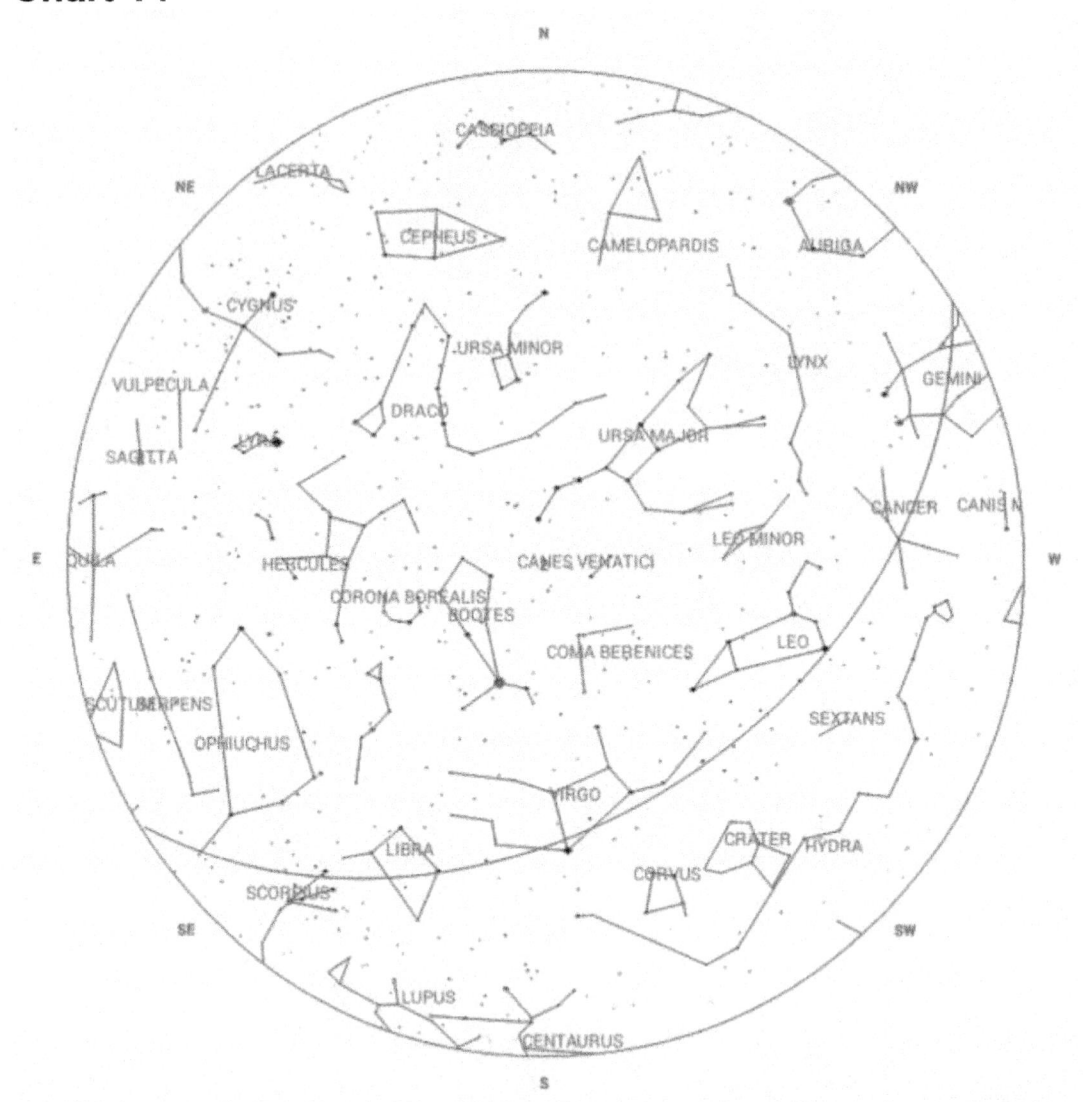

The following constellations are well-placed for observation at this time: Boötes, Canes Venatici, Cepheus, Coma Berenices, Corona Borealis, Corvus, Crater, Draco, Hercules, Leo, Libra, Lyra, Ursa Major, Ursa Minor and Virgo.

Chart 15

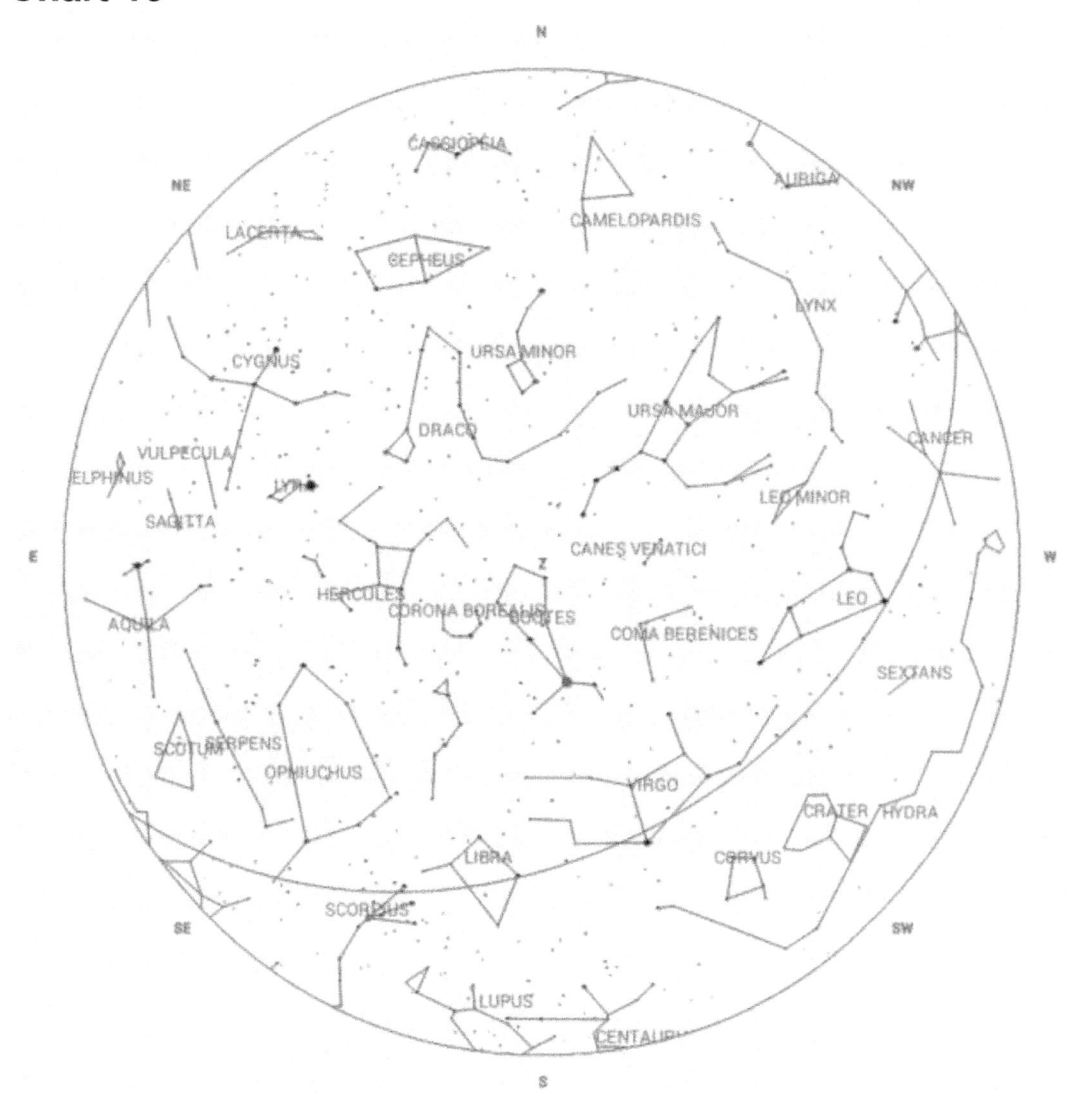

The following constellations are well-placed for observation at this time: Boötes, Canes Venatici, Cepheus, Coma Berenices, Corona Borealis, Corvus, Crater, Cygnus, Draco, Hercules, Leo, Libra, Lyra, Ursa Major, Ursa Minor, Virgo and Vulpecula.

Chart 16

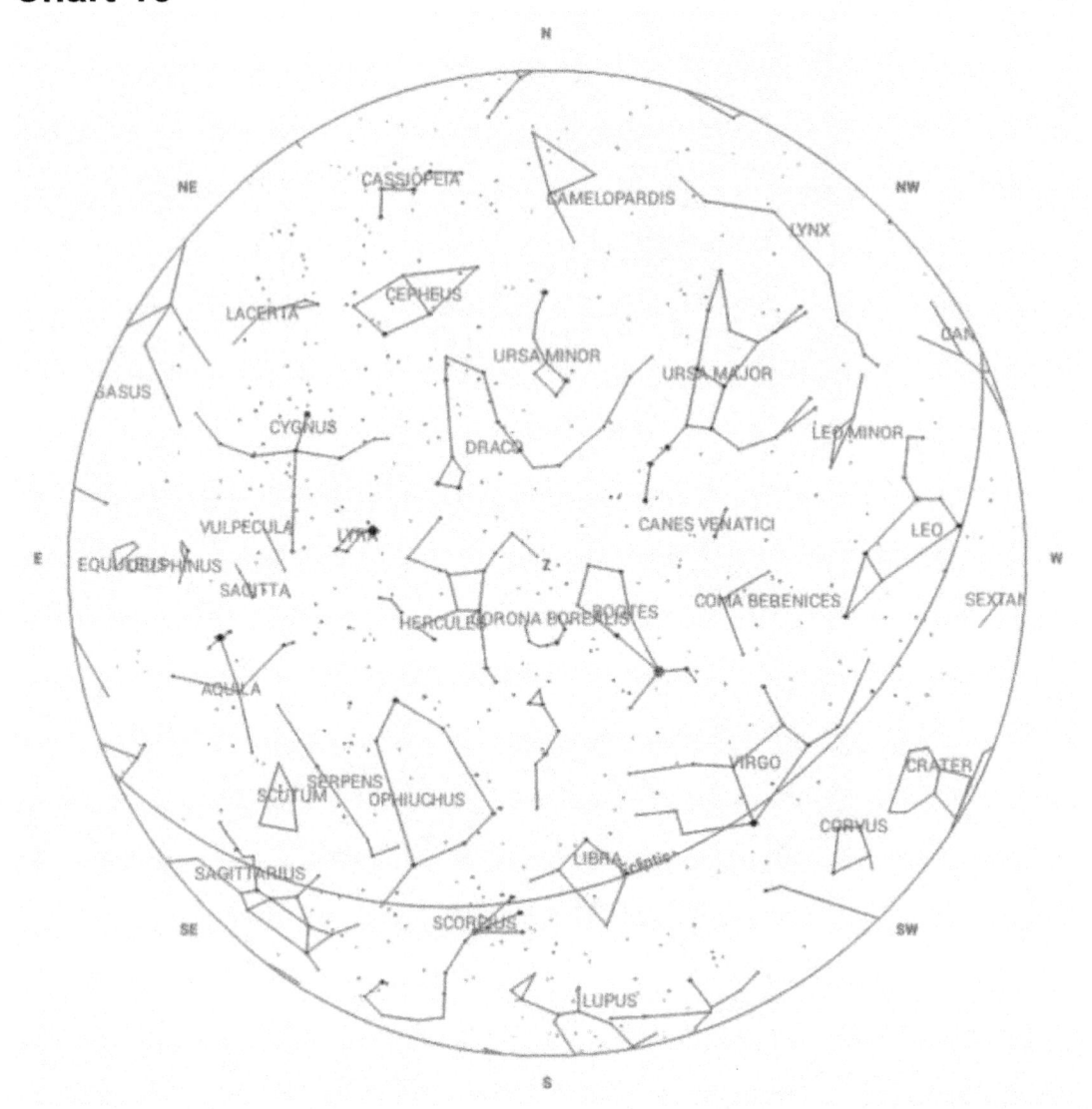

The following constellations are well-placed for observation at this time: Boötes, Canes Venatici, Cepheus, Coma Berenices, Corona Borealis, Cygnus, Delphinus, Draco, Hercules, Leo, Libra, Lyra, Ophiuchus, Sagitta, Scorpius, Serpens, Ursa Major, Ursa Minor, Virgo and Vulpecula.

Chart 17

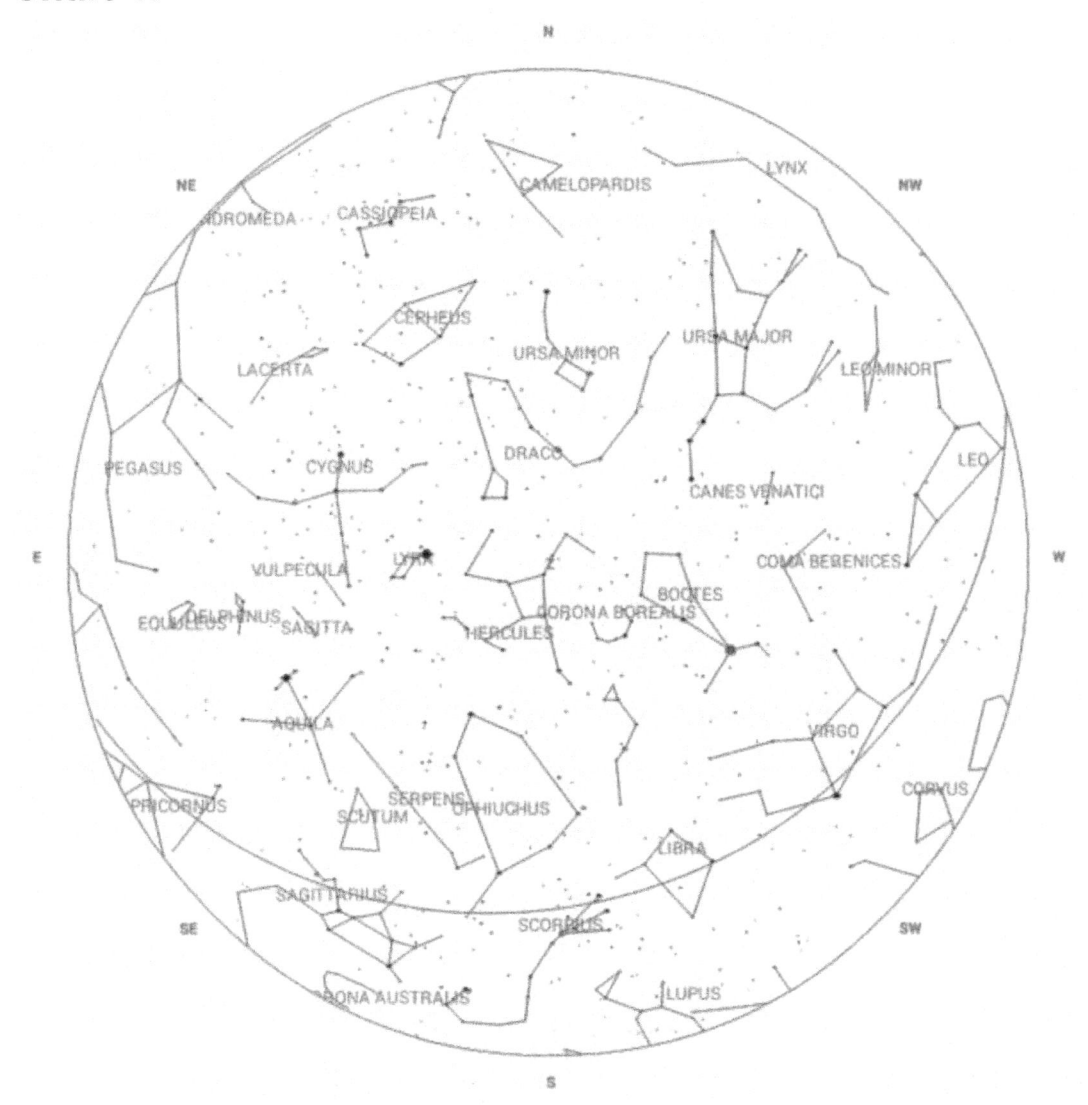

The following constellations are well-placed for observation at this time: Aquila, Boötes, Canes Venatici, Cepheus, Coma Berenices, Corona Borealis, Cygnus, Delphinus, Draco, Hercules, Libra, Lyra, Ophiuchus, Sagitta, Sagittarius, Scorpius, Serpens, Ursa Major, Ursa Minor, Virgo and Vulpecula.

Chart 18

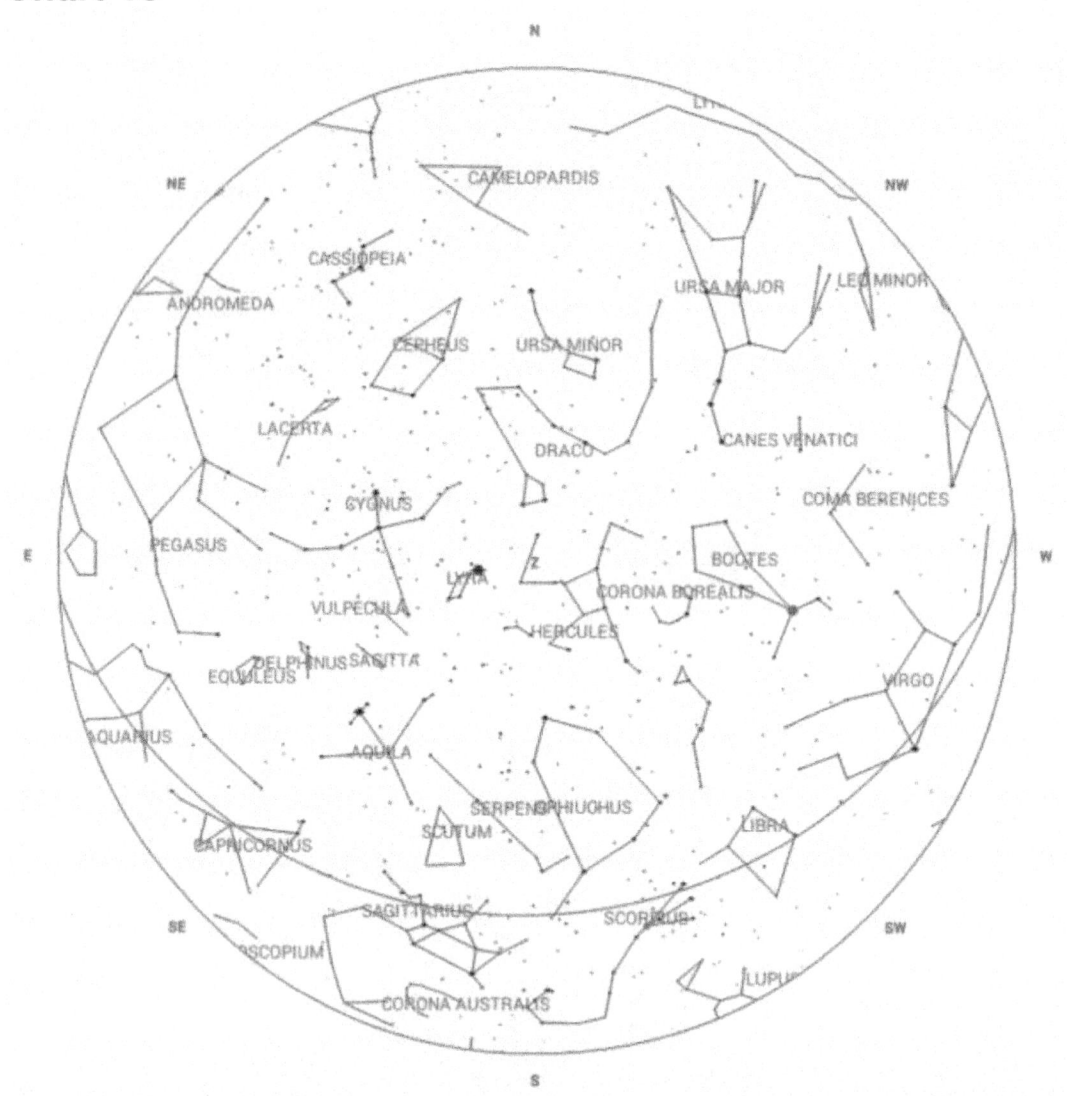

The following constellations are well-placed for observation at this time: Aquila, Boötes, Canes Venatici, Cassiopeia, Cepheus, Coma Berenices, Corona Borealis, Cygnus, Delphinus, Draco, Equuleus, Hercules, Libra, Lyra, Ophiuchus, Sagitta, Sagittarius, Scorpius, Serpens, Ursa Major, Ursa Minor and Vulpecula.

Chart 19

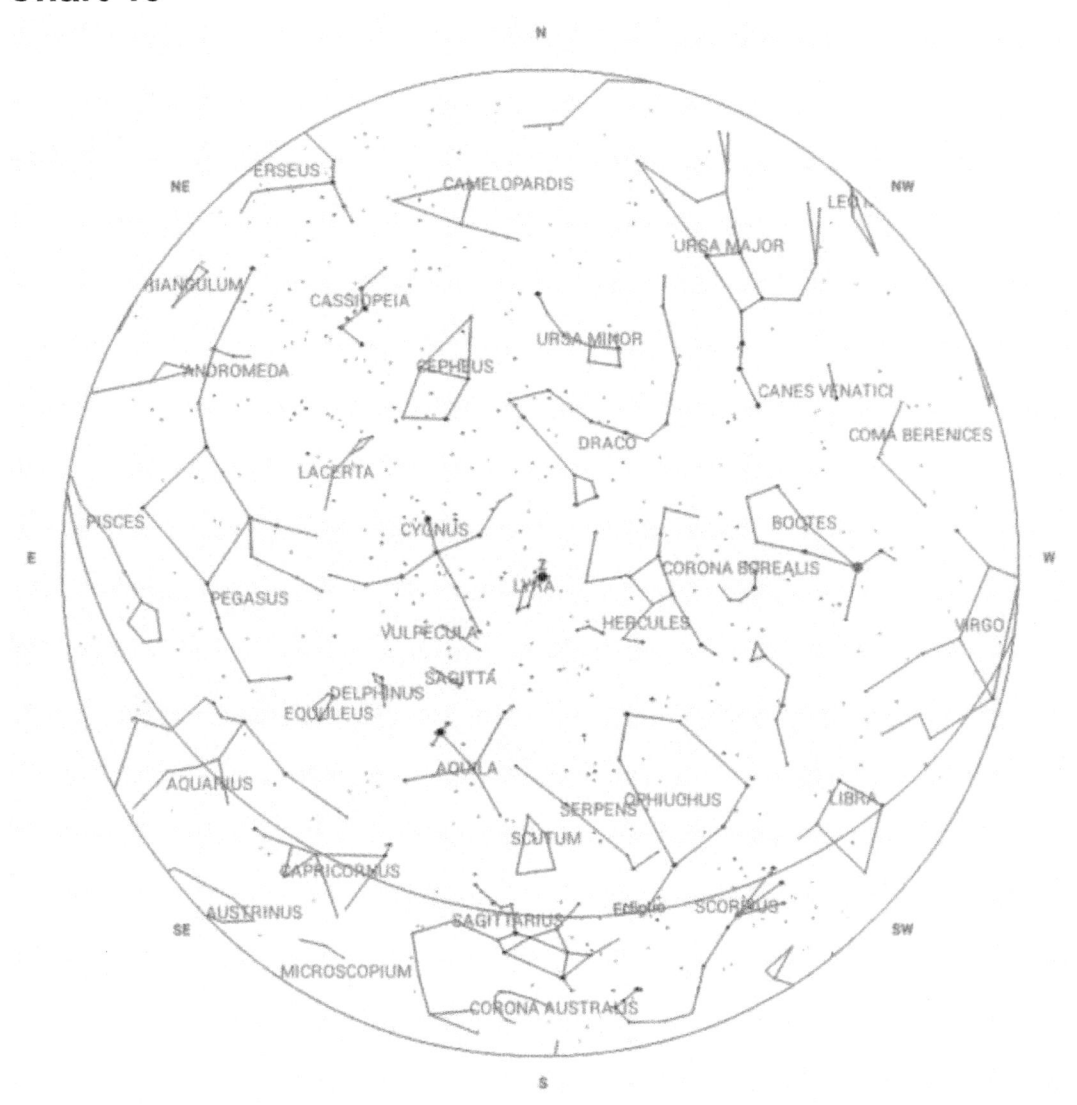

The following constellations are well-placed for observation at this time: Andromeda, Aquila, Boötes, Canes Venatici, Capricornus, Cassiopeia, Cepheus, Corona Borealis, Cygnus, Delphinus, Draco, Equuleus, Hercules, Lyra, Ophiuchus, Pegasus, Sagitta, Sagittarius, Scorpius, Serpens, Ursa Major, Ursa Minor and Vulpecula.

Chart 20

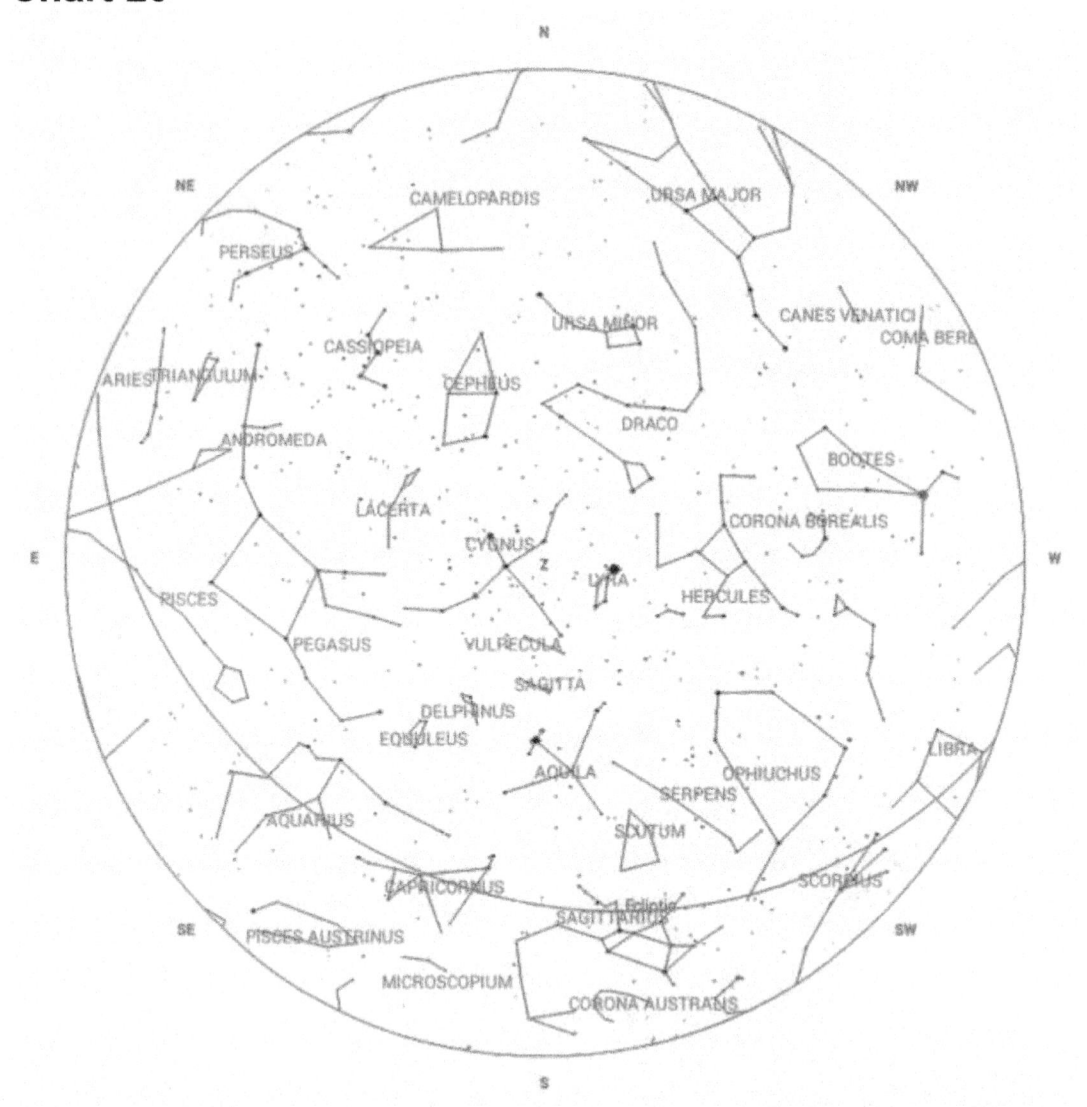

The following constellations are well-placed for observation at this time: Andromeda, Aquarius, Aquila, Boötes, Capricornus, Cassiopeia, Cepheus, Corona Borealis, Cygnus, Delphinus, Draco, Equuleus, Hercules, Lyra, Ophiuchus, Pegasus, Sagitta, Sagittarius, Serpens, Ursa Major, Ursa Minor and Vulpecula.

Chart 21

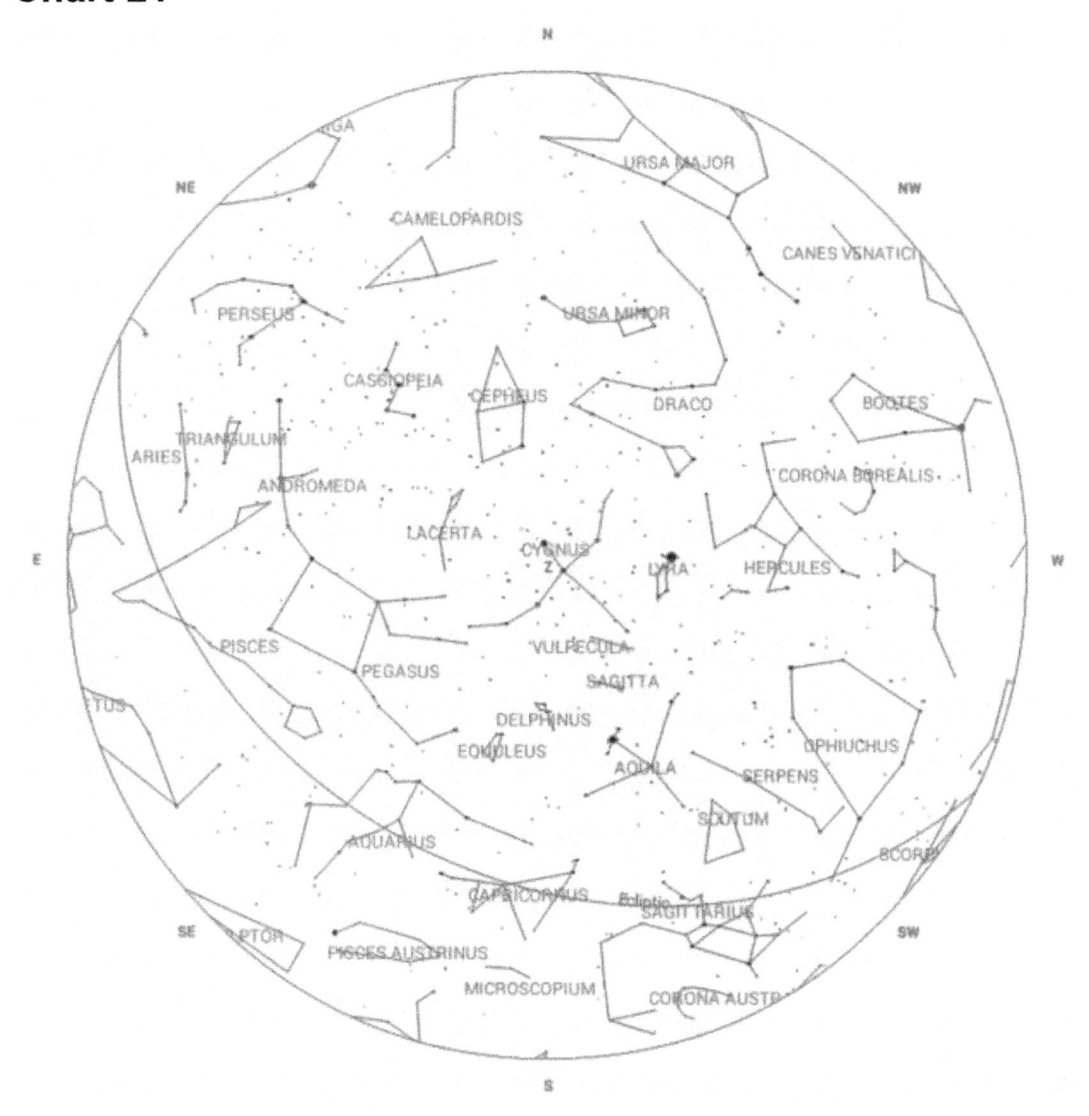

The following constellations are well-placed for observation at this time: Andromeda, Aquarius, Aquila, Aries, Capricornus, Cassiopeia, Cepheus, Corona Borealis, Cygnus, Delphinus, Draco, Equuleus, Hercules, Lyra, Ophiuchus, Pegasus, Perseus, Pisces, Sagitta, Sagittarius, Serpens, Ursa Major, Ursa Minor and Vulpecula.

Chart 22

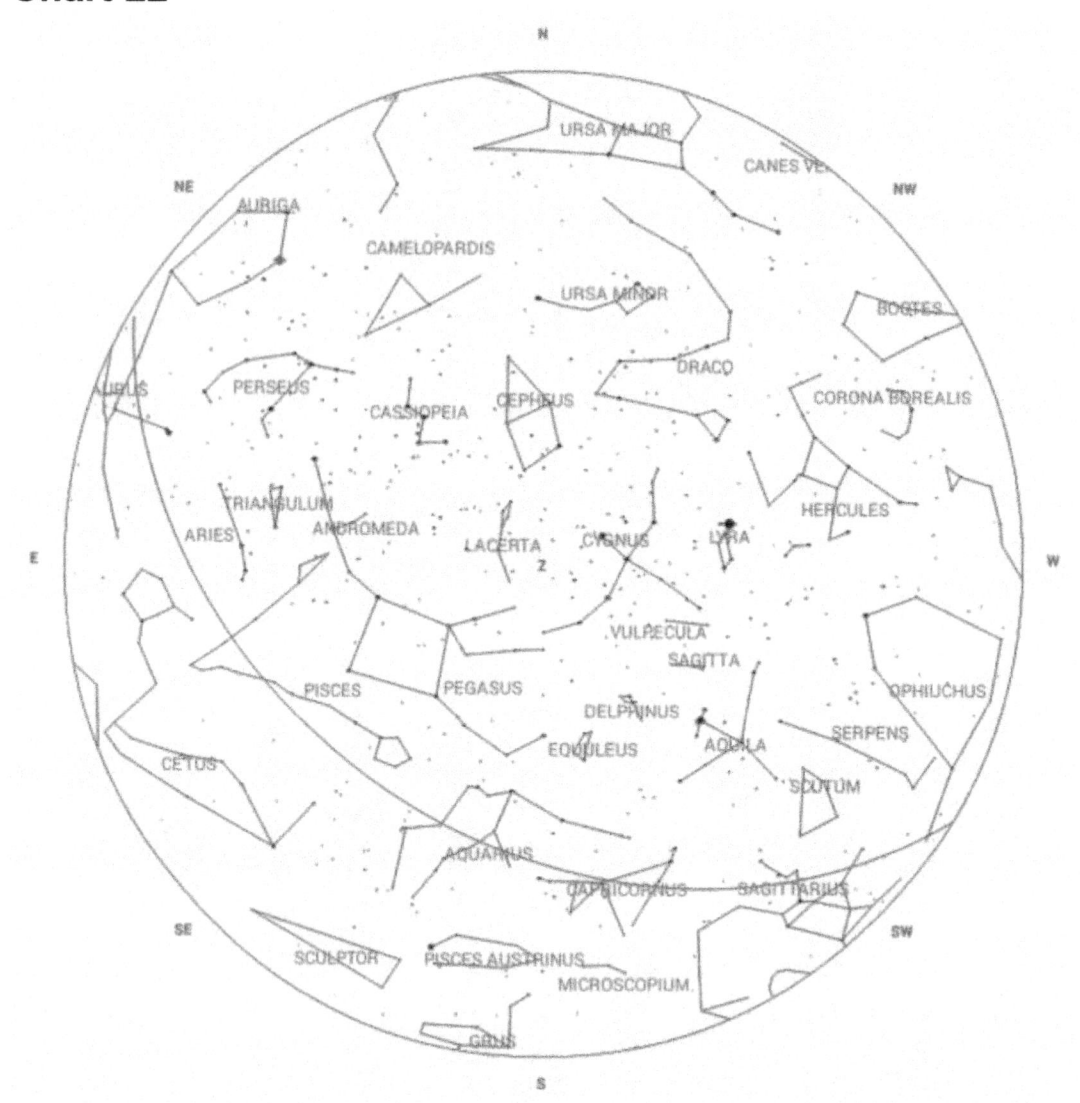

The following constellations are well-placed for observation at this time: Andromeda, Aquarius, Aquila, Aries, Capricornus, Cassiopeia, Cepheus, Corona Borealis, Cygnus, Delphinus, Draco, Equuleus, Hercules, Lyra, Pegasus, Perseus, Pisces, Sagitta, Ursa Minor and Vulpecula.

Chart 23

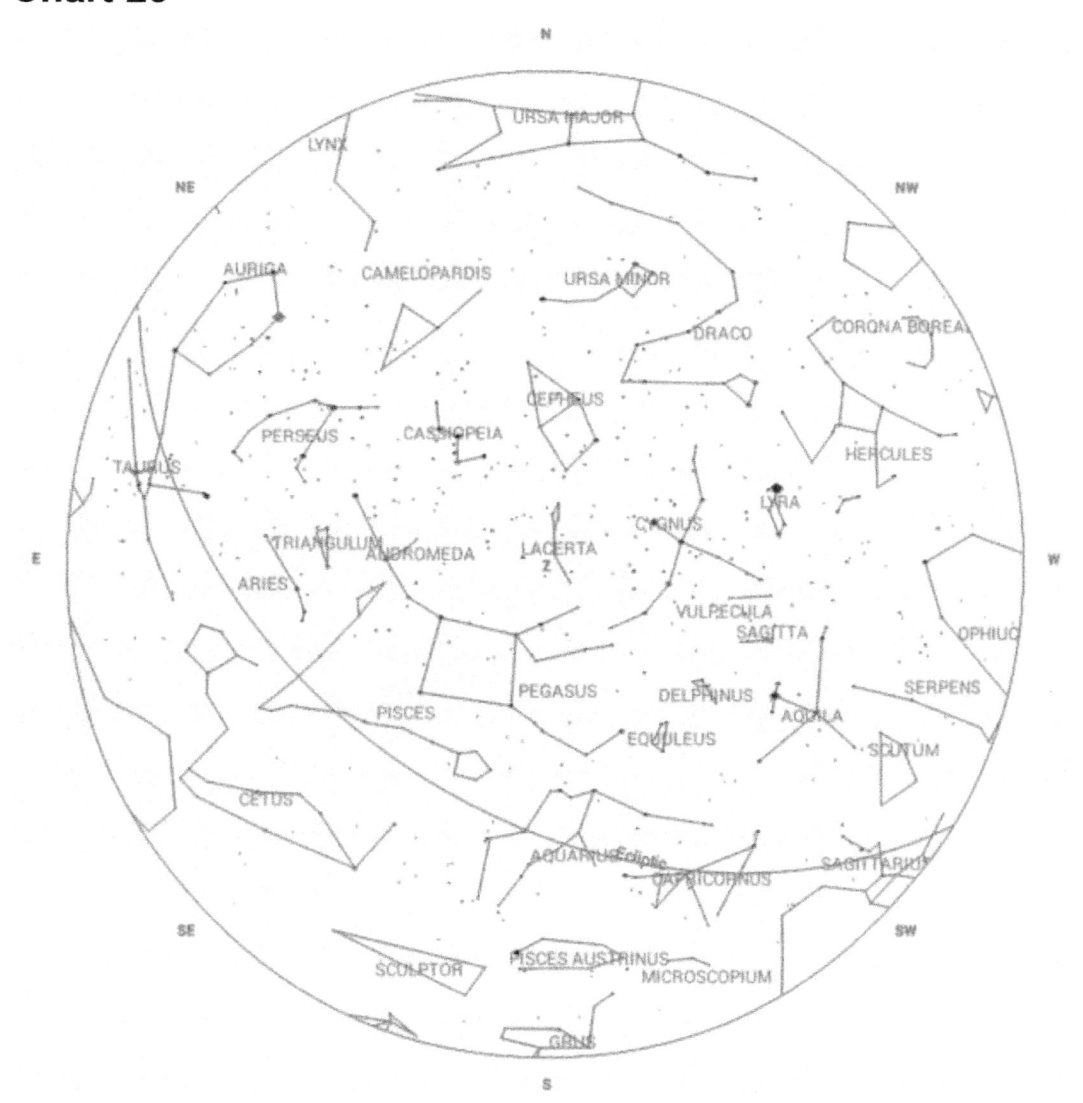

The following constellations are well-placed for observation at this time: Andromeda, Aquarius, Aquila, Aries, Auriga, Capricornus, Cassiopeia, Cepheus, Cetus, Cygnus, Delphinus, Draco, Equuleus, Hercules, Lyra, Pegasus, Perseus, Pisces, Sagitta, Ursa Minor and Vulpecula.

Chart 24

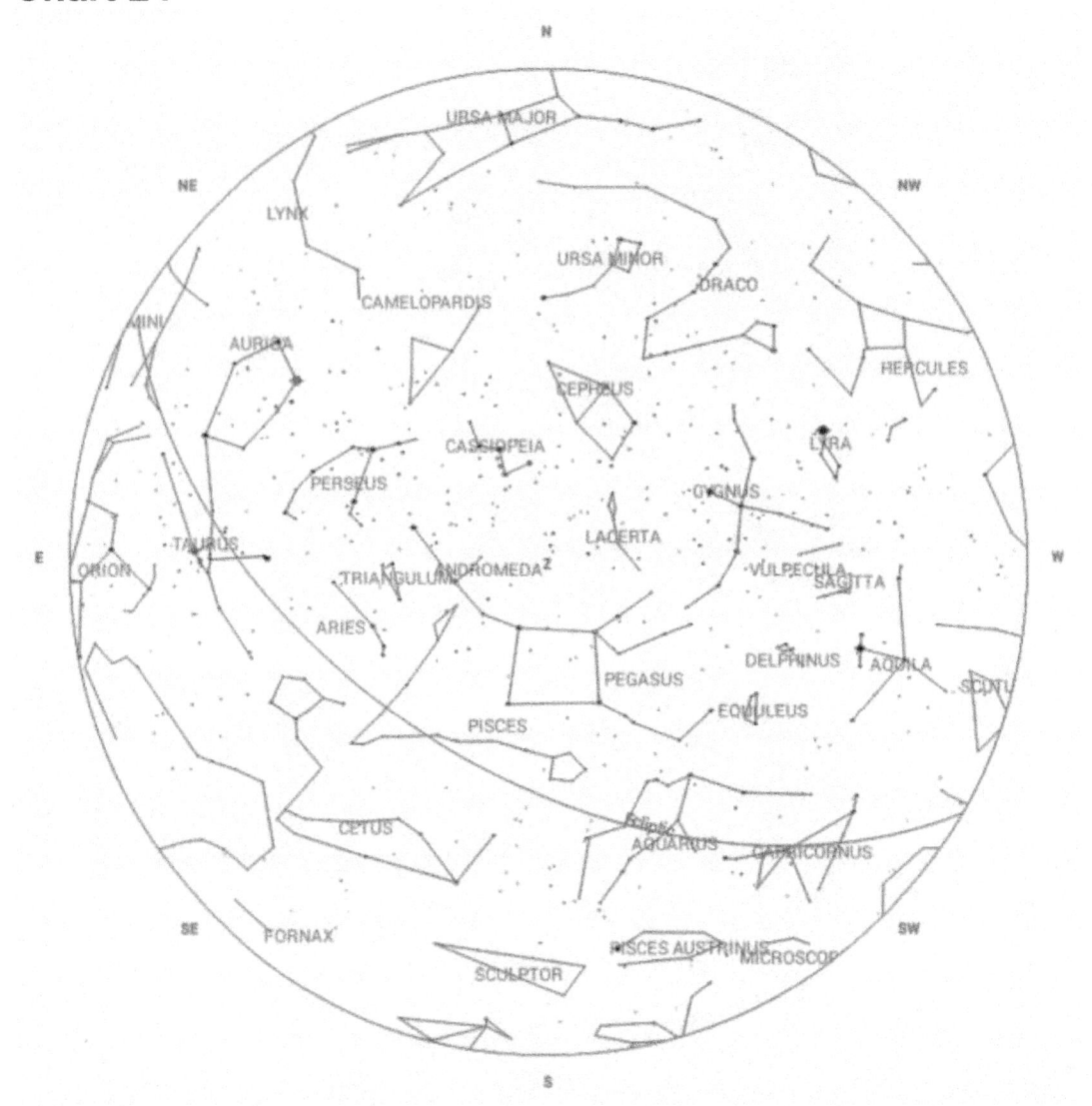

The following constellations are well-placed for observation at this time: Andromeda, Aquarius, Aquila, Aries, Auriga, Capricornus, Cassiopeia, Cepheus, Cetus, Cygnus, Delphinus, Draco, Equuleus, Lyra, Pegasus, Perseus, Pisces, Sagitta, Taurus, Ursa Minor and Vulpecula.

The Constellations

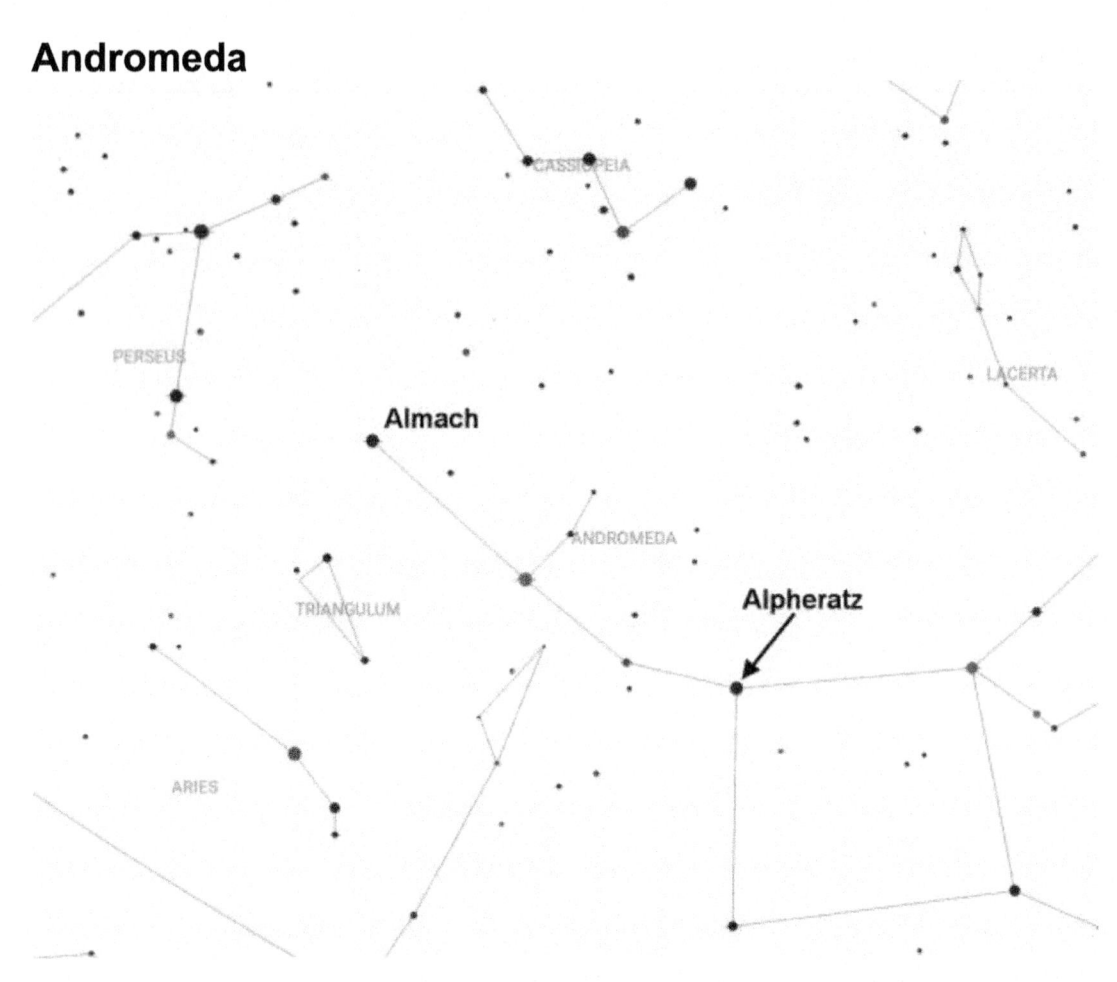

Andromeda

Andromeda is one of the more prominent constellations of the autumn sky and is conveniently located close to Cassiopeia and Pegasus. In Greek mythology, Andromeda was a princess and her story was made famous by the movie *Clash of the Titans*.

The legend involves a number of other constellations, all found nearby, most notably Cassiopeia, Cepheus, Pegasus and Perseus.

Andromeda was the daughter of Cassiopeia, the Queen and Cepheus, the King. Cassiopeia was a vain woman who boasted that her daughter was more beautiful than the sea-nymphs, thereby angering the god Poseidon.

In retribution, Poseidon sent a monster, sometimes associated with Cetus, to terrorize the kingdom. Cepheus consulted an oracle who advised him to sacrifice his daughter to the monster. This would appease the god and save his kingdom.

Poor Andromeda was chained to a rock and was about to be devoured when Perseus came to her rescue. Perseus was returning from slaying the Medusa, a half-woman/half-serpent whose gaze could turn living creatures to stone.

Swooping down on his trusty steed, Pegasus the Flying Horse, Perseus pulled the head of Medusa from his bag and turned the monster to stone, thereby saving the princess. Of course, in true fairy tale fashion, the pair fell in love, married and lived happily ever after.

The constellation has a distinctive curve that outlines the princess's body, but in a game of stellar join-the-dots, if you look closely you can see a second curved line of fainter stars just to the north.

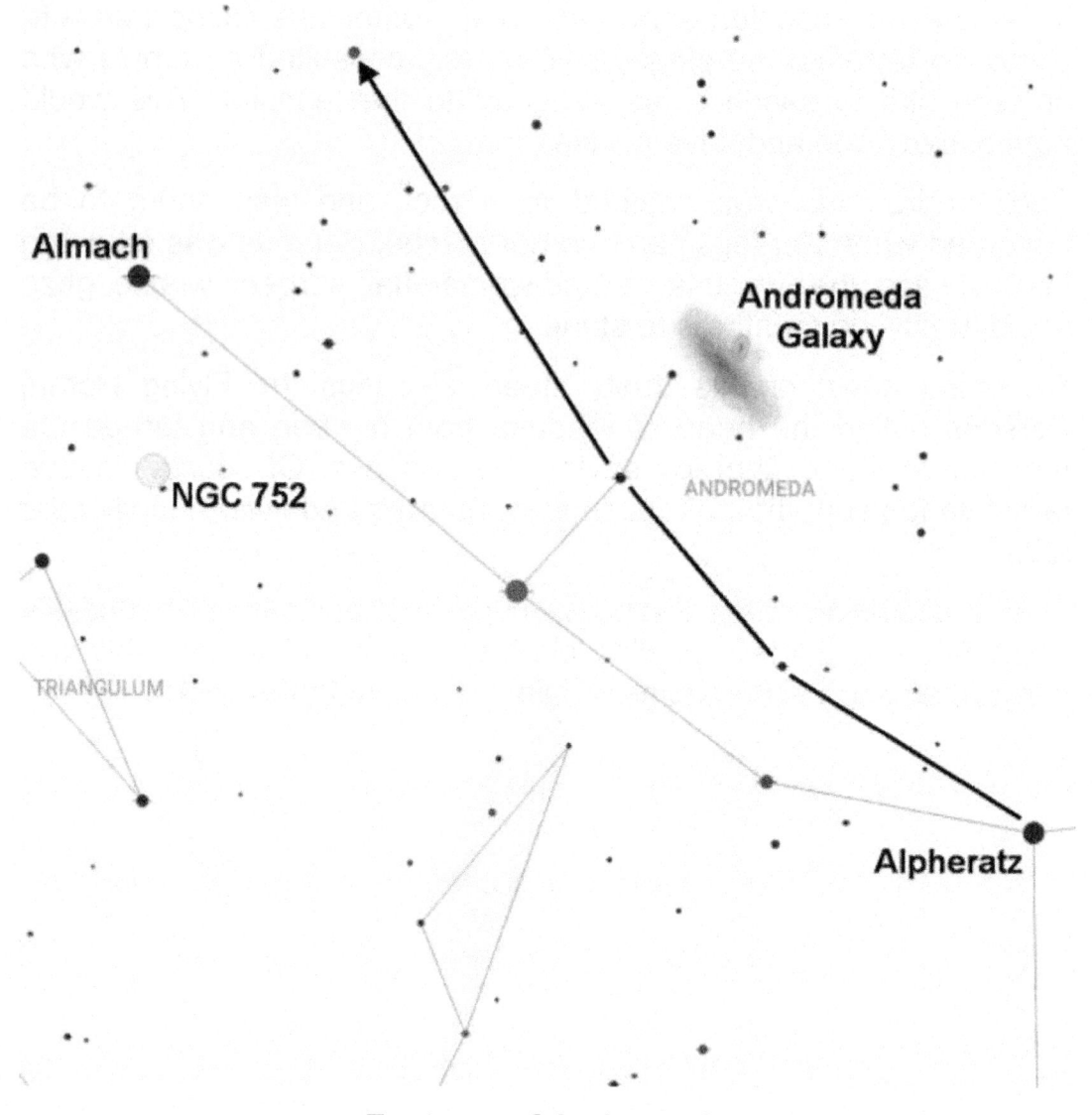

Features of Andromeda

It's one of only two pairs of constellations that share a star. Alpha Andromedae actually marks the north-eastern corner of the square of Pegasus, the Flying Horse and is more commonly known as Alpheratz, from the Arabic for "the navel of the mare" – a reminder of its role in that constellation.

Although it appears to be a single magnitude 2.1 star to your eyes, it's actually a binary system about 100 light years away.

Besides Alpheratz, Andromeda is notable for containing the most distant object easily seen with just your eyes. Messier 31, the Andromeda Galaxy, is a sister galaxy to our own Milky Way and is thought to be about 2 ¼ million light years away.

If you look carefully, you can barely glimpse it as a very faint, misty patch but you'll need to be away from the lights of your town or city to see it. If you can't get away, try scanning the area with binoculars or a small telescope.

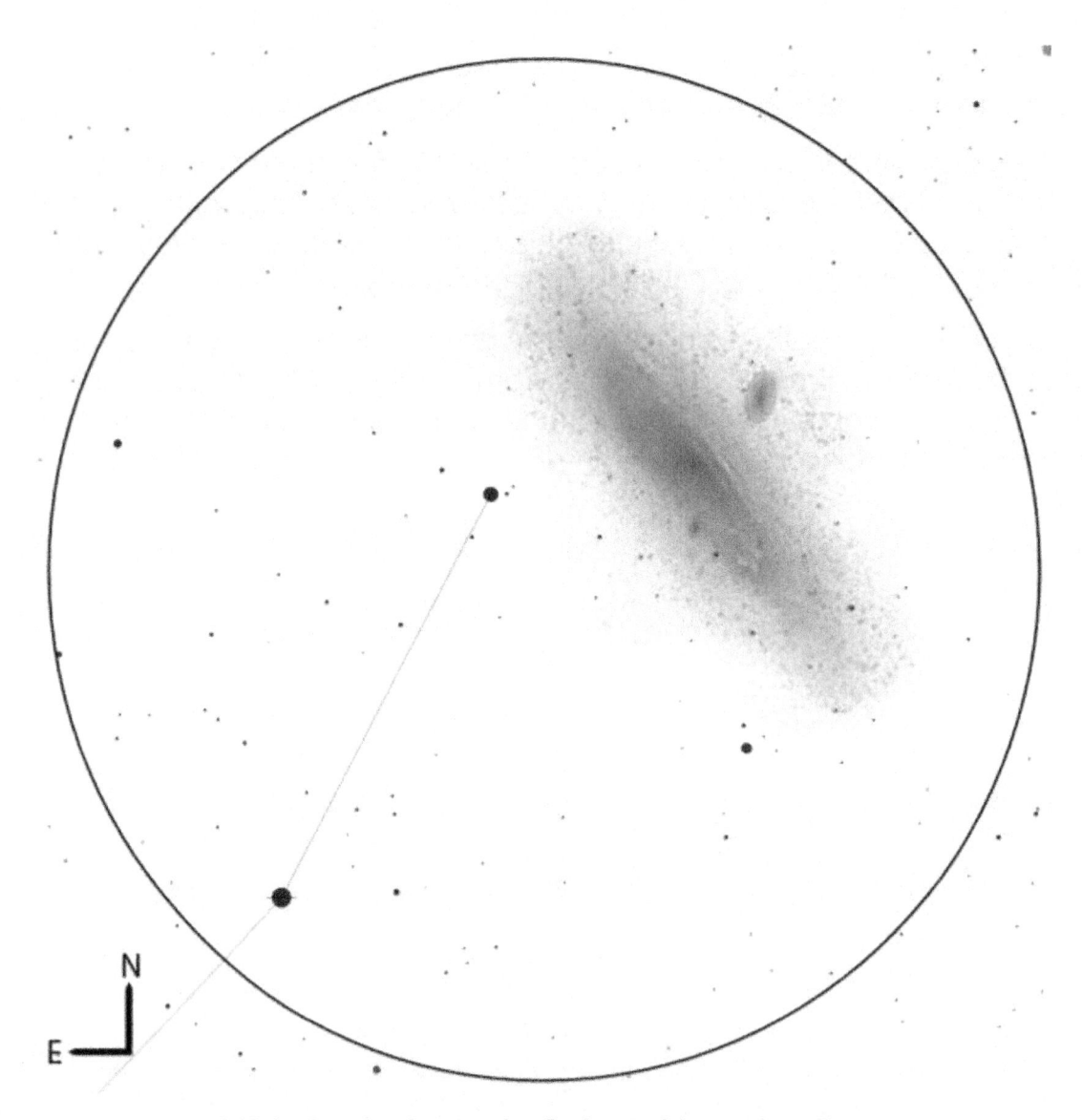

M31, the Andromeda Galaxy, binocular view

Further to the east is Gamma, also known as Almach, a magnitude 2.3 star that's a fine double in small telescopes. Close to Almach is NGC 752, a binocular star cluster that appears large but faint through a regular pair of 10x50's. Like Almach, this cluster is also a fine target for small telescopes with even a low power eyepiece providing an attractive view.

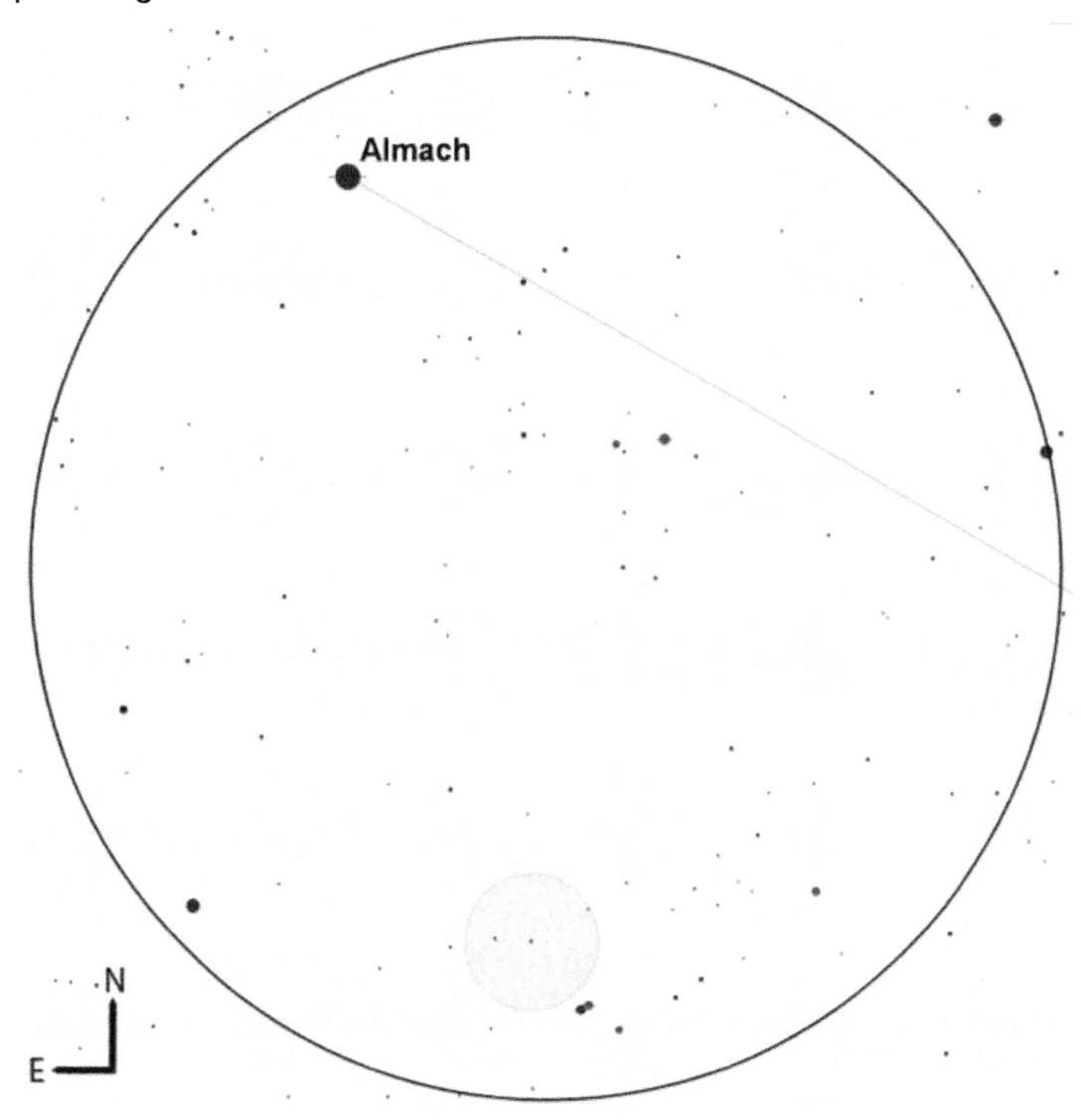

NGC 752, binocular view

Aquarius

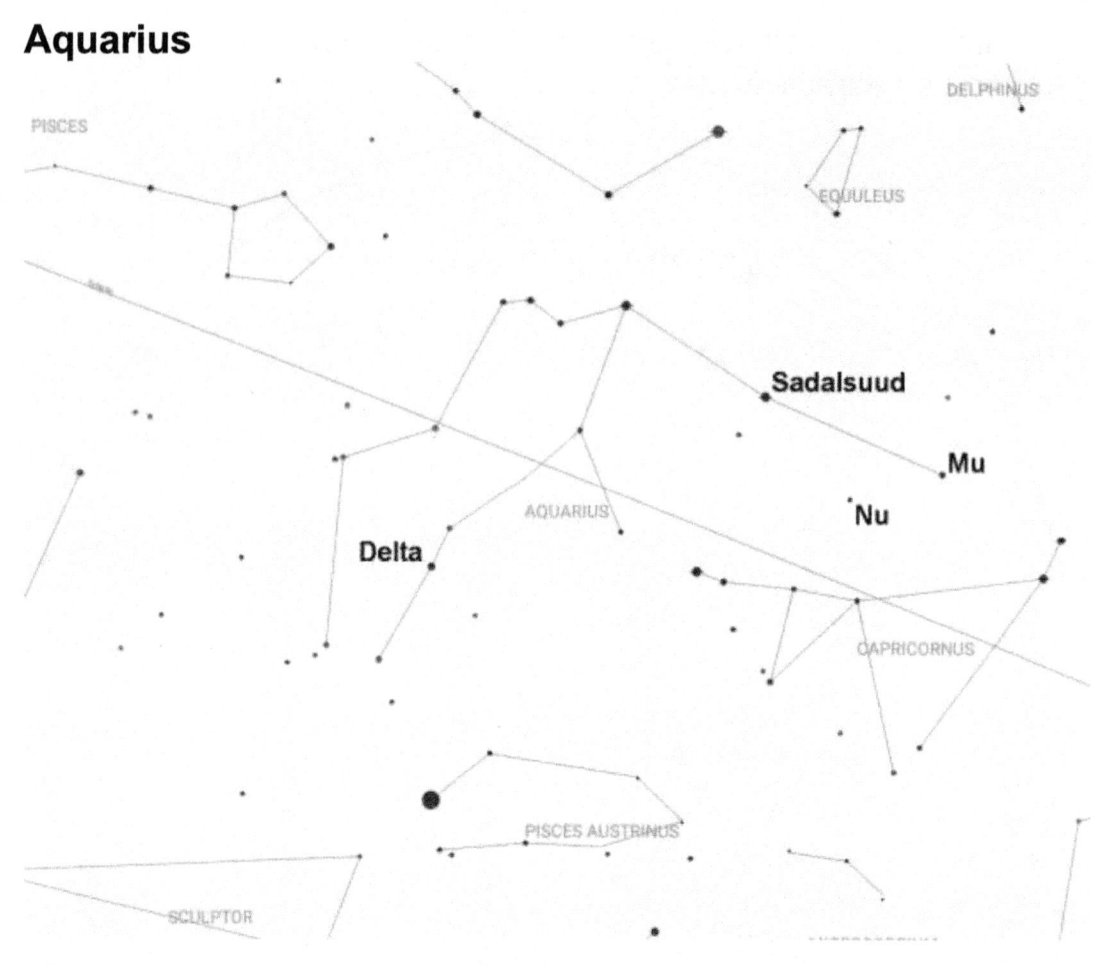

Aquarius is also known as "the water carrier" and, in Greek mythology, it's often associated with Ganymede, a Trojan boy who was kidnapped by Zeus to be the cup bearer of the gods.

Aquarius is one of the faint autumnal constellations and is not easily seen or recognized. You'll probably need to get away from the lights of your nearest town or city to identify its outline.

It's a sprawling constellation, 10th in size overall, that can be found to the east of Capricornus. If you can find the square of Pegasus, draw a line diagonally down through the top right and bottom right stars of the square. Keep going down until you come to a bright star.

This is Fomalhaut, the brightest star in Pisces Austrinus, the Southern Fish. Midway between the two is Aquarius.

The brightest star in Aquarius is Beta, called Sadalsuud, an Arabic name that means "luck of lucks." Located some 550 light years away, it's a yellow star some fifty times the size of the Sun that's over 2,000 times brighter than our own star.

It's also pretty young – only about 60 million years old – which means if you could travel back in time and walk the Earth with the dinosaurs, you wouldn't see this star in the sky!

To our eyes today, it appears as a pretty ordinary star, just under magnitude 3 in brightness.

Aquarius is home to a number of deep sky objects but you'll need at least a pair of binoculars or a telescope to see them.

Brightest of these is Messier 2, a large globular cluster that should be within the range of a decent pair of binoculars. It's located about 3/4 of the way between Enif, in Pegasus and Sadalsuud. You can also try scanning westward from Sadalmelik.

Through binoculars I've noted that it appears as a small, grey misty patch while a small telescope can reveal a little more detail.

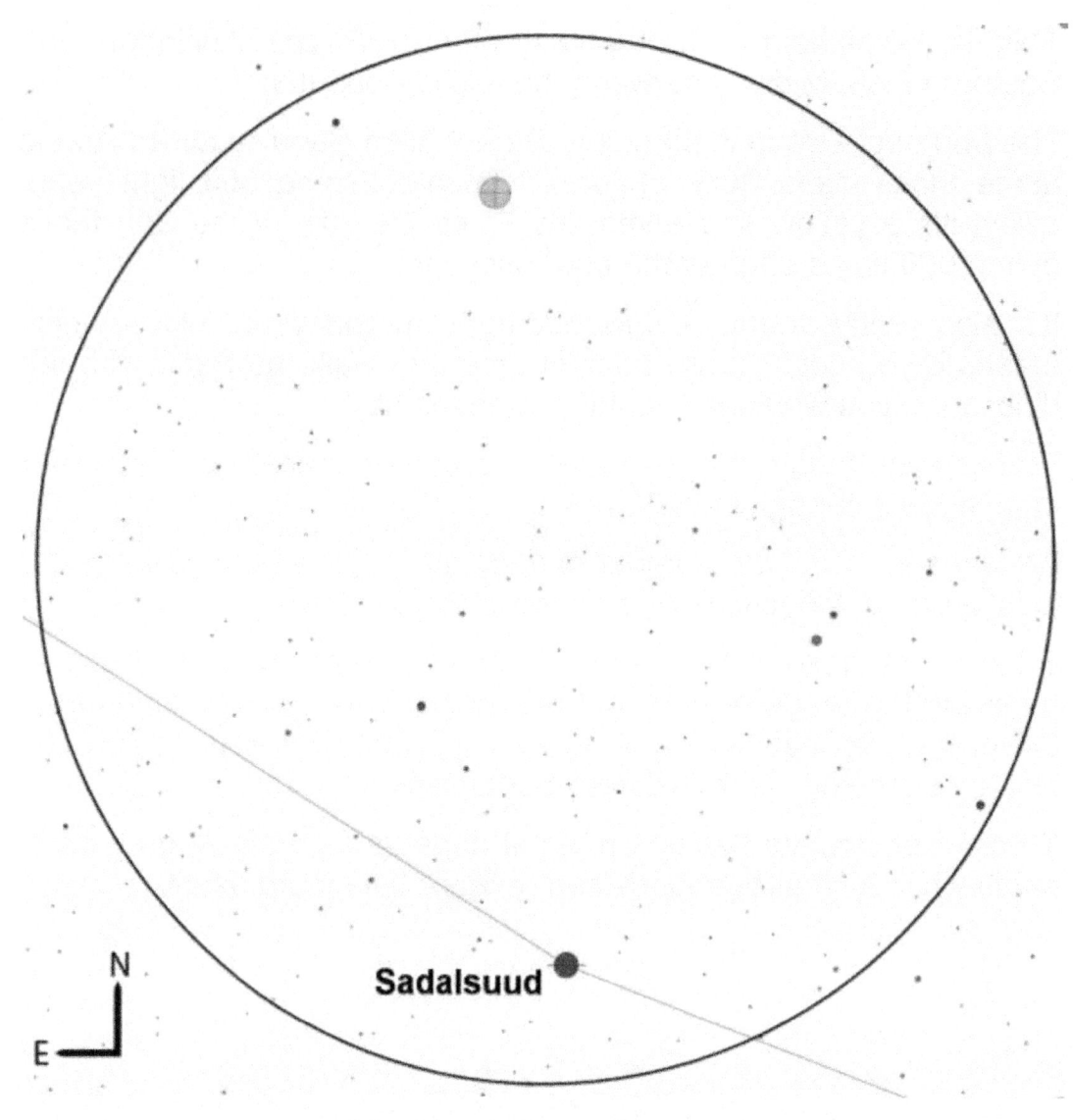

Messier 2, binocular view

Of the other objects, two in particular stand out. The Helix Nebula is very large (almost the size of the full Moon) but is also very faint. You'll certainly need binoculars and you'll definitely need to be as far away from any lights as possible. Try to catch it close to Delta Aquarii with 66 Aquarii midway between the two.

This is a planetary nebula, which means it's the shell of a dying star that's slowly expanding outwards into space. This shell is now thought to be nearly three light years in diameter!

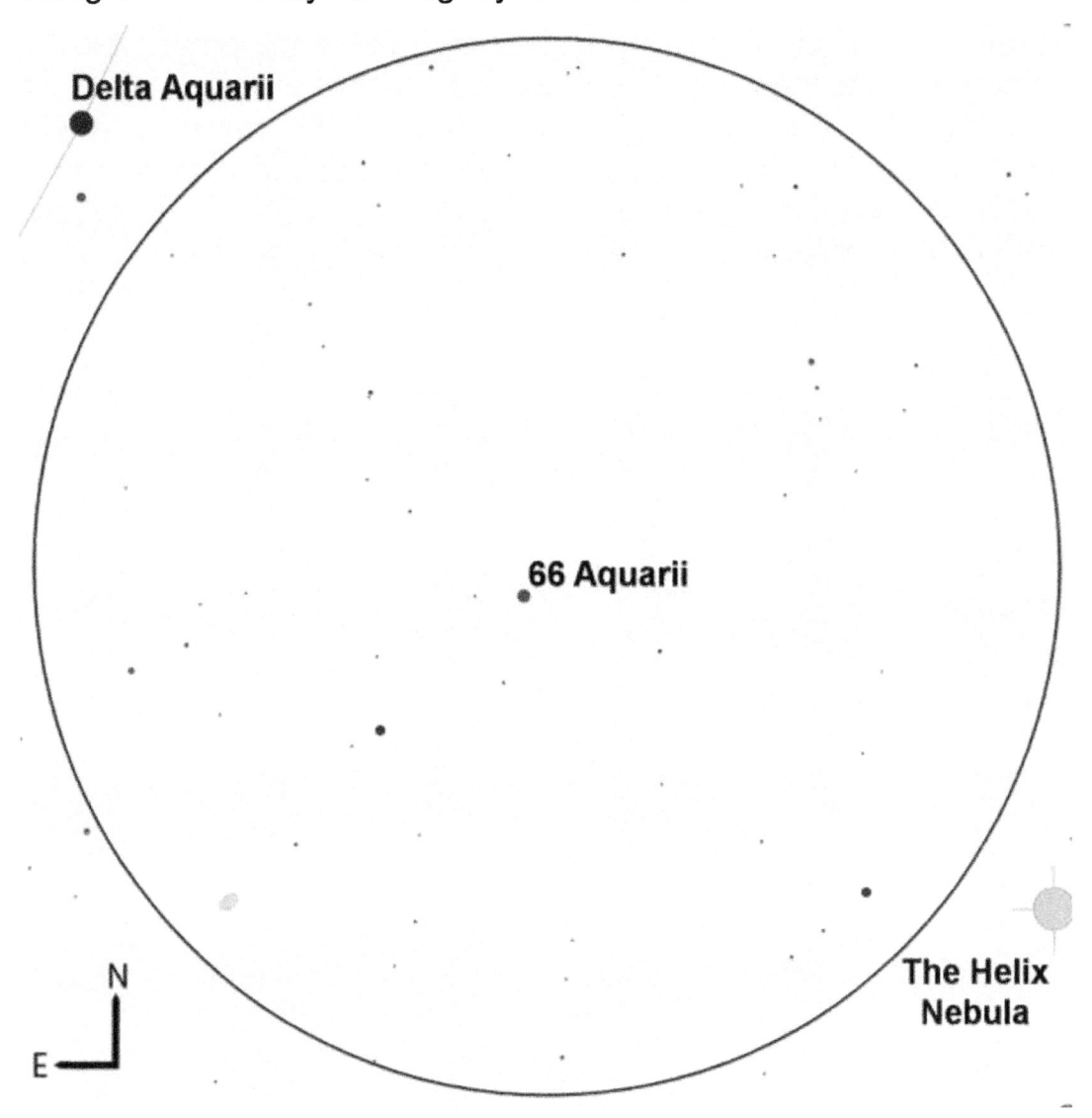

Locating the Helix nebula, binocular view.

Another planetary is called the Saturn nebula. It's much smaller than the Helix, but has the appearance of that famous planet when observed with a telescope.

Through binoculars it can appear as a small, fairly bright star-like point, but it has the distinction of having a yellow-greenish hue. Like the Helix, this is the shell of a dying star but this particular stellar remnant is only a half light year in diameter. Look for it close to Mu and Nu Aquarii, but again, it's best to get away from any lights if you want to try your luck!

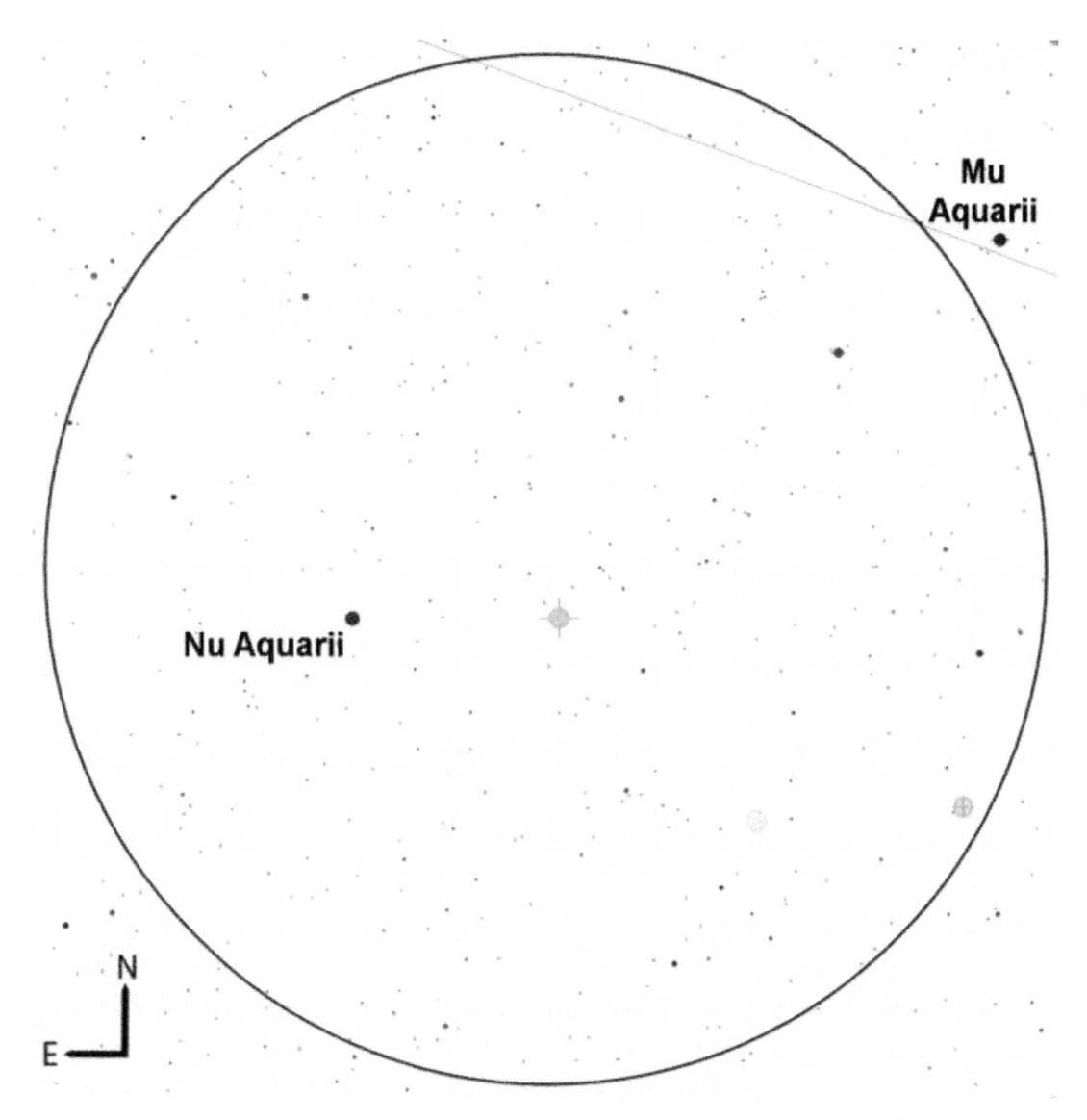

Locating the Saturn nebula, binocular view.

Aquila

In Greek mythology, Aquila represents the eagle that carried the thunderbolts of Zeus. This was the same eagle that carried the boy Ganymede away from his home to be the cup bearer for the gods (and was consequently immortalized in the constellation of Aquarius.)

Aquila is one of the main constellations of summer and is easily visible until the autumn. Its brightest star, Altair, marks one corner of the Summer Triangle with Vega (in Lyra) and Deneb (in Cygnus) completing the pattern.

Altair itself is associated with its own legend, but not one of Greek origin. In several Asian cultures, Altair represents a cow herder who fell in love with a weaver girl (or in some versions, a princess), as represented by the star Vega.

There are a number of variations, but the tale goes something like this: the girl spent all her time weaving and despaired of finding true love. Her father, the God of Heaven, wishing her to be happy, arranged for her to meet the cow herder but he didn't anticipate what happened next.

Falling deeply in love, the pair married and the girl stopped weaving and the cows wandered all over Heaven. This angered her father and so he separated them by placing the cow herder and the weaver girl on opposite sides of a river, represented by the Milky Way.

Consequently, the pair can only meet once a year, on the 7th day of the 7th month. On that day, all the magpies come together to form a bridge across the river. If it rains on that day, it's said to be the tears of the lovers, unable to meet.

In reality, Altair is the 12th brightest star in the sky and, at just under 17 light years away, one of the closest to our own. It's a pale yellow magnitude 0.8 star, nearly twice the mass of the Sun, that spins on its axis once every nine hours. This has the curious effect of flattening the star at its poles!

Altair is accompanied on either side by two stars: Alshaid (Beta Aquilae) to the east and Tarazed (Gamma Aquilae) to the west. In the legend recalled earlier, these two stars sometimes represent the two children of the forbidden lovers.

Keeping with the avian theme, Alshaid's name is derived from the Arabic for "the raven's neck" while all three stars are collectively known as the "family of Aquila."

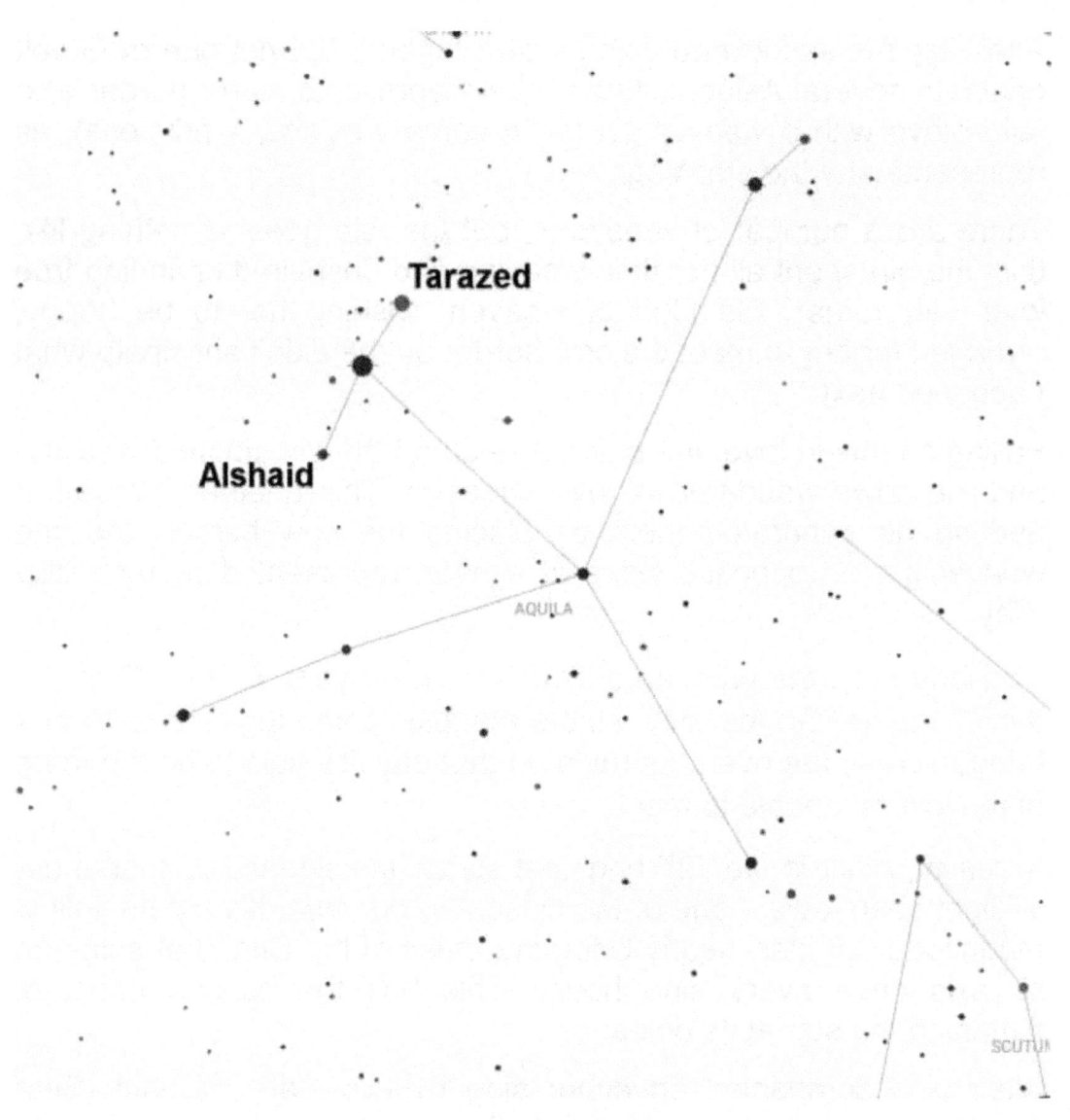

Alshaid and Tarazed

There isn't a conspicuous deep sky object that's easily seen in the constellation; however, if you scan with binoculars just to the southwest, you'll encounter the small constellation of Scutum the Shield.

Here, quite close to Lambda Aquilae and Beta Scuti, is the Wild Duck Cluster. Discovered in 1681 by the German astronomer Gottfried Kirch, it has an estimated 2,900 stars and is over 6,000 light years away.

Through binoculars it appears as a small, faint globular patch but it's better observed with a small telescope under low or moderate power.

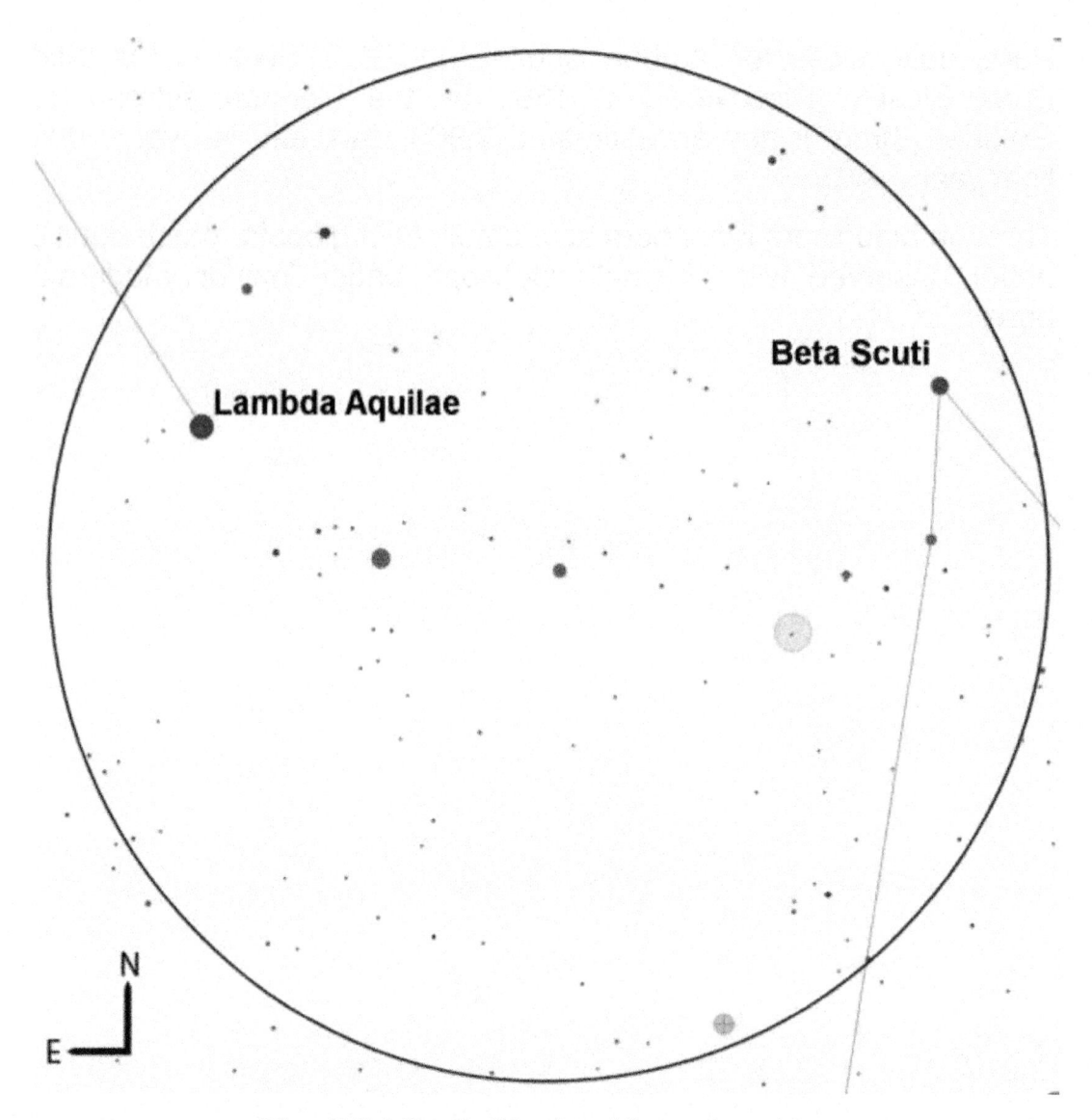

The Wild Duck Cluster, binocular view.

88

Aries

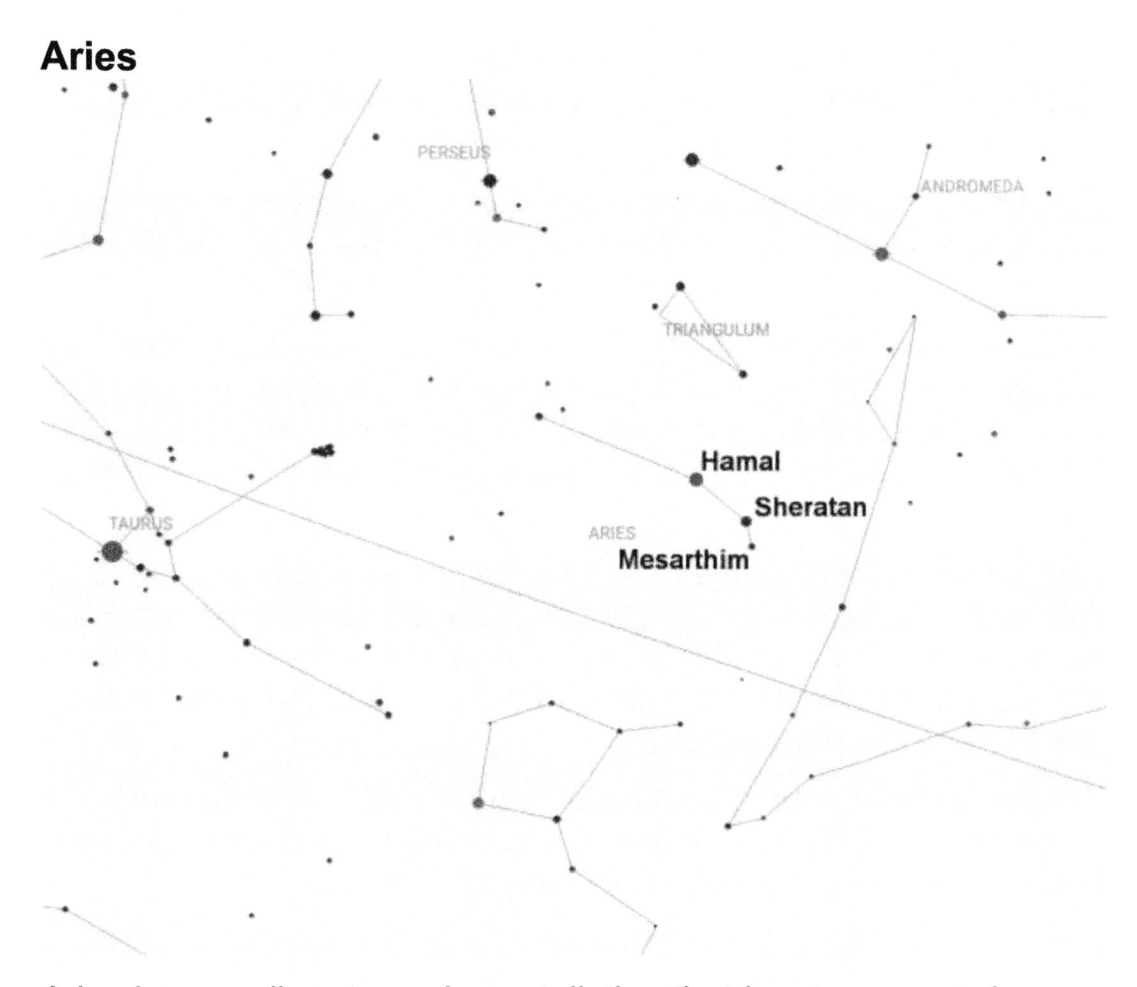

Aries is a small, autumnal constellation that has represented a ram across numerous cultures and civilizations since antiquity. Nowadays it's commonly associated with the ram that saved the lives of the twins Helle and Phrixus in Greek mythology.

The fleece of the ram became known as the Golden Fleece and features prominently in the legend of Jason and the Argonauts.

Aries is the first of twelve zodiac constellations and, as such, the Sun, Moon and planets all pass through it as they traverse across the sky.

Aries is particularly noteworthy as it once contained the First Point of Aries. This is where the Sun would cross from the southern celestial hemisphere to the north during the Spring equinox.

First noted over two thousand years ago, this point has since moved backwards into the constellation of Pisces but it still retains the name.

The constellation predominantly consists of three main stars that form a curved line between Taurus and Pegasus. From west to east, they are Mesarthim (the faintest of the three, magnitude 3.9), Sheratan (magnitude 2.7) and Hamal (the brightest, at magnitude 2.0)

Hamal means "head of the ram" and is an orange giant star some 66 light years away. It's thought to have at least one planet orbiting it once every 380 days. This planet is also about the same distance from its parent star as the Earth is from the Sun, but unfortunately, that's where the similarities end.

This planet is thought to be a giant about the size of Saturn and with nearly twice the mass of Jupiter. It also orbits the star far outside the habitable zone, so alien life is not likely to be there.

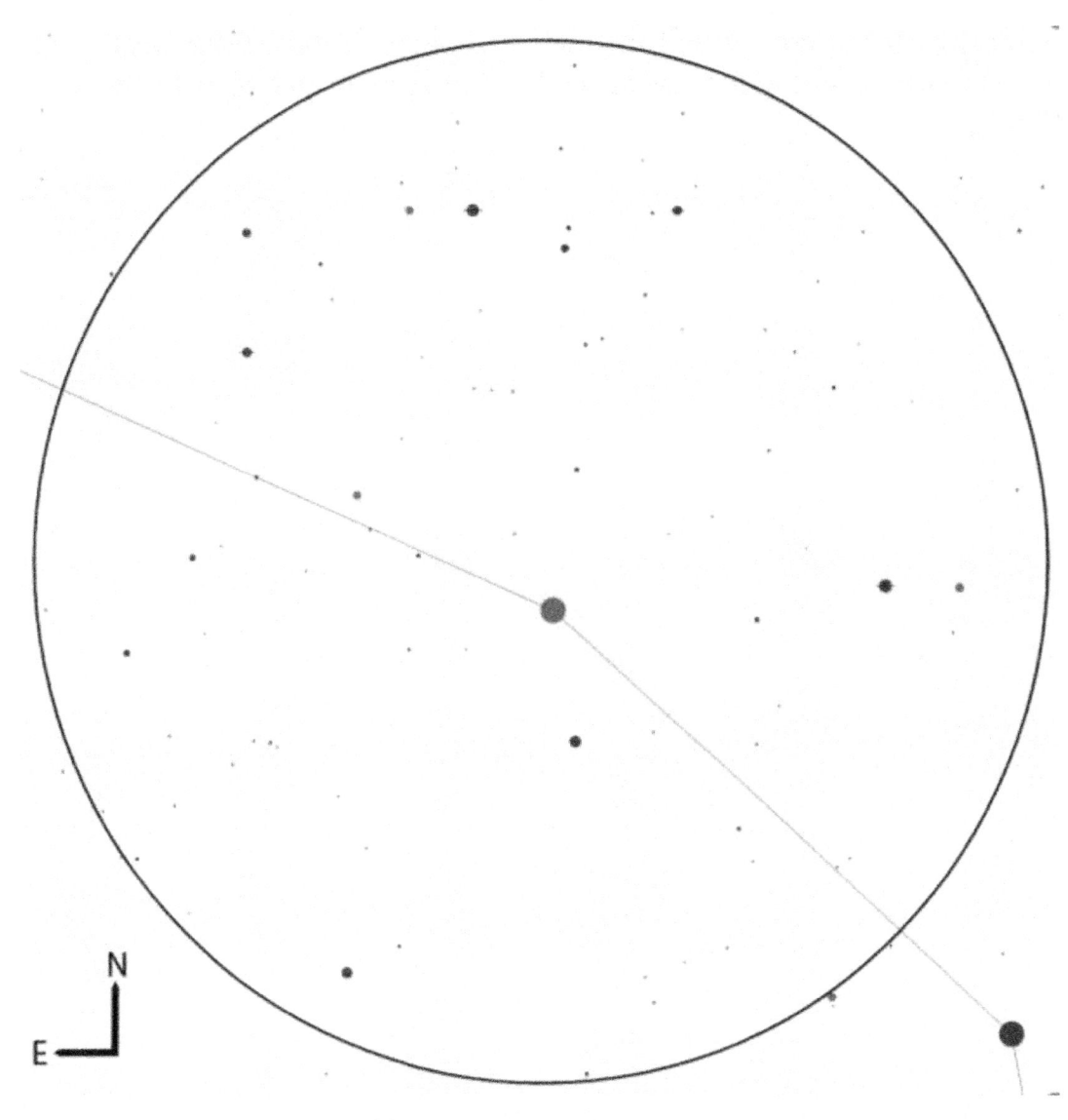

Hamal, binocular view.

Sheratan, the second brightest star in the constellation, is slightly closer at about 60 light years away. It consists of a close pair of stars that orbit one another once every 107 days.

Unfortunately, you won't be able to see them both with only binoculars or a small telescope, but Aries is home to a particularly fine gem.

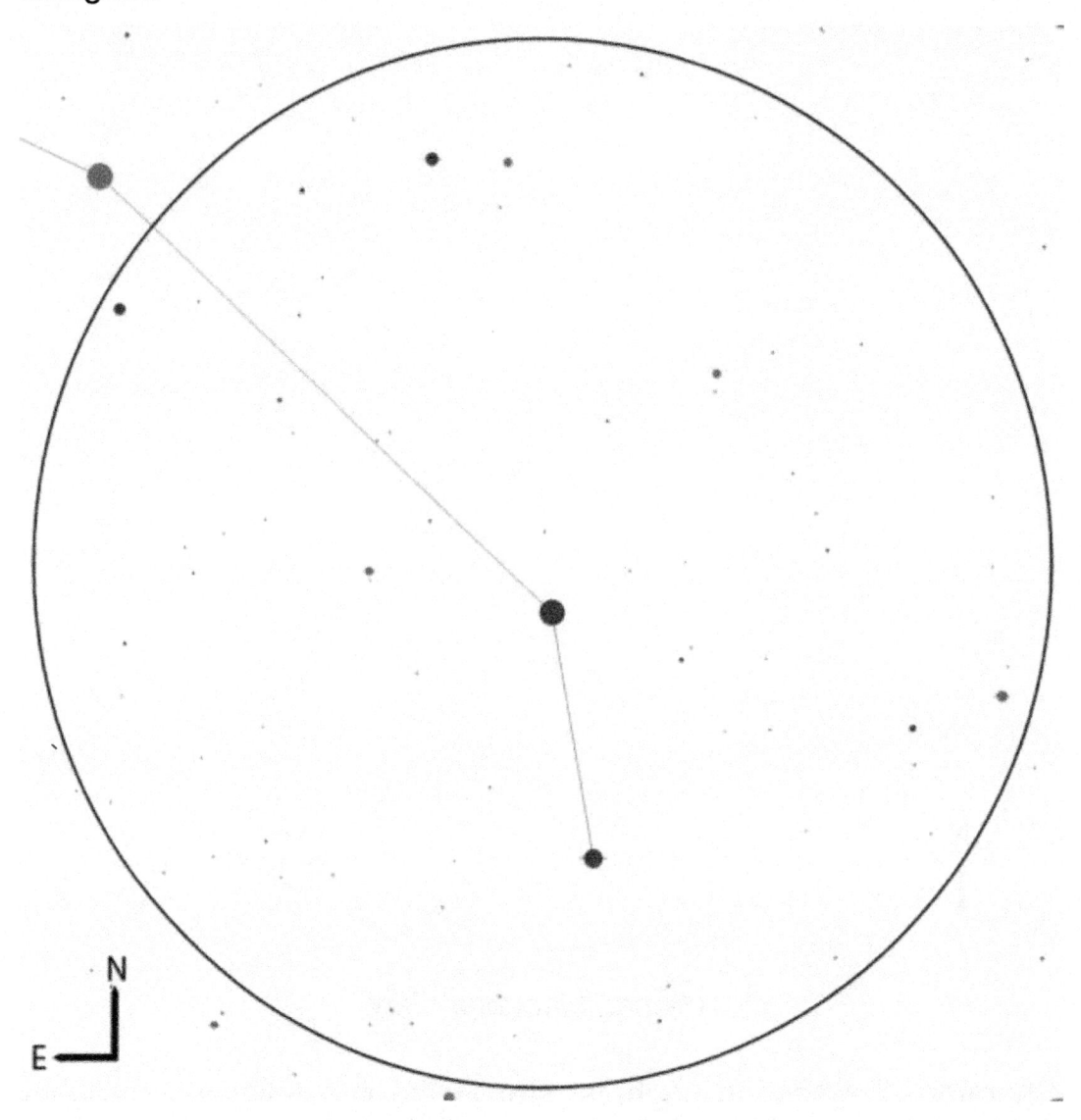

Sheratan, binocular view.

If you have a telescope, take a look at Mesarthim, the faintest of the three stars. With medium power (about 50x), you can easily split the star into two bright white components of equal brightness.

This is a genuine double star system that lies about 165 light years away with the two stars taking more than 5,000 years to orbit one another.

As for the name, its origins are not definitively known with links to the Arabic and Sanskrit words for ram.

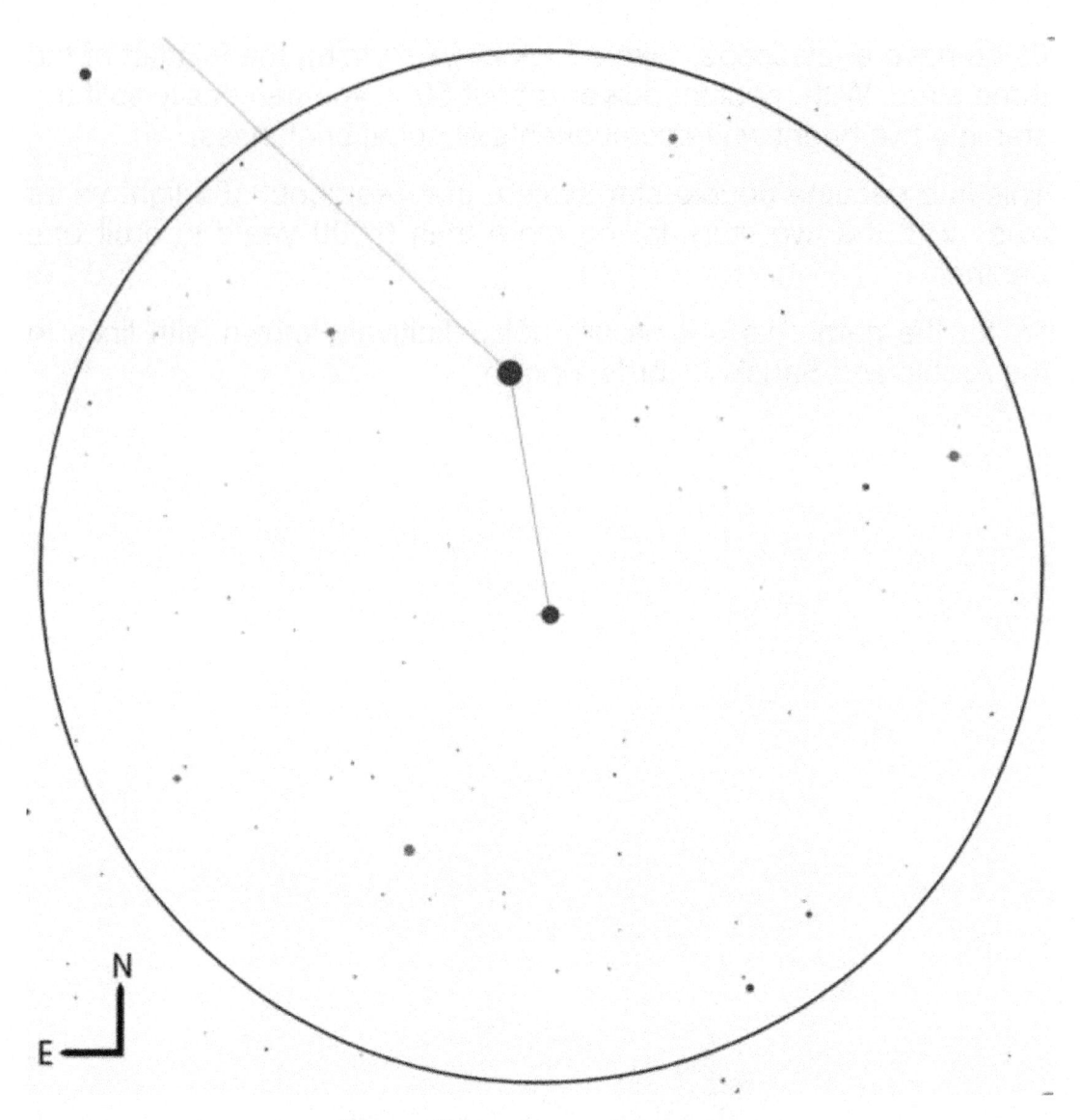

Mesarthim, binocular view.

One other star deserves a mention: Teegarden's star is a very faint red dwarf star, far beyond the limits of your eyes or binoculars. It wasn't discovered until 2003 but, at 12 light years away, is one of our closest neighbors in space.

Auriga

Auriga, the Charioteer, is thought to represent Erichthonius, the lame footed king of Athens who invented the chariot as a means of transport.

It's a mis-shapen hexagon halfway between Perseus and Gemini, easily visible throughout the entire winter and made distinctive by its brightest star, Capella.

Not only is Capella the brightest star in the constellation, but at magnitude 0.1, it's also the sixth brightest in the entire night sky.

Like many other bright stars, at just under 43 light years, Capella is one of our closest neighbors but its most fascinating feature is invisible to us. To the naked eye it appears as a single star but it's actually a quadruple system made up of two pairs of stars.

The first pair are two yellow stars, similar to the Sun but each about 2-3 times more massive. They orbit one another once every 100 days or so with a gap of about ¾ the distance of the Earth to the Sun between them.

The other pair consists of two red dwarfs, thousands of times further out from the first pair.

Capella is also one of the few stars that has its own mythological associations.

According to Greek myth, the star represents the she-goat Amalthea who nursed the baby Zeus.

If you look closely at Capella you'll see a small elongated triangle of three stars, just to the west and on the Perseus side of the constellation.

Known as the *Haedi* (or "the kids") the bottom two stars represent the young goats sometimes depicted in the arms of the charioteer himself.

The northernmost star in the triangle may also be worth a look. Epsilon Aurigae is a variable star; in other words, it appears to grow dim and then brighten again. Unfortunately, it doesn't happen very often – in fact, it only happens to Epsilon once every 27 years and it won't happen again until approximately 2036.

At that time, the star will appear to fade from magnitude 3.0 to 3.8 and will stay this way for about a year or so. This is because the star is actually a binary system. Once every 27 years the fainter companion passes in front of the brighter primary star and eclipses it, causing the star's magnitude to drop.

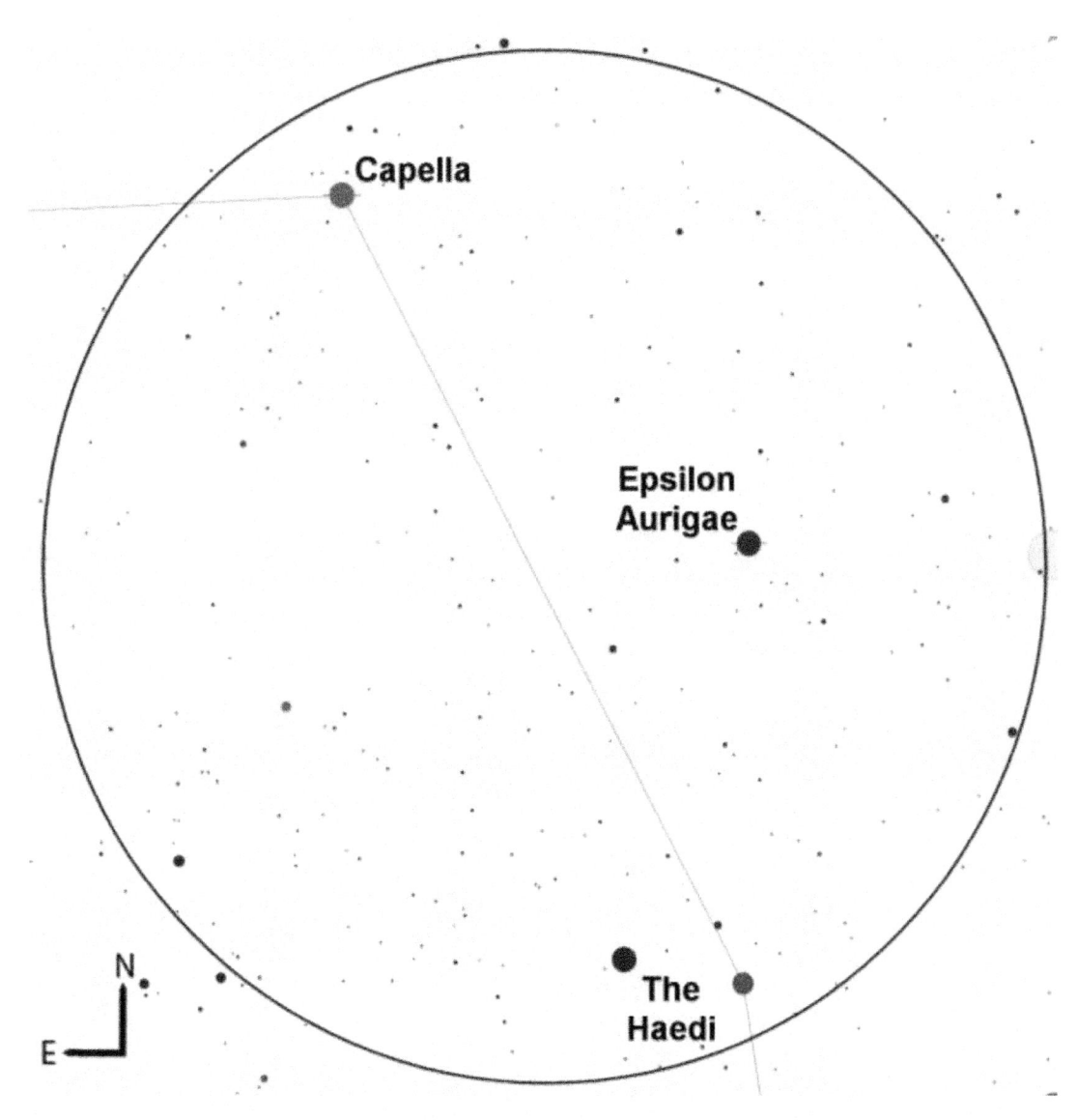

Capella, Epsilon and the Haedi, binocular view.

Auriga, like Andromeda, actually shares one of its stars with another constellation. If you look carefully at the star chart for Auriga, you'll notice that the southernmost star, El Nath, is also a part of Taurus the Bull.

Once known as Gamma Aurigae, it now officially belongs to only Taurus and is known as Beta Tauri.

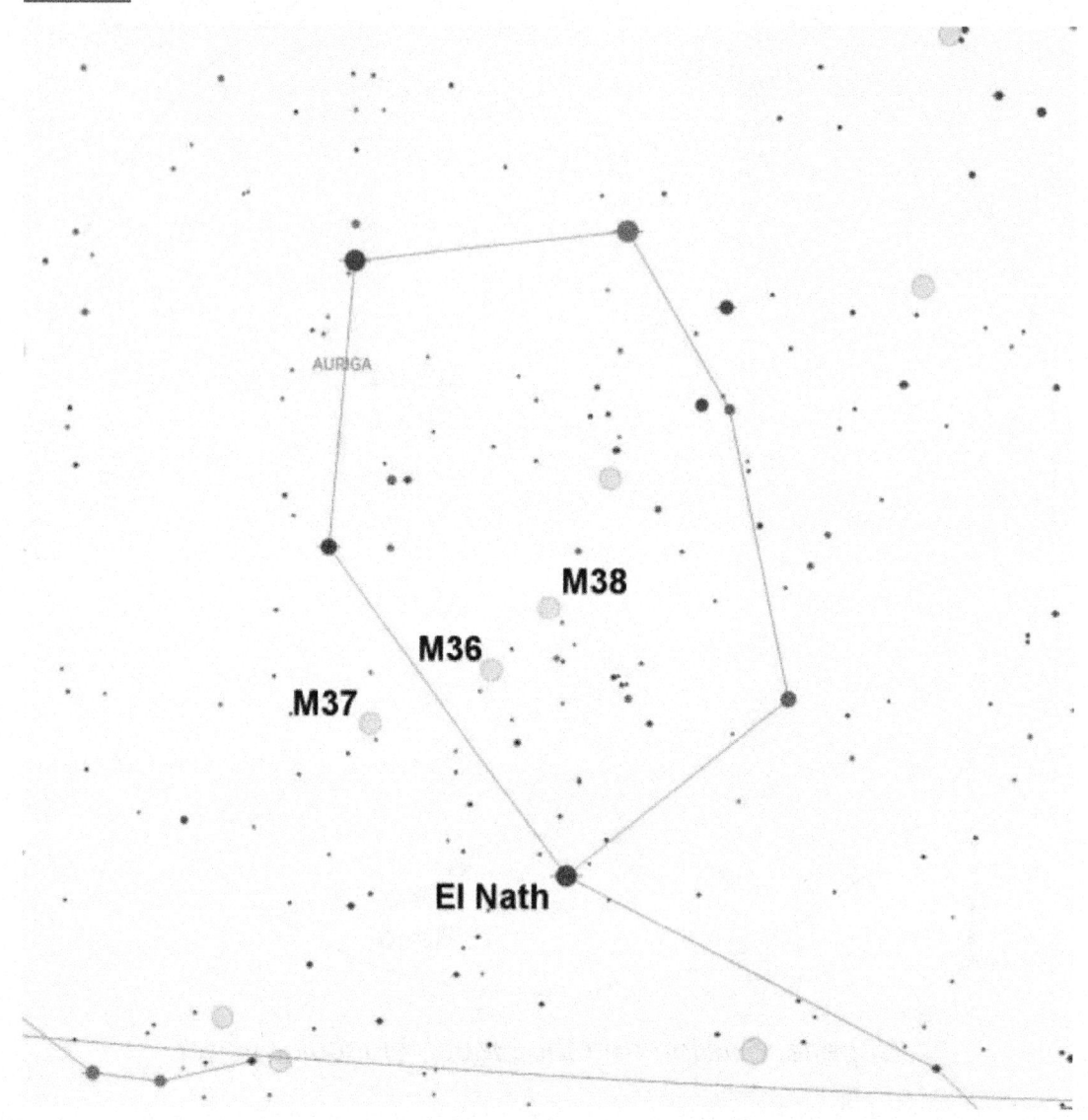

The location of El Nath, M36, M37 and M38

Lastly, if you have binoculars be sure to track down Auriga's three open star clusters – M36, M37 and M38. Of the three, M37 is the brightest and densest but M36 is smaller and, hence, its light is more condensed and the cluster can be easier to spot. M38 may only appear as a faint glow. All are best seen with a small telescope.

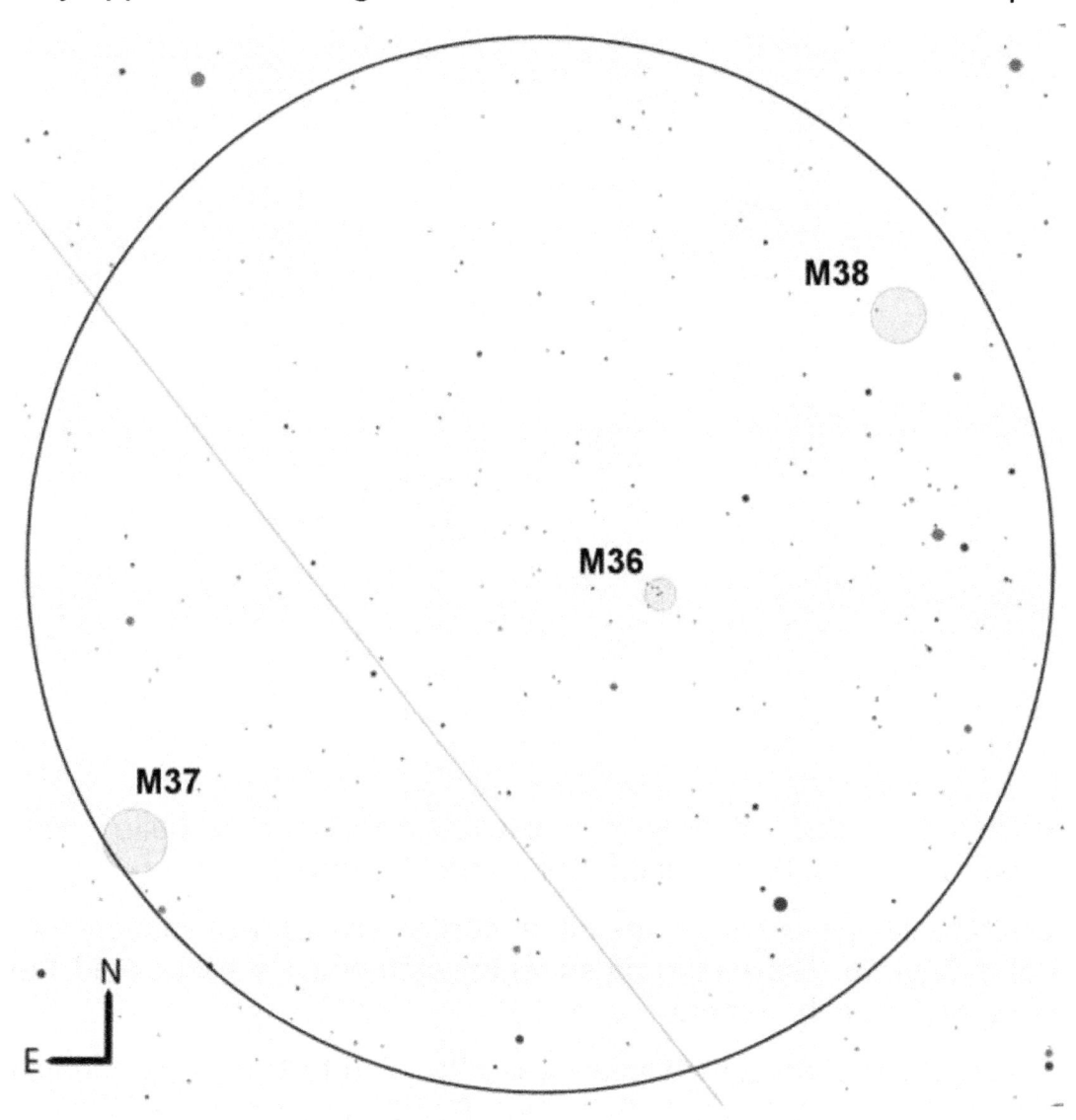

M36, M37 and M38, binocular view.

Boötes

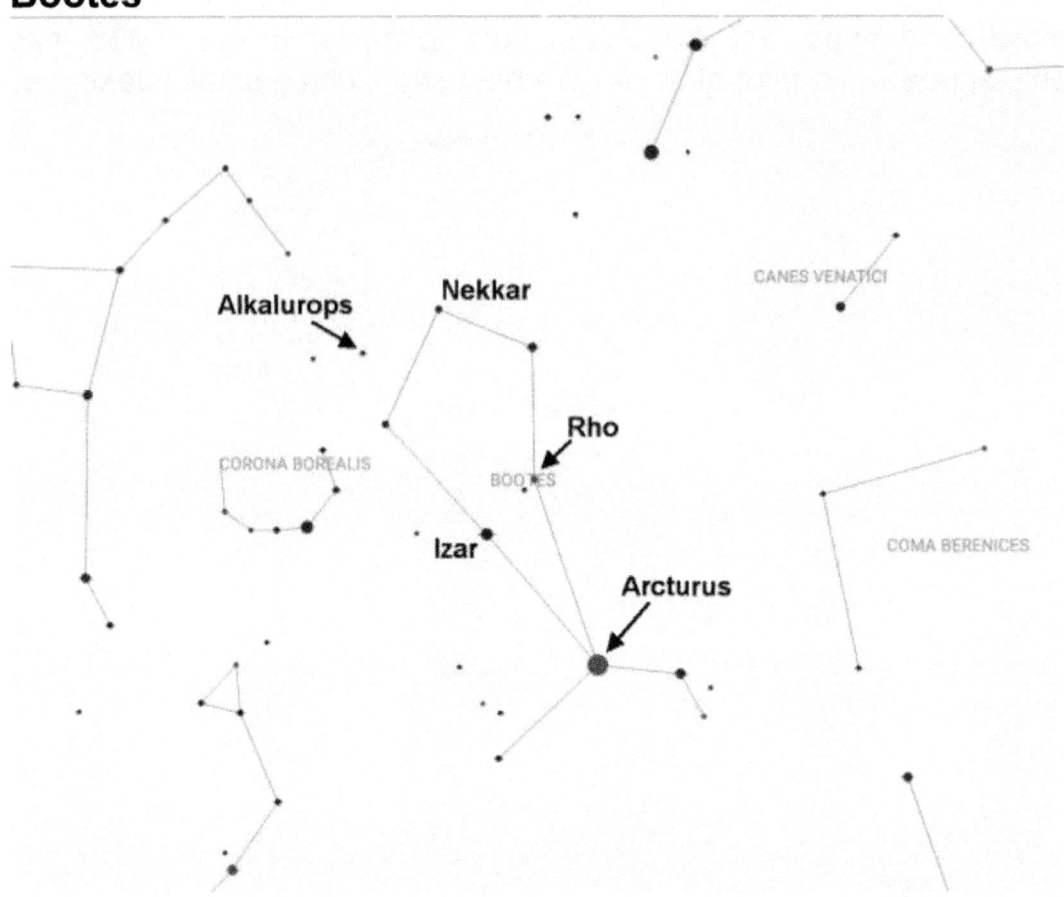

Boötes is a large, kit-shaped constellation that can be quite easily seen overhead throughout the Spring and Summer.

Collectively the stars represent a herdsman, an association that dates back to Babylonian times when astronomers associated the constellation with farmers.

To the Greeks the constellation was often tied to Ursa Major, which was sometimes represented as oxen. Boötes was seen to be driving the oxen or, sometimes a plough – which would explain why the seven brightest stars in Ursa Major are known as the Plough in Europe today.

In fact, to find Boötes you only have to first find the Plough and you can use the three stars of its handle to curve down to Arcturus, the brightest star in Boötes. (If it helps, remember to "arc down to Arcturus." See here for more details.)

Arcturus itself is the fourth brightest star in the entire night sky and is hard to miss on a Spring or Summer evening.

An orange giant star only 37 light years away, it has a distinctive hue when observed with the naked eye. The name is derived from an ancient Greek word meaning "guardian of the bear" – an obvious reference to nearby Ursa Major.

Many other cultures across the world are also familiar with the star and it's one of the few stars mentioned in some versions of the Bible (Job 38:32, "or canst thou guide Arcturus with his sons?")

Perhaps most curiously, light from Arcturus was actually used to open the 1933 World's Fair in Chicago. It was thought the light from the star had started on its journey during the last World Fair in 1893.

Unfortunately, this was wrong as the star is only 37 light years away – not the required 40 – although it's possible that contemporary astronomers believed it to be that distance.

Of the other stars there are a number of multiples that might be worth seeking out in binoculars or a small telescope. For starters, take a look near the top of the kite for two easy-to-see binocular doubles.

Firstly, there's Nu^1 and Nu^2 Boötis, a relatively wide pair of stars of equal brightness. Both have appeared white to me but others have reported hints of blue and orange.

Within the same field of view is Alkalurops (Mu Boötis), another easy binocular double with the primary appearing about twice as bright as the secondary.

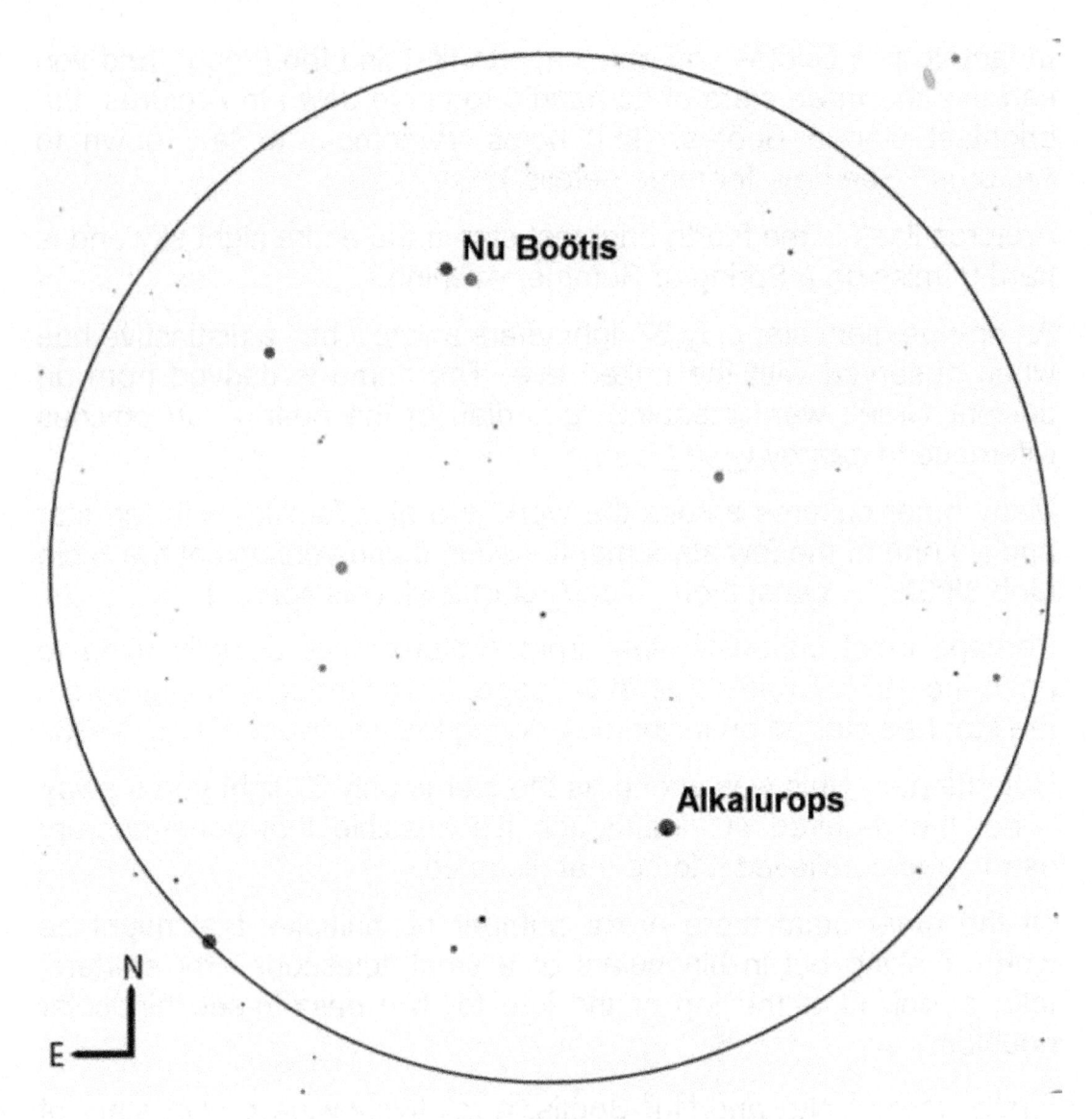

Alkalurops and Nu Boötis, binocular view.

While you're in the area, take a look at Beta, also known as Nekkar. This slightly variable star has a curved trail of fainter stars to the south and a close pair of magnitude 8 stars to the south-west.

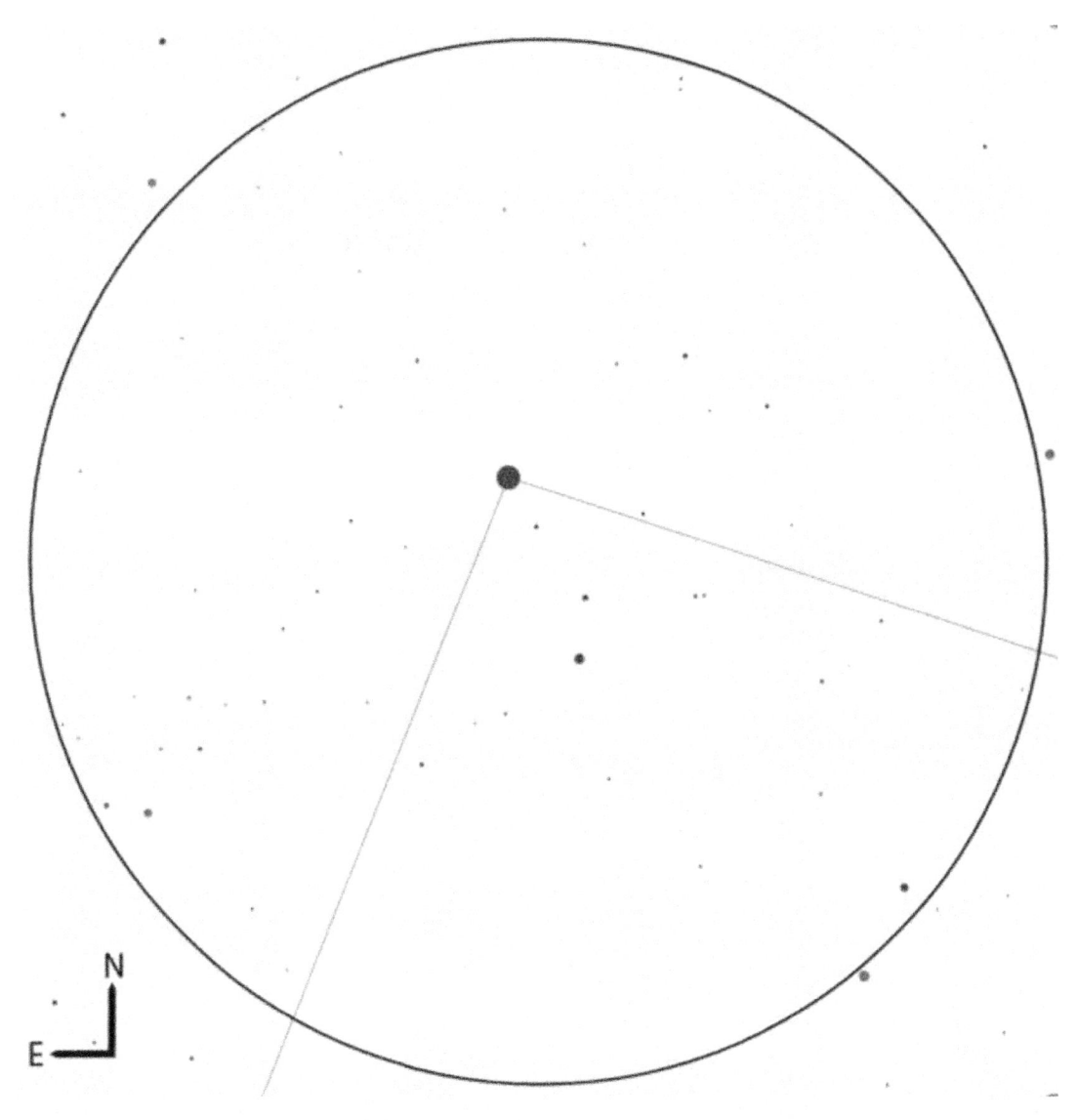

Nekkar, binocular view.

Lastly, move south to Epsilon (Izar) and Rho. Izar is a white star with an unrelated companion to the south. A magnitude 4.5 star appears close to Rho and a much closer magnitude 7.8 companion may also be within binocular reach.

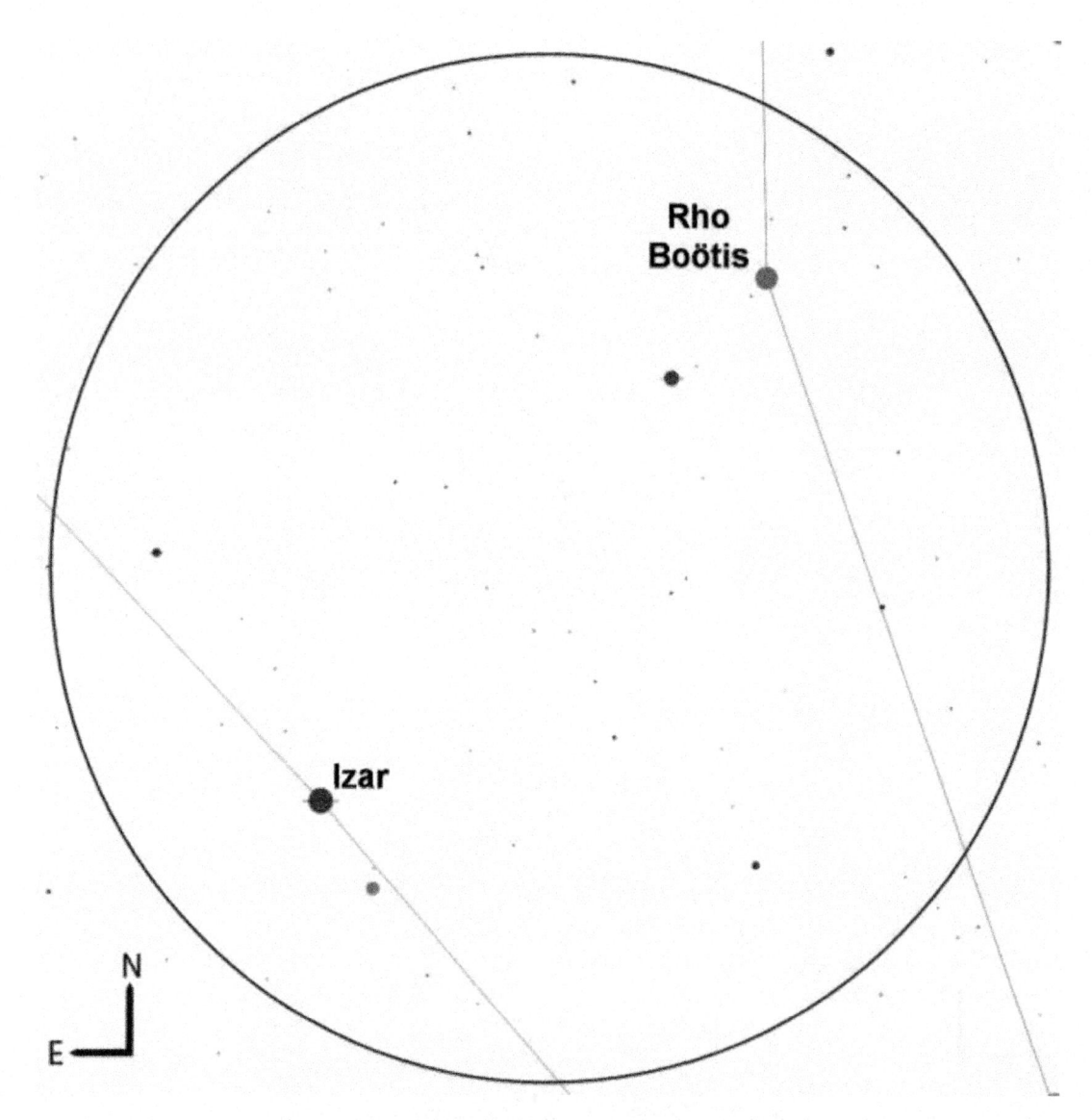

Izar and Rho Boötis, binocular view.

Cancer

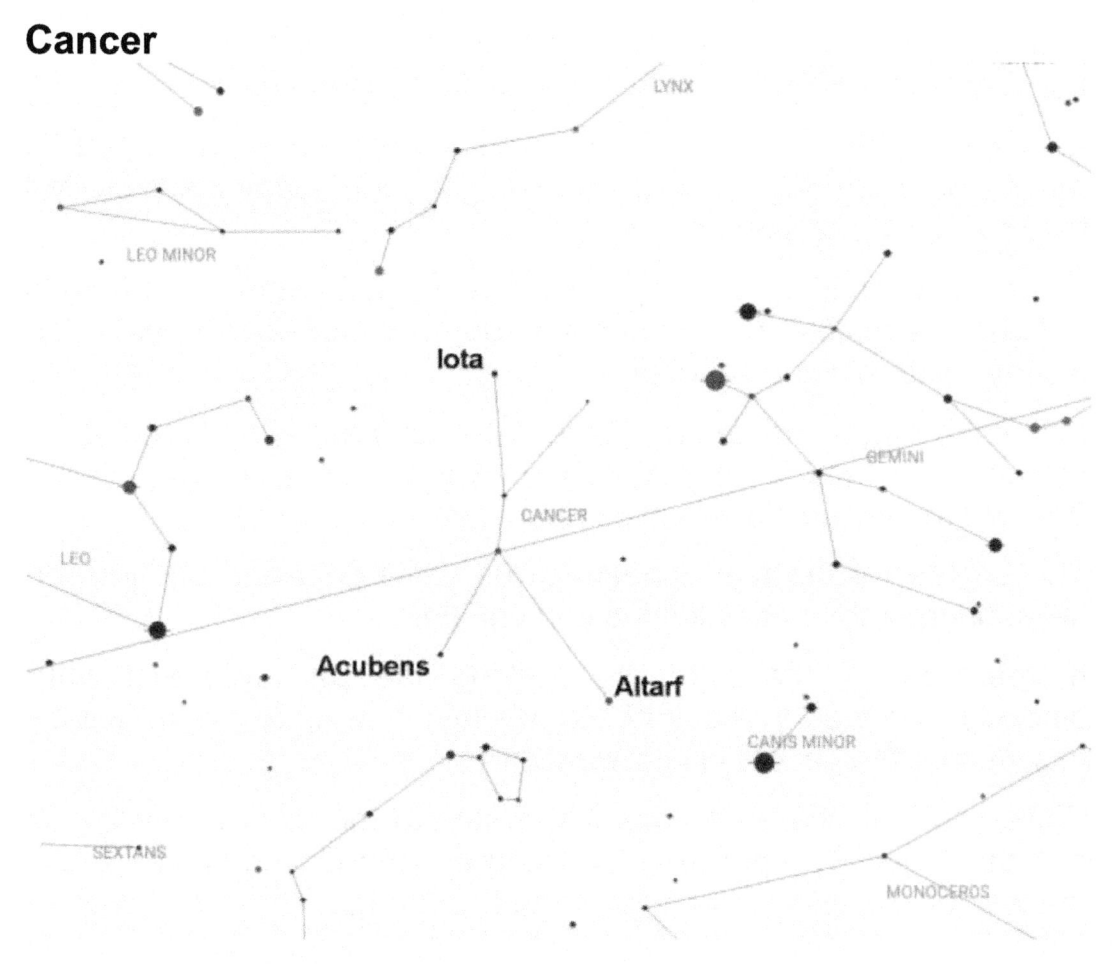

Cancer, as many people know, represents a Crab and is one of the twelve signs of the zodiac. It's also the faintest, with no stars brighter than magnitude 3.5.

Poor Cancer suffers mythologically too as there are no grand stories associated with it. It's said to be the crab that Hercules crushed with his foot after the poor creature nipped him with its claws as he battled the sea-serpent Hydra.

Unlike many of the other constellations, it does at least partly resemble the crab it represents. Get away from the lights of the city and you should see a faint K shaped constellation midway between the bright stars of Pollux in Gemini and Regulus in Leo.

Its own brightest star is Altarf, also known as Beta Cancri, a magnitude 3.5 orange star some 290 light years away that's orbited by a red dwarf companion.

The companion is too faint to be seen by most amateurs, but there's at least one double that's an easy target for small telescopes – and it comes with a binocular double nearby.

Iota is the northernmost star of the K and can easily be found, even without optical aid. Turn a telescope toward it and low power (about 27x) will reveal the star's two components.

The brighter of the two appears to be white-gold and about three times brighter than its pale blue companion.

If you want a challenge, try splitting the pair with just your binoculars. In theory, a pair of 10x50's might be up to the job but it's tricky under the best of circumstances.

While you're in the area, look just a little to the east of Iota for 53 and 55 Cancri. The pair is often listed as Rho Cancri in books and makes for an easy binocular target. Through a regular pair of 10x50's, you'll see two coppery stars of almost equal magnitude.

53 Cancri is itself a double but you'll need a telescope to split it and the companion is pretty faint. 55 Cancri, also a binary, was one of the first stars discovered to have its own system of planets. At only 41 light years away, this star is currently known to have five planets orbiting it but, unfortunately, none of them are good candidates for extra-terrestrial life.

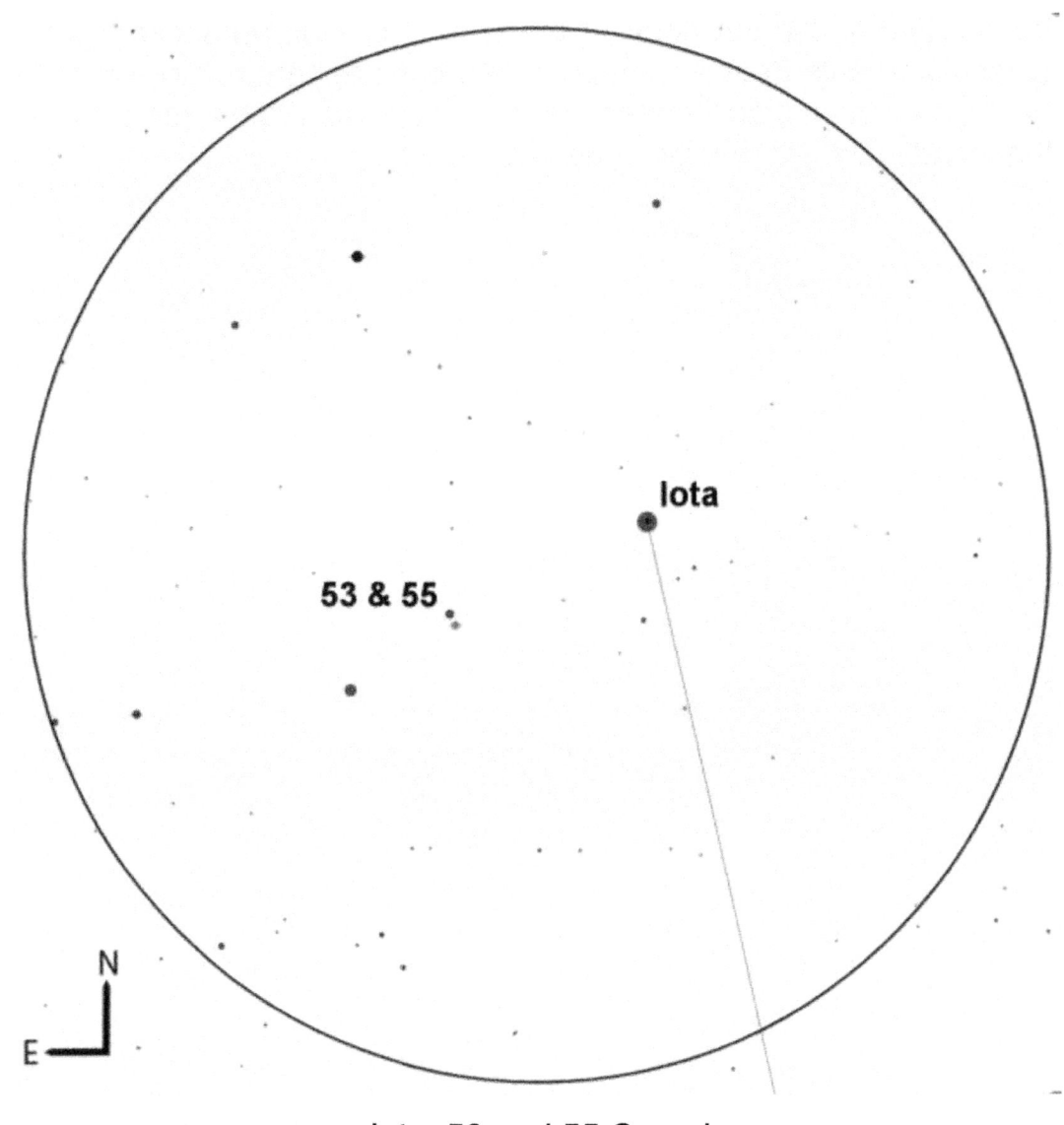

Iota, 53 and 55 Cancri

Double stars aside, the real gem of Cancer is the Praesepe open star cluster, also known as the Beehive or, occasionally, the Manger. Seen with just the unaided eye under clear dark skies, it was once used to predict the weather. If the cluster could not be seen on a clear night, it was said that rain was on its way.

It's easily found in the heart of the crab and is an attractive sight in binoculars as its Beehive shape is becomes apparent. However, it's best seen in a small telescope at low power when many of its thousand stars will readily come into view.

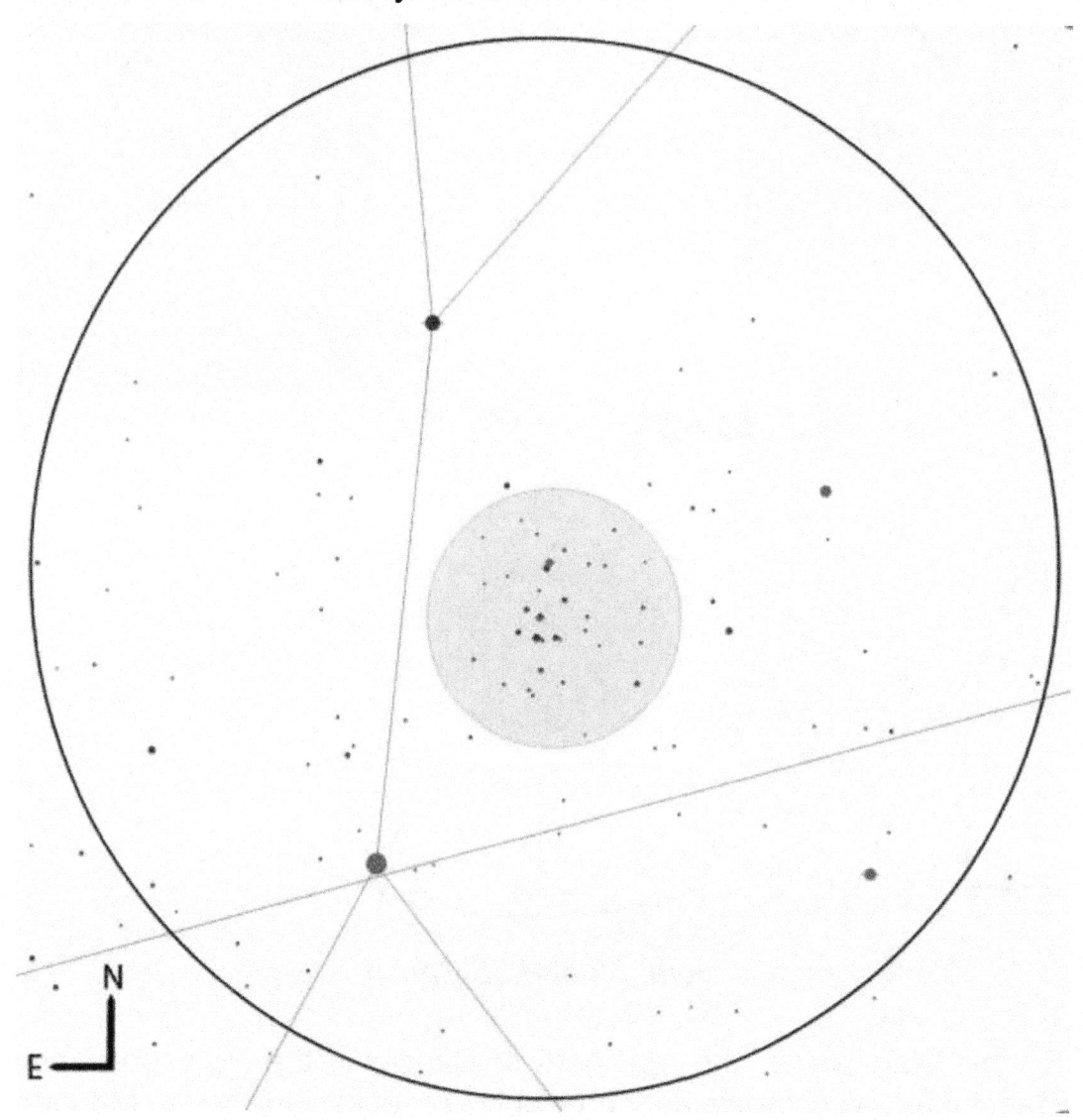

The Praesepe, binocular view.

Lastly, be sure to also look out for Messier 67, a tightly packed star cluster close to Acubens at the southern-eastern edge of the constellation. A faint cluster, it's also one of the oldest clusters known with an estimated age of 10 billion years!

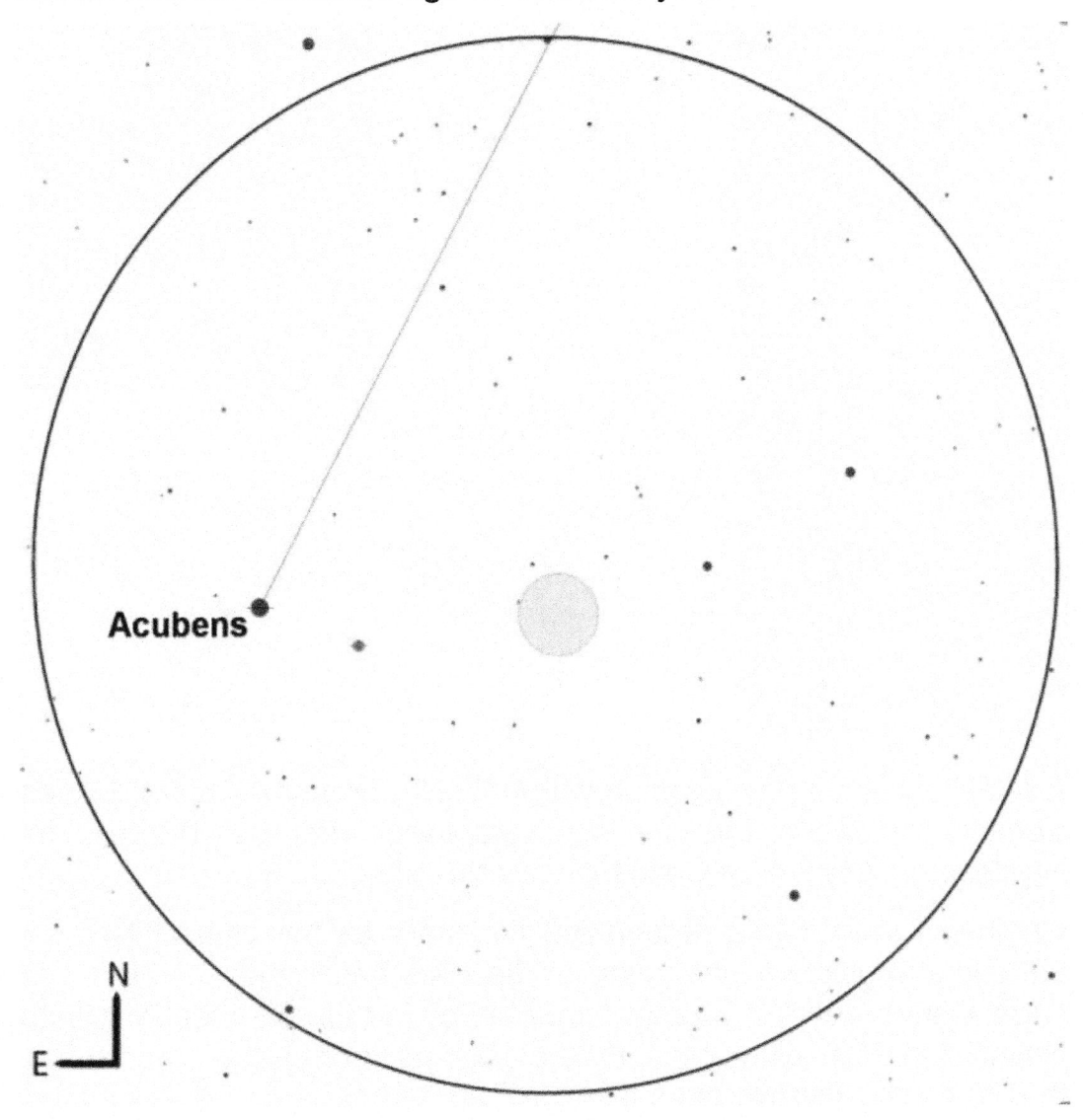

Messier 67, binocular view.

Canes Venatici

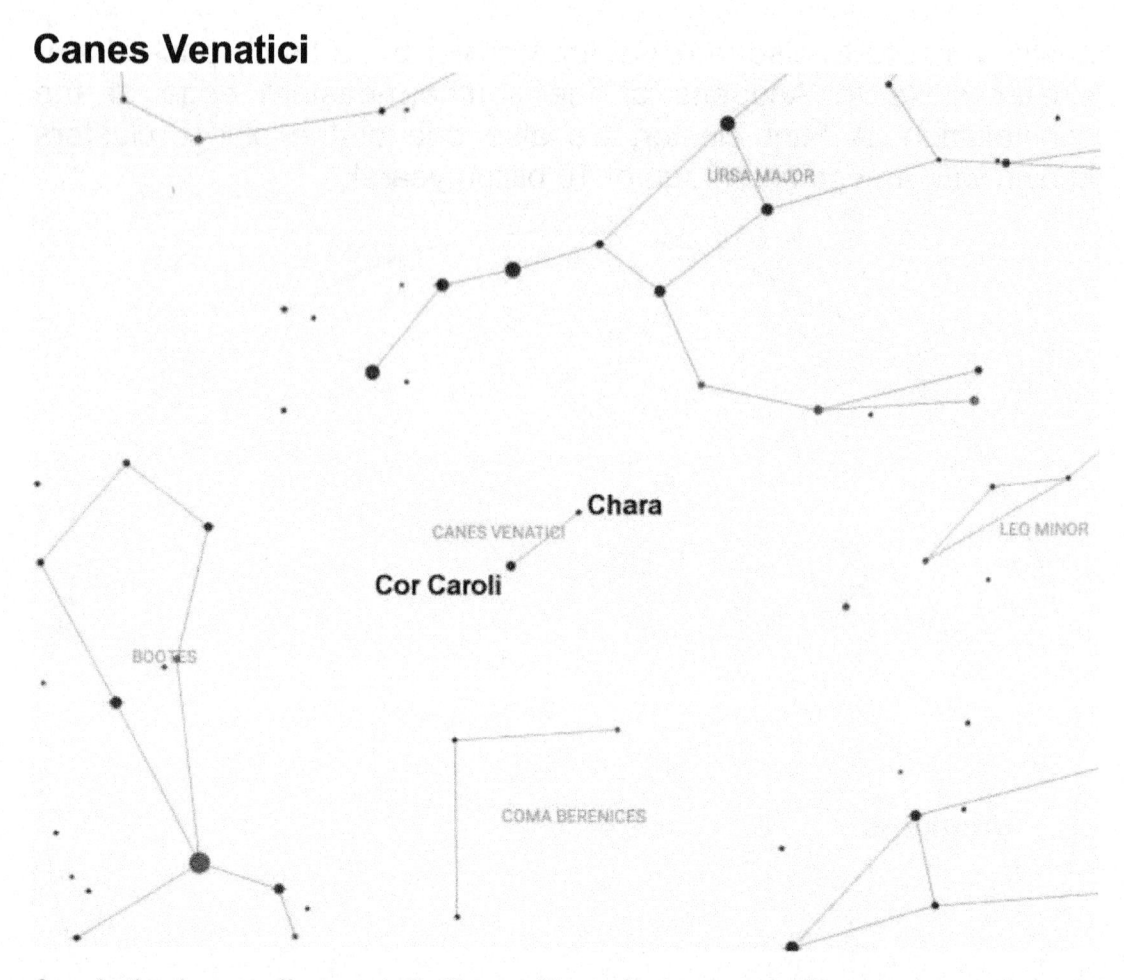

A relatively small constellation with only two prominent stars, Canes Venatici represents the Hunting Dogs associated with Boötes, the Herdsman. However, it wasn't always this way.

Originally, the Greeks recognized the stars as the club of Boötes, but due to multiple mistranslations the stars became associated with dogs. Canes Venatici was then created by the astronomer Johannes Hevelius in 1687 when he set the stars apart from Boötes and made the stars into their own constellation.

There are two dogs depicted here and, traditionally, both the two brightest stars Cor Caroli (Alpha) and Chara (Beta) represented the southern hound. In fact, the name Chara refers to the name of the dog itself as Beta originally had no name. Hevelius named the northern dog Asterion, which means "little star" – an appropriate name since no bright stars mark its position!

The star Chara is relatively unremarkable. At magnitude 4.3 it might be tricky to spot from the light polluted skies of a town or city and there's not much else to set it apart from the surrounding stars.

It's a yellow star, similar to the Sun, that's only 27 light years away and, as such, it's a potential candidate for nearby alien civilisations. Unfortunately, so far there's been no indication of any planets, much less little green men.

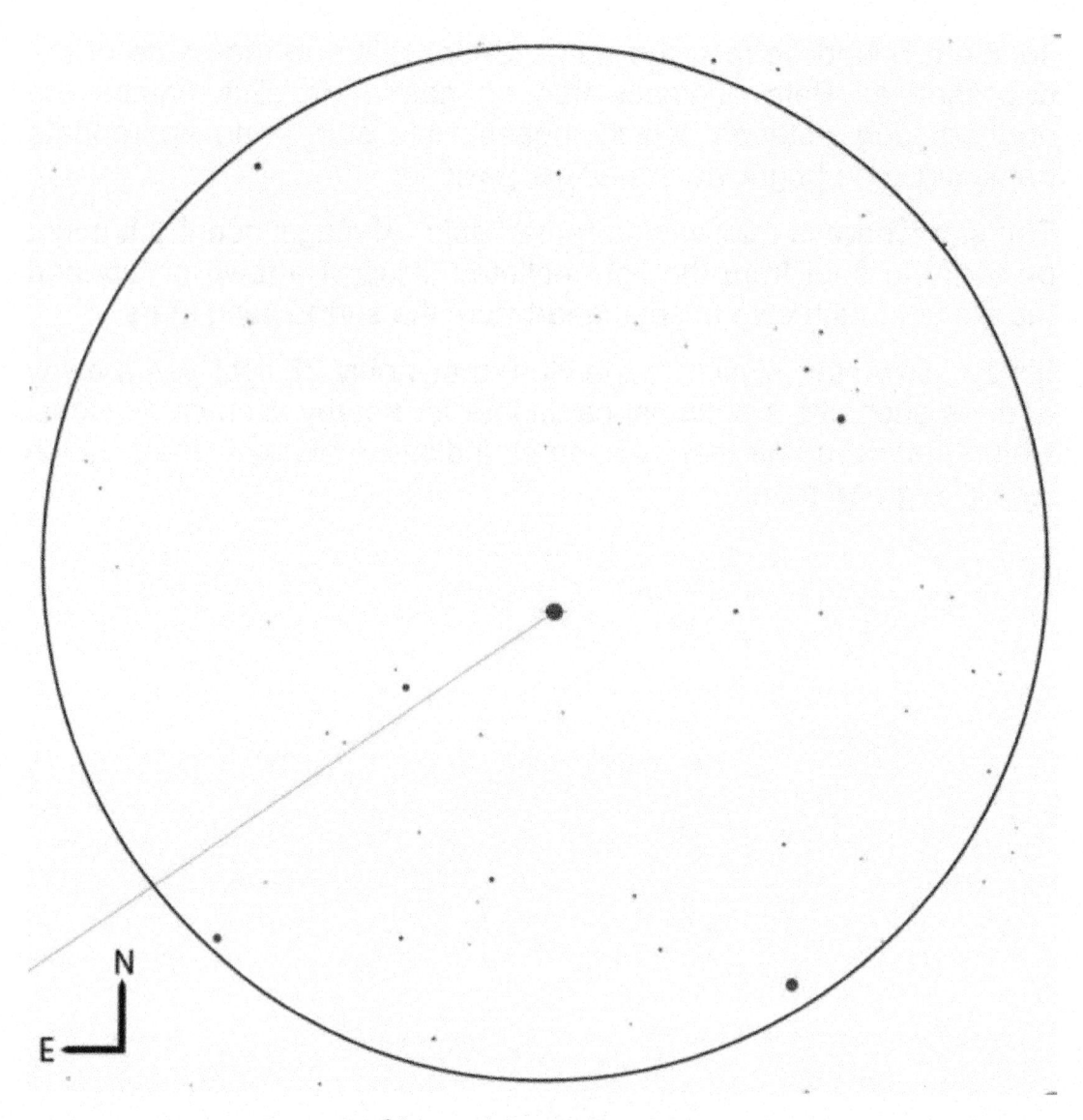

Chara, binocular view.

Now move a little toward the north-west and try looking for the appropriately named La Superba. It's a variable star that changes magnitude from 4.9 to 7.3 over a period of roughly 160 days. Try observing the star's brightness and comparing it with the surrounding stars in the area. Then come back a few weeks later – does it seem brighter or fainter than before?

If you're looking for the star, you might be wondering how to recognize it. Fortunately, La Superba makes it easy, thanks to its deep red color. It's a rare type of carbon-rich star that, despite its low surface temperature, shines with a luminosity several thousand times that of the Sun.

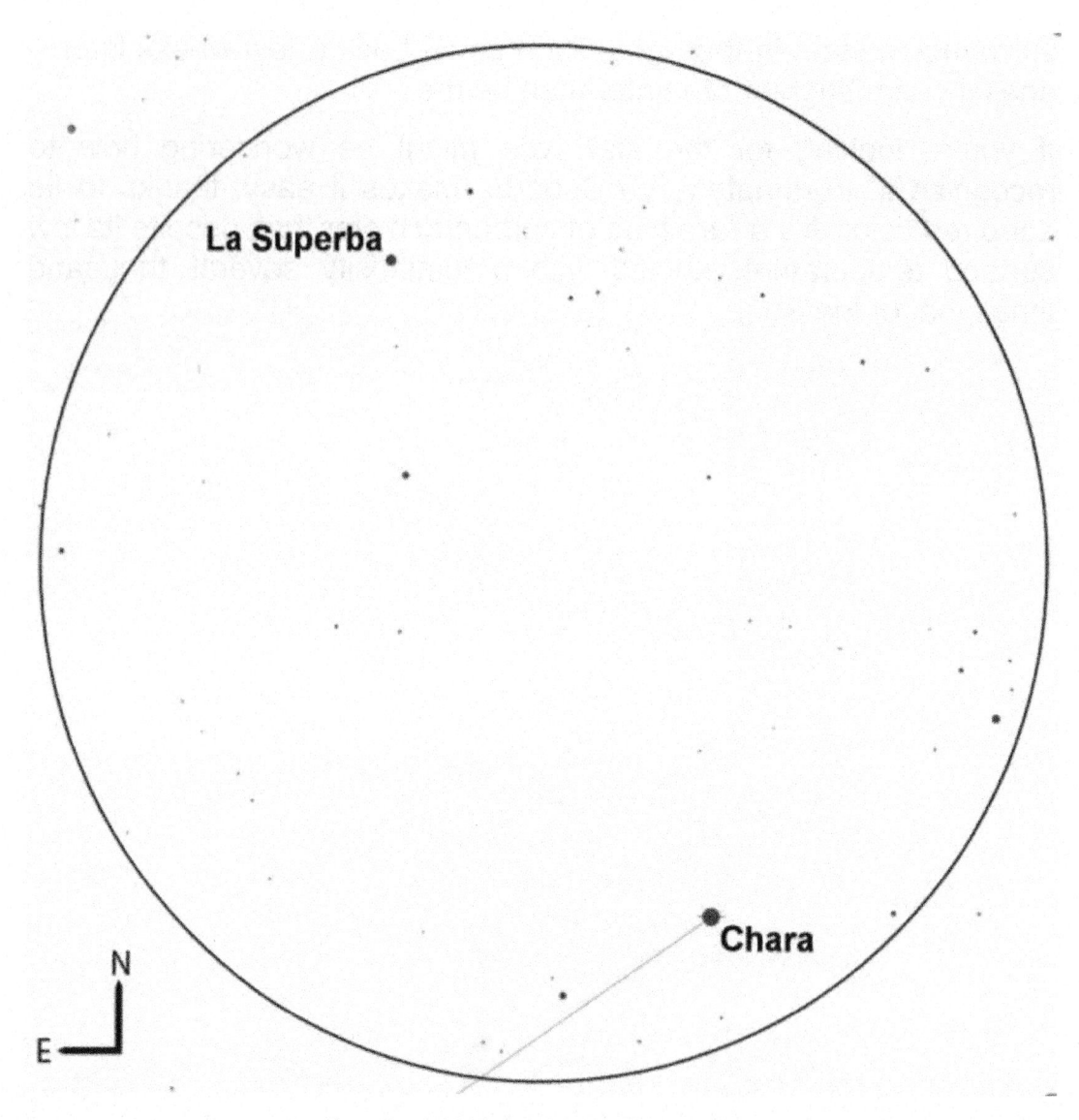

La Superba, binocular view.

Alpha, commonly known as Cor Caroli, the brightest star in the constellation, is a stellar gem for observers with a small telescope. Its name means "Charles's Heart" and was given to the star in 1660 when it's said the star brightened upon the return of King Charles to England. To the naked eye, it's a moderately bright star of magnitude 2.8 and although it *does* change a little in brightness, it's too slight to be seen with just your eyes.

At about 110 light years, it's another nearby star but unlike Chara, this one's a beautiful double, easily split with a small telescope. If you have binoculars, look out for 15 & 17 Canum Venaticorum, a close pair of stars to the east.

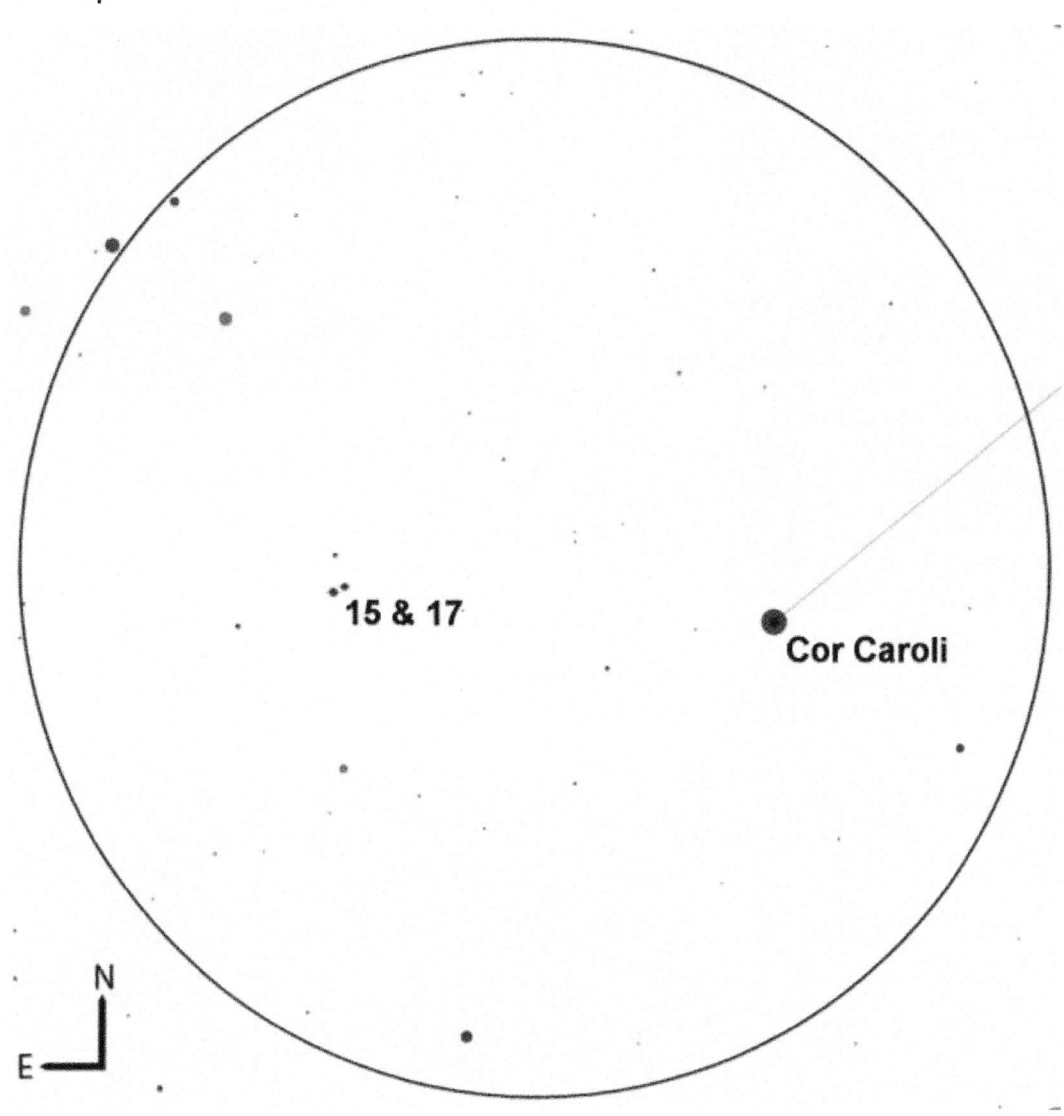

Cor Caroli with 15 and 15 Canum Venaticorum, binocular view.

The constellation is also home to a number of other deep sky objects, but unfortunately none are easily seen with just your eyes. However, you may be able to glimpse the bright globular cluster, Messier 3, with a pair of binoculars.

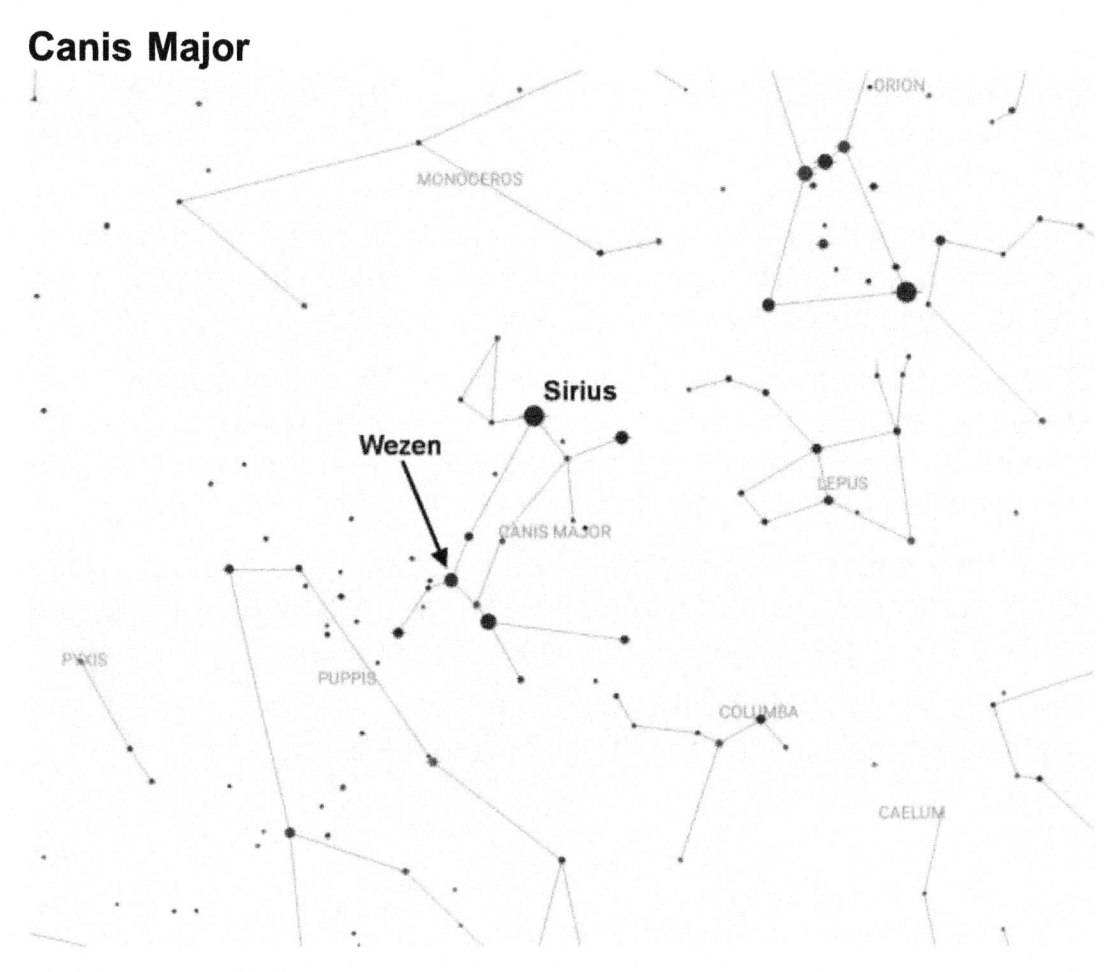

Canis Major

Canis Major is the most prominent of three canine constellations (the other two being Canis Minor and Canes Venatici) and represents the greater of Orion's two hunting dogs.

Arguably, the constellation would not be so prominent if it weren't for two things: its location and its brightest star – the brilliant Sirius, also known as "the dog star."

With the constellation being conveniently located to the south-east of his master, Sirius can be easily found by following the three stars of Orion's belt downward.

Not only is the star the brightest in the constellation, but as many folks know, it's also the brightest star in the sky and can be a dazzling sight. In fact, its very name is derived from the Greek word for "searing."

This can be especially true when the star is close to the horizon. At this time, it appears to flash a myriad of colors, including red, white and blue, and has even been mistaken for a UFO.

Given its prominence, it's not surprising to learn that the star was known to ancient civilizations around the world. It was particularly revered by the Egyptians, who associated it with their goddess Isis and used its pre-dawn rising to predict the flooding of the Nile.

What they couldn't know is that Sirius actually has a small, white dwarf companion, affectionately known as "the pup" and all but invisible to the vast majority of amateur telescopes.

They were also blissfully unaware that the system is a mere 8 light years away, making it one of the closest to the Sun.

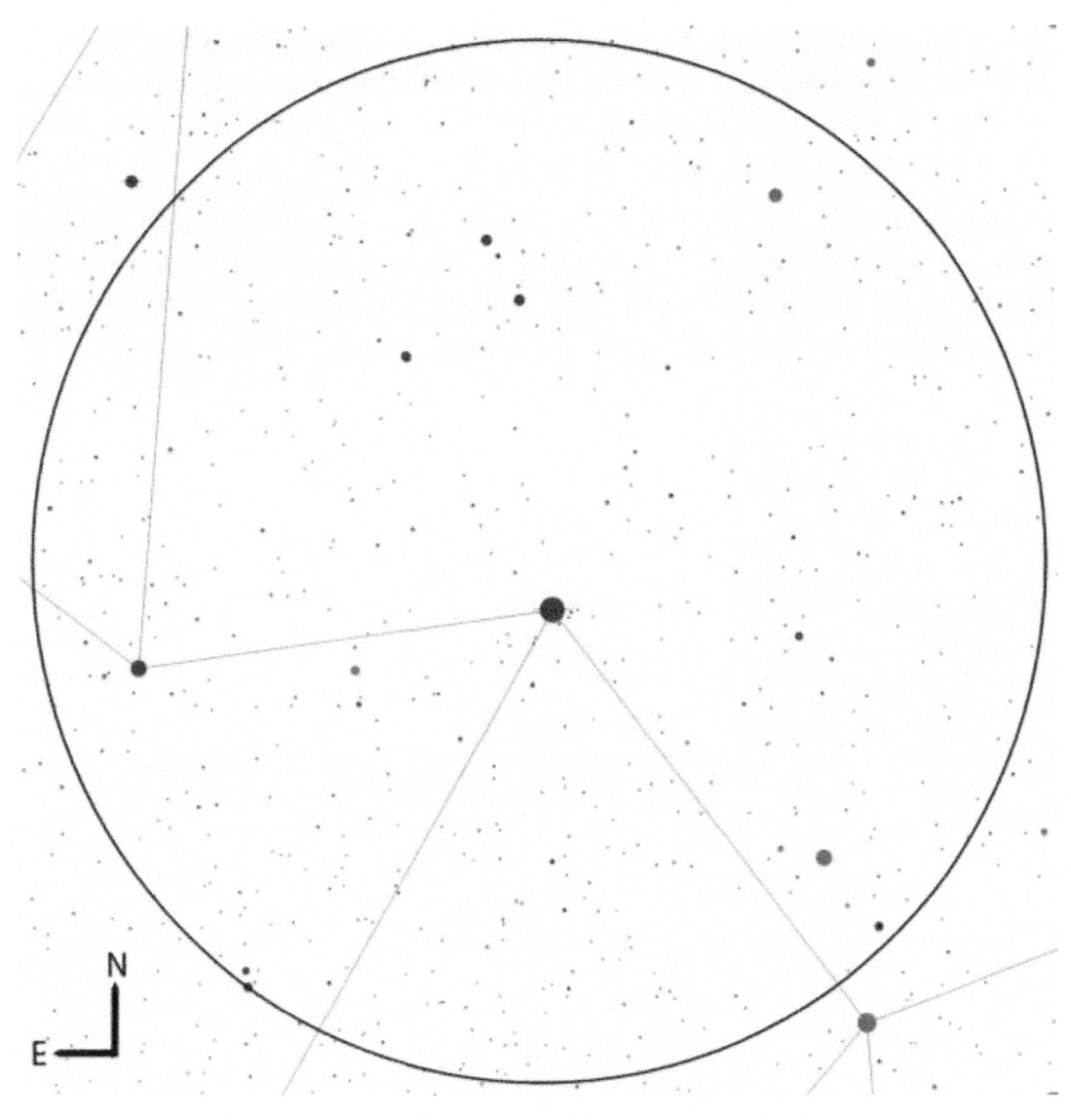

Sirius, binocular view

Canis Major contains a number of deep sky objects. The easiest to observe is Messier 41, an open star cluster found almost directly due south of Sirius and midway between that star and Wezen.

This cluster is a highlight of winter skies but is often overlooked in favor of the larger and brighter Pleiades. Even from the suburbs it's visible as a small, conspicuous patch in binoculars and has even reminded me of a lobster on occasion.

That being said, the cluster truly shines when observed with a small telescope. Low power will reveal a large cluster, predominantly made up of uniformly bright blue-white stars with a couple of older orange stars thrown in for good measure.

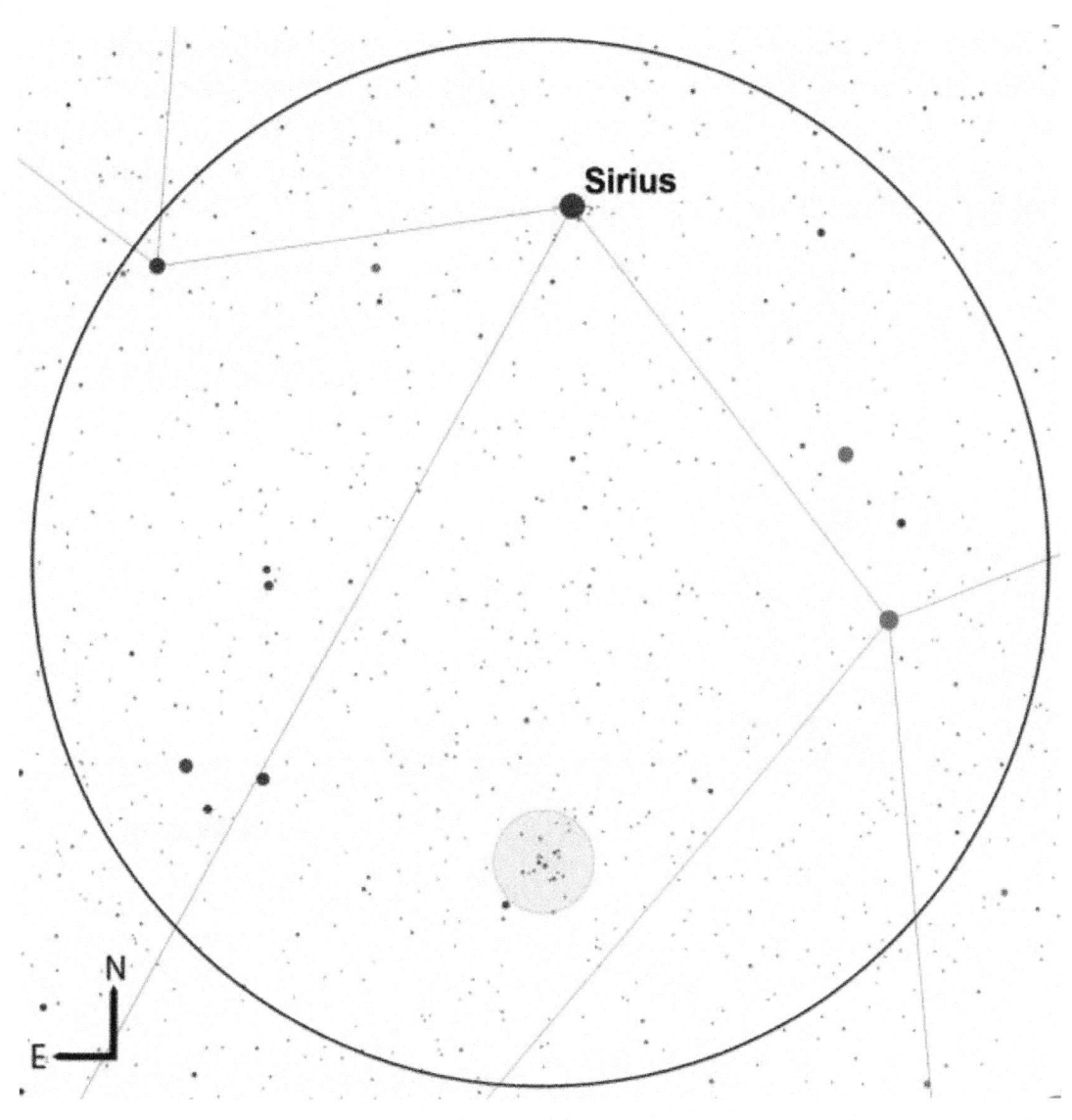

Messier 41, binocular view.

There are a number of other highlights for binocular observers. If Sirius is one of our closest neighbors, then VY Canis Majoris – at a distance of 3,900 light years - is one of our most distant and most fascinating.

Shining with the light of over 60,000 suns and with a diameter of over 600 suns, it's one of the largest and most luminous stars known. It's also variable, fading from magnitude 6.5 to 9.6 roughly every 2,000 days. Tricky to find, look for it within the same binocular field of view as Delta, also known as Wezen.

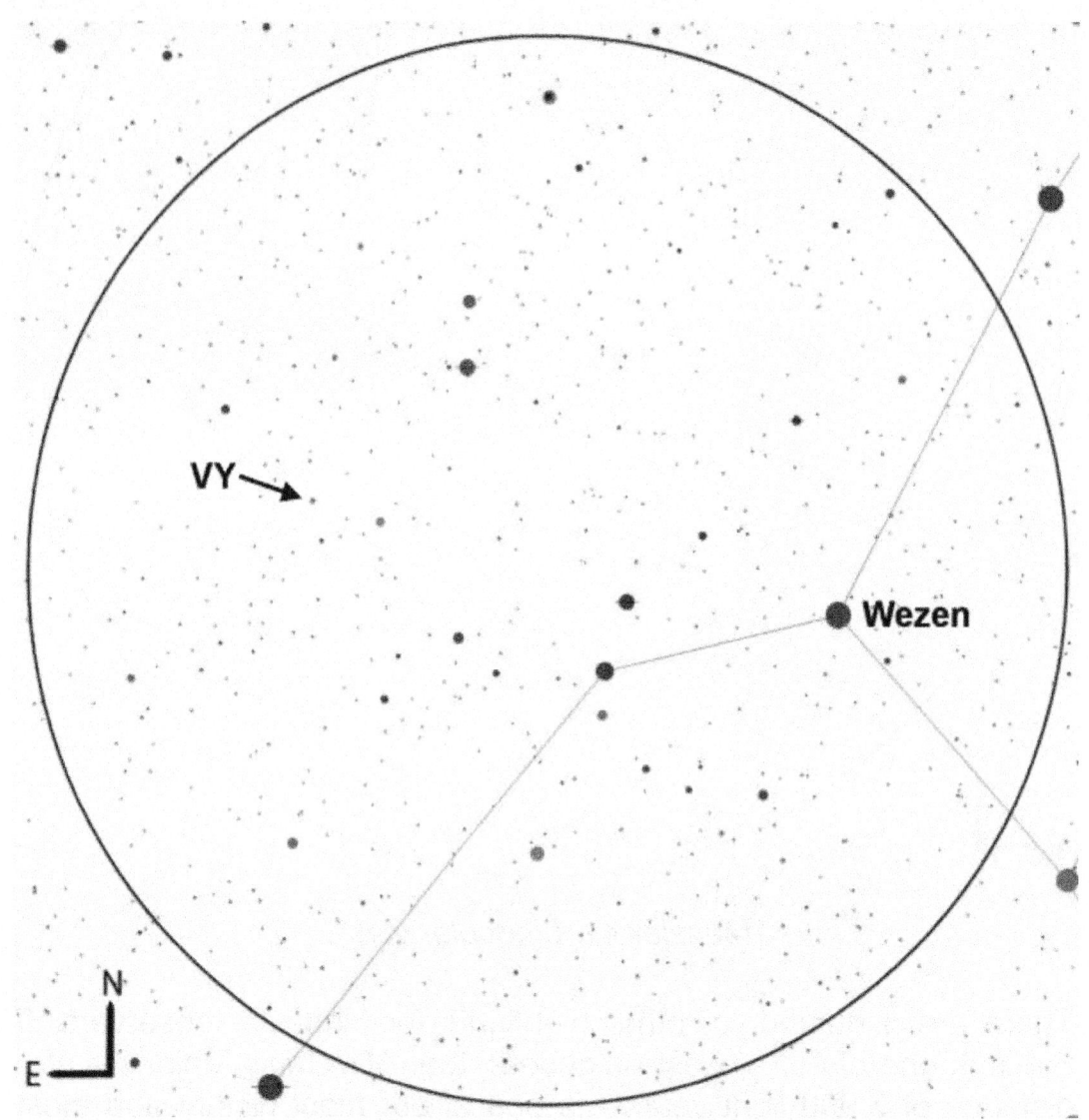

VY Canis Majoris, binocular view.

Canis Minor

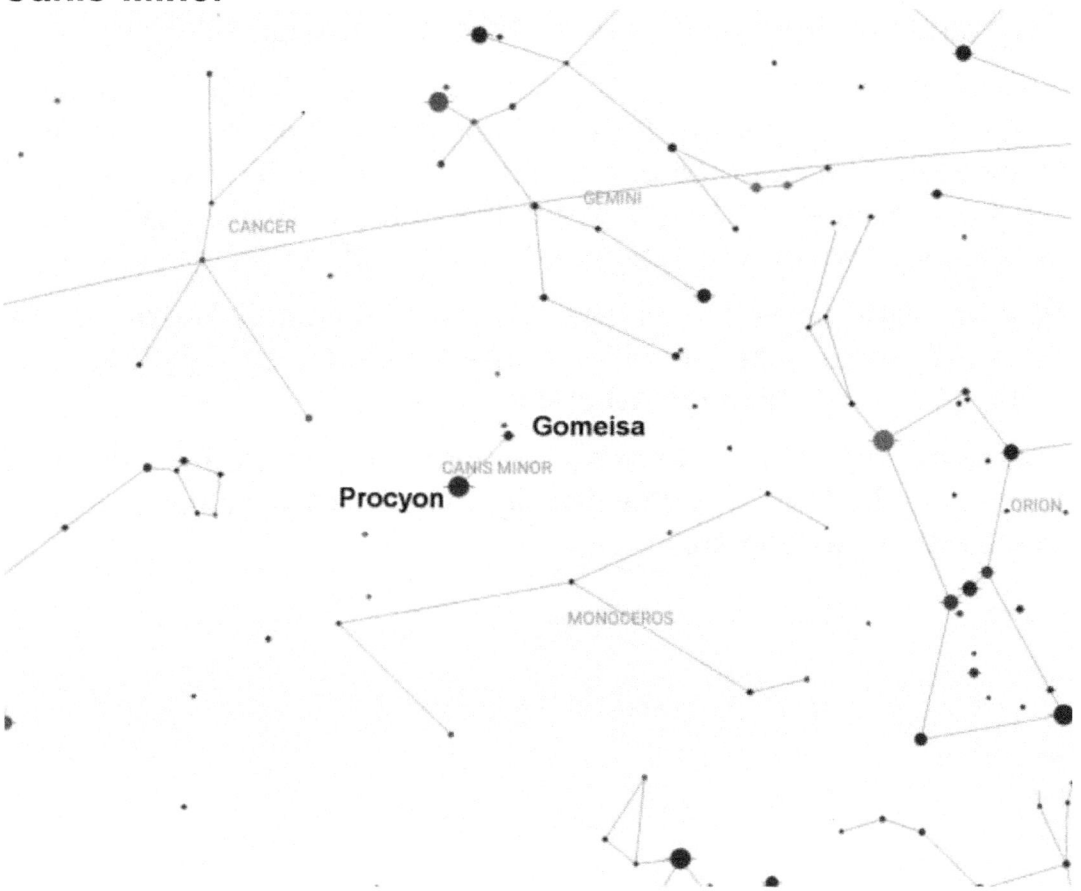

Representing the second of Orion's hunting dogs, this constellation depicts the lesser and presumably smaller canine. Out of the 88 constellations in the sky, it ranks 71st in size and, like Canes Venatici, another hunting canine constellation, it consists of only two bright stars.

Its brightest is Procyon, the 8th brightest star in the sky and, like its neighbor Sirius, at just under 11 ½ light years it's also one of the nearest. Its name was originally given to the whole constellation by the Greeks and means "coming before the dog." This is a reference to Canis Major as Procyon and Canis Minor will always rise before Sirius and the larger (and more southerly) constellation.

A white star just moving into the subgiant stage, Procyon also has a white dwarf companion (like Sirius) that's invisible to amateur telescopes. The pair orbit one another once every 41 years at about the same distance as that between the Sun and Uranus. Binoculars reveal a faint white companion that's unrelated to Procyon itself.

Procyon also marks one corner of what's commonly known as the Winter Triangle with the other corners marked by Betelgeuse in Orion and Sirius, the brightest star in the sky.

The other bright star is Gomeisa, an unremarkable blue-white star of magnitude 2.9 that lies some 162 light years away. Its name means "the bleary-eyed woman."

The Winter Triangle

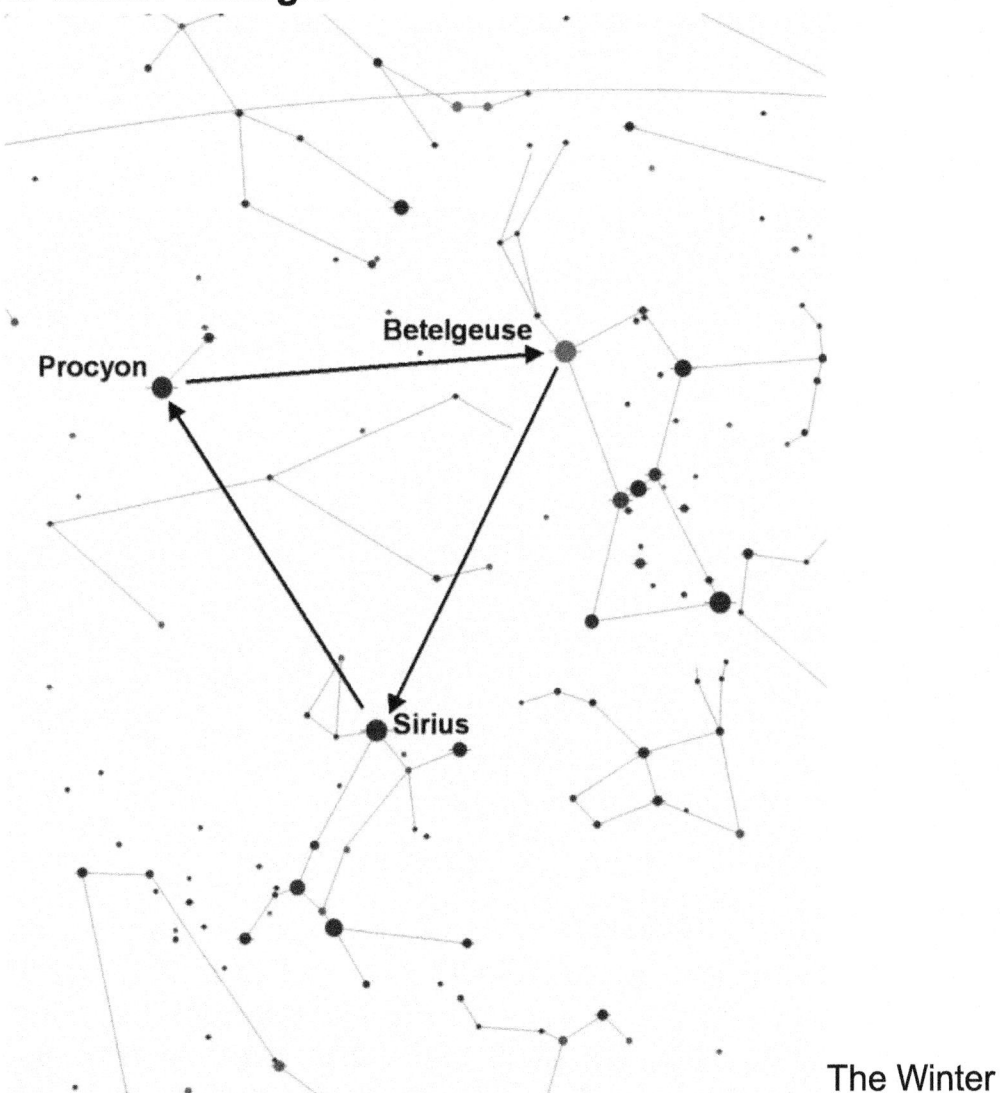

The Winter Triangle is a prominent feature of the winter sky and can be easily seen right through to early Spring. It consists of Procyon in Canis Minor, Betelgeuse in Orion and Sirius in Canis Major, three of the brightest stars in the entire sky. This large asterism is best seen in the evening hours throughout January and February. It has its counterpart in the Summer Triangle.

Capricornus

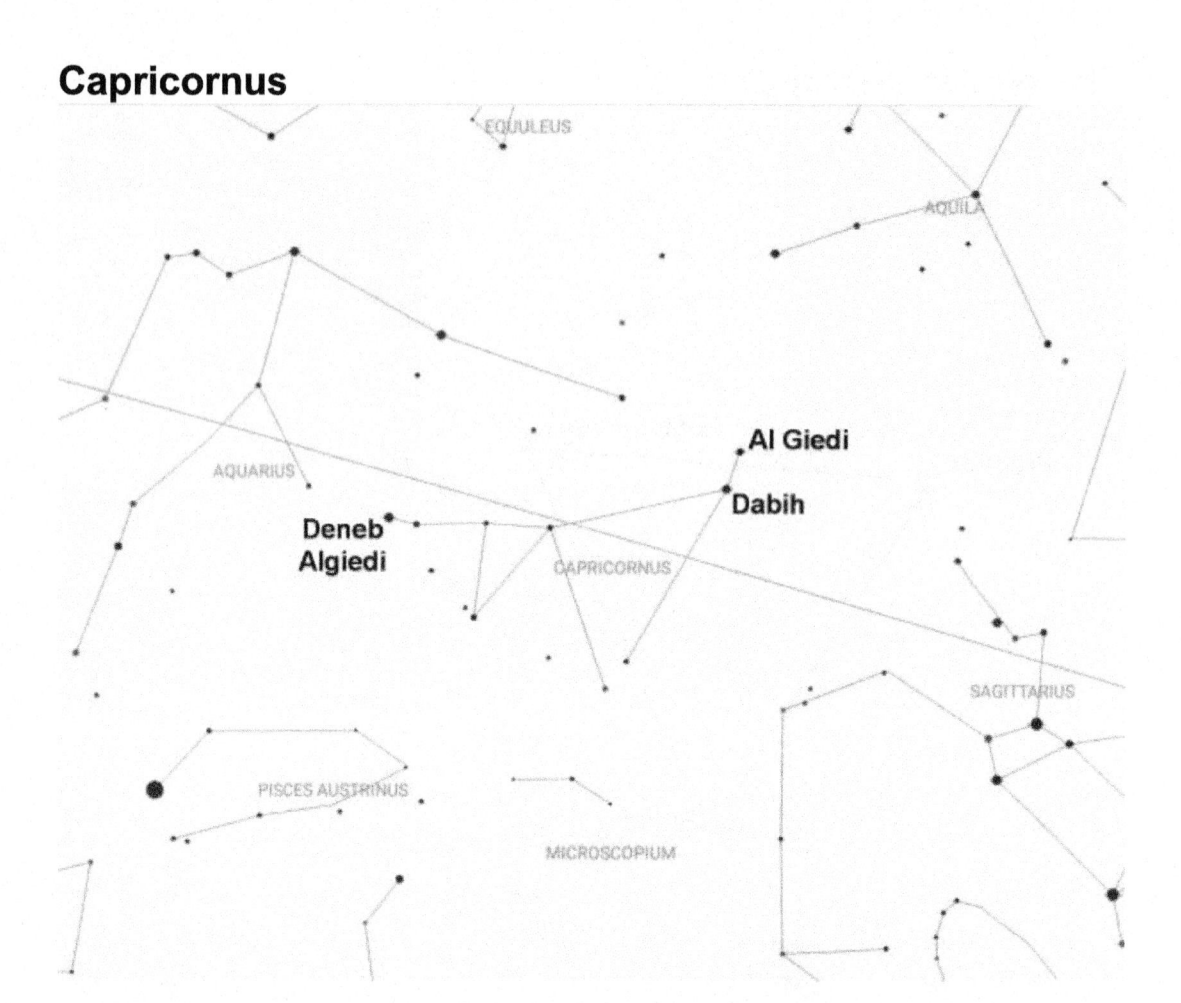

Capricornus, one of the twelve signs of the zodiac, represents quite a bizarre creature. Half goat, half fish, it's said to be the goat-like god Pan who jumped into a river to save himself from the monster Typhon. In doing so, he panicked and didn't give himself enough time to properly change into a fish; hence the half-goat, half-fish combination.

Sometimes affectionately known as "the smile in the sky," Capricornus is a mid-sized constellation of fairly inconspicuous stars.

It's often thought of as being an autumnal constellation, but in fact, it can be easily seen in the evening sky from mid to late Summer onwards and is found to the south-east of Aquila.

Its brightest star is Delta Capricorni. Commonly known as Deneb Algiedi, its name is Arabic for "the tail of the goat" and it is appropriately located on the eastern edge of the constellation. Like many stars, it's actually a double star system with both components taking just one day to orbit one another. The stars lie about 38 light years away.

Of greater interest is Alpha Capricorni, also known as Al Giedi, an Arabic name that translates to "the kid." Al Giedi is actually a wide pair of stars that, like Mizar & Alcor in Ursa Major, can be seen without optical aid by sharp-eyed observers.

The most westerly is known as Alpha^1 Capricorni (or Prima Giedi) while the easterly star is Alpha^2 Capricorni (Secunda Giedi.)

The pair make for a good binocular target with both stars appearing creamy-white and of almost equal brightness.

In reality, these stars are not a true double star system and only appear close together due to a chance alignment. Alpha^1 is nearly 700 light years away while Alpha^2 is a lot closer at 109 light years. Alpha^1 must therefore be the much brighter of the two and, in fact, is about 1,000 times more luminous than the Sun.

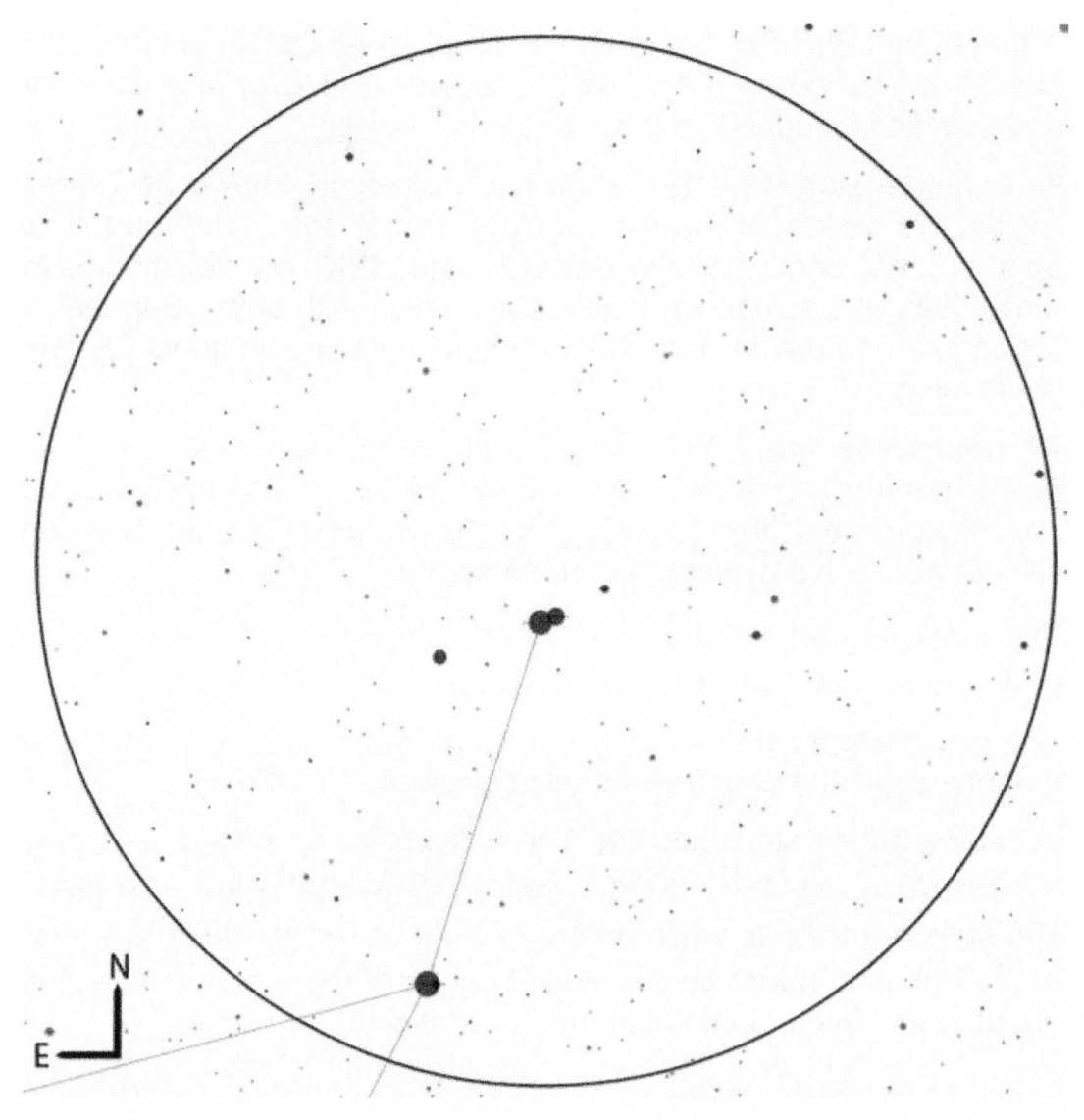

Al Giedi, binocular view.

While you're in the area, be sure to look for another double. Beta Capricorni (aka Dabih) has two components, separated by a third of a light year and taking about 700,000 years to orbit one another. An easy target for binoculars, the primary appears pale yellow and about two or three times brighter than the white secondary.

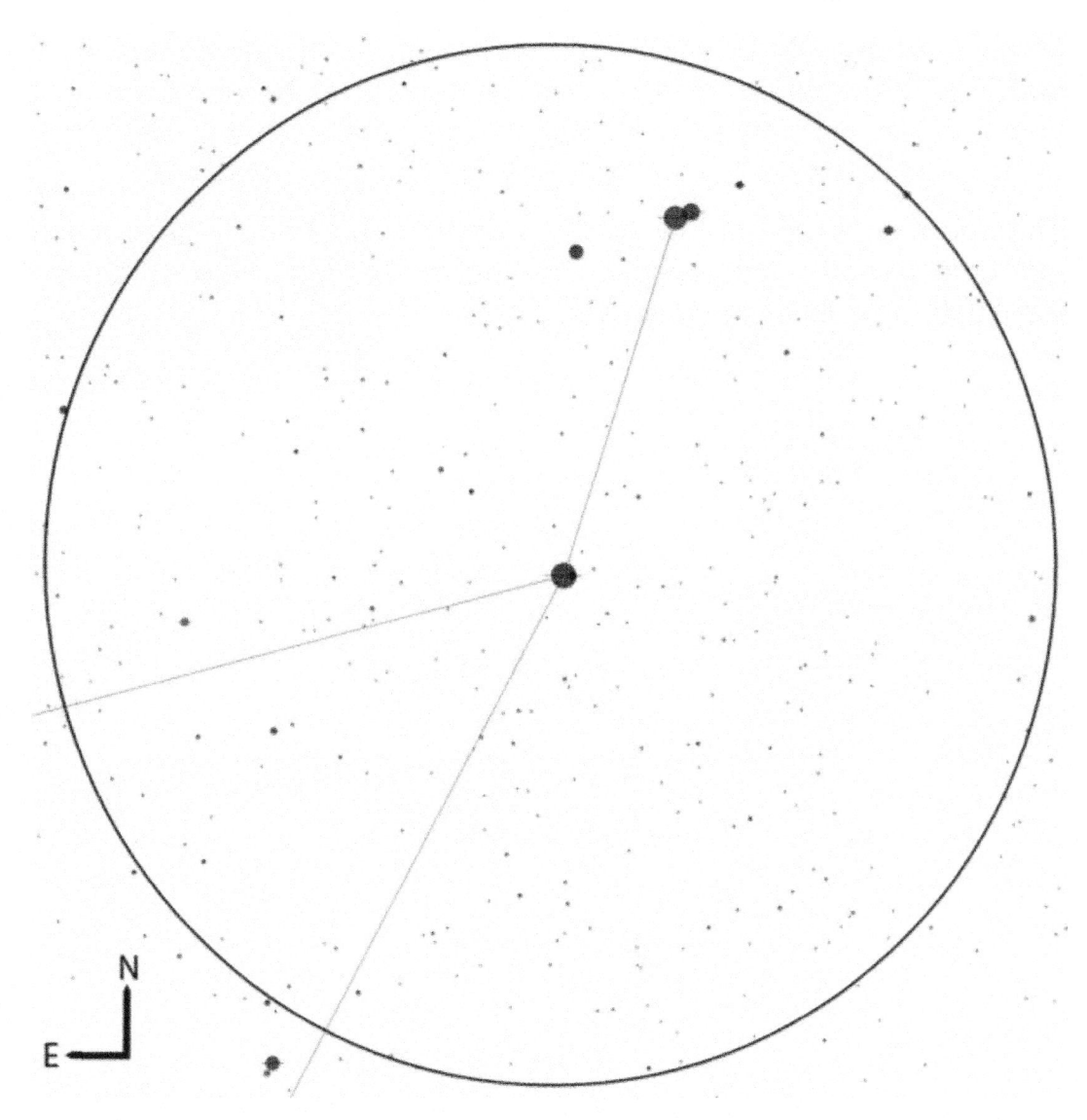

Dabih, binocular view.

If doubles don't appeal, try your hand at a globular cluster. Messier 30 is magnitude 7.7 and well within reach of binoculars. It can be found within the same field of view as Zeta and close to the magnitude 5 star 41 Capricorni.

Discovered in 1764 by the French astronomer Charles Messier, it's about 27,000 light years away and is thought to be about 93 light years across. As with other globulars, these stars are typically much older – this cluster is thought to be nearly 13 billion years old!

Through a telescope at low power, it appears as a small, hazy patch but increasing the magnification to about 100x may help to resolve the cluster into its individual stars.

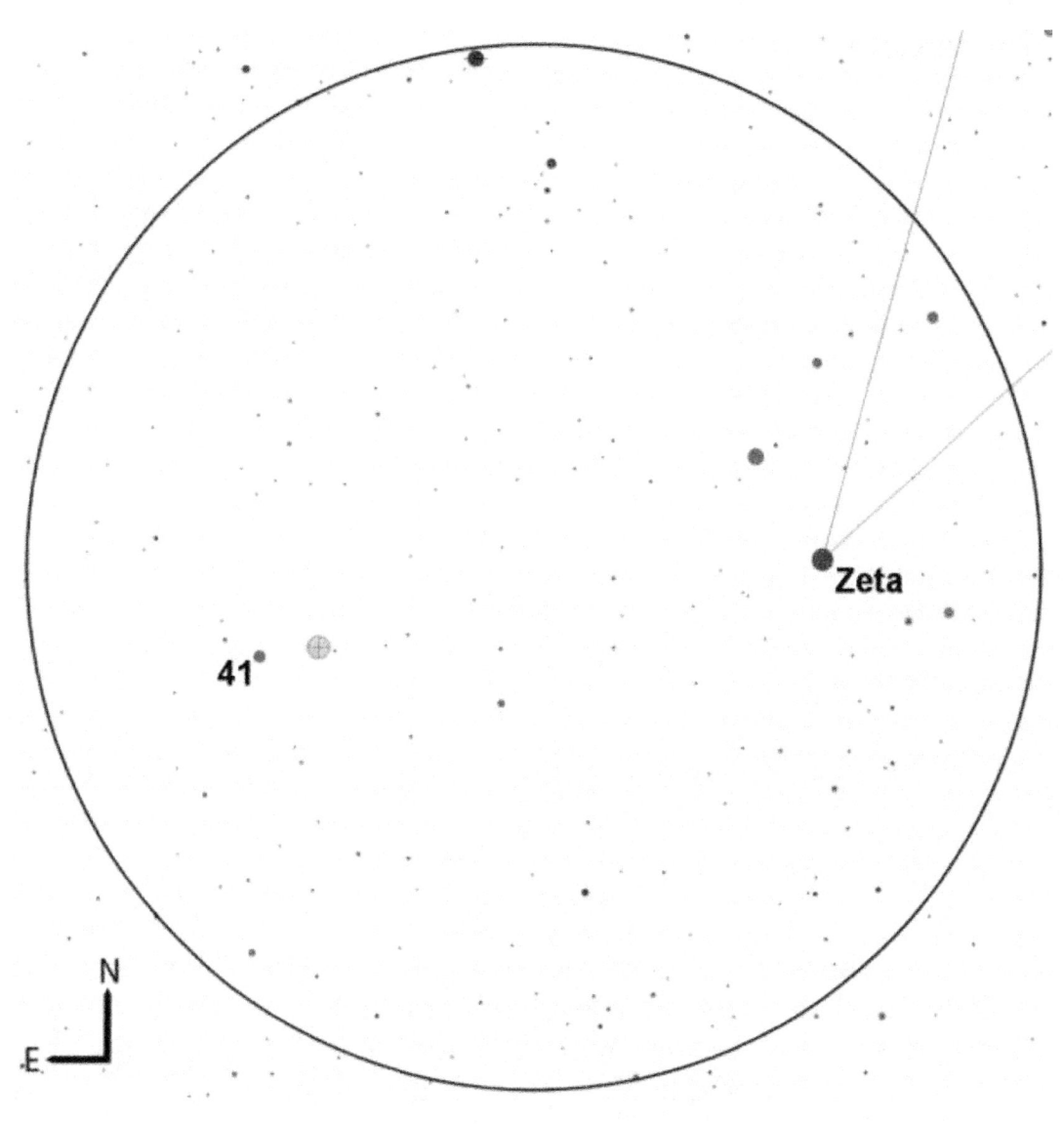

Messier 30, binocular view.

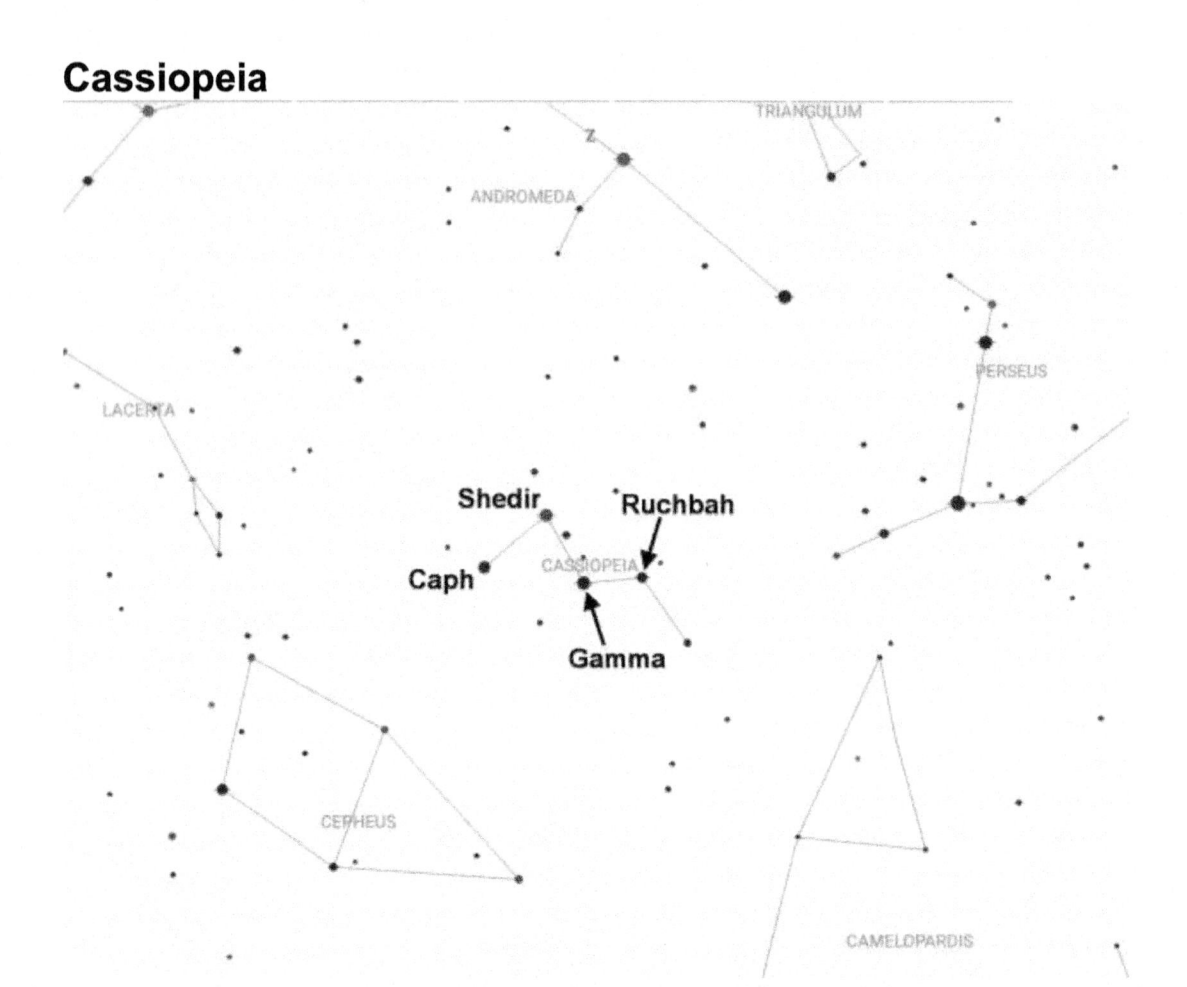

Cassiopeia

Cassiopeia represents the mother of Andromeda the Princess and a central player in that constellation's mythological story. It was Cassiopeia's vain boasts that angered Poseidon and put her daughter in mortal danger. (See here for the full story.)

The constellation is distinctive for a number of reasons. Firstly, it's what's known as a circumpolar constellation. In other words, it circles Polaris, the North Pole star and never appears to set when observed from much of the northern hemisphere.

For example, if you live in the United Kingdom or the northern United States and could see the stars shine through both the day and the night, you'd see it move around Polaris throughout the twenty-four hours of the day.

Which leads us to its second distinctive feature: its shape. The five brightest stars form an easily recognizable W in the sky… or M… or 3… or E… depending on its position in relation to Polaris.

For example, in the autumn it appears as an M above Polaris. In the Winter, it's an E, to the west of the star. In the Spring, it's a W below the star and just above the horizon. Finally, during the Summer months it begins its climb again and appears as a 3 to the east of the pole star.

Its last distinctive feature is the stars themselves as its five main stars are quite bright. With an average magnitude of 2.5 between them, Cassiopeia is easily found and the stars can provide convenient markers for some nice deep sky objects.

The brightest star – for now - is actually Gamma Cassiopeiae, the central star in the constellation. Curiously, unlike its neighbors, it has no name, almost as though the ancient astronomers forgot to assign it one.

I say it's brightest for now because Gamma is an unpredictable, irregular variable star. In other words, it can vary in brightness between magnitude 1.6 and 3.0 over a period of years. It's now gradually brightening and is slightly brighter than Alpha Cassiopeiae, also known as Shedir.

The Milky Way runs through Cassiopeia and we can use Shedir to find one of the constellation's open star clusters. By drawing a line through that star, moving through Beta (Caph) and continuing for about the same distance again, we come to Messier 52. This cluster appears in the same binocular field of view as Beta and may appear as a small misty patch.

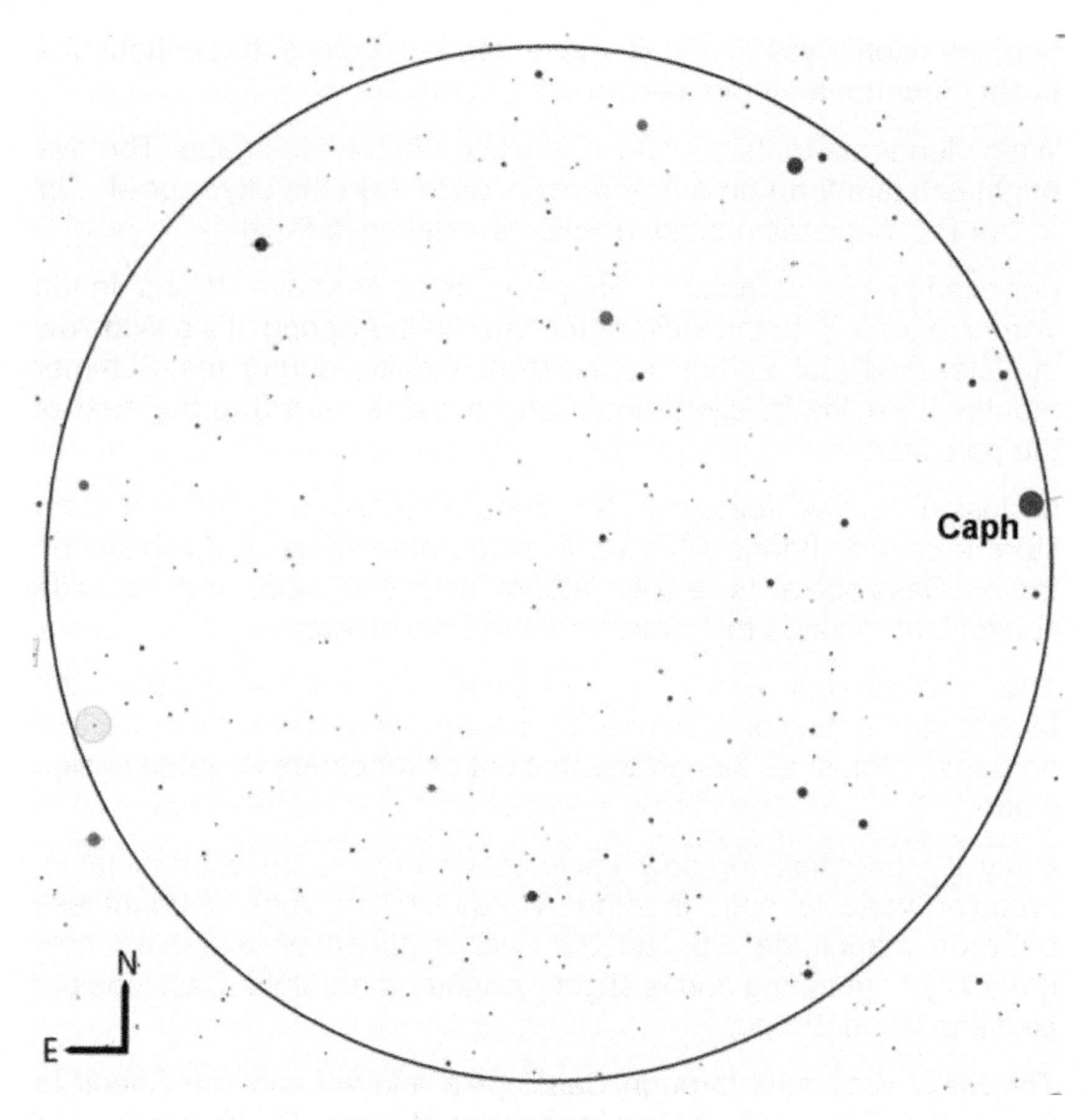

Messier 52, binocular view.

Another sight for binoculars is the open cluster NGC 457. Also known as the Owl Cluster, this can be found close to Delta (Ruchbah) and Gamma Cassiopeiae. Although it can be seen with binoculars under suburban skies as a tiny, very faint smudge, it's best observed with a small telescope.

Look carefully and you'll see the double star Phi Cassiopeiae that marks the eyes of the Owl with the remaining stars forming the body of the bird. It's a large, attractive and fairly bright cluster that – somehow – Charles Messier missed as he was compiling his famous catalog.

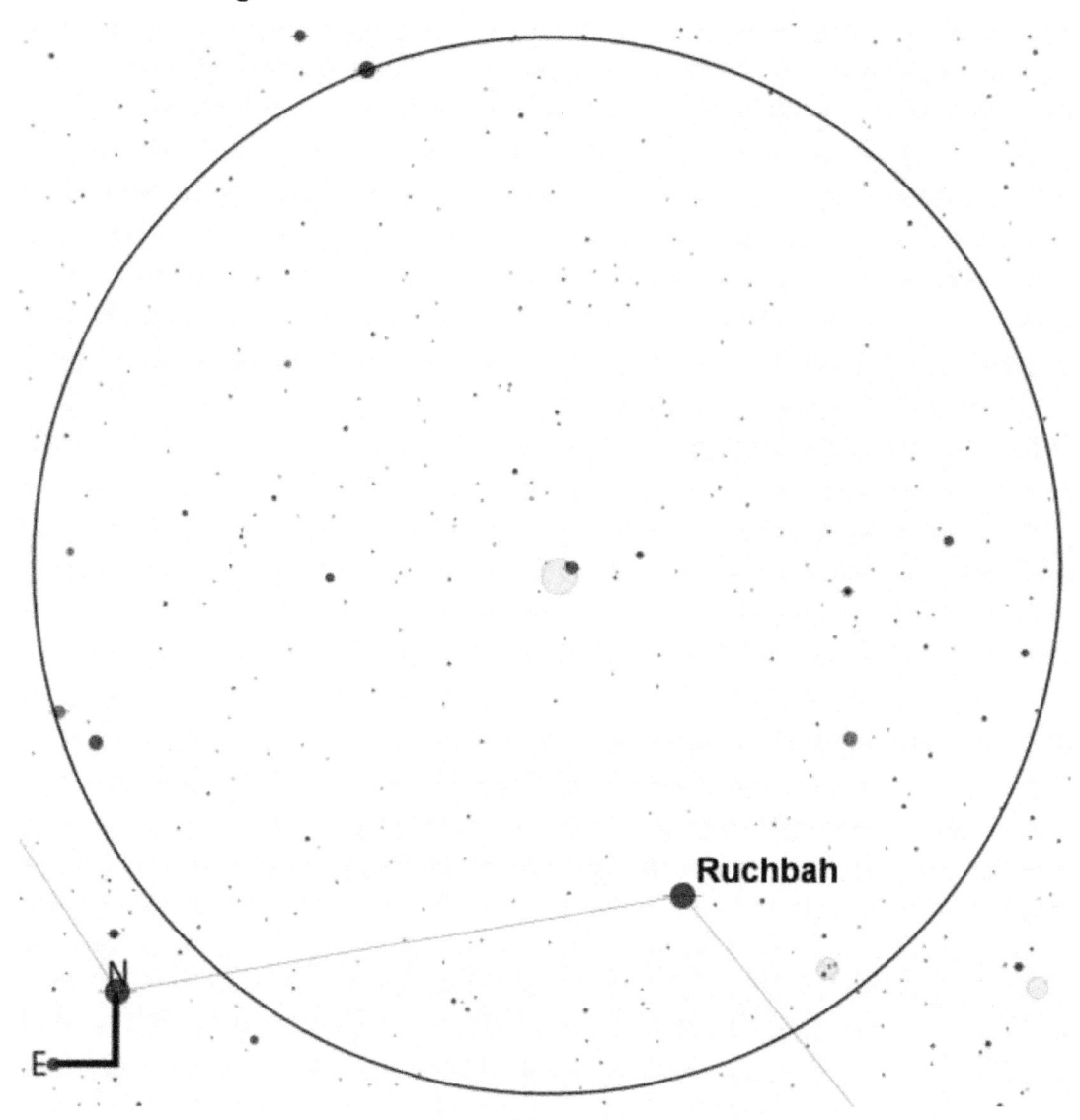

The Owl Cluster, binocular view.

Cepheus

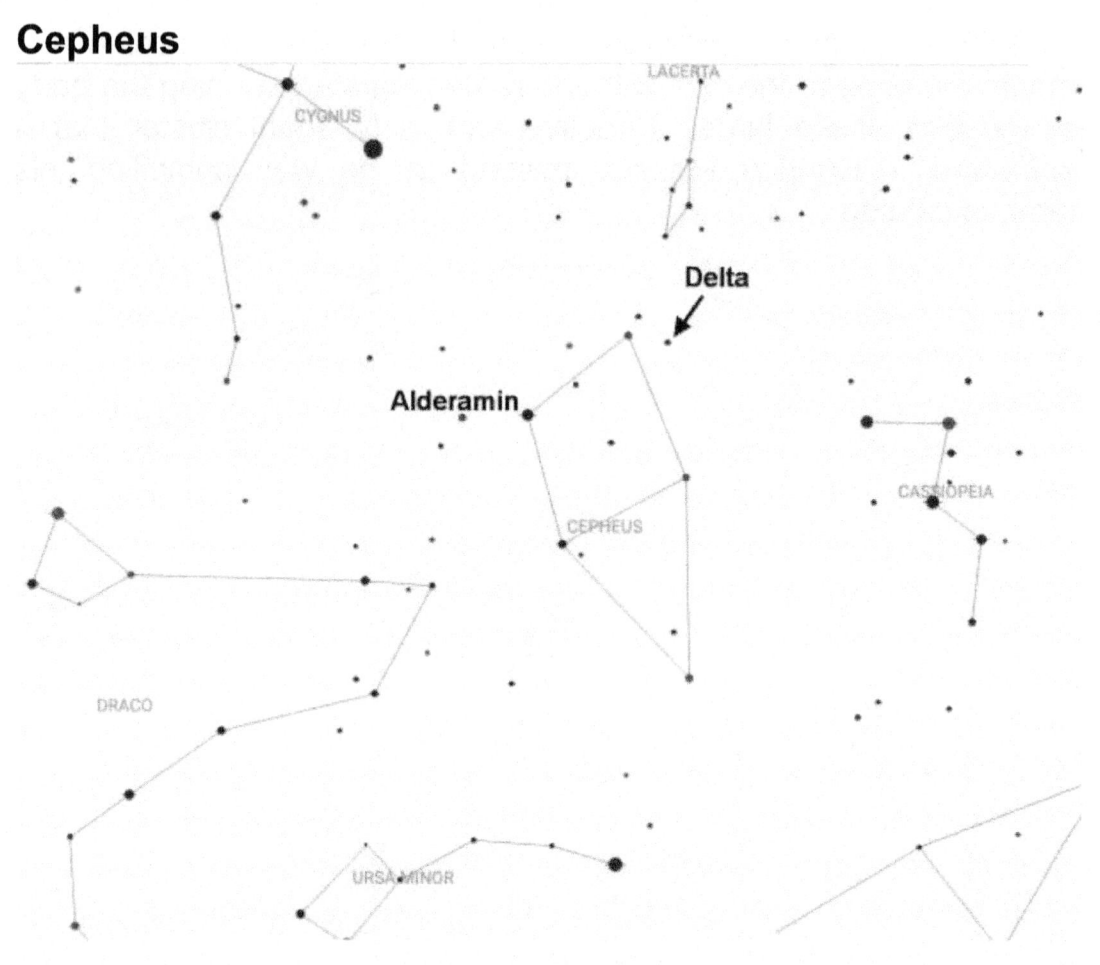

The constellation of Cepheus depicts the husband of vain Queen Cassiopeia and father to poor princess Andromeda. As with his wife, he plays a pivotal role in Andromeda's story as he is primarily responsible for agreeing to her sacrifice. (See here for the whole story.)

It's not a particularly conspicuous constellation but it does have a fairly distinctive shape as it looks like a small child's drawing of a house.

There are no particularly bright stars to be seen here; the brightest is Alpha, a magnitude 2.5 white star only 49 light years away. Also known as Alderamin (derived from the Arabic for "the right arm") it's primary claim to fame is that it was once the celestial pole star (as Polaris is now) and, in about 5,500 years, will be once again.

Of the other stars, Delta Cepheid is certainly worthy of mention as it's the prototype of a class of variable star that bears its name. As first noted by the English astronomer John Goodricke in 1784, Delta varies in brightness from magnitude 3.48 to 4.37 over a period of 5.37 days. Today, you can track the changes with binoculars.

A quadruple star nearly 900 light years away, the brightness change is due to gas and dust smothering the light from the distant star system.

The Constellations of the Andromeda Legend

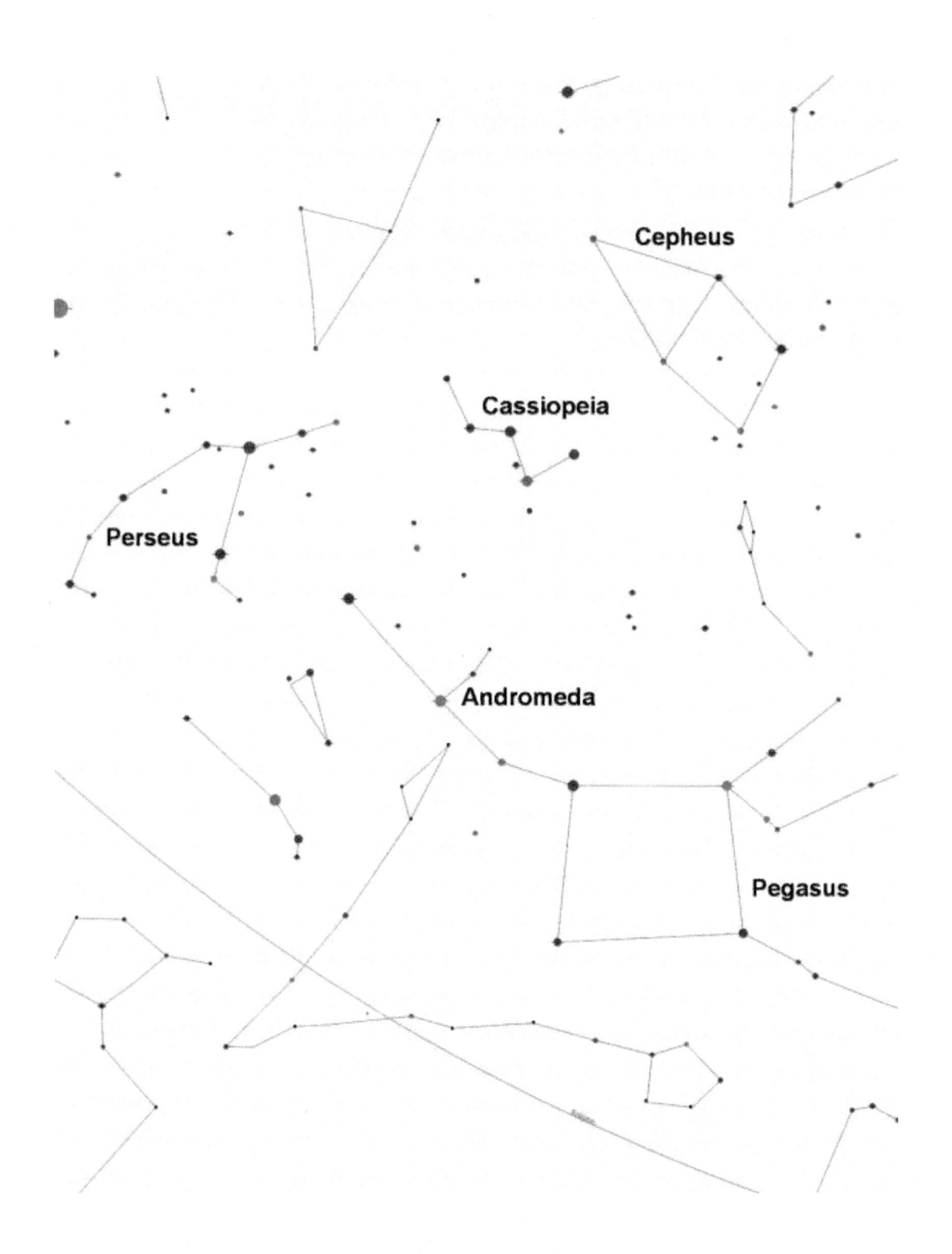

The five major players in the legend of Andromeda can be seen in the late autumn and early winter sky. Andromeda's vain mother, Cassiopeia, appears to the north while her father, Cepheus, appears to the north-west.

Her hero, Perseus is to her east while his trusty steed, Pegasus, is just to the west. This image simulates the overhead view at 10pm in early November, 9pm in mid November, 8pm in early December and 7pm in mid December.

Cetus

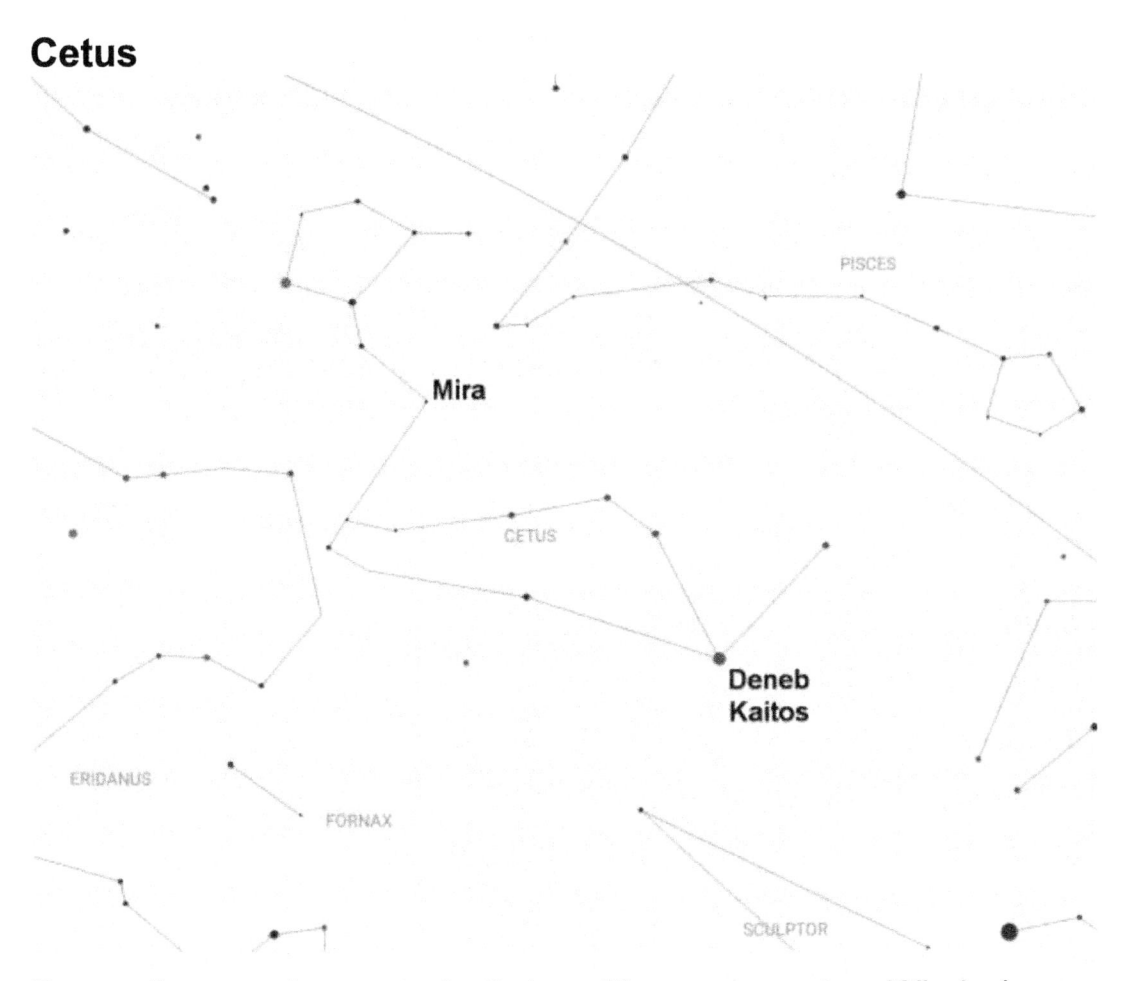

Depending on who you ask, Cetus either represents a Whale (some associate it with the Whale that swallowed Job in the Bible) or the sea monster that nearly consumed poor Andromeda.

Either way, it's a large but rather unimpressive constellation, 4th in size and found beneath another faint autumnal constellation, Pisces.

Its brightest star is Beta Ceti, also known as either Deneb Kaitos (derived from the Arabic for "the tail of the whale") or Diphda, which is taken from the Arabic word for "frog." Only 96 light years away, this magnitude 2.0 orange giant is otherwise quite unremarkable.

However, there is one star in the constellation that's famous with astronomers across the globe. Omicron Ceti, also known as Mira (which very aptly means "the wonderful") was one of the first variable stars to be discovered.

A red giant star hundreds of light years away, on average it shines at about magnitude 8 –beyond naked eye visibility but within reach of binoculars. However, every 11 months (332 days, to be precise) it brightens to naked eye visibility, usually to around magnitude 3, but sometimes as high as 2.0.

Upcoming dates of maximum brightness for are listed below. (Data calculated using *Sky Tools 3* by Skyhound, http://www.skyhound.com)

March 26th, 2017	June 23rd, 2024
February 11th, 2018	May 21st, 2025
January 9th, 2019	April 18th, 2026
December 7th, 2019	March 16th, 2027
November 3rd, 2020	February 11th, 2028
October 1st, 2021	January 8th, 2029
August 29th, 2022	December 6th, 2029
July 27th, 2023	November 3rd, 2030

Coma Berenices

Coma Berenices (or just "Coma") is a mid-sized but very faint constellation at its best visibility during the Spring and Summer months.

Many of the constellations were created and named by the Greeks and Coma is no exception. However, what sets it apart is that it doesn't represent a mythological figure at all, but rather the hair of Queen Berenice.

Queen Berenice was an historical figure who lived in the third century B.C.E. Married to King Ptolemy of Egypt, she swore to the goddess Aphrodite that she would cut off her beautiful hair if her husband safely returned from battle.

Sure enough, the king came home and Berenice cut off her hair and left it for Aphrodite in her temple. The hair vanished overnight and was said to have been placed amongst the stars by the goddess herself.

Located to the west of Boötes, the constellation has no bright stars and will require dark skies to find it. Its brightest star is actually Beta, which shines (if you can call it that) at a dim magnitude 4.3.

That doesn't mean it's not interesting – far from it, because Beta is only 30 light years from Earth and is actually remarkably Sun-like.

There are a few minor differences. The Sun is approximately 4½ billion years old whereas Beta is only three and Beta is also slightly larger and brighter. However, liquid water could exist on a hypothetical planet at the same distance as the Earth is from the Sun. (Alas, no planets are known to orbit the star.)

Coma's second brightest star, Alpha, is only slightly fainter and is commonly known as Diadem. The name refers to the crown or headband that Berenice wore upon her head.

Very close to Alpha is Messier 53, a globular cluster that should be within range of binoculars. Look for a faint, fuzzy star within the same field-of-view as Alpha. A small telescope will help, but you'll need a mid-sized 'scope to see the individual stars within the cluster.

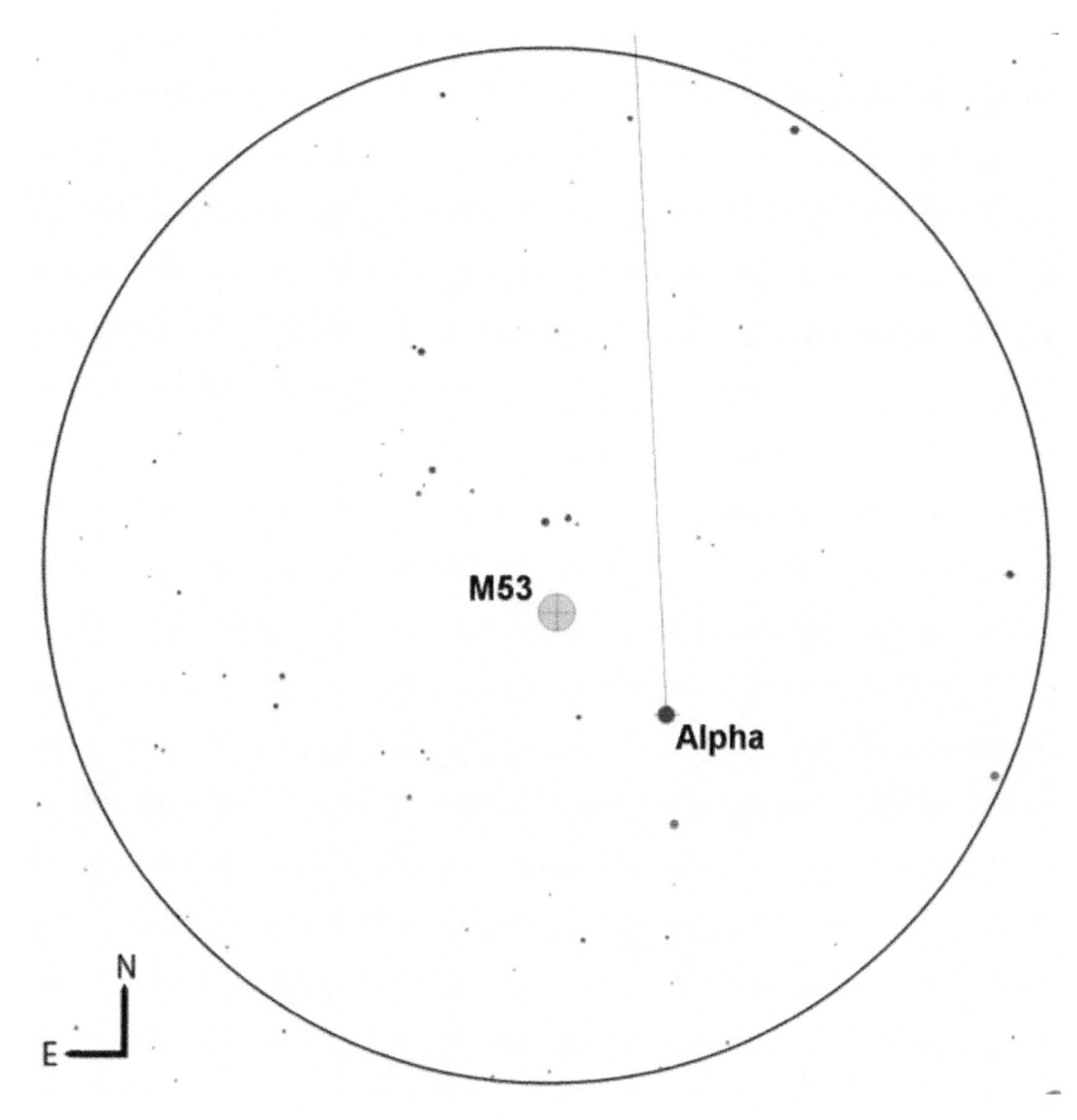

Messier 53, binocular view.

Coma is also well-known for containing a high concentration of galaxies, including seven from Charles Messier's famous catalog. One (M64, the Blackeye Galaxy) may be glimpsed with binoculars but as it lies in such a barren area of sky, it might be quite difficult for the inexperienced astronomer to find.

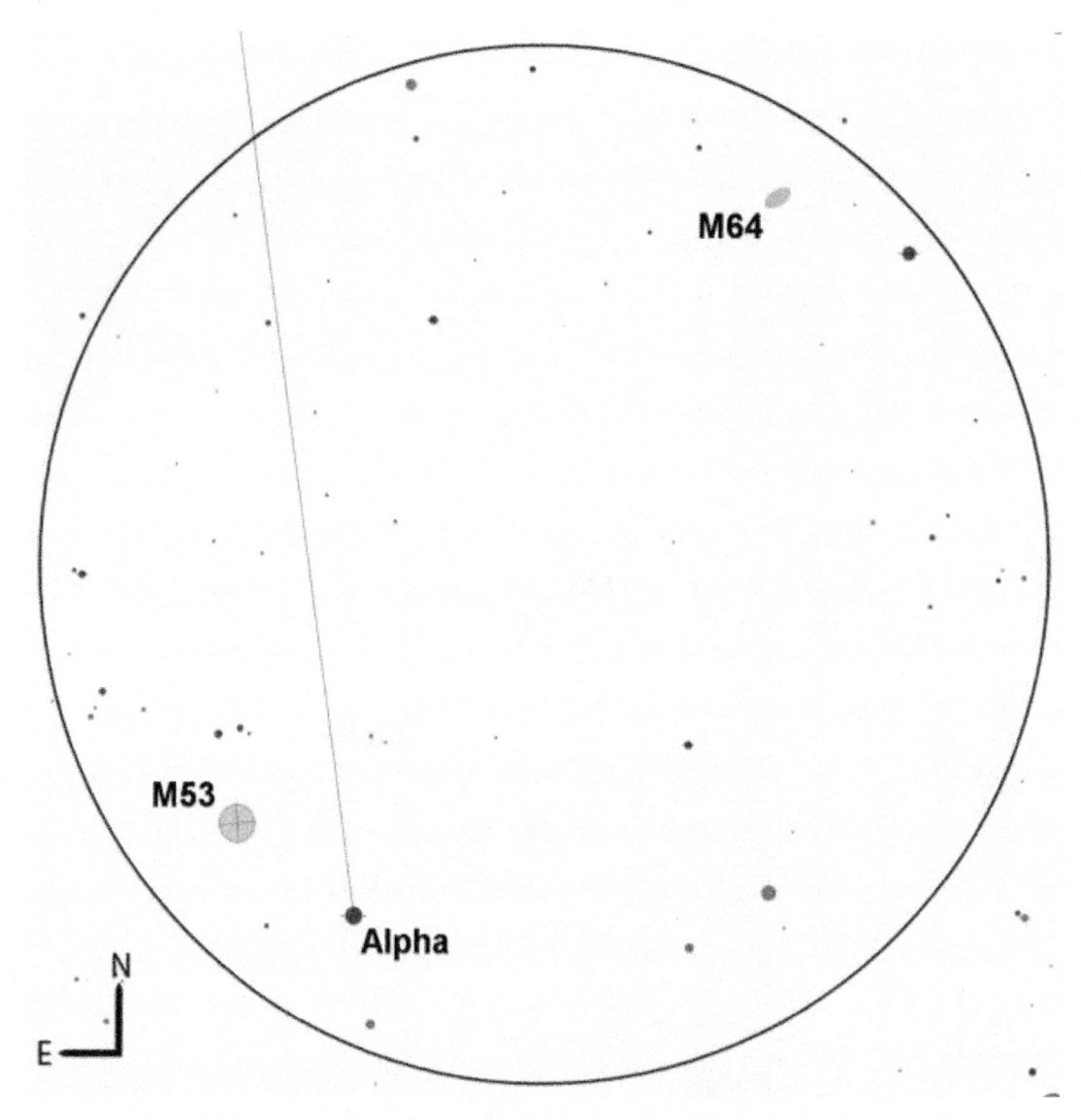

The Blackeye Galaxy, binocular view.

The reason for the multitude of galaxies has to do with our own Milky Way. The heart of our galaxy is best seen in the summer, but during the Spring you're actually looking directly over the north pole of our galaxy and into the deep depths of the universe itself!

While you're using your binoculars, scan to the north-west for Gamma and the Coma Star Cluster (Melotte 111). A large sprinkling of faint stars barely visible under dark skies with the unaided eye, it's worth a look with binoculars when more of its fifty members will come into view. A true cluster, it lies only 288 light years away.

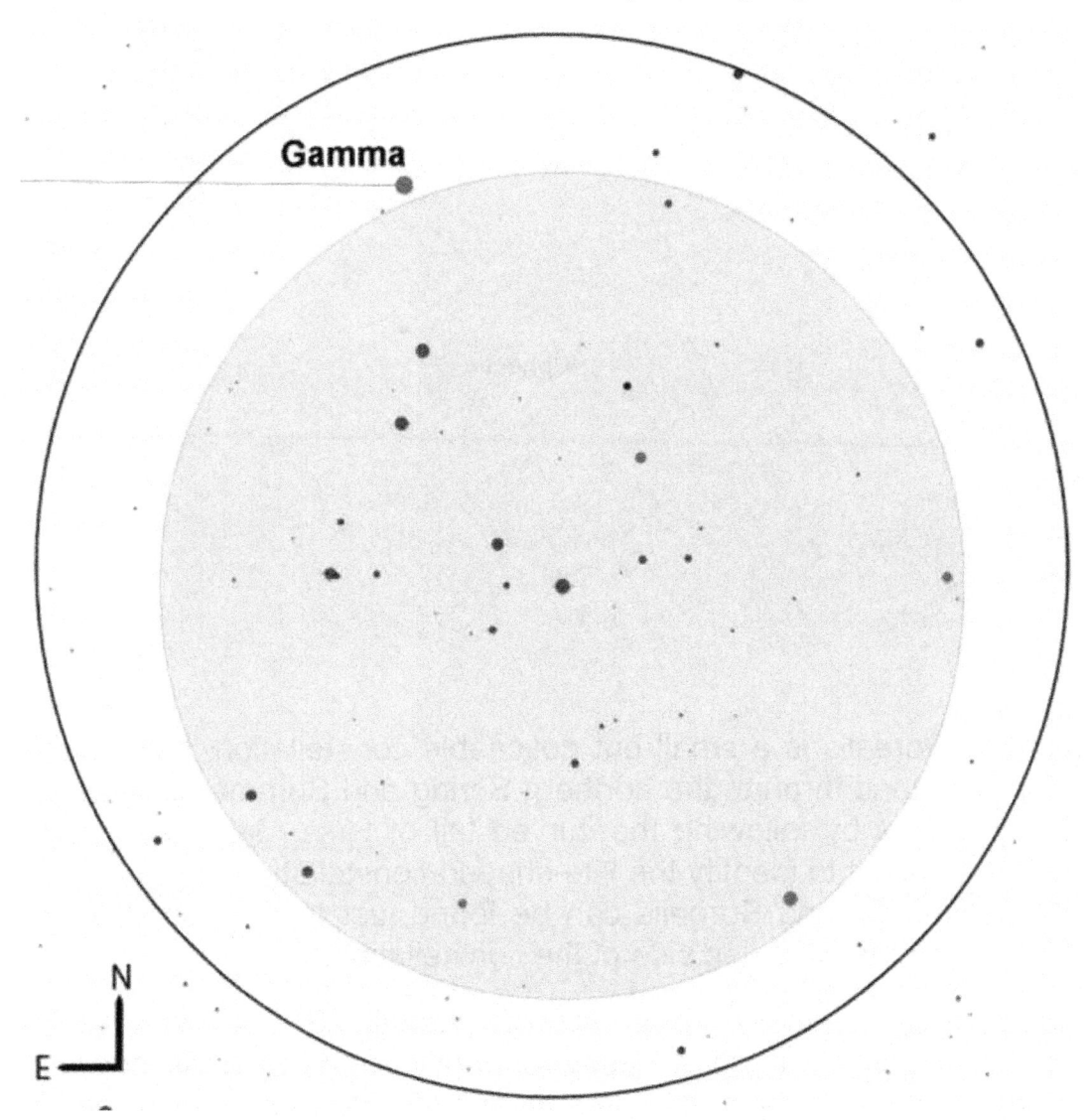

The Coma Star Cluster, binocular view.

Corona Borealis

Alphecca

Corona Borealis is a small but noticeable constellation that passes high overhead through the northern Spring and Summer skies. First find Arcturus by following the curved tail of Ursa Major (see here) and then use it to identify the kite-shaped constellation of Boötes the Herdsman. Corona Borealis can be found just to the north-east of Boötes, on the Hercules side of the constellation.

Despite its relatively small size (it ranks 73rd out of the 88 constellations) it's relatively easy to identify as it has a distinctive C shape. Not surprisingly, its name means the "northern crown" and is said to represent the crown once worn by the Cretan princess Aridane.

According to Greek myth, the crown was given to her by her husband, Theseus, but when he left her and she re-married, the crown was transferred into the starry heavens above.

It wasn't always identified with a crown; originally, the ancient Greeks saw a wreath here while other cultures saw a platter, sisters and, to the indigenous people of Australia, a boomerang.

Unfortunately, the constellation is a little bereft of deep sky wonders. Its brightest star, Alpha, is known as Alphecca and shines at a respectable magnitude 2.2. The name is derived from Arabic for "the bright one of the dish" but others know it more appropriately as Gemma – literally, the jewel.

A binary system some 75 light years away, the primary component is a white star about three times the size of the Sun while its companion is a yellow star of about the Sun's size.

It's thought the system might be surrounded by a disk of gas and dust, which might indicate a young solar system in the process of forming.

There are several double stars for small telescopes in the area but they lie away from the main constellation. However, Omicron Coronae Borealis lies near the eastern tip of the crown and reveals two tiny unrelated companion stars through binoculars. The star has one confirmed planet orbiting it.

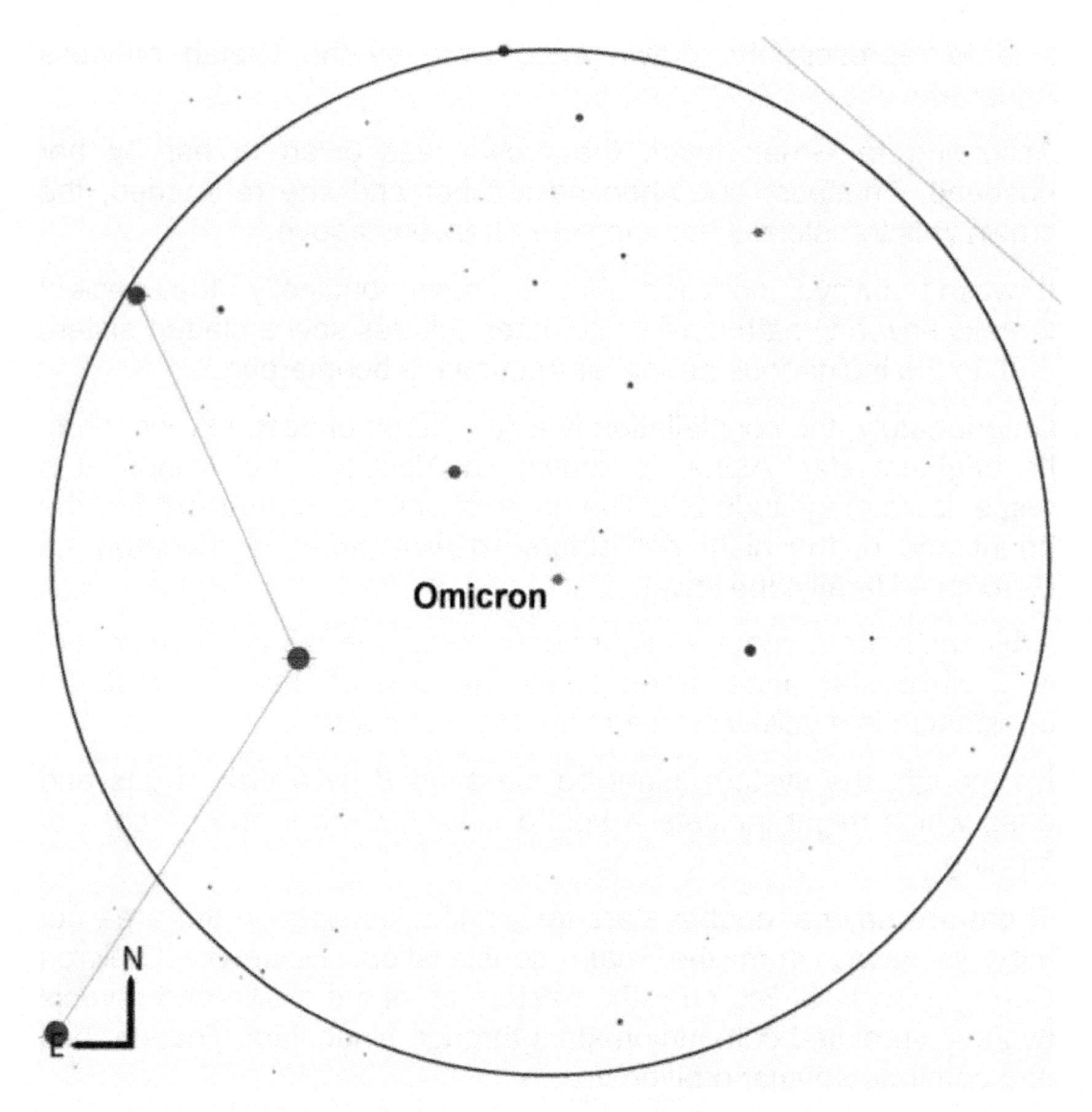

Omicron Coronae Borealis, binocular view.

There's also R Coronae Borealis. An irregular variable, it normally shines at about magnitude 6 but it will unpredictably fade to magnitude 13 or 14 over the course of several months– making it almost invisible to all but the largest of amateur telescopes. This fading is thought to be caused by a build-up of carbon dust in the star's atmosphere.

At the moment (March 2016) it's still quite faint (around magnitude 8 or so) and has been randomly brightening and fading by several magnitudes for nearly ten years now. Take a look – can you see it?

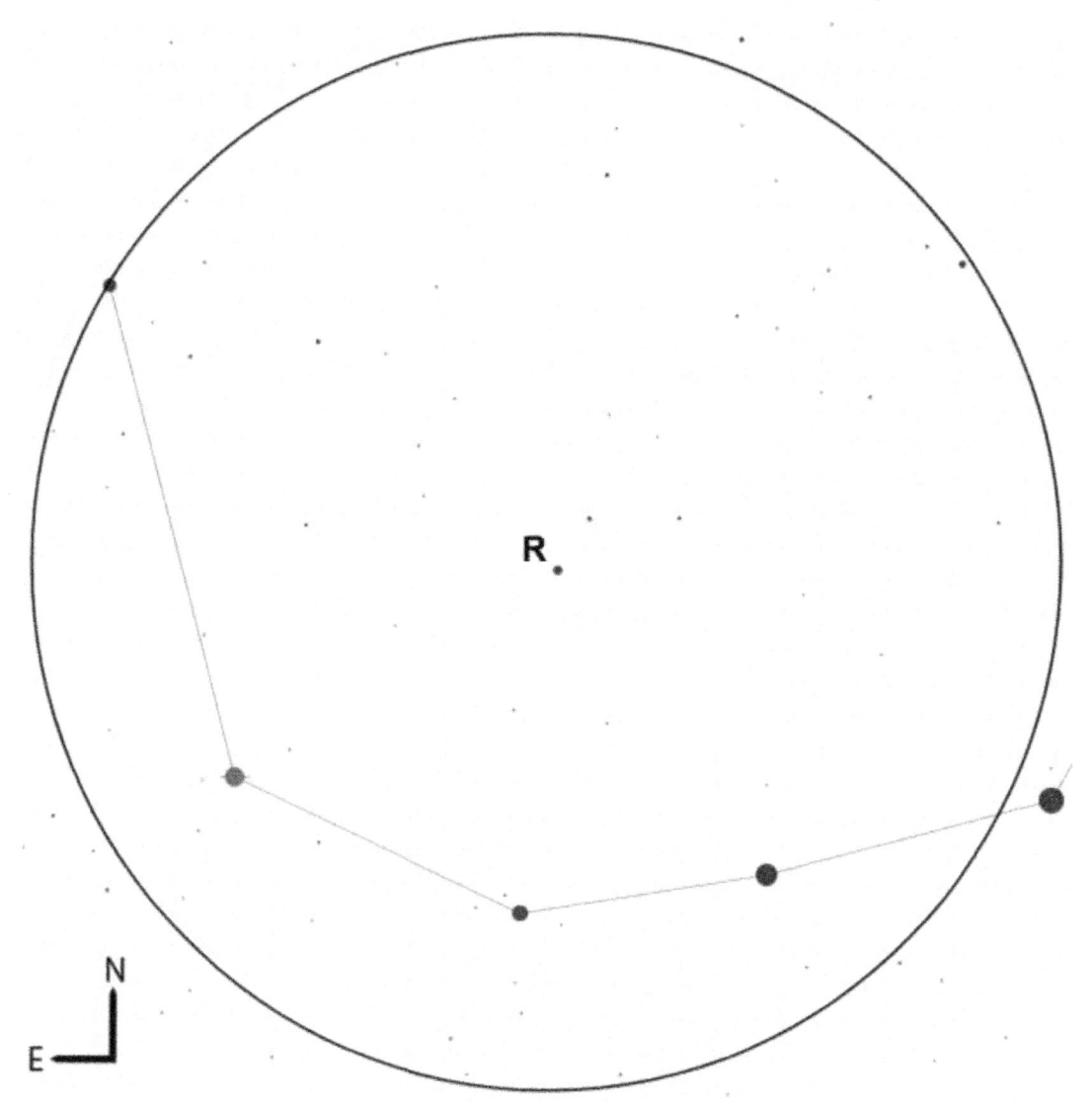

R Coronae Borealis, binocular view.

Similarly, T Coronae Borealis is known as the Blaze Star and is a recurring nova. In other words, it randomly and suddenly brightens to around magnitude 2 or 3. However it's most recent outburst was in 1946 and, at a regular magnitude of about 10, it may be tricky to spot in binoculars.

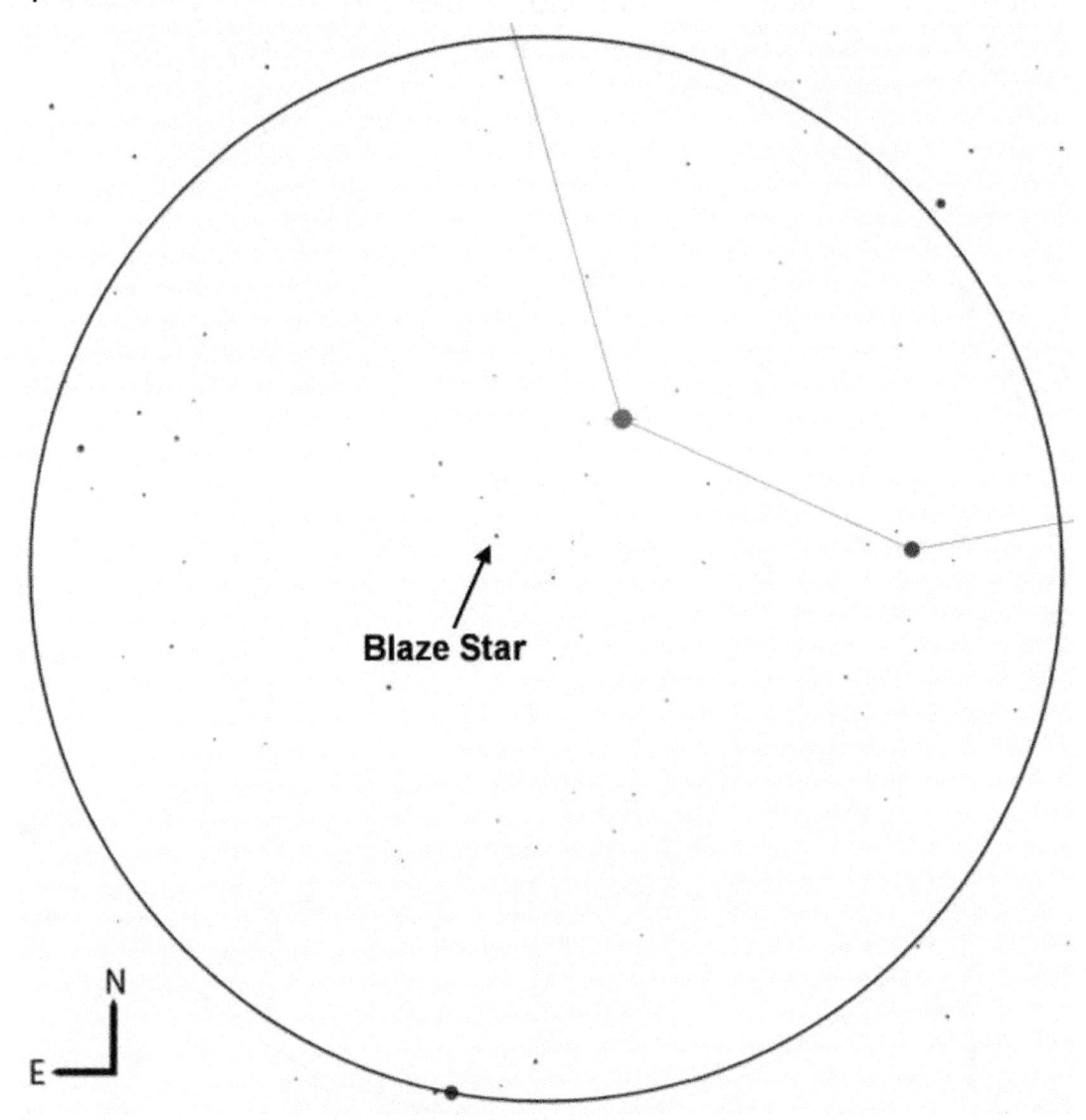

The Blaze Star, binocular view.

Corvus & Crater

Corvus and Crater are two relatively small constellations predominantly visible in the Spring sky.

Corvus, the brighter and more easterly constellation of the two, represents a crow while Crater depicts a cup. According to myth, the god Apollo sent the bird with the cup to bring him some water.

However, the bird stopped along the way to eat some figs, which delayed his return and made Apollo angry. Furthermore, rather than telling the truth, the bird claimed that a snake had temporarily prevented him from gathering the water. As proof, he held in his talons a snake.

Apollo, in his anger, threw the snake into the sky where it can still be seen today. He then cursed the bird to be eternally thirsty before throwing both it and the cup into the sky. The cup is to the west, always out of reach of the thirsty bird, while Hydra, the snake, slithers to the west.

Of the two constellations Corvus is smaller, being ranked 70th in size out of the 88 recognized constellations. Its four main stars – Beta, Gamma, Delta and Epsilon – form an asterism known as Spica's Spanker. An odd name, a spanker is actually a sail flown from the aftmost mast of a ship or yacht. Spica refers to the brightest star in the constellation of Virgo, the Virgin.

At magnitude 2.6, the brightest star in Corvus is Gamma. Also known as Gienah, the name is appropriately derived from the Arabic for "the right wing of the crow."

Like many others, this giant blue-white star is part of a double star system and has a Sun-sized orange companion. The pair orbit one another once every 158 years and lie about 150 light years away.

If you have binoculars, look out for Zeta Corvi, a white magnitude 5.2 star near the southern end of the constellation. Just to the west you should easily see a slightly fainter, unrelated orange companion.

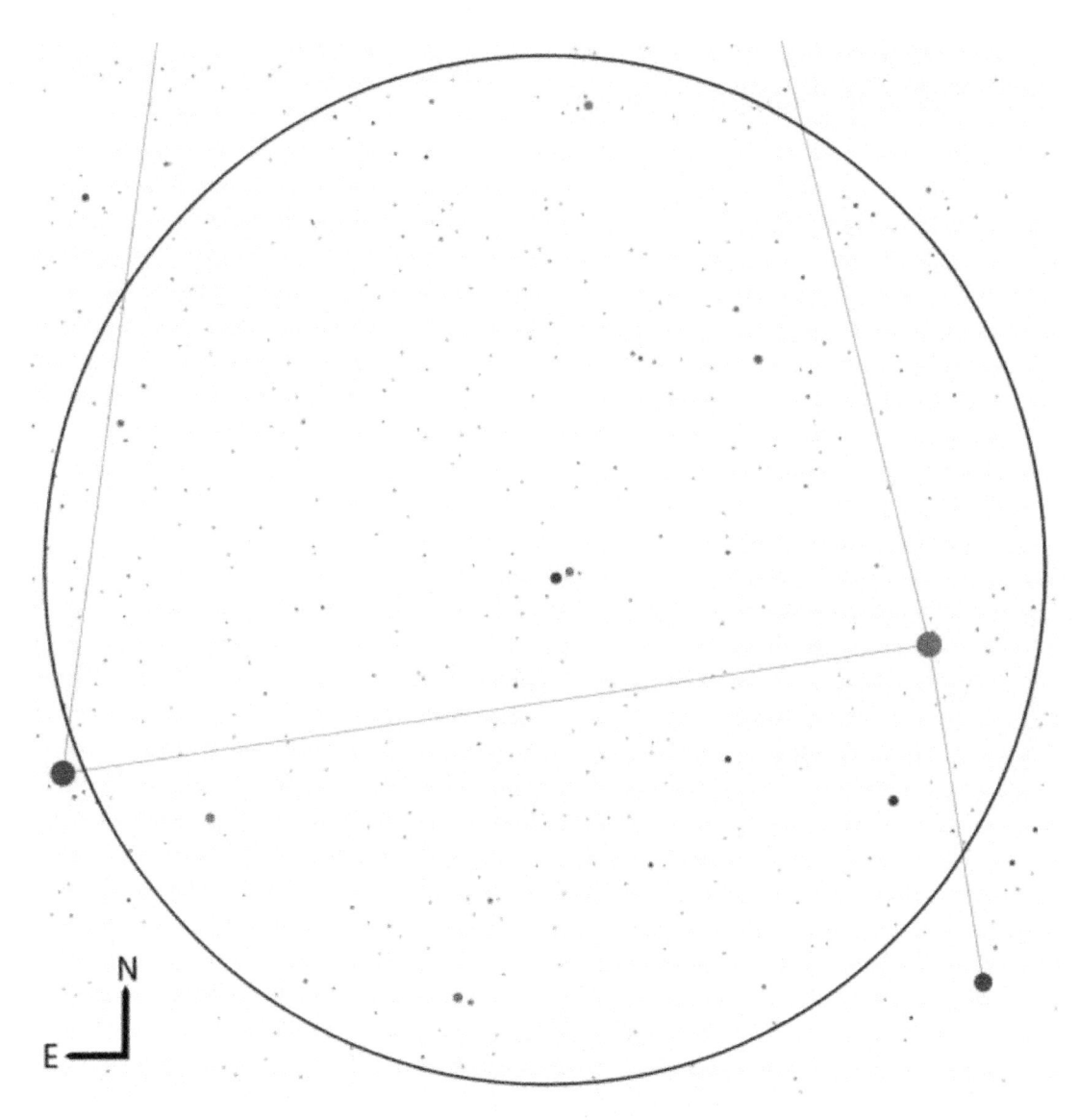

Zeta Corvi, binocular view

An easier target is Delta Corvi, better known as Algorab from the Arabic word for "crow." Binoculars will show the wide, magnitude 4.3 unrelated star Eta Corvi, but turn a telescope toward it with a medium power eyepiece (about 50x) and Algorab may reveal a close companion. The primary is a brilliant white and the much fainter secondary appears bluish.

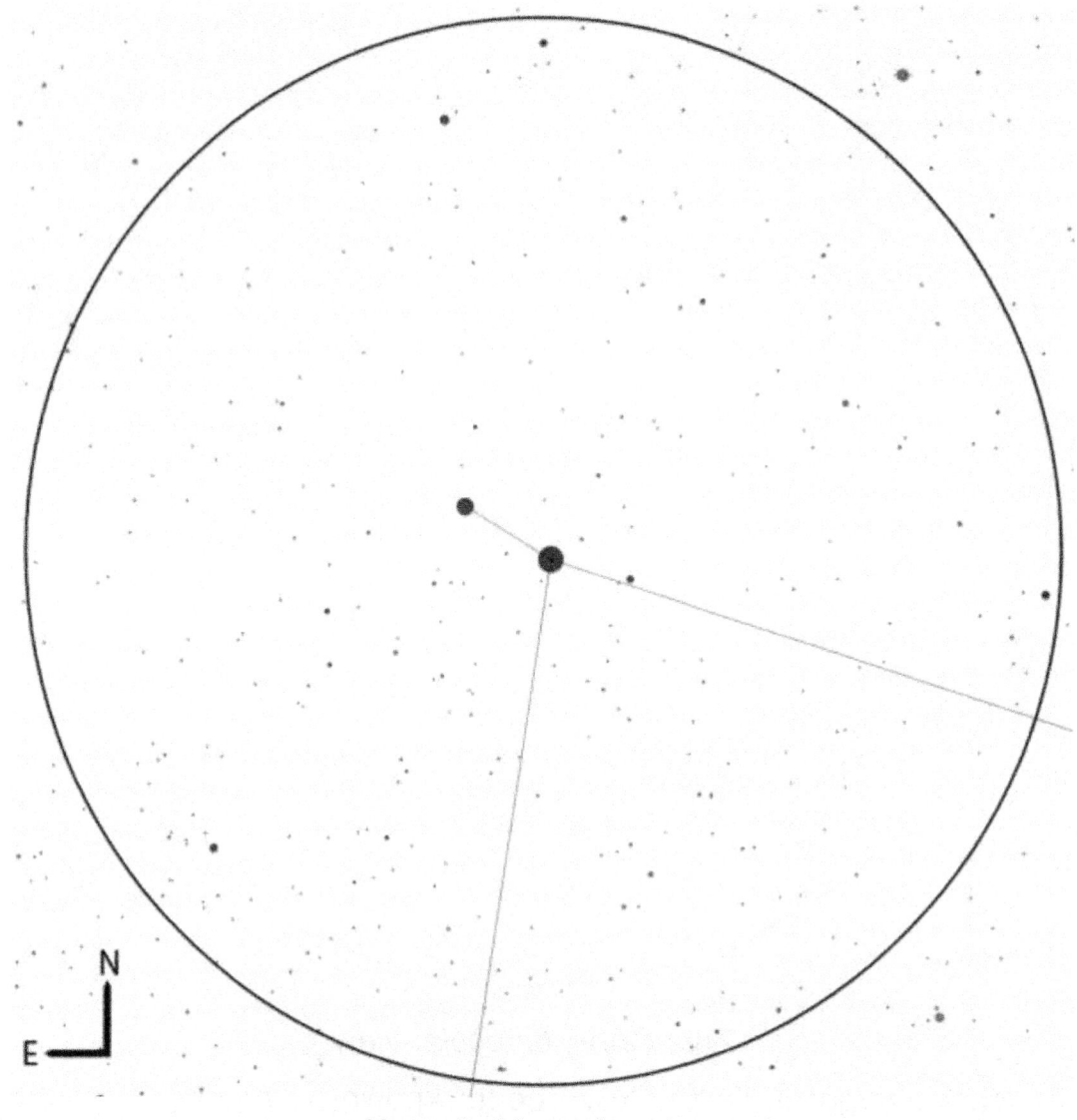

Algorab, binocular view.

If you want a challenge, try your hand at spotting Messier 68, a small and relatively faint globular cluster that's just over the border in neighboring Hydra. You can use Algorab and Beta as pointers and the cluster is conveniently located within the same binocular field of view as the latter star.

Meanwhile, over in Crater, its brightest star is Delta, which glimmers at magnitude 3.5. Named Labrum, "the lip (of the cup)", it's an orange giant star just under 200 light years away.

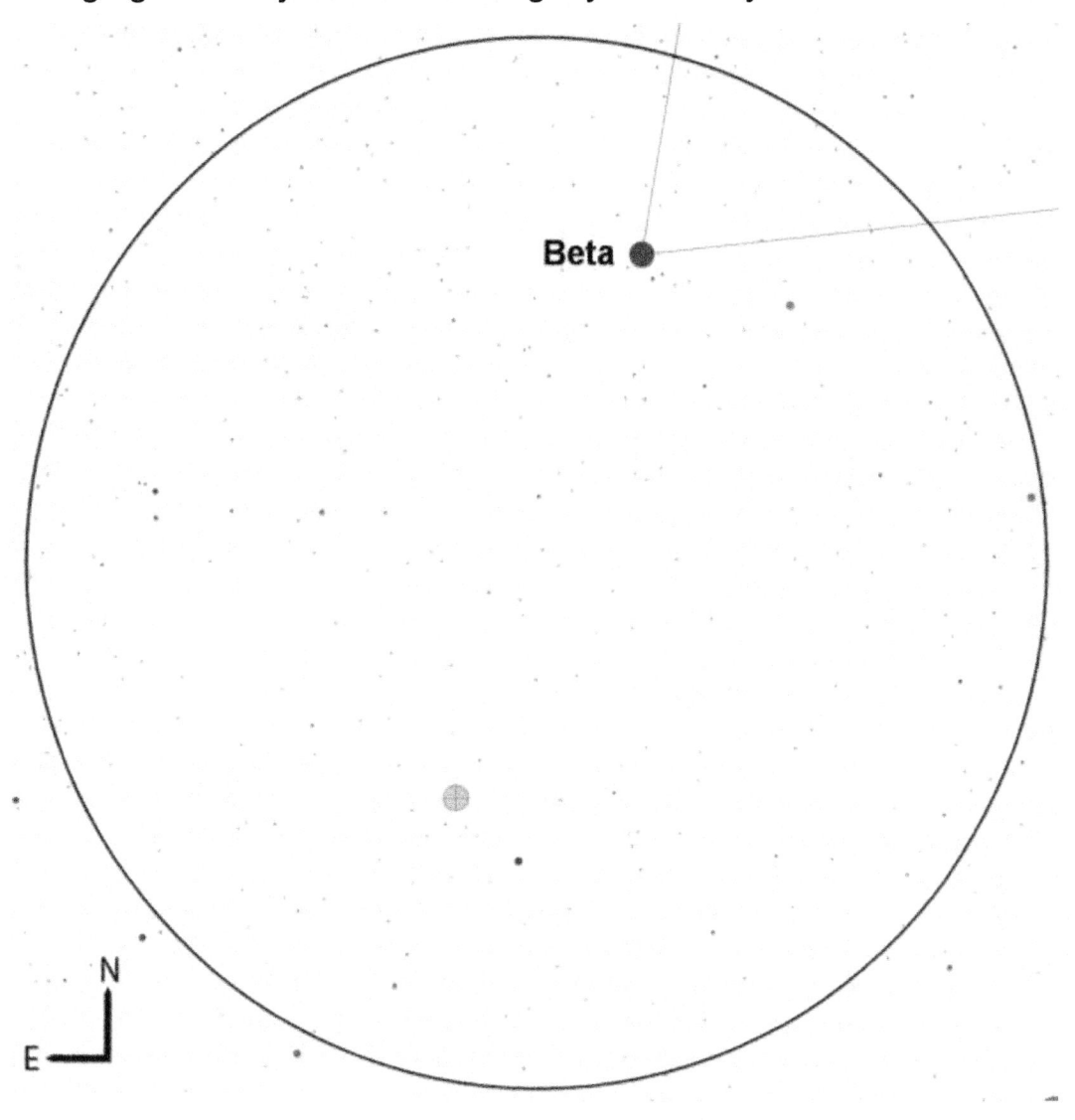

Messier 68, binocular view.

At magnitude 4.1, Alpha Crateris is fainter and is known by the name Alkes, which is derived from the Arabic word for cup. Like Delta, it's an orange giant star, but slightly closer to Earth at 174 light years.

Cygnus

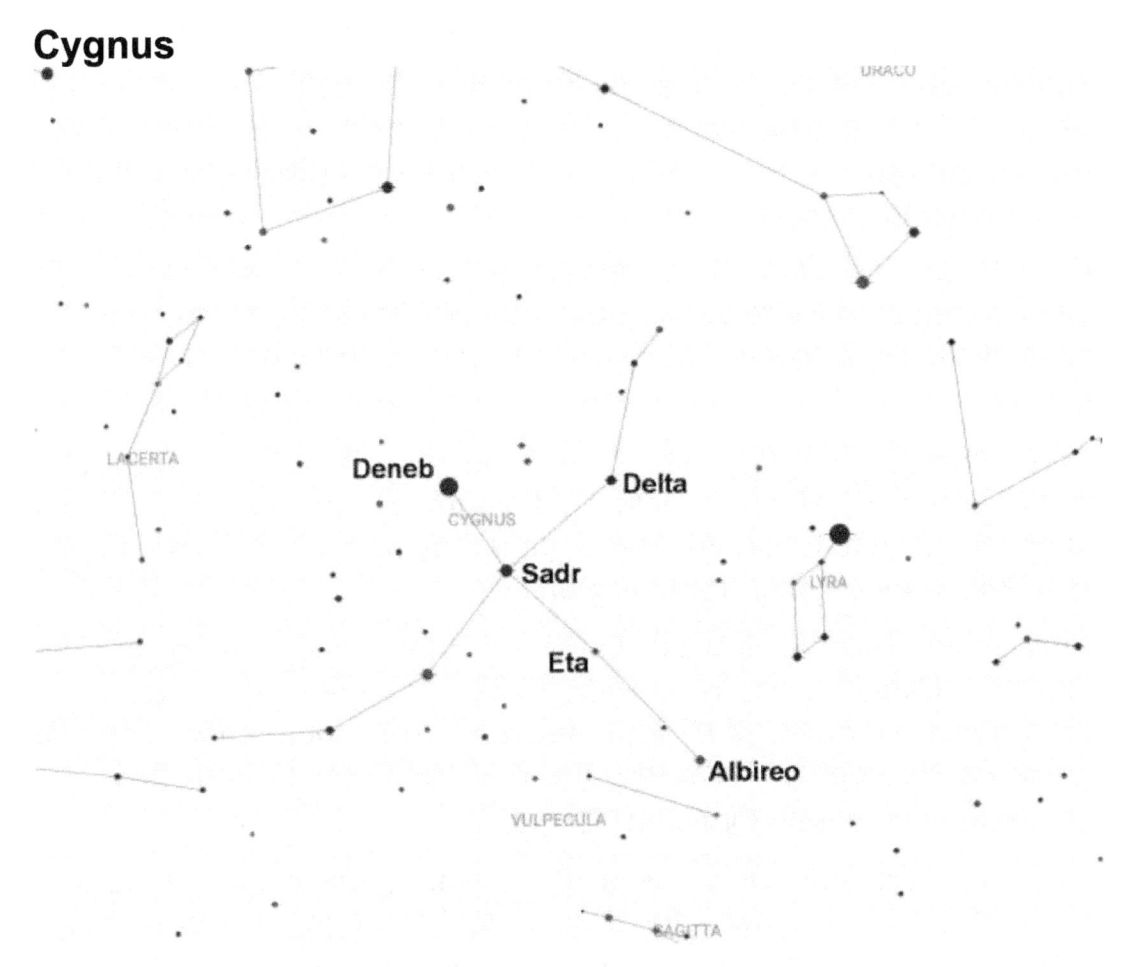

Cygnus, the Swan, is a large, bright constellation easily seen throughout the Summer and Autumn months. From the northern hemisphere the celestial bird flies high overhead and its distinctive cross-shape makes it an unmissable sight on any warm summer night.

There are a number of myths associated with the constellation but one of the most common concerns yet another amorous adventure of Zeus. Transforming himself into a swan, he seduced Leda, Queen of Sparta, who later gave birth to the twins Castor and Pollux. (See Gemini.)

However, the constellation is known for something far more spectacular. Get yourself away from the city lights on an August night and you'll see our own Milky Way galaxy streaming down toward the south like a river. Under the right conditions, it is literally breathtaking.

Cygnus is rich with stars and sweeping the constellation with binoculars can be a rewarding experience. At the northern tip is the constellation's brightest star, Alpha, more commonly known as Deneb.

Part of the Summer Triangle of stars, Deneb is the 19th brightest star in the sky and, at about 800 light years away, one of the most luminous known. Estimates vary, but it may shine with a light nearly 200,000 times brighter than the Sun.

Now move halfway toward Delta on the western wing to find Omicron Cygni. If you're using 10x50 binoculars, you can have Deneb just on the edge of your view and you should easily see two golden stars nearby. However, the real treat comes from the southern component, Omicron^1 Cygni.

Look carefully and you'll see a third, slightly fainter pale blue star very close to it. It makes for a nice sight through binoculars but a small telescope at low power only improves the view.

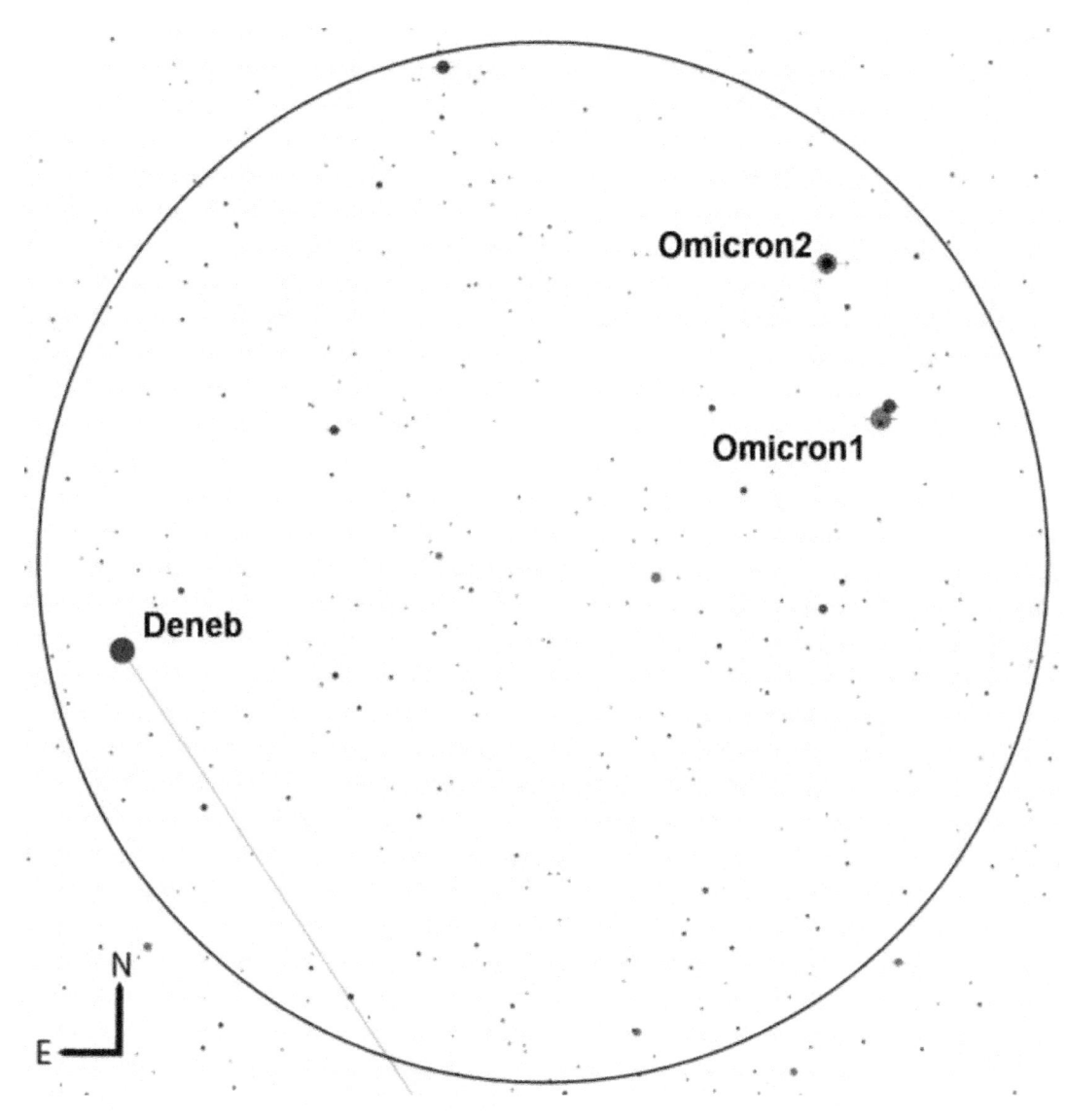

Omicron Cygni, binocular view.

Move back toward the center of the cross to find magnitude 2.2 Sadr. This area of Cygnus is particularly rich with stars and provides a very nice view in binoculars. Can you see tiny Messier 29 close by?

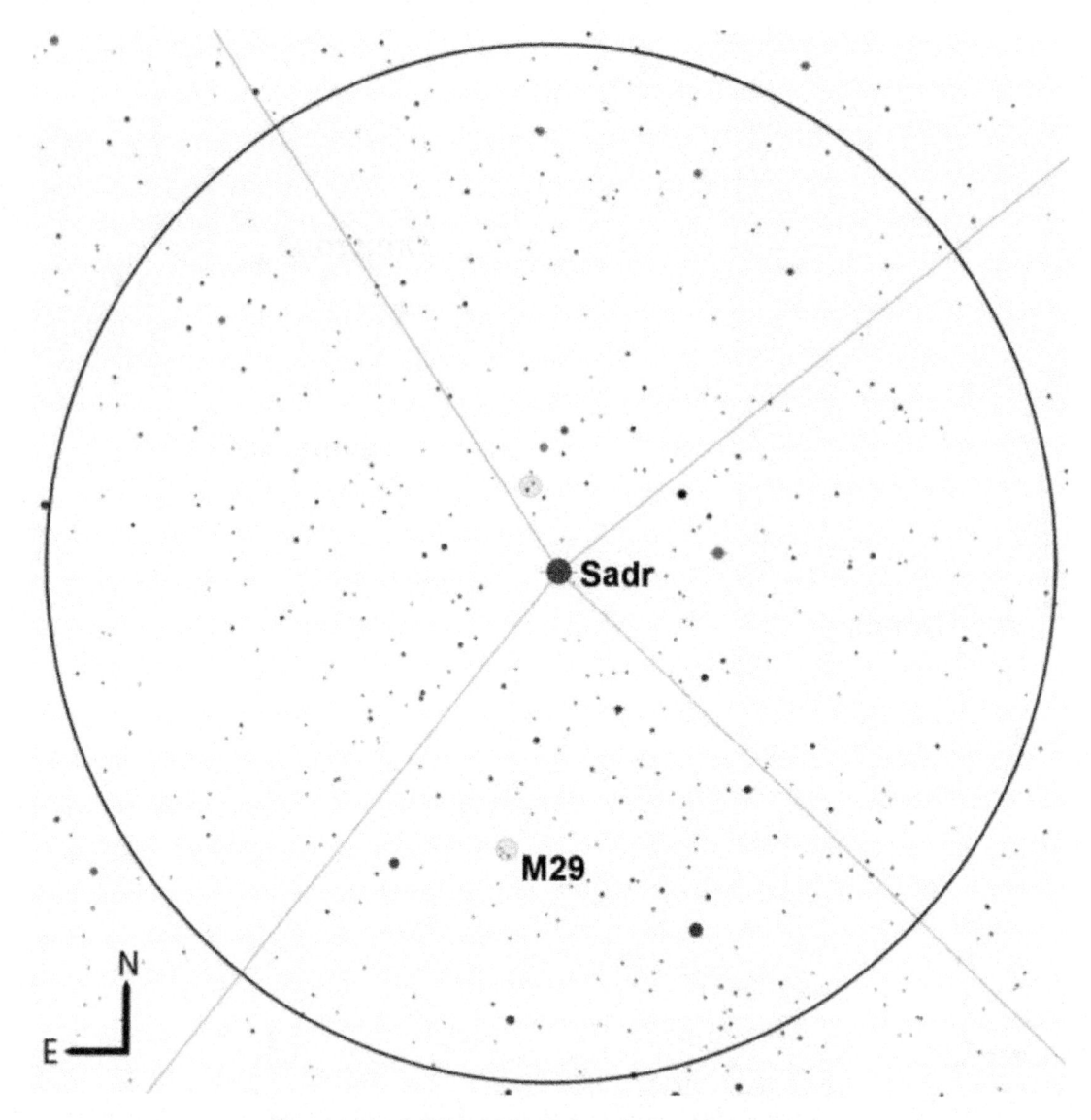

Sadr and Messier 29, binocular view.

Further south along the neck of the swan, we come to Chi Cygni. Appearing close to Eta, it lies about midway between Sadr in the center and Albireo at the bottom.

Chi is a red giant variable star which typically ranges between roughly magnitude 5 to magnitude 14 over a period of about 408 days. However, on rare occasions it has been known to flare up to magnitude 3, making it easily visible to the naked eye.

Upcoming dates of maximum brightness for Chi Cygni are listed below. (Data calculated using *Sky Tools 3* by Skyhound, http://www.skyhound.com)

October 27th, 2017	July 10th, 2024
December 9th, 2018	August 22nd, 2025
January 21st, 2020	October 4th, 2026
March 4th, 2021	November 16th, 2027
April 16th, 2022	December 28th, 2028
May 29th, 2023	February 9th, 2030

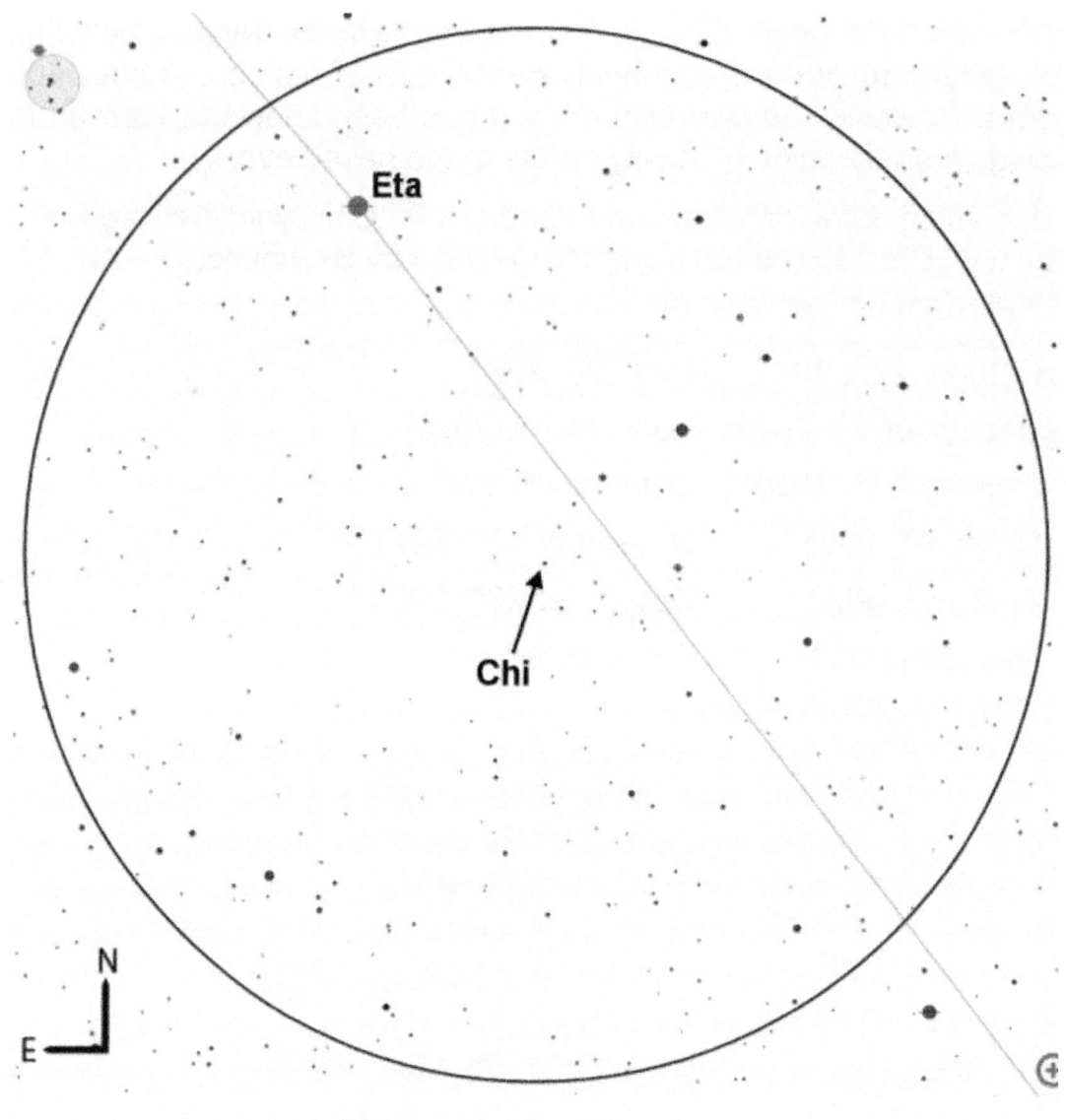

Chi Cygni, binocular view.

Lastly, no words on Cygnus would be complete without mentioning Beta, also known as Albireo. One of the most popular double stars in the sky, every amateur astronomer knows it as a Summer showcase for small telescopes. Low power will reveal a golden primary with a stunning sapphire blue companion. But try your hand with binoculars – held steady under excellent conditions, you might get lucky!

Delphinus

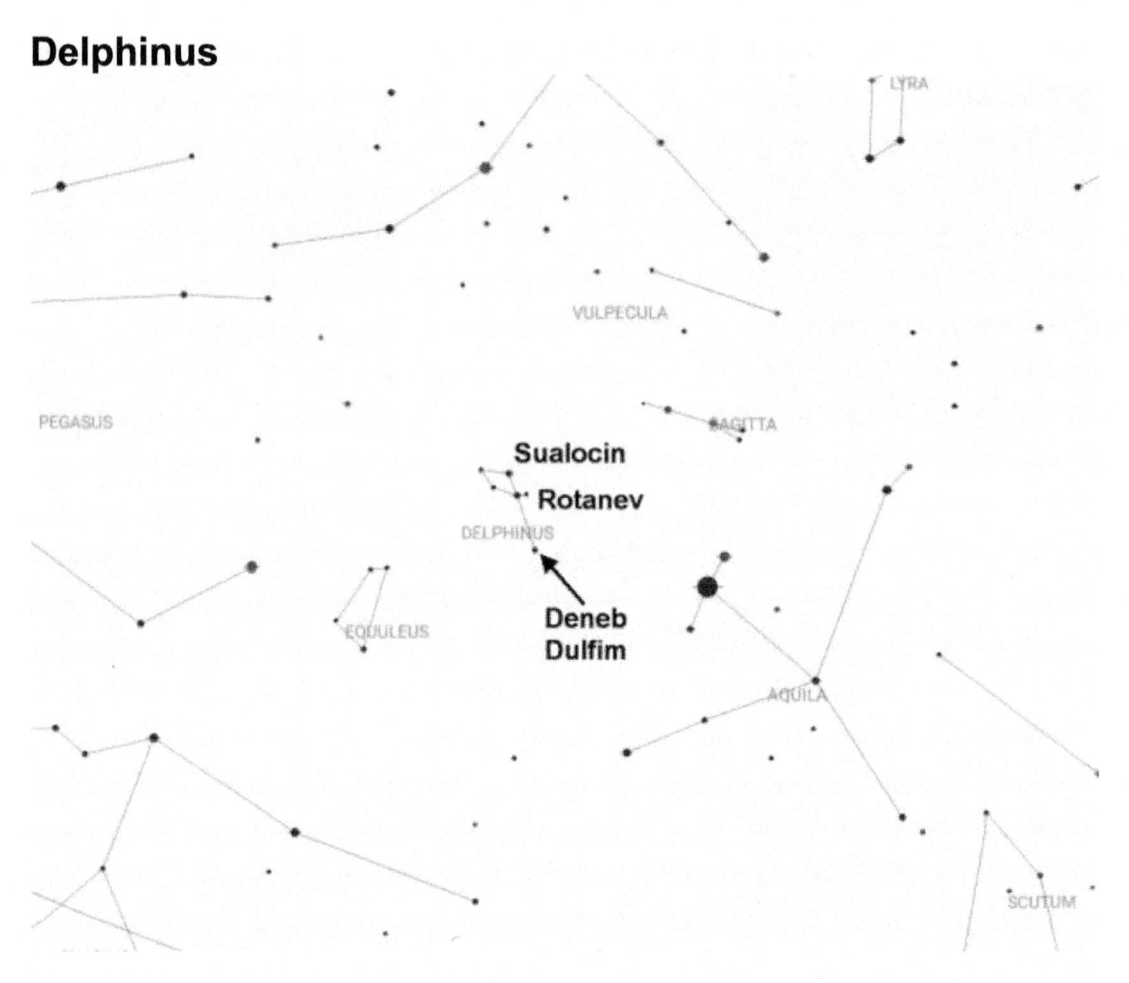

One of the smallest constellations in the sky, it ranks 69th in size and the entire constellation can comfortably fit into the field of view of a pair of 10x50 binoculars. Delphinus represents a dolphin and is one of the few constellations that at least partially looks like the creature or object it's meant to depict.

One legend tells of how Poseidon, god of the sea, fell in love with the sea nymph Amphitrite but unfortunately, not feeling quite the same way, Amphitrite fled to the mountains to escape his advances. Being a god, this didn't deter Poseidon, who then sent out a number of sea creatures to find her. Not only did Delphinus successfully find her, but was also able to persuade the nervous nymph to return to the god. In gratitude, Poseidon placed the dolphin amongst the stars.

Delphinus is not particularly bright, but thanks to its position, just east of Cygnus the Swan and north-east of Aquila the Eagle it's relatively easy to find and has a distinctive shape. Visible throughout the summer and autumn, I tend to think of it as being the last of the summer constellations and the first of the aquatic autumn constellations.

At magnitude 3.6, its brightest star is Beta, a double star system just slightly more than 100 light years away that consists of a white giant star with a subgiant companion. Unfortunately, the pair are too close to be split with all but the largest of amateur telescopes.

Second brightest is Alpha. It appears as a single magnitude 3.8 star to the unaided eye but is actually a complicated system comprised of seven stars some 74 light years away.

Both these stars have unusual names that deserve a mention. Alpha is also known as Sualocin while Beta is also known as Rotanev. Like Cor Caroli in Canes Venatici these are not names with Arabic or Greek origins but date back to the early 19th century. The names were given to the stars by the Italian astronomer Niccolò Cacciatore who was helping to compile the second edition of the Palermo Star Catalogue.

Taking the Latinized version of his name, Nicolaus Venator, he simply reversed the names before applying them to Alpha and Beta respectively. The names were consequently printed in the catalogue and their origins were a mystery for years.

Alpha and Beta are not the only stars with odd names; Epsilon, sometimes known as Deneb (not to be confused with the brightest star in Cygnus the Swan) was known to the Chinese as Pae Chou, "the rotten melon."

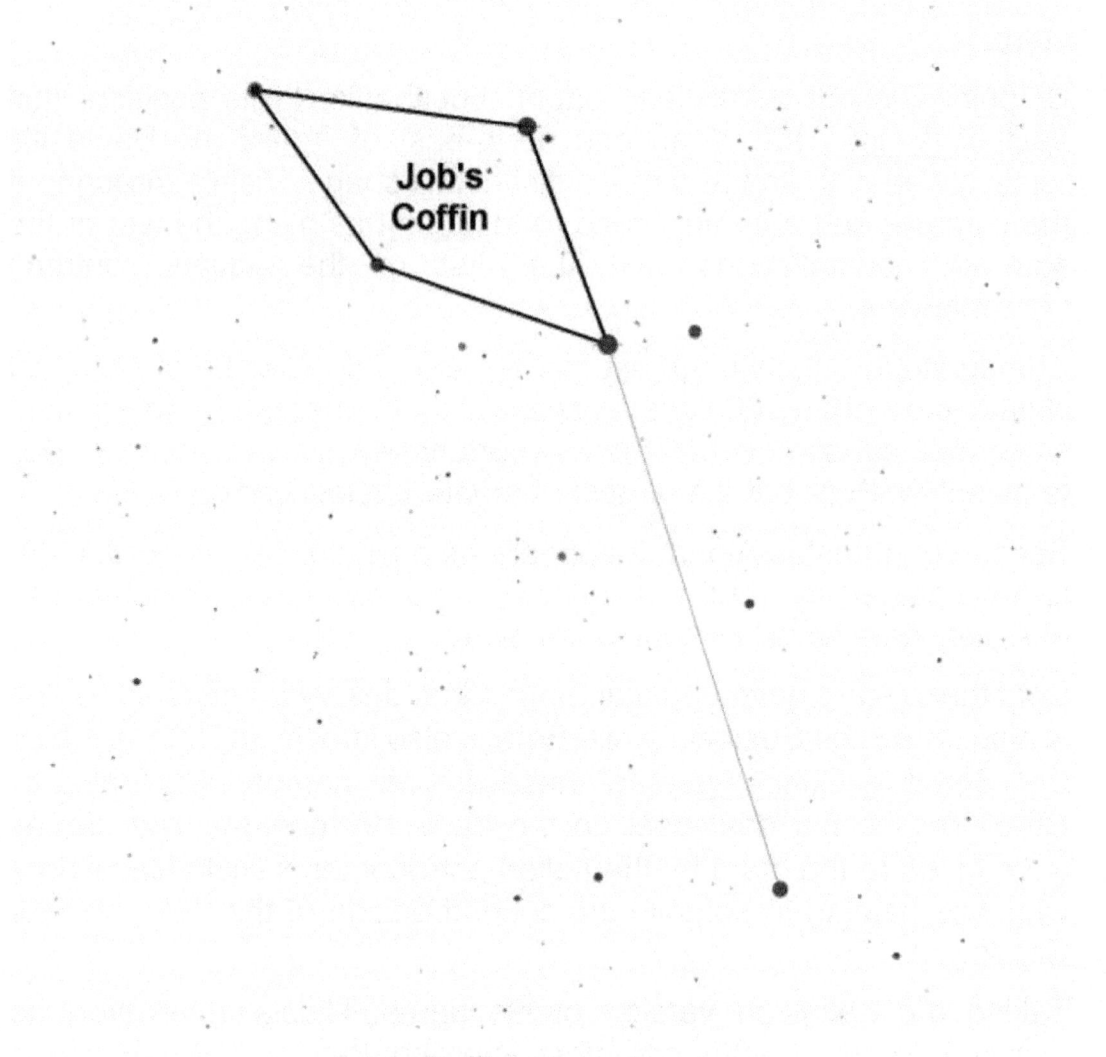

Job's Coffin, binocular view.

Alpha, Beta, Gamma and Delta collectively form an asterism known as Job's Coffin; despite being an obvious reference to the Biblical character, the exact origins of its name remain a mystery.

If you have binoculars, take a look at Sualocin and you should see a fainter, magnitude 6.0 white star just to the west of it.

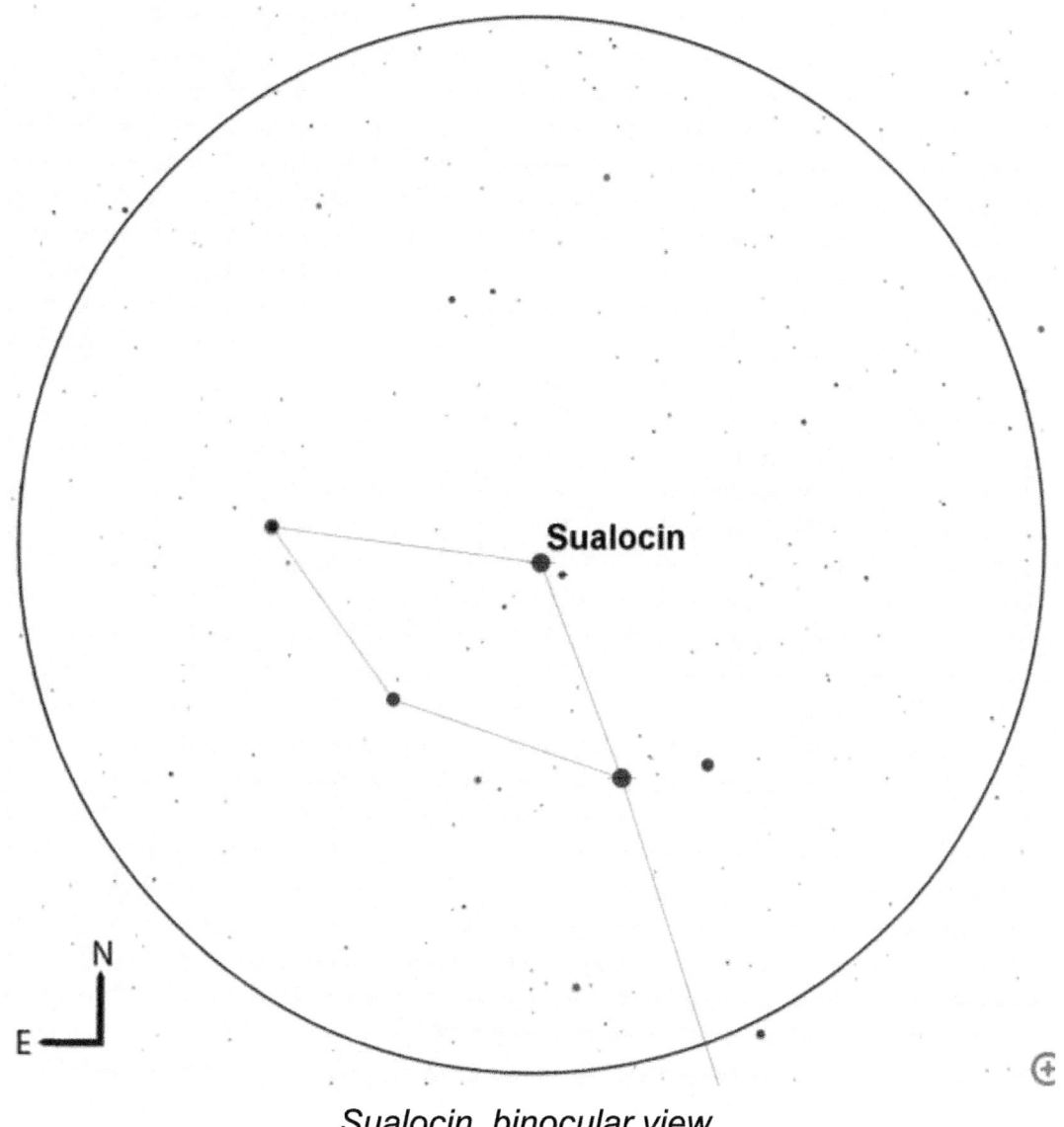

Sualocin, binocular view.

Meanwhile, to the south of Epsilon, also known as Deneb Dulfim, lies NGC 6934, a small and faint globular cluster of magnitude 8.9

that should prove a worthy challenge on a clear, dark night.

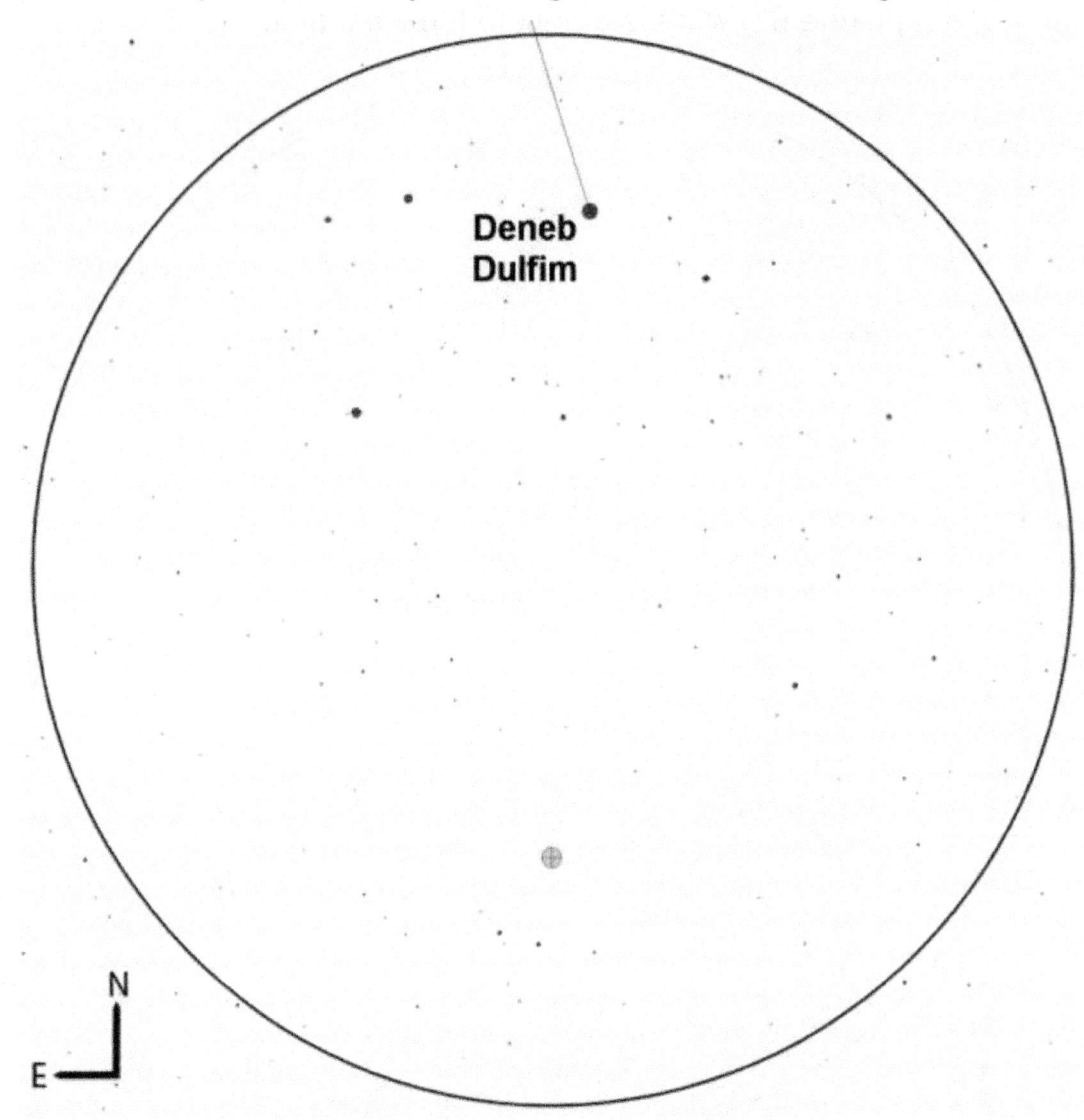

NGC 6934, binocular view.

Draco

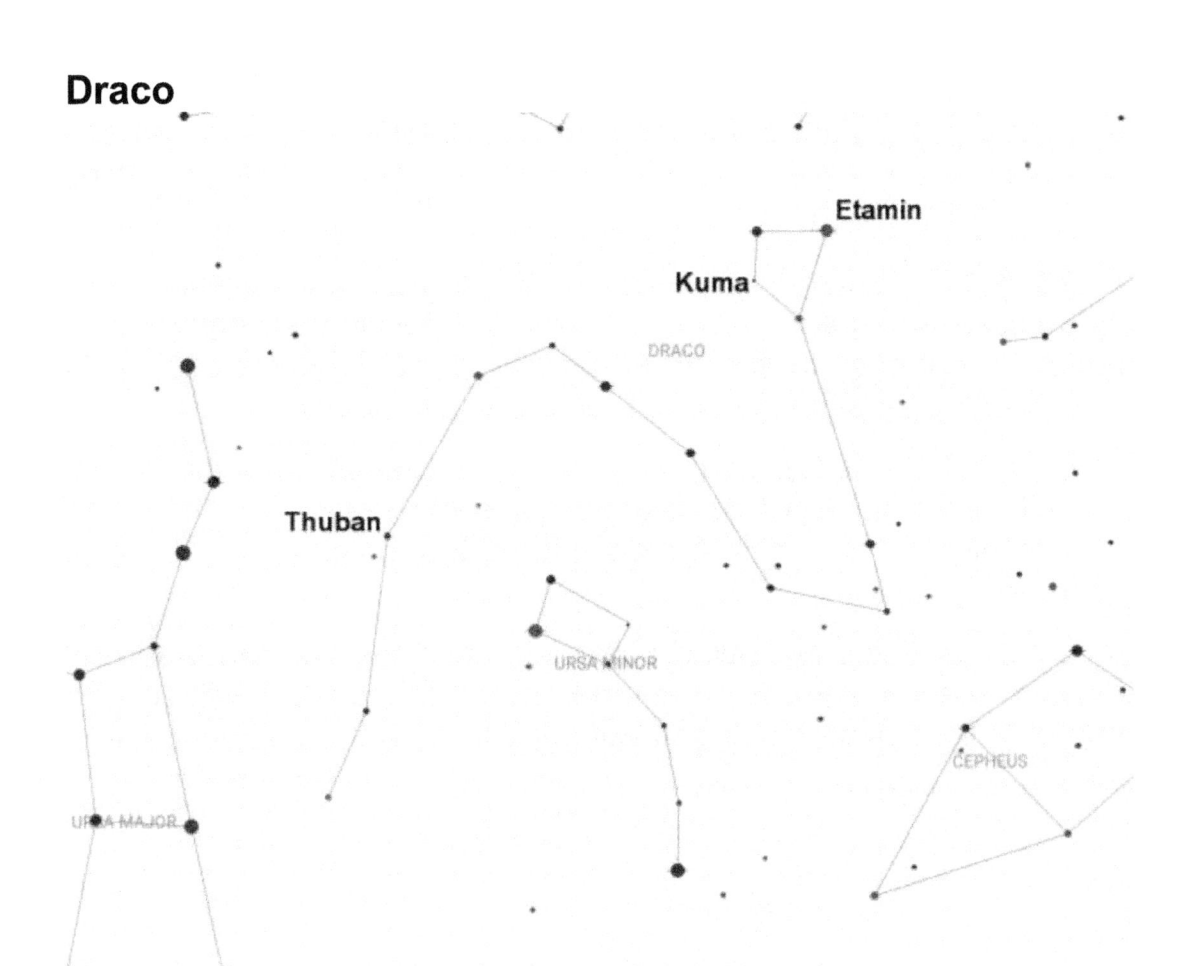

Draco, the Dragon, is an unusual constellation in that you could start to observe it in the spring, when it's tail appears high above the northern horizon, work your away along its body throughout the summer and then finish with its head in the autumn.

That being said, perhaps the best time to spot the constellation as a whole (as depicted in the image above) is early July, when the entire constellation arches over Ursa Minor at about 10pm.

In Greek mythology, Draco represents Ladon, the dragon tasked with guarding the golden apples that grew in the garden of Hesperides. The garden contained an orchard owned by Hera, wife of Zeus, who had placed the dragon there to stop the Hesperides from taking the apples for themselves. Unfortunately, the dragon was slain by Hercules who was tasked with stealing the apples as one of his twelve labors.

Draco is a very large constellation, 8th in size and covering over 1,000 square degrees of sky. But, with the possible exception of its head, it's not easy to spot from the city, a fact compounded by its long, twisting serpentine body of relatively faint stars.

Its brightest star is Gamma, also known as Etamin, from the Arabic for "the great serpent." An orange giant star nearly fifty times the size of the Sun, it shines at magnitude 2.2 and lies about 150 light years away.

It has a suspected red dwarf companion and the pair are gradually moving closer toward us. In another 1.5 million years, it will only be about 28 light years away and will appear to be the brightest star in the sky.

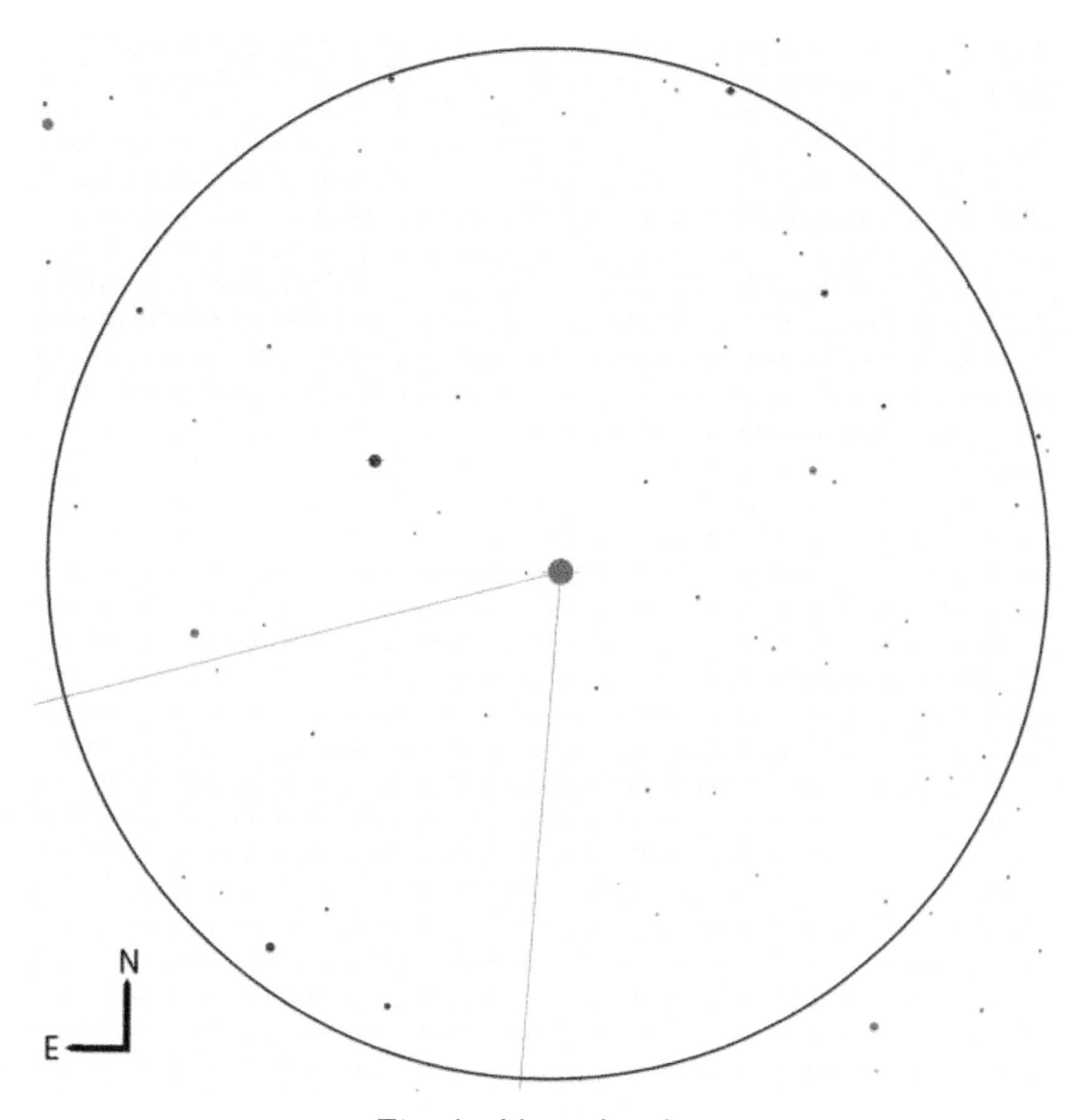

Etamin, binocular view.

Meanwhile, the fainter Alpha Draconis, also known as Thuban (from the Arabic for "the snake"), has its own claim to fame. As every astronomer knows, our north pole star is the appropriately named Polaris, the brightest star in the constellation of Ursa Minor.

This is the star that appears directly overhead from the north pole, but this wasn't always the case. Over the course of 26,000 years, the Earth actually wobbles slightly in a circular motion on its axis. Known as the precession of the equinoxes, this causes the north pole star to change over the course of those years.

So, for example, right now the closest star to the celestial north pole is Polaris. But from 3942 BCE to 1793 BCE the pole star was Thuban and all the other stars appeared to spin about it. In approximately another 7,000 years, this will be the case again (but not before other stars take their turn!)

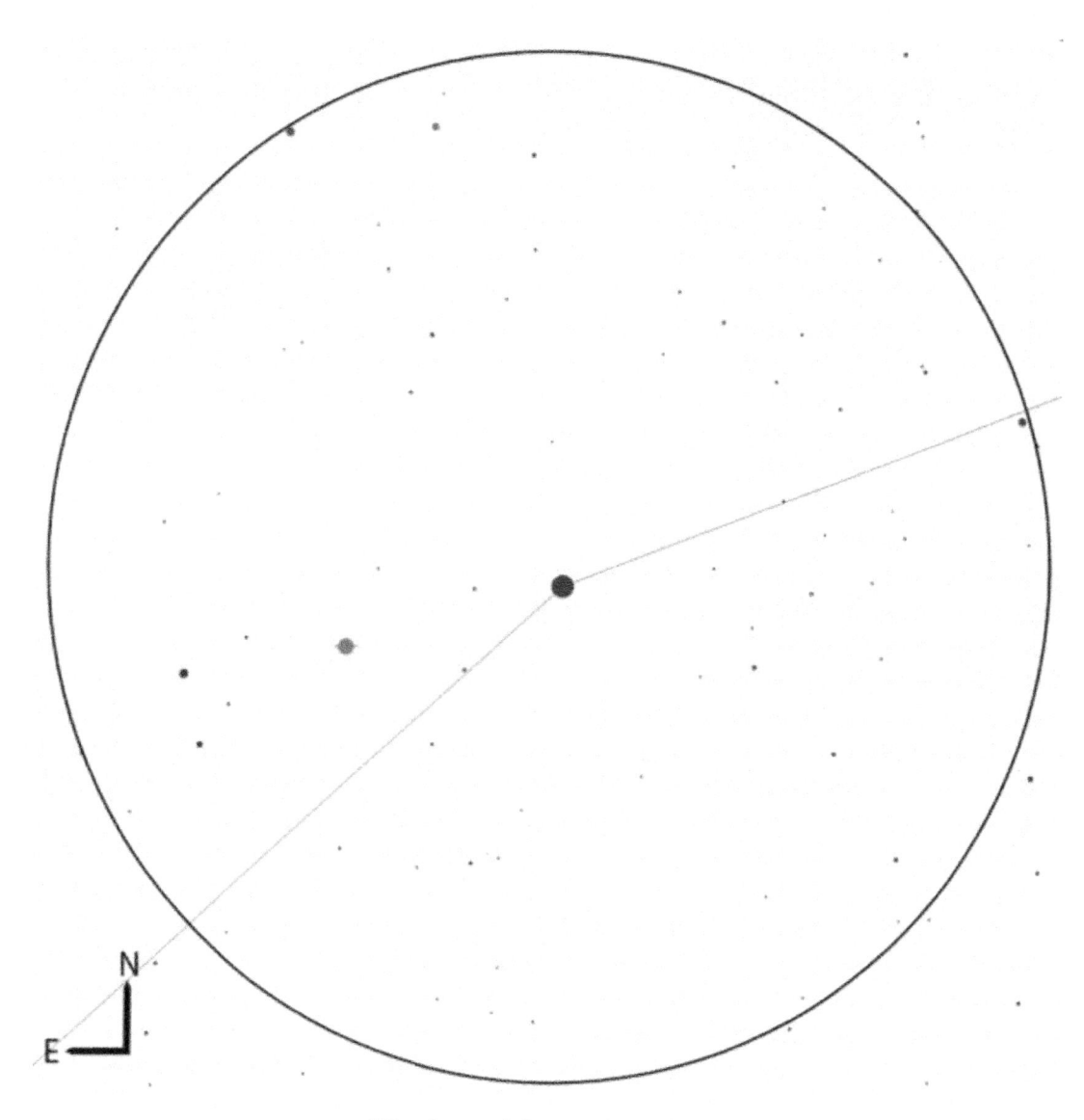

Thuban, binocular view.

Lastly, close to Etamin, in the head of the dragon, is Nu Draconis, also known as Kuma. This is a favorite double star for both binoculars and small telescopes. A regular pair of 10x50 binoculars, held steady, should be able to split this magnitude 4.9 star into two brilliant white components of equal brightness.

A true double star system about 100 light years away, this famous double has rightfully earnt itself the nickname "the dragon's eyes." Take a look for yourself and you'll soon see why!

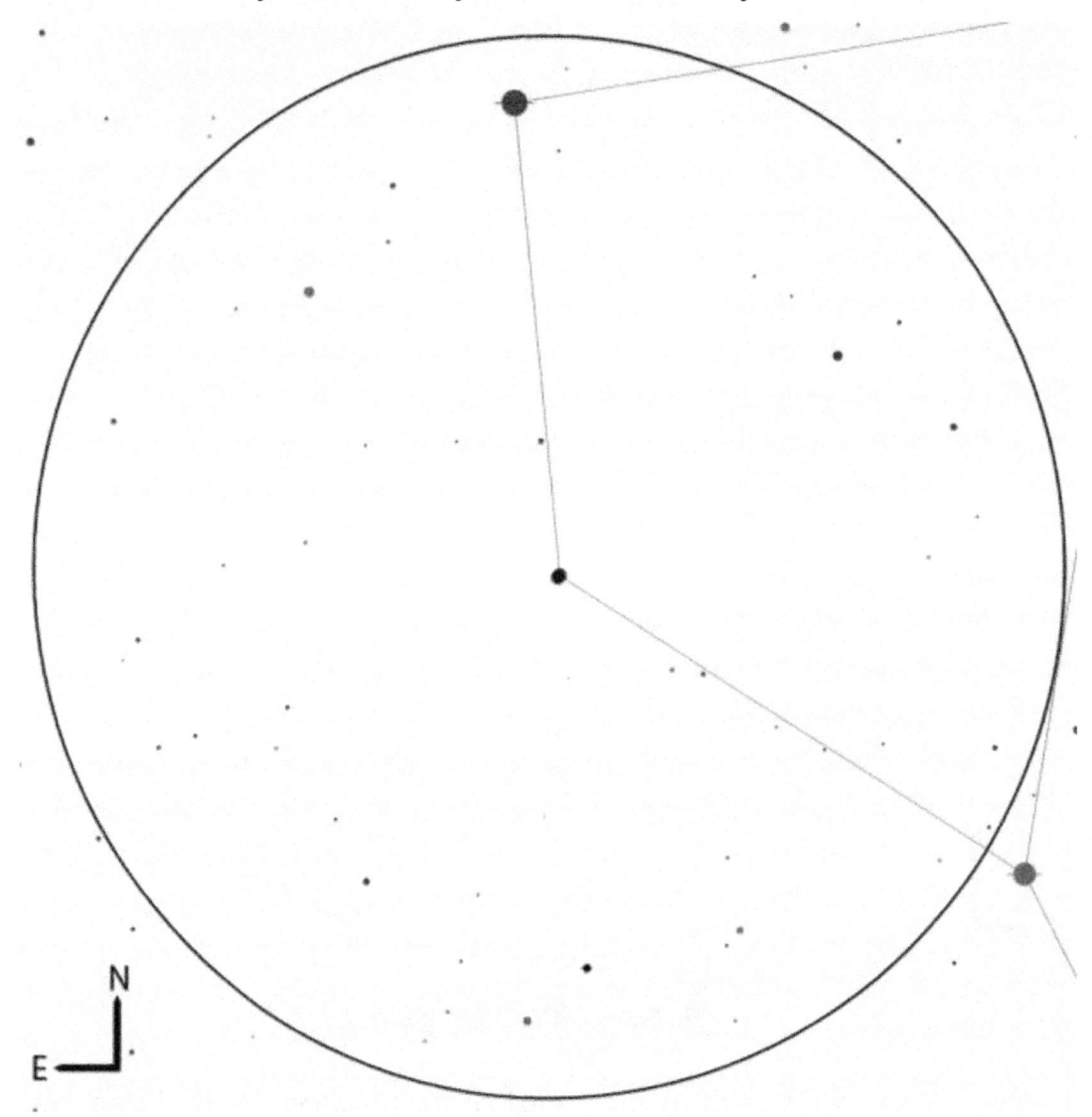

Kuma, binocular view.

Gemini

Gemini, as almost everyone knows, is one of the twelve signs of the zodiac and is a prominent feature of the winter and early spring skies. Thanks to its two brightest stars, it's been associated with twins across a number of civilizations but the constellation is now most commonly linked to the Greek myth of Castor and Pollux.

Curiously, despite being twins, they have different fathers. Although both were born to Leda, Castor was the mortal son of Tyndareus, the King of Sparta, while Pollux was the demigod son of Zeus who had seduced Leda while disguised as a swan. The twins embarked on many adventures together throughout their lives, including rescuing their sister Helen and joining the crew of the *Argo*.

Despite all their heroic escapades, the end came tragically while the twins were attempting to steal cattle from their cousin. During the raid, Castor was fatally wounded, causing the distraught Pollux to plead with his father Zeus to help them both. Zeus took pity and immortalized the twins by placing them among the stars.

Gemini is a bright, mid-sized constellation, easily found close to Orion the Hunter with the two bright stars of Castor and Pollux marking the heads of the respective twins. At magnitude 1.1, Pollux is the brighter and closer of the two. The 17th brightest star in the sky, it's an orange giant some 34 light years away with a single planet, twice the mass of Jupiter, unofficially named Thestias. The planet takes 590 days to orbit its parent star.

Meanwhile, Castor is a complex multiple star system about 51 light years away. To the naked eye, it's a single magnitude 1.6 white star but, in reality, there are three pairs of stars, making for a system of six in all.

Observers with a small telescope can see the two brightest components for themselves, but it requires a reasonably high magnification of about 100x to split the primary.

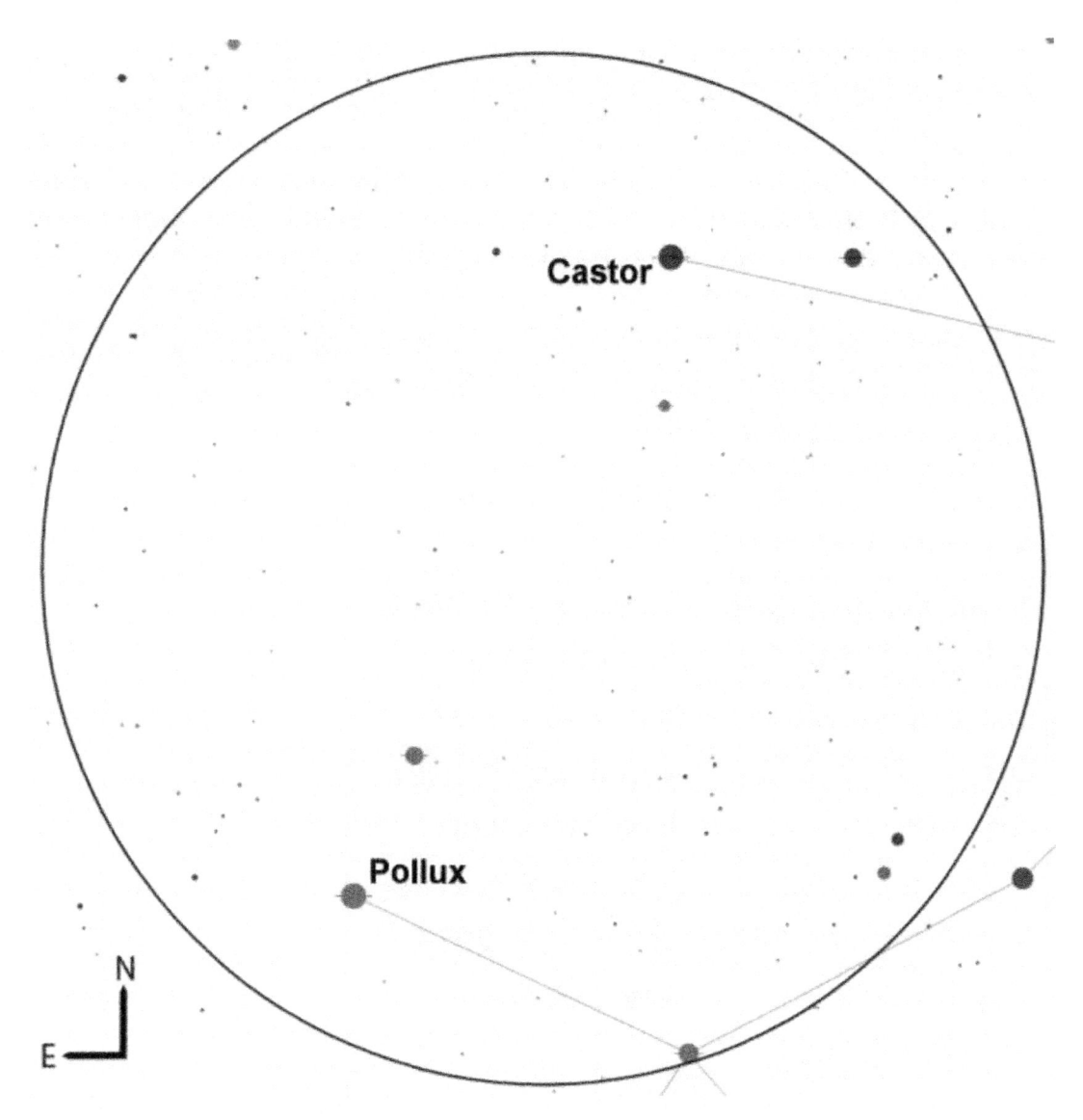

Castor and Pollux, binocular view.

Near Castor's foot is Eta, also known as Propus. This variable star is easily found but its changes in brightness are subtle and may require regular observations over a prolonged period to be noticed.

The reason for this is it only ranges in magnitude from 3.1 to 3.9 over a period of 233 days. Take a close look at this orange star and then compare it to Epsilon (Mebsuta) and Kappa. Which star is closest to Propus in magnitude? Mebsuta is magnitude 3.0 while Kappa is magnitude 4.0. Record your observation and then come back in about a month. What has changed?

Upcoming dates of maximum brightness for Propus are listed below. (Data calculated using *Sky Tools 3* by Skyhound, http://www.skyhound.com)

August 21st, 2017	August 26th, 2024
April 11th, 2018	April 16th, 2025
November 30th, 2018	December 5th, 2025
July 21st, 2019	July 26th, 2026
March 10th, 2020	March 16th, 2027
October 29th, 2020	November 4th, 2027
June 19th, 2021	June 24th, 2028
February 7th, 2022	February 11th, 2029
September 27th, 2022	October 2nd, 2029
May 18th, 2023	May 23rd, 2030
January 6th, 2024	

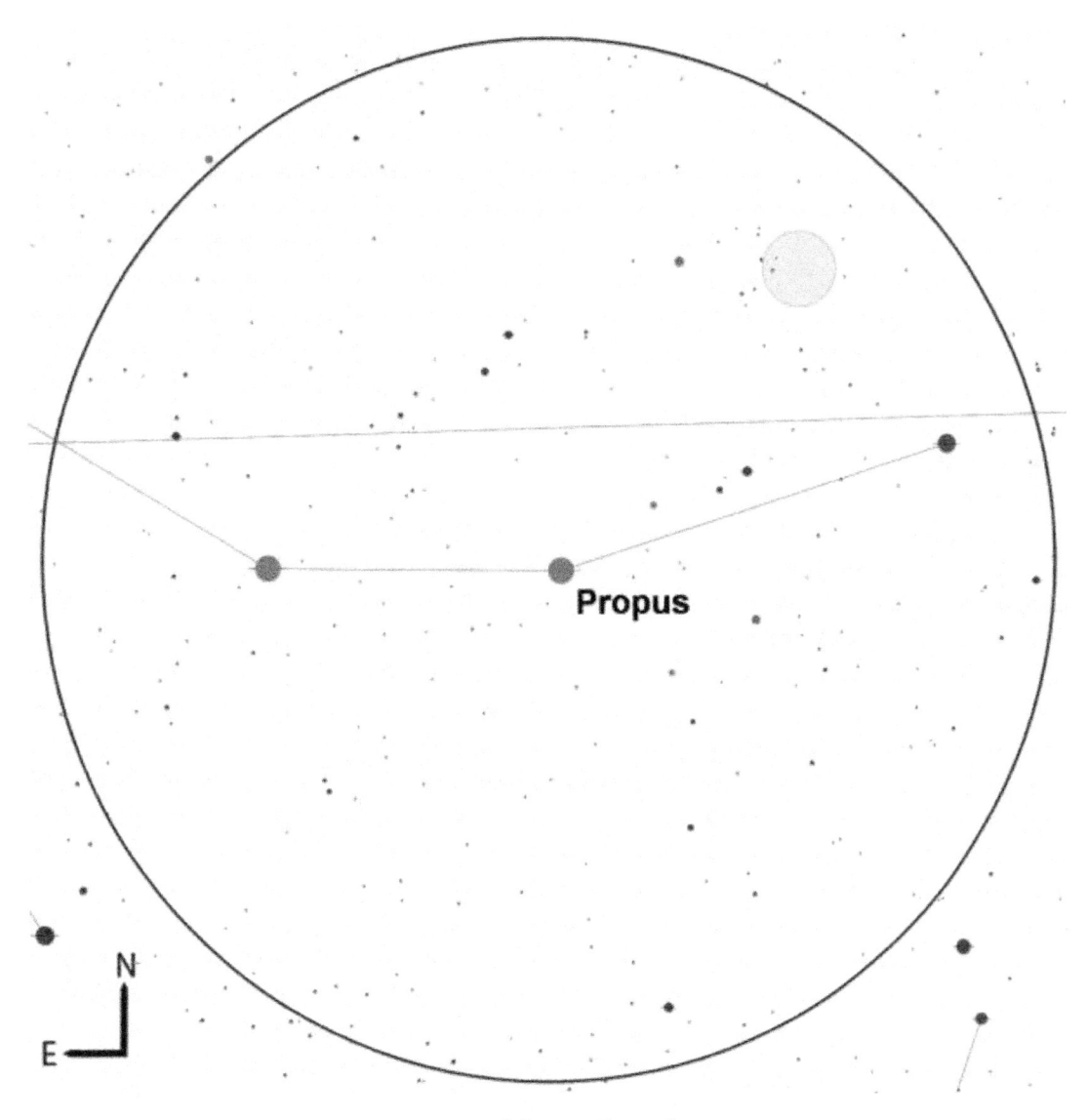

Propus, binocular view.

The constellation isn't devoid of objects for binocular observers either. Close to Propus is Messier 35, a large, reasonably bright open cluster of magnitude 5.3.

Discovered by the French astronomer Phillippe Loys de Chêseaux in 1745, it lies about 2,800 light years away and contains approximately 200 stars. Through 10x50 binoculars under suburban skies I've seen it as a faint, grey, hazy hourglass shaped misty patch with a number of individual stars being visible.

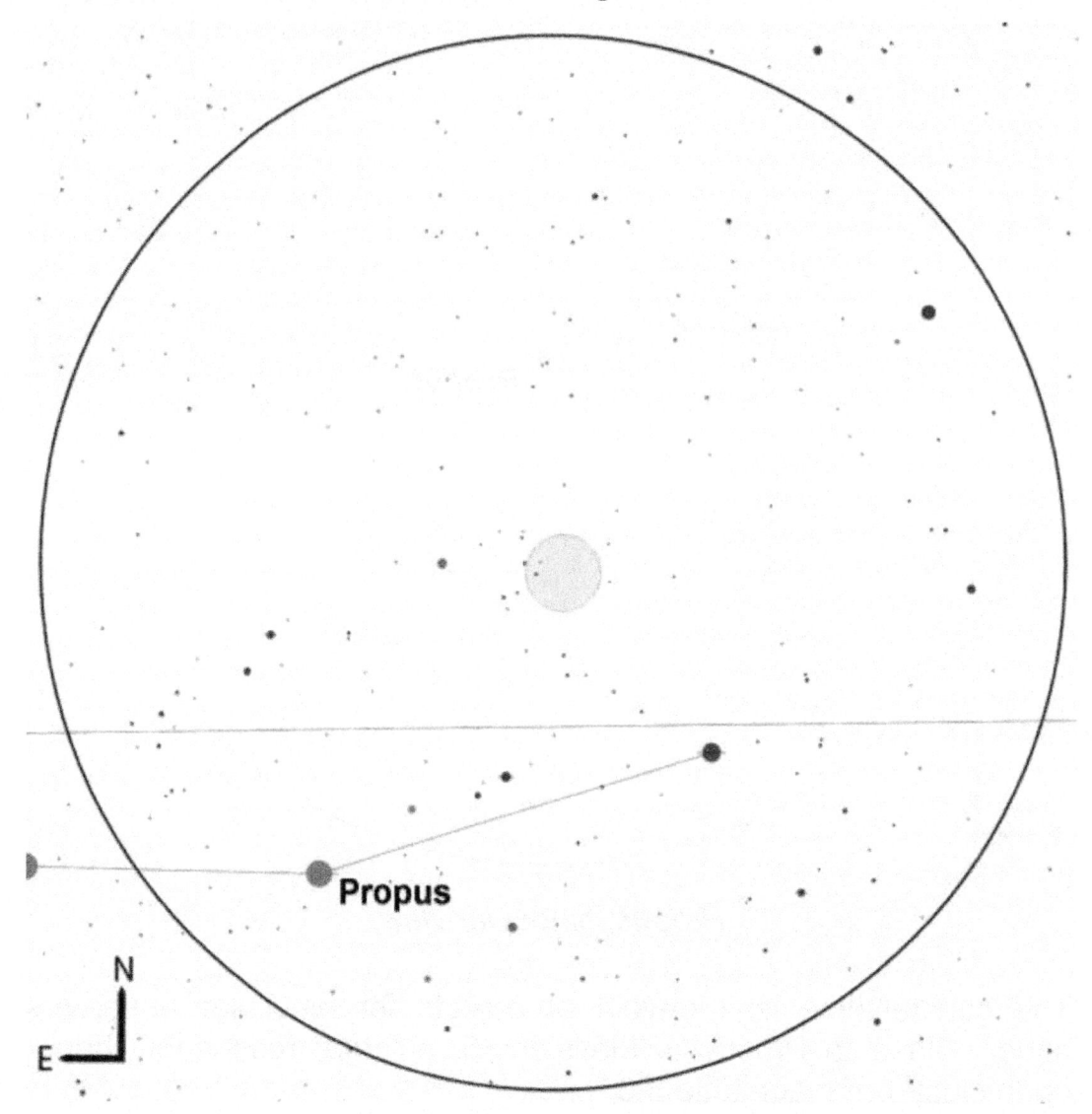

Messier 35, binocular view.

Hercules

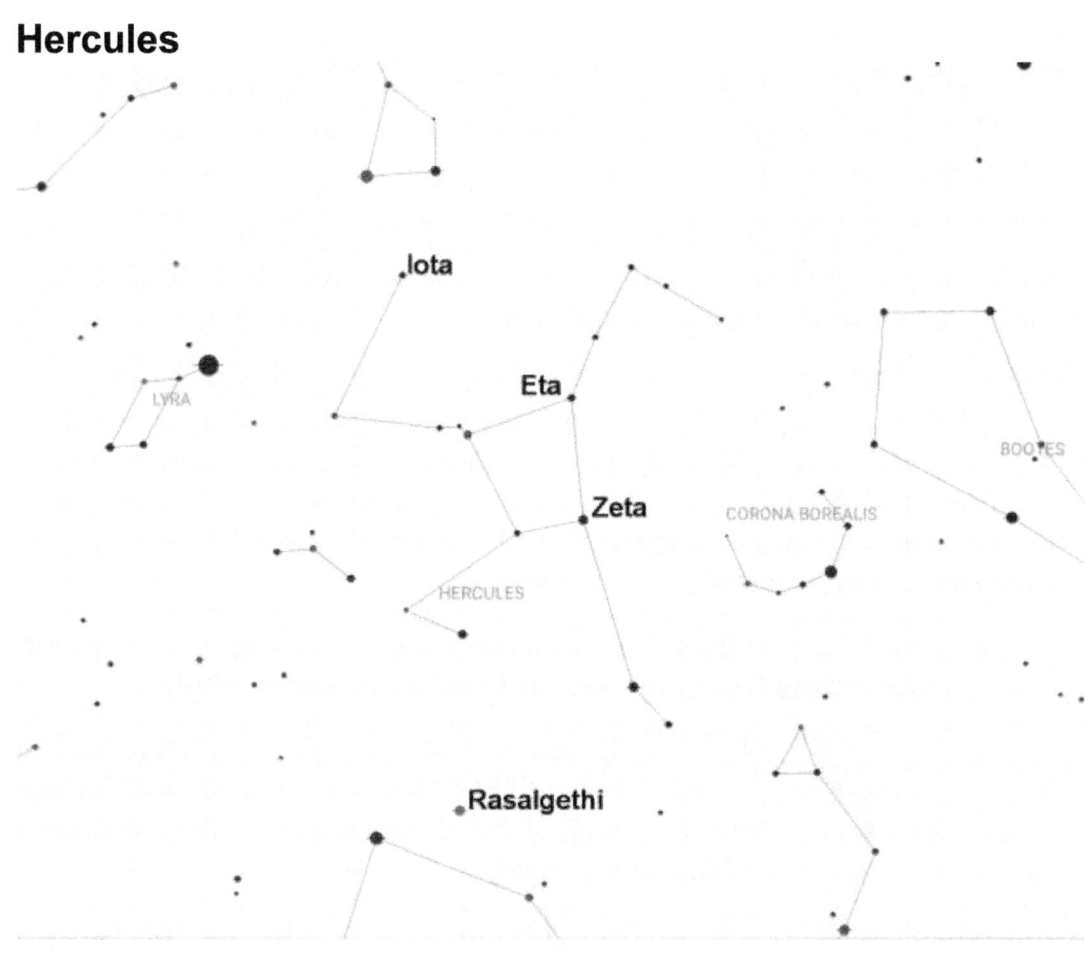

As many know, this constellation represents the hero Hercules (originally known as Heracles in Greece), son of the god Zeus and the mortal woman Alcmene. Poor Heracles did *not* have a happy life, mostly as a result of the anger directed at him by Hera, the wife of Zeus, who had decided to punish Zeus for his infidelity by persecuting his illegitimate son.

Heracles served King Eurystheus for ten years and it was during this time that the King assigned Heracles the labors for which he is well known. Some of these, like Heracles himself, have been immortalized in the sky – specifically, the slaying of the Nemean lion

(Leo), the nine-headed hydra (Hydra), capturing the Cretan bull (Taurus) and also stealing the golden apples of the Hesperides after first slaying Ladon, the dragon guarding them (immortalized as the constellation Draco.)

Hercules is surprisingly large. Covering approximately 1,225 square degrees, it's ranked 5th out of the 88 recognized constellations making it one of the largest in the sky.

Despite its size, it has no stars brighter than magnitude 2 and even its brightest – Alpha, also known as Rasalgethi – barely scrapes through magnitude 3 by shining at magnitude 2.9. Its name is Arabic and means "the head of the kneeler," which seems a little odd given that the star appears at the bottom of the constellation as seen from the northern hemisphere.

This is because, traditionally, Hercules is often depicted upside down on star charts (although no one seems to know why!)

A red giant star some 350 light years away, it has a companion that may be revealed with amateur telescopes. I've found that under steady skies and medium to high power the orange primary appears to have a fainter, pale blue companion.

A far easier target is the famous globular cluster, Messier 13. Known as the Keystone Cluster, it gets its name from the distinctive asterism of four stars that marks Hercules' torso.

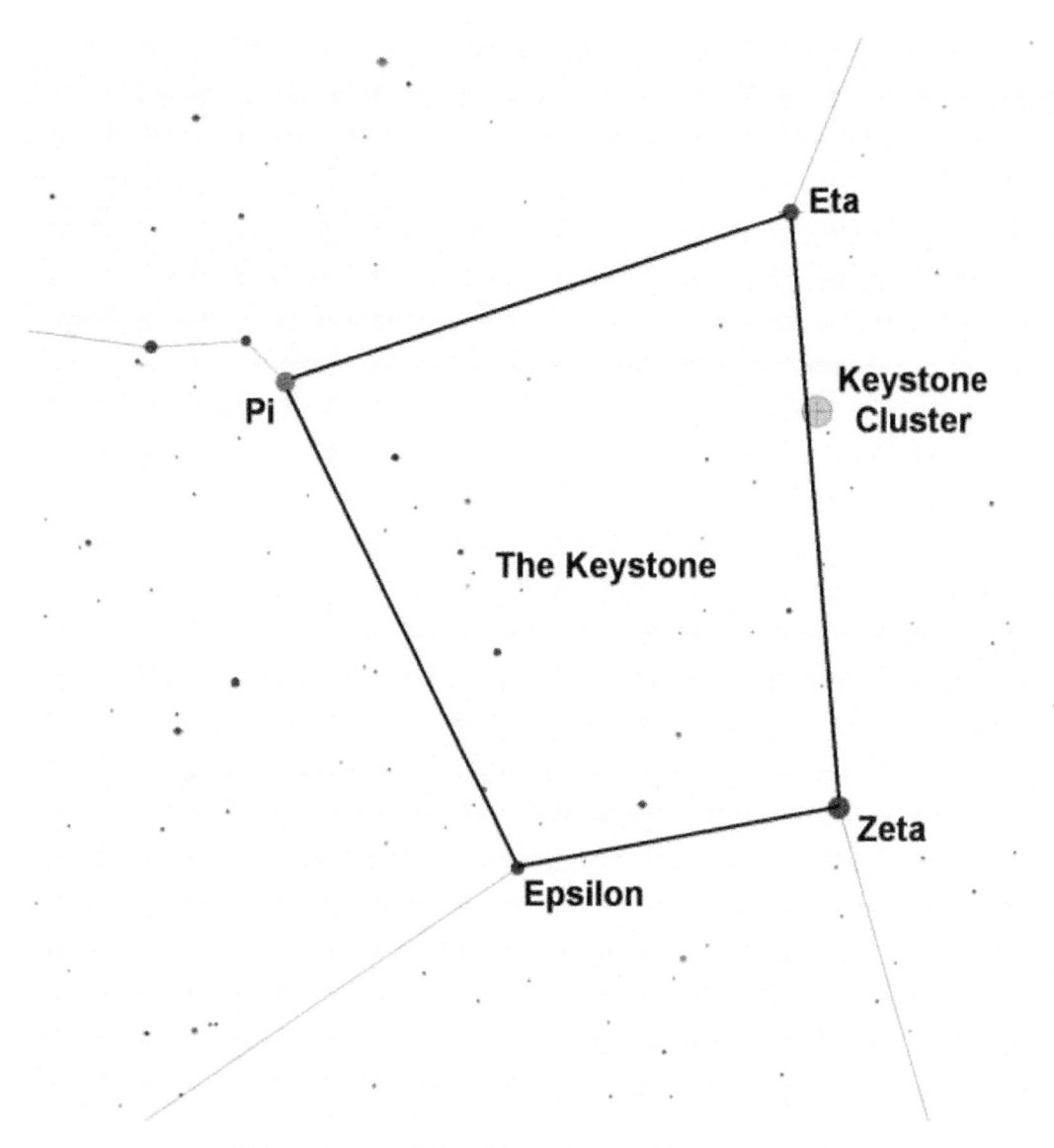

The stars of the Keystone, binocular view.

At magnitude 5.8, the cluster may be seen by sharp-sighted observers under clear, dark skies but for the rest of us, a pair of binoculars is required.

Discovered by Edmund Halley (of comet fame) in 1714, the cluster appears as a small, hazy circular patch with a star-like core. It can be found between Eta and Zeta when observed with 10x50 binoculars.

Through a small telescope – even at low power – it can be stunning. Depending upon your conditions and equipment, it's easy to see chains of stars within the cluster, snaking away from the cluster's center like the tentacles of some deep sea creature.

If nothing else, it's worth seeking out for the challenge and, like Messier 13, can be glimpsed with binoculars under suburban skies.

Of the two, Messier 13 is the closest at 22,000 light years while Messier 92 is 5,000 light years more distant.

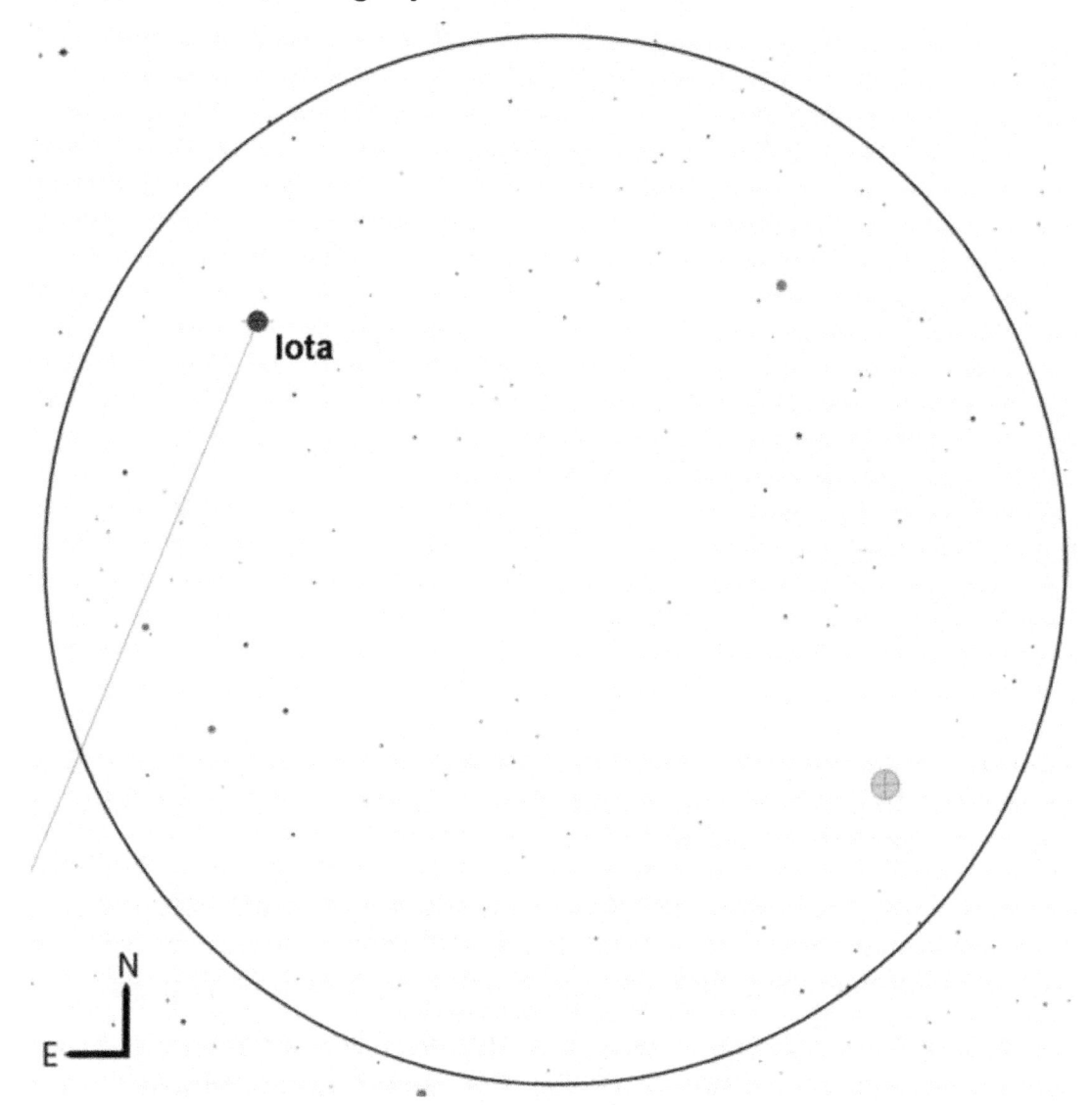

Messier 92, binocular view.

Leo

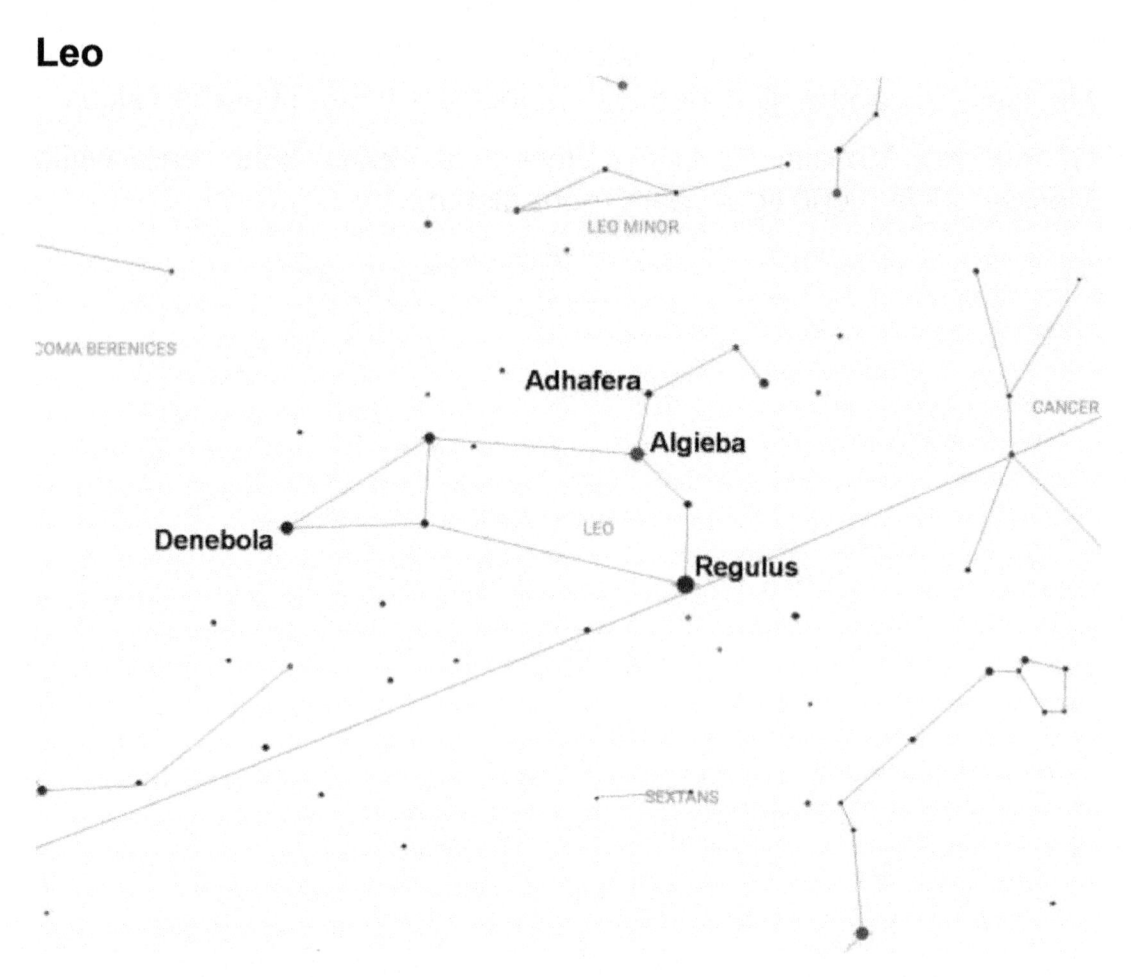

Leo, a constellation of the zodiac, ranks fifth in overall size and is prominent throughout the spring. (See here for a guide on how to use Ursa Major to locate it.)

It also has the rare distinction of resembling the creature it represents, which is, as almost everyone knows, a lion. In fact, its shape is so distinctive that it's hard to imagine it as anything else.

To the ancient Greeks it was the Nemean lion impervious to all weapons, thereby almost making the beast undefeatable. After killing a large number of warriors, the lion was eventually slain by

Heracles (aka, Hercules) who killed it with his bare hands as one of his labors.

The constellation contains a number of bright stars that make it easily recognizable. In particular, look out for the backwards question-mark asterism that forms the head and front of the lion. Also known as the Sickle, it's punctuated by the constellation's brightest star, Alpha (Regulus) at the bottom.

Regulus is the 21st brightest star in the sky and, at only 79 light years away, one of the nearest. A magnitude 1.4 blue-white star about 3½ times the size of the Sun, it's a multiple star system made up of two pairs of stars that take several million years to orbit one another.

Unfortunately, you won't see all four stars with amateur equipment, but binoculars will reveal a wide, faint bluish companion.

Regulus appears only half a degree away from the ecliptic, which is the path the Sun, Moon and planets take to traverse across the sky. What does this mean? Well, depending on the position of the planets, you can get some rather nice sights as the Moon and planets will sometimes group together near the star.

Equally entrancing is an occultation of Regulus by the Moon. This happens when the Moon appears to pass in front of the star, thereby hiding it from view. It's not uncommon, but your location and timing will determine its visibility and it's best to check online for upcoming events.

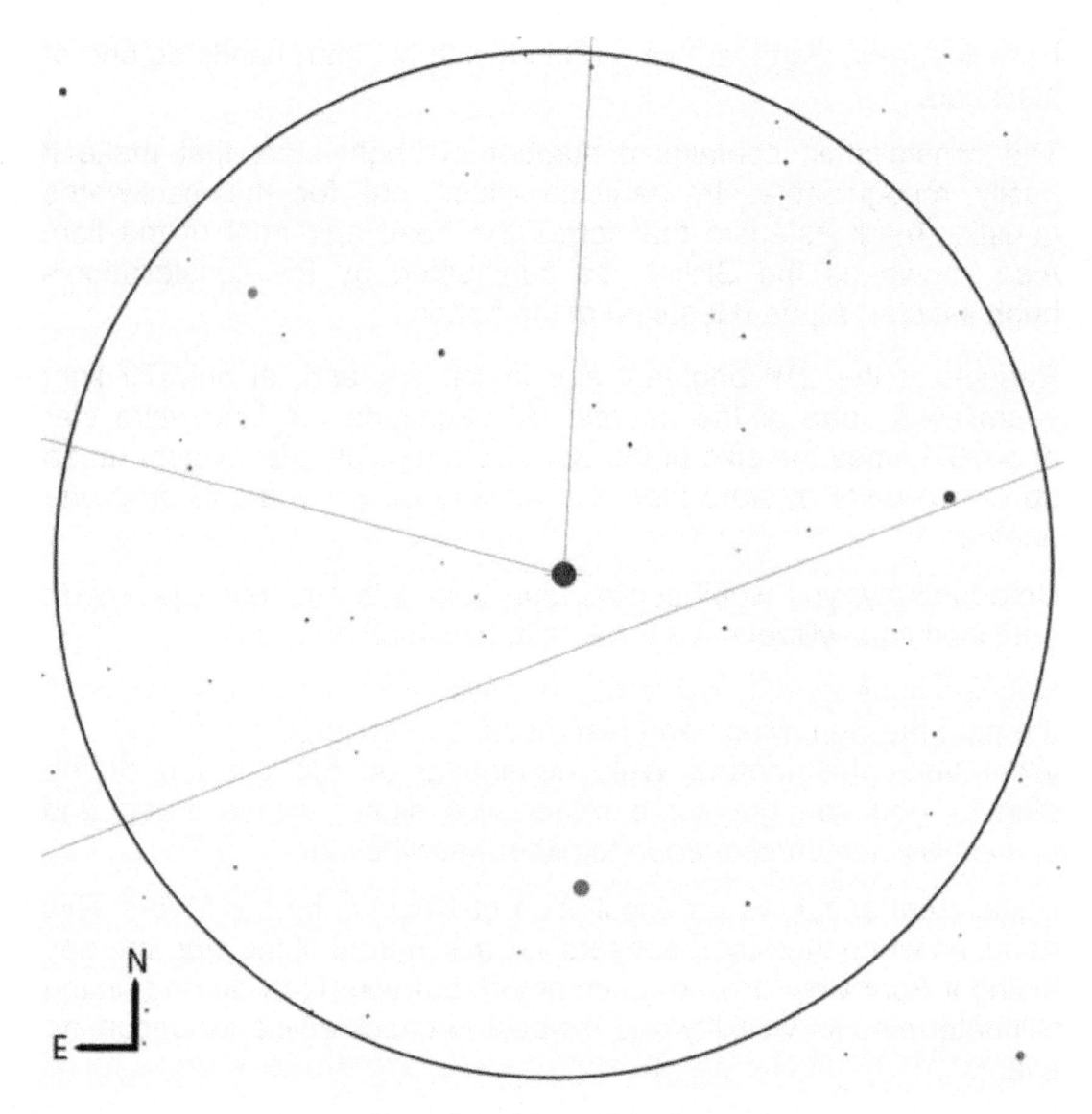

Regulus, binocular view.

Another double appears nearby in the Sickle asterism. Gamma, (aka Algieba, from the Arabic for "the forehead") is a famous multiple star best observed with a small telescope. A medium to high magnification will reveal two gold stars of equal brightness.

Binoculars won't allow you to split the pair, but you *can* see an unrelated magnitude 4.8 star, 40 Leonis, just to the south of Algieba itself. If you have good eyesight, you may even be able to spot it without optical aid.

Within the same binocular field of view is Zeta, commonly known as Adhafera. This lemony-white magnitude 3.4 star has a white, unrelated magnitude 5.8 companion.

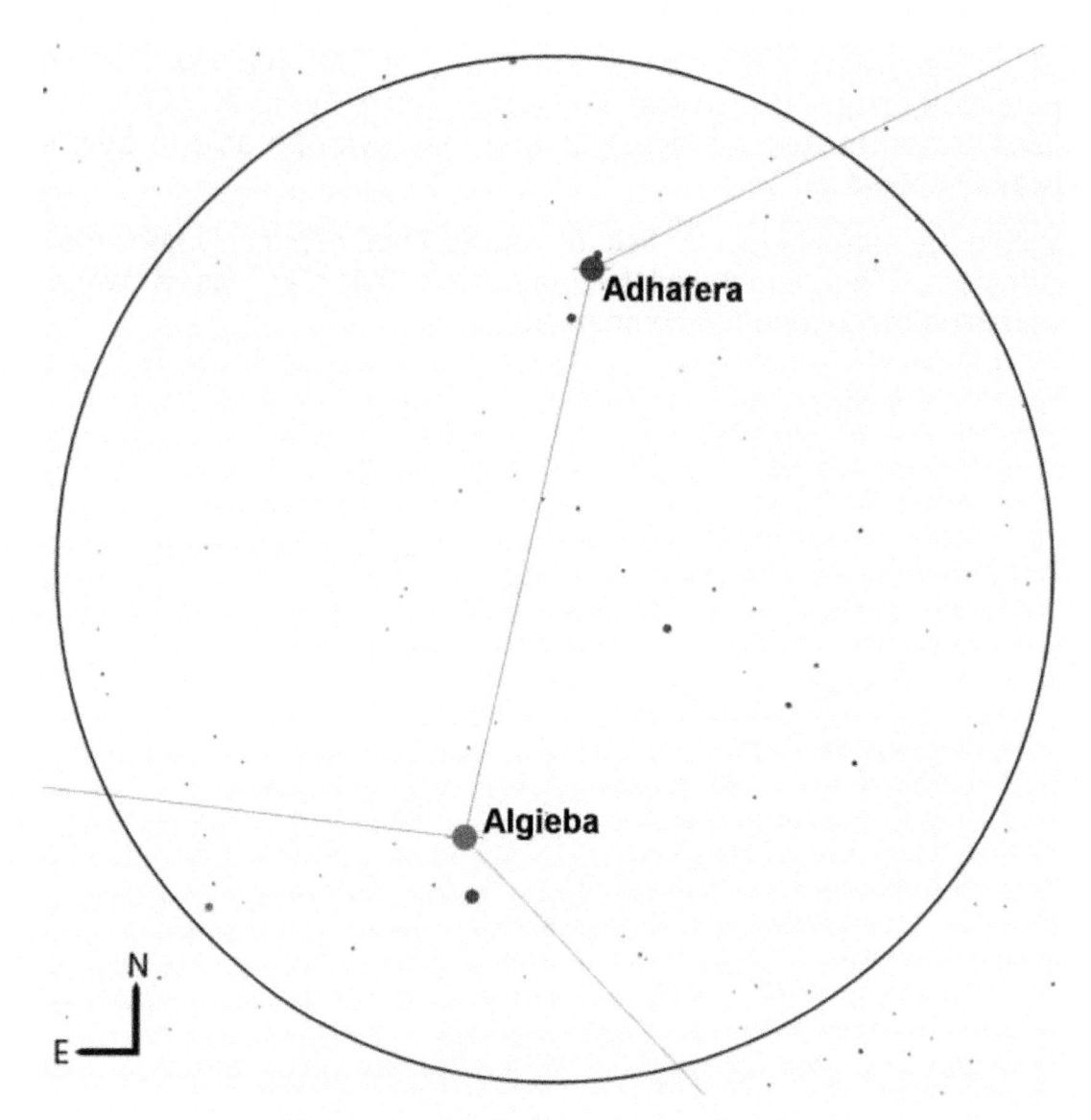

Algieba and Adhafera, binocular view.

At the opposite end of the constellation, Beta (aka, Denebola, from the Arabic for "tail of the lion") is a white magnitude 2.2 star. Like Algieba, binoculars will reveal an unrelated companion but with a third, fainter star between them.

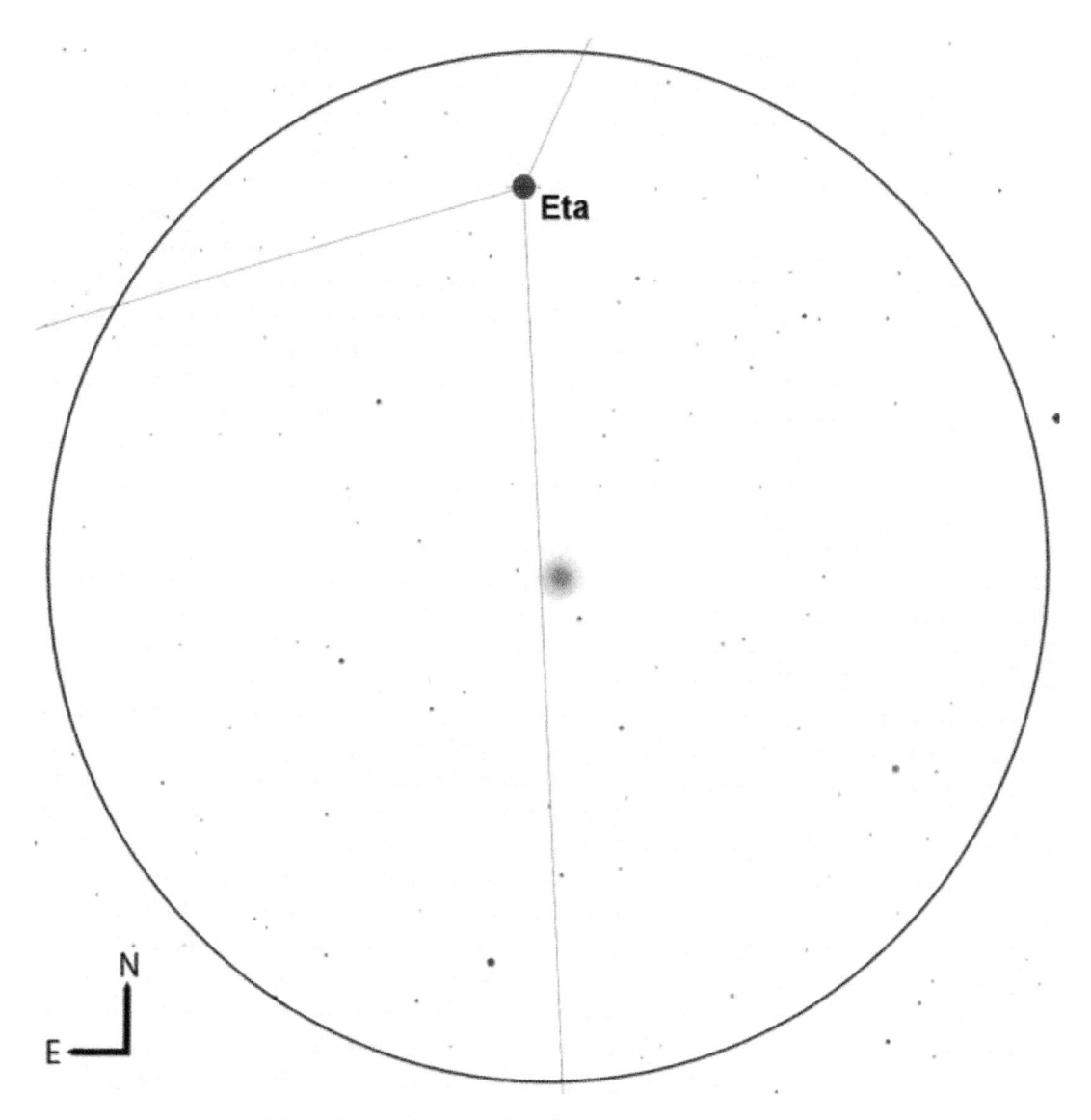

The Keystone Cluster, binocular view.

Also within binocular reach is its smaller neighbor, Messier 92. At magnitude 6.3 it's a little fainter but can be conveniently found within the same binocular field of view as Iota.

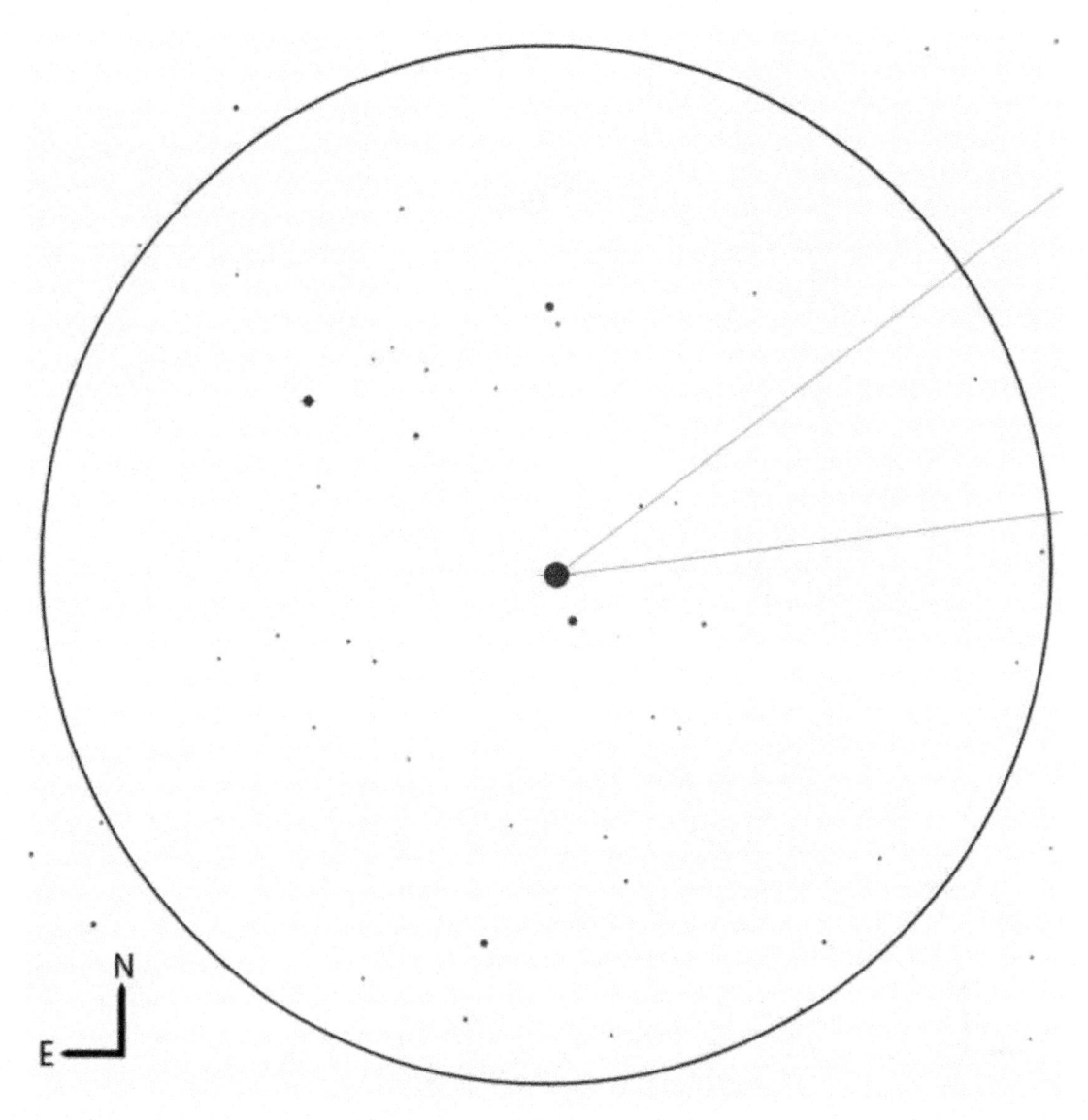

Denebola, binocular view.

Lepus

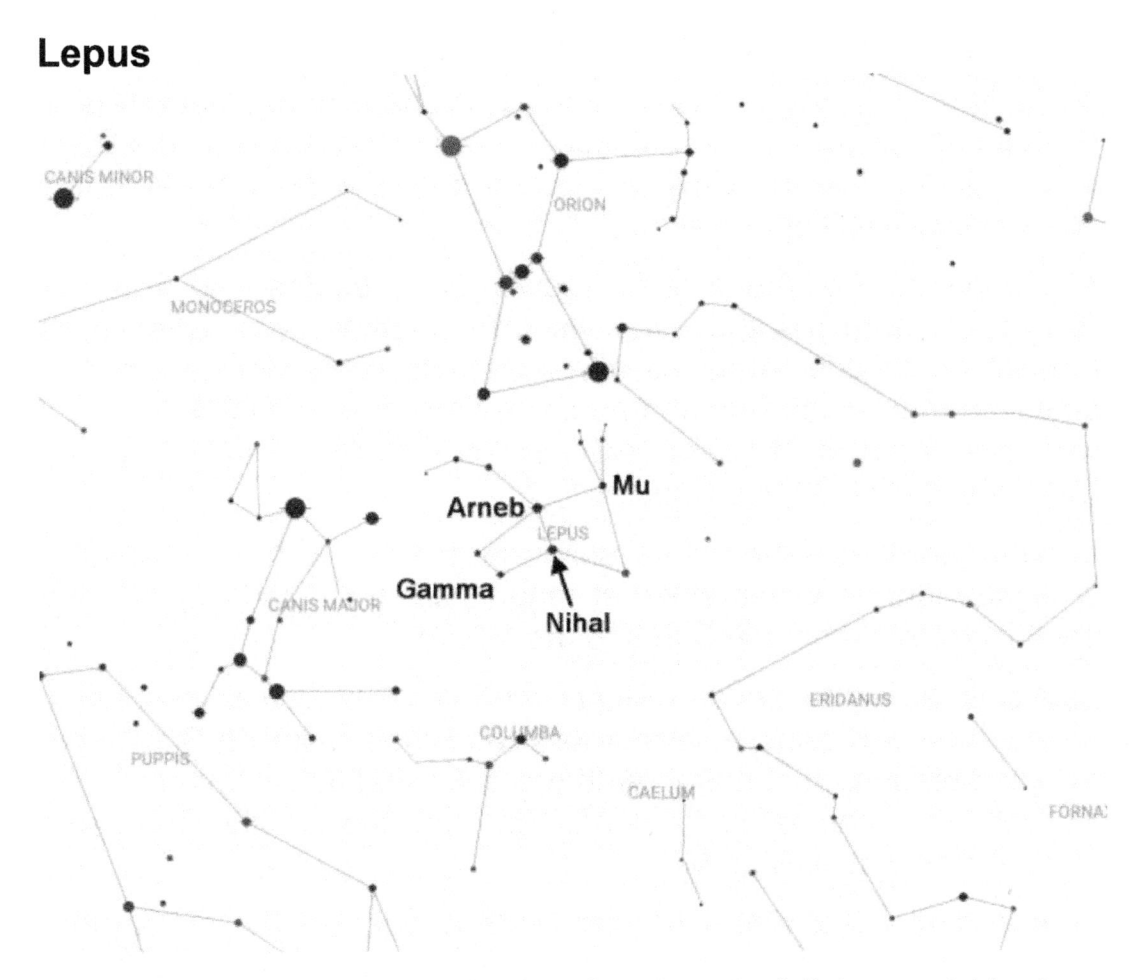

Lepus represents a hare, the hunting target of Orion and his dogs Canis Major and Canis Minor.

The constellation is thought to originate from the Greeks of ancient Sicily, which once suffered from an infestation of the furry critters, but there are no clear myths or legends associated with it.

Perhaps one of the reasons Sicily suffered was because the hare was able to out-smart the hunters. I say this because Lepus is clearly hiding in plain sight, directly beneath Orion himself! (Although, in Orion's defence, he appears to be fending off Taurus the Bull at the same time.)

It's a mid-sized constellation (51st in ranking) but given its location, it's fairly easy to spot. Four of its stars, Alpha (Arneb), Beta (Nihal), Gamma and Delta form an asterism known to the Arabs as the Chair of the Giant while the Egyptians knew it as the Boat of Osiris (as represented by Orion above it.)

At magnitude 2.6, Alpha, also known as Arneb (derived from the Arabic for "hare") is the constellation's brightest star. Despite its modest magnitude, Arneb is a yellow-white giant star, nearly 130 times larger than the Sun and about 14 times more massive. It lies a whopping 2,200 light years away, which means it also has a very high luminosity – 32,000 Suns!

In other words, if Arneb were only one parsec away (equivalent to 33 light years), it would shine at magnitude -6.5 – far brighter than anything else except the Sun and the Moon!

Lepus is home to several sights worthy of binocular observers. Firstly, there's R Leporis, also known as Hind's Crimson Star – and for good reason, as it has a deep red color that its discoverer, John Russell Hind, compared to blood. You can find it within the same binocular field of view as Mu.

That in itself would make the star worth a look, but like many other red giant stars in the waning years of its life, it's also a variable. At its brightest, it glows at a reasonable magnitude 5.5 but will then fade to magnitude 11.7, making it invisible in binoculars. It period has been known to vary, from 418 to 441 days, but is currently estimated at 427 days.

Upcoming dates of maximum brightness for R Leporis are listed below. (Data calculated using *Sky Tools 3* by Skyhound, http://www.skyhound.com)

| May 7th, 2017 | May 12th, 2024 |
| July 8th, 2018 | July 13th, 2025 |

September 8th, 2019	September 13th, 2026
November 8th, 2020	November 14th, 2027
January 9th, 2022	January 14th, 2029
March 12th, 2023	March 17th, 2030

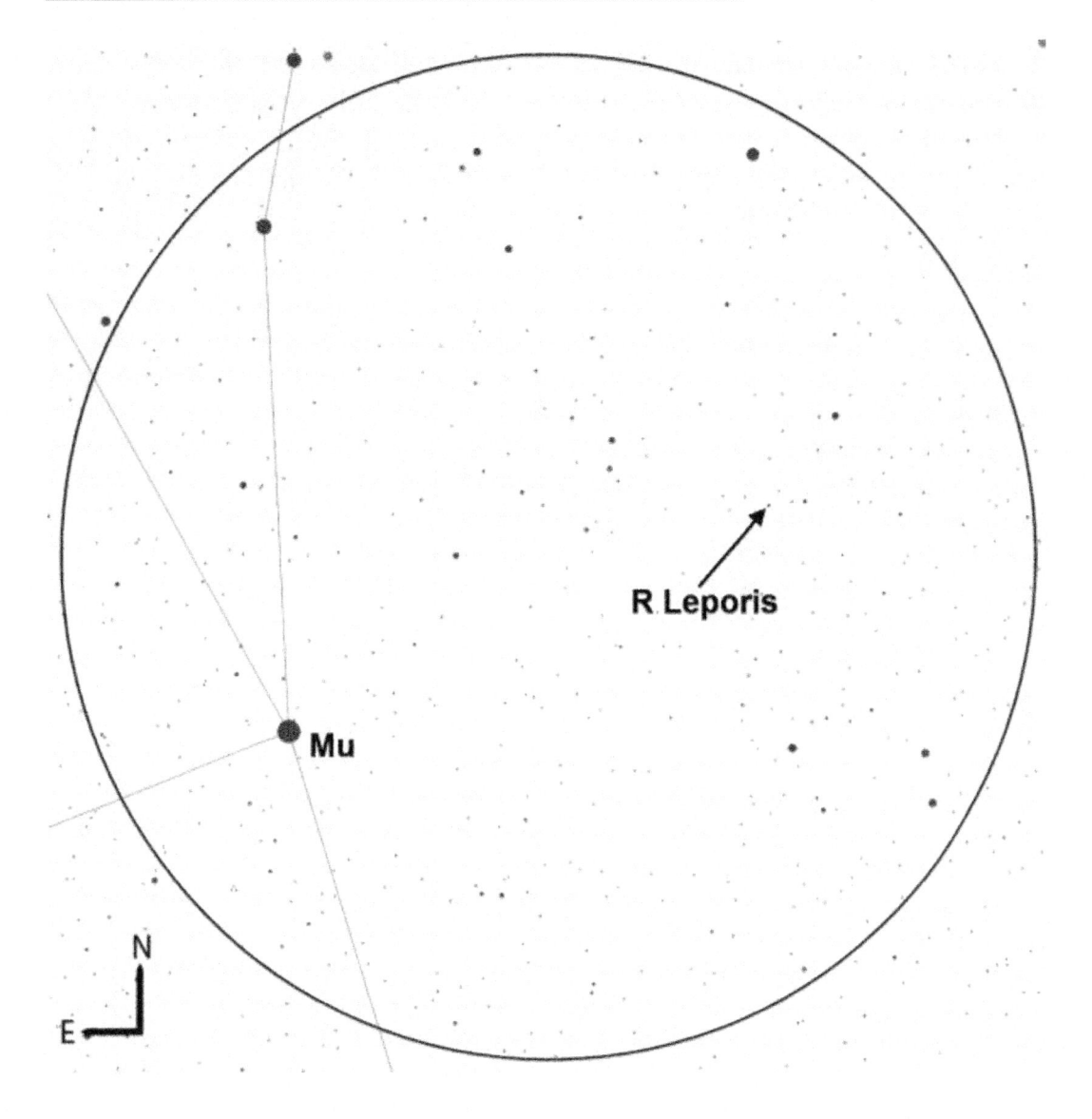

Hind's Crimson Star, binocular view.

If you're under dark skies, trying looking for M79, the brightest deep sky object in an otherwise fairly barren constellation. Unfortunately, M79 is not only fainter but less than half the size of the Keystone Cluster, its summer cousin.

However, it can be glimpsed close to Nihal as a small, hazy star, almost comet-like in appearance. At 41,000 light years away, M79 might not belong to our Milky Way galaxy at all. Studies have shown that it might be a member of the Canis Major Dwarf Galaxy, which just so happens to be passing close to our own, much larger galaxy, at this time.

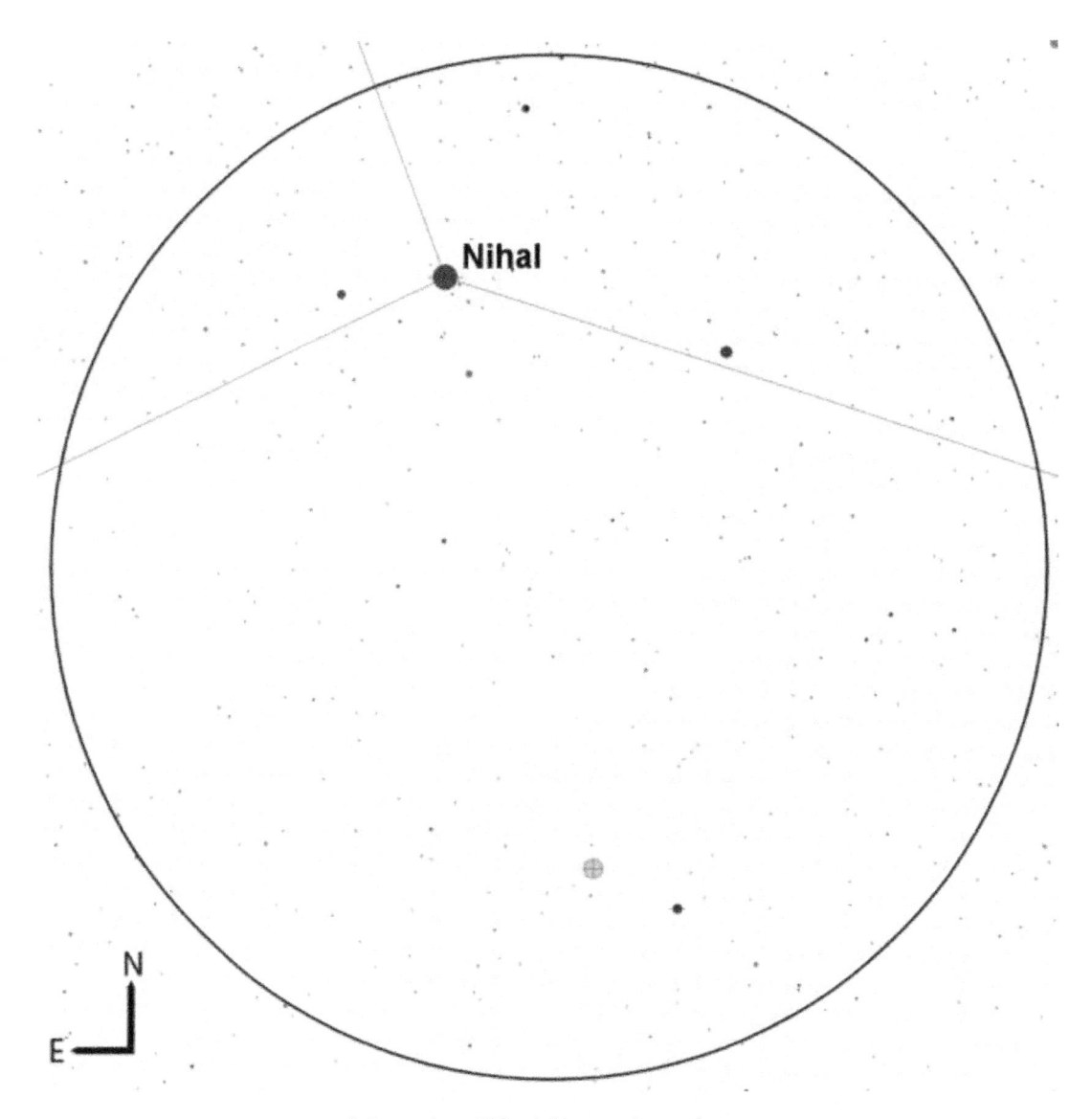

Messier 79, binocular view.

Lastly, there's Gamma, a fairly well-known double that can be split with 10x50 binoculars. The primary appears creamy and much brighter than the coppery companion, which appears to the southeast. If you have a small telescope, two other components may also be visible.

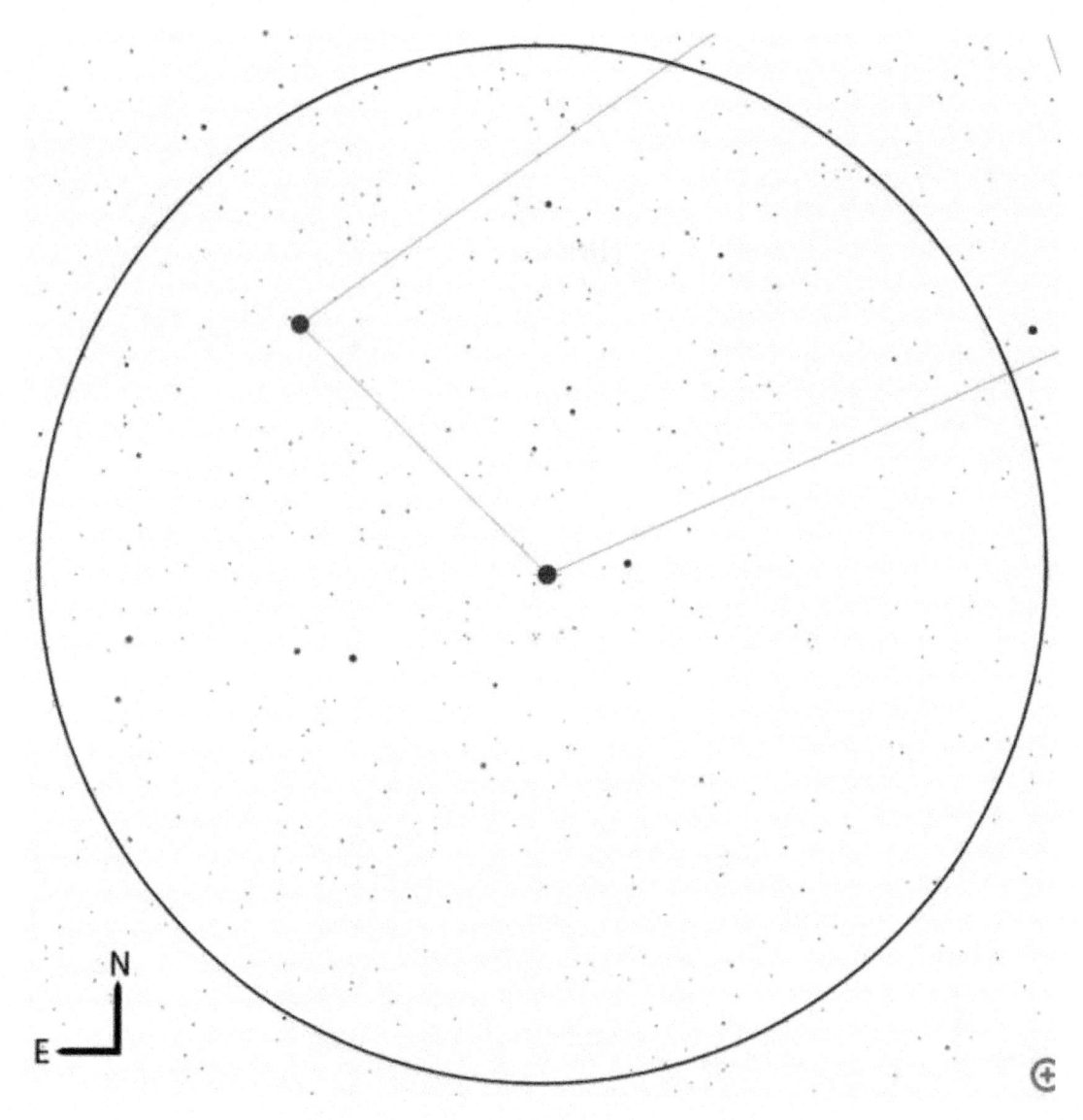

Gamma Leporis, binocular view.

Libra

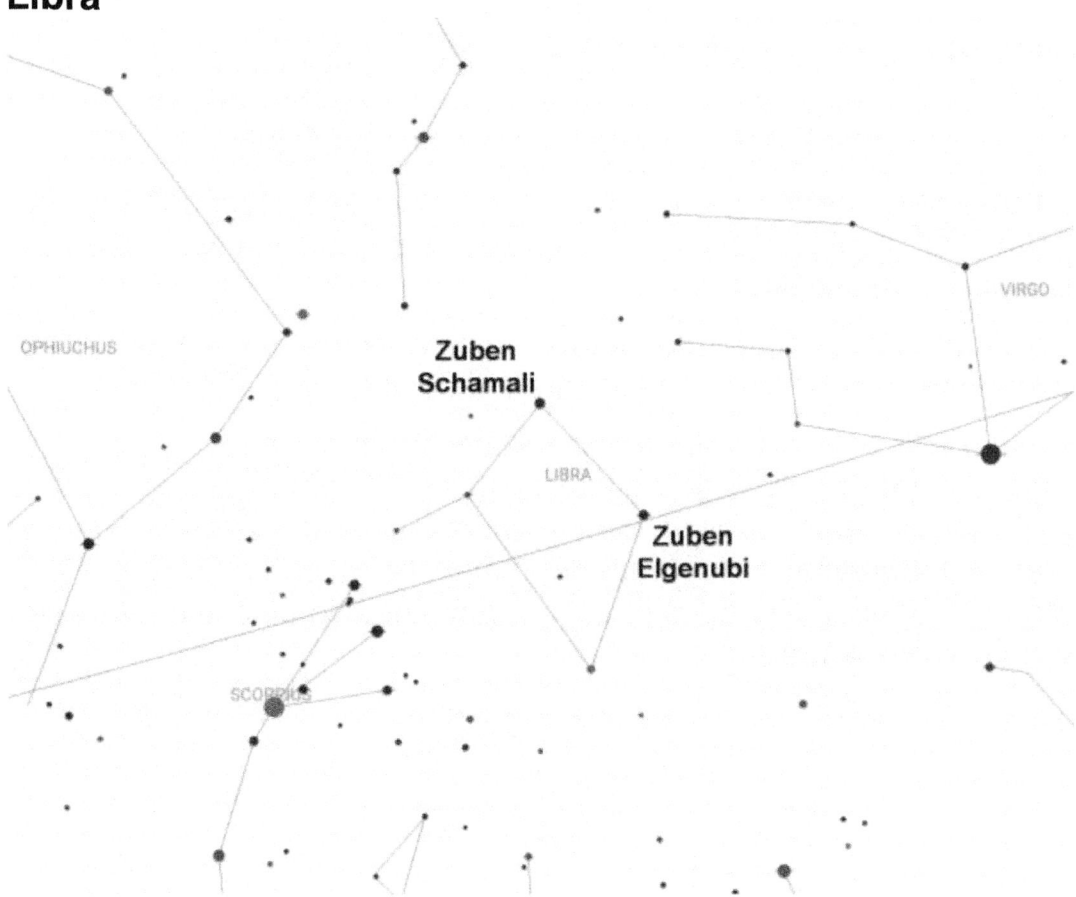

Perhaps not surprisingly, Libra, the Scales, doesn't have any myths or legends associated with it as the ancient Greeks identified the stars as the claws of nearby Scorpius.

It's thought the constellation became known as the Scales (or the Balance) at a time when the Sun would pass through the constellation on the spring equinox. With the days and nights being of equal length on that date, it must have seemed an appropriate way for the ancients to commemorate the event.

Libra is also a curious constellation in that it probably wasn't one of the original signs of the zodiac but may have been added by the

Romans as part of their Julian calendar.

It's a mid-sized constellation, found midway between white Spica in Virgo and orange-red Antares in Scorpius. Unfortunately, it's not particularly bright, with no stars brighter than magnitude 2.

Its brightest star is Alpha, also known as Zuben Elgenubi from the Arabic for "southern claw" – an obvious reference to when the star was still a part of Scorpius.

To almost everyone, it appears as a single star of magnitude 2.7 but a standard pair of 10x50 binoculars will easily split the star in two.

What you'll see is a pair of white stars of almost equal magnitude. This is a true multiple star system, some 77 light years away, with both components forming their own binary star systems. Beyond that, a theoretical fifth component may be a part of the system, making a total of five stars in all, but only the two binocular stars are visible to amateurs.

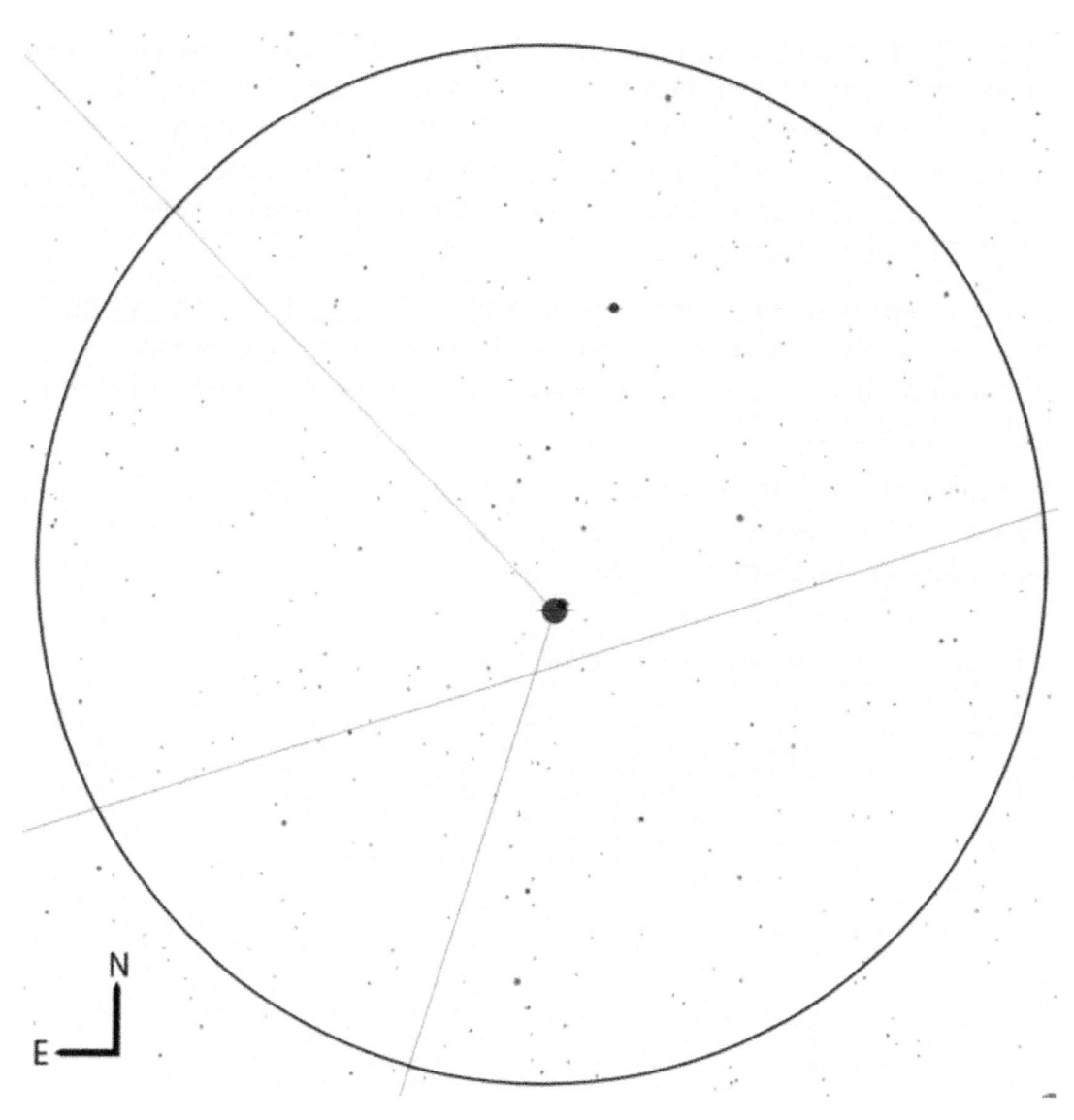

Zuben Elgenubi, binocular view.

What color are the stars? Many are white, or blue-white, with the occasional yellow star or even an orange or red giant thrown in for good measure. So why are there no green stars?

The reason is a little complicated (and I simply don't have the room to explain it here!) – suffice it to say, a star's color depends upon its surface temperature. A hot star will literally glow white hot (just the same as metal does) but as it cools, the color fades to yellow, orange and then red. Just as metal (typically) doesn't glow green when it's hot, neither do stars.

Except, perhaps Beta Librae, also known as Zuben Schamali, from the Arabic for "northern claw." Nicknamed "the emerald star," numerous observers have noted a pale green color, visible with just the unaided eye.

In reality, it's a blue-white star, five times larger than the Sun and about 185 light years away. Not everyone sees its green light, but it's worth taking a look for yourself!

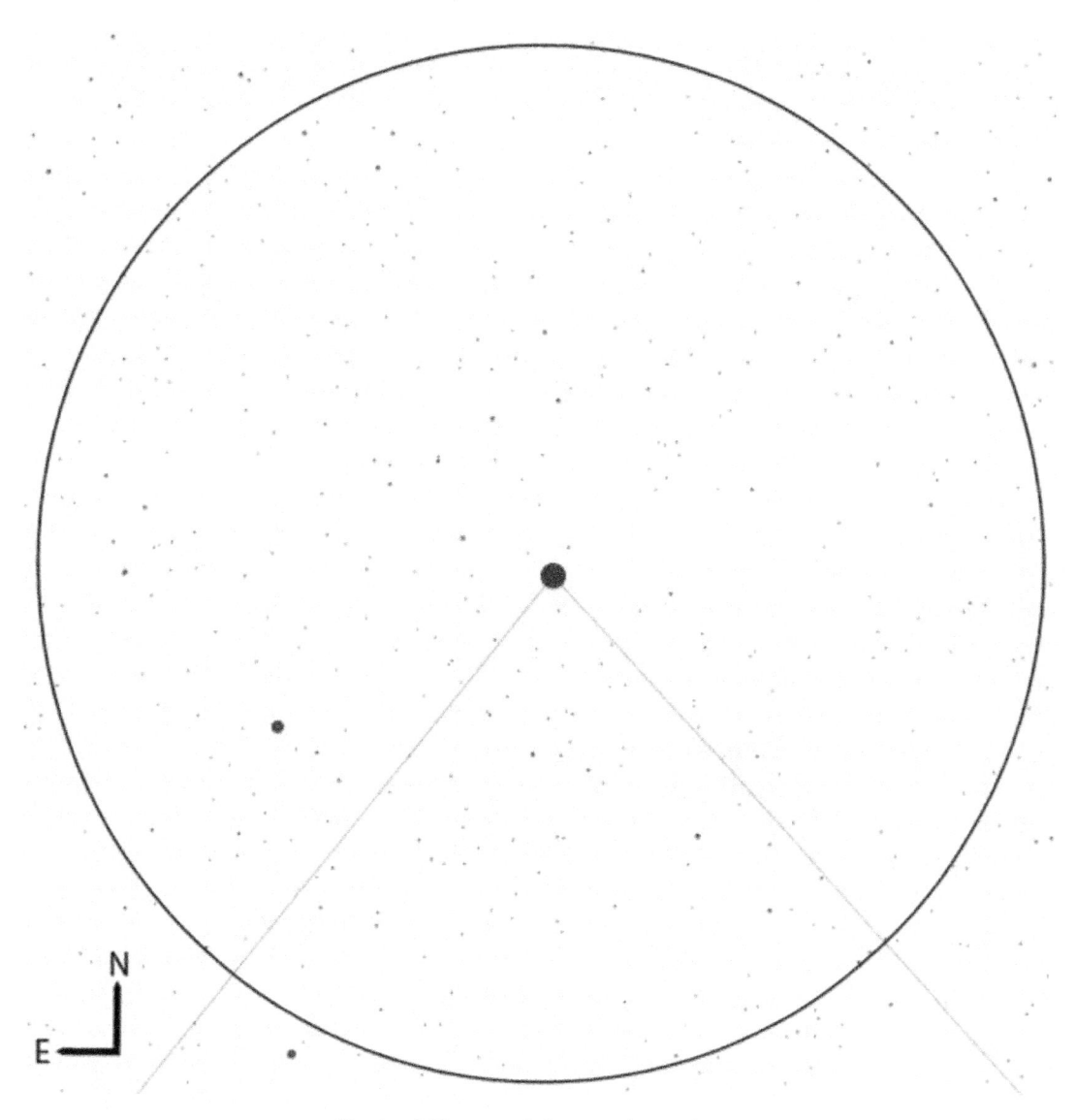

Beta Librae, binocular view.

Lastly, Libra is home to Delta Librae, a variable star much like Algol in Perseus. At its brightest, it glows at magnitude 4.4, which might make it tricky to spot without optical aid from the light polluted skies of a town or city.

If you can see it, come back to it tomorrow night and look for it again. It'll drop to magnitude 5.8 and then return to its former glory over a period of 2.3 days.

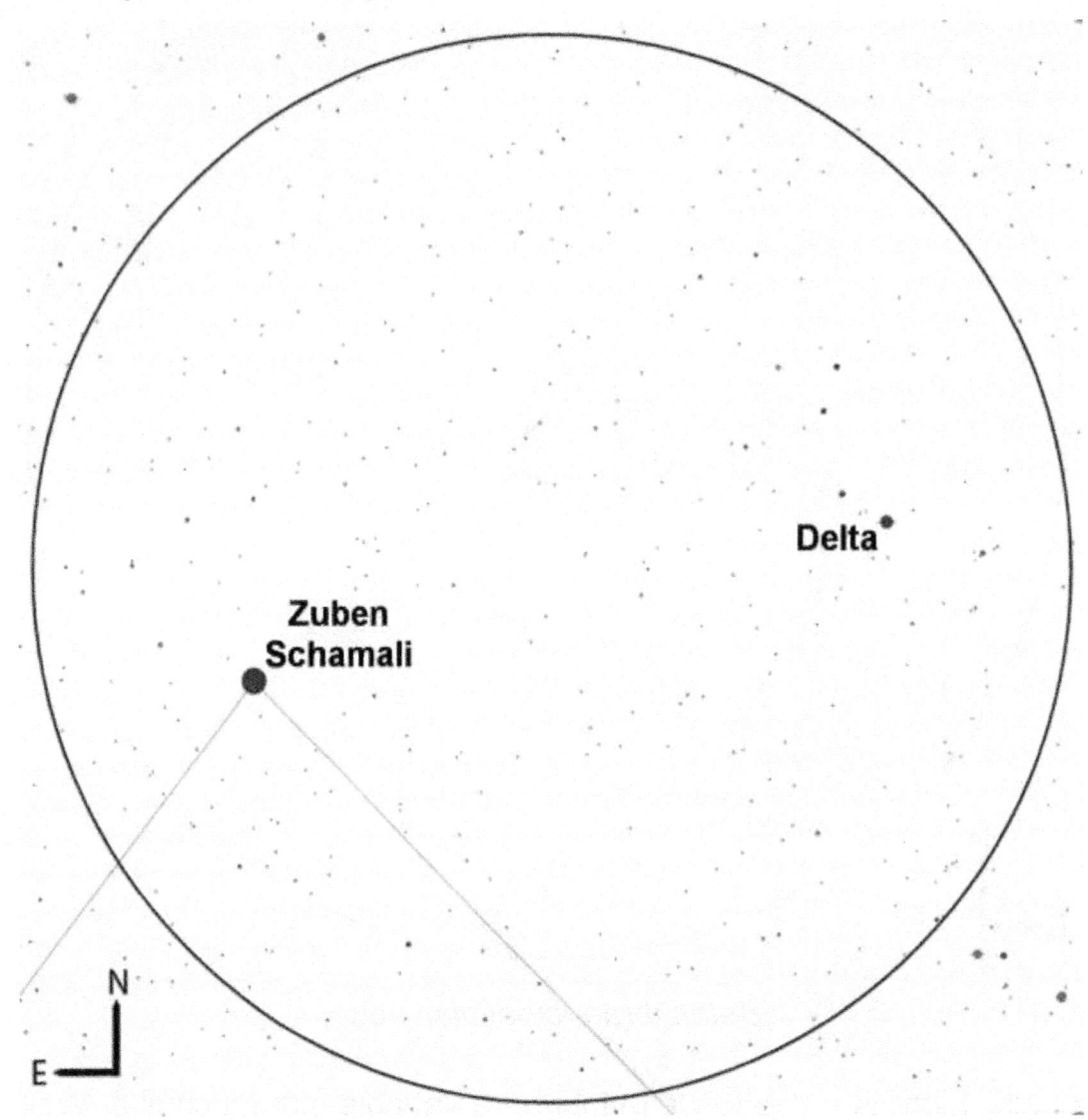

Delta Librae, binocular view.

Lyra

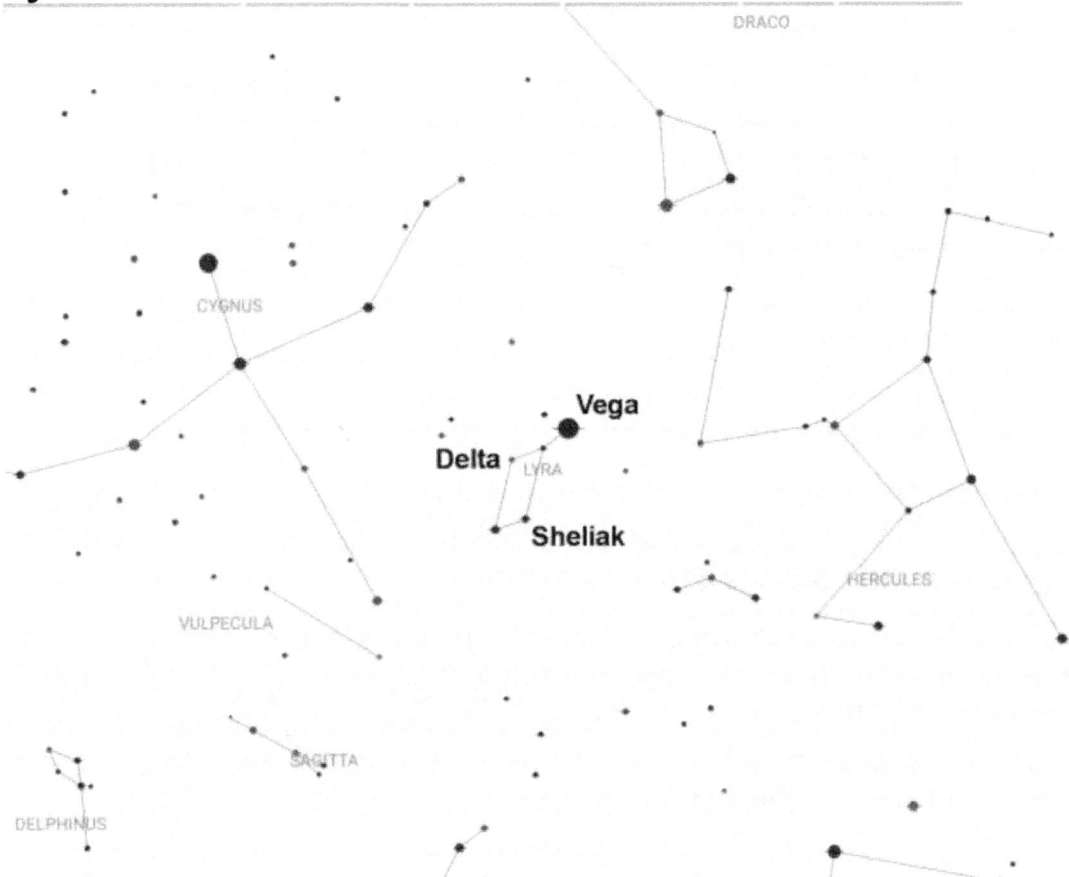

Lyra represents the lyre given to Orpheus by his father, the god Apollo. With this musical instrument, Orpheus was able to charm pretty much everyone and everything, including Hades, the god of the Underworld. When Eurydice, beloved wife of Orpheus, was killed by a snake, Orpheus entered the Underworld and used his lyre to charm Hades into releasing her.

Hades only agreed on the condition that, as Orpheus left, he would not look back. However, Orpheus could not resist temptation and did indeed look back, causing Hades to keep Eurydice in the Underworld forever. Heart-broken Orpheus then spent the rest of his life wandering throughout the land, playing his lyre and forever mourning her loss.

This summer constellation is relatively small, but bright and easily found, midway between Hercules the Hero and Cygnus the Swan. Its brightest star is Alpha, a brilliant white star of magnitude 0.0 also known as Vega, the fifth brightest star in the entire night sky and one of the three stars of the Summer Triangle.

At only 25 light years away, it's one of the closest stars to Earth and, at just under 500 million years old, one of the younger stars known. Like Altair in Aquila the Eagle, another bright star of summer it spins rapidly on its axis, causing the star to be flattened at the poles.

Another fascinating feature of Vega is the disk of dust that surrounds the star. No one knows for sure, but the disk may be a planetary system in the early stages of formation.

Close to Vega is another fascinating star system, Epsilon Lyrae. Popularly known as "the double double" this is a multiple star system some 160 light years away. Its two brightest components are easily seen in binoculars as a pair of identical, bright white stars. Turn a small telescope toward them and crank up the magnification to about 150x and you'll see that each star is itself a double with all four stars appearing white and of almost equal brightness. In all, there may be as many as ten stars in this system!

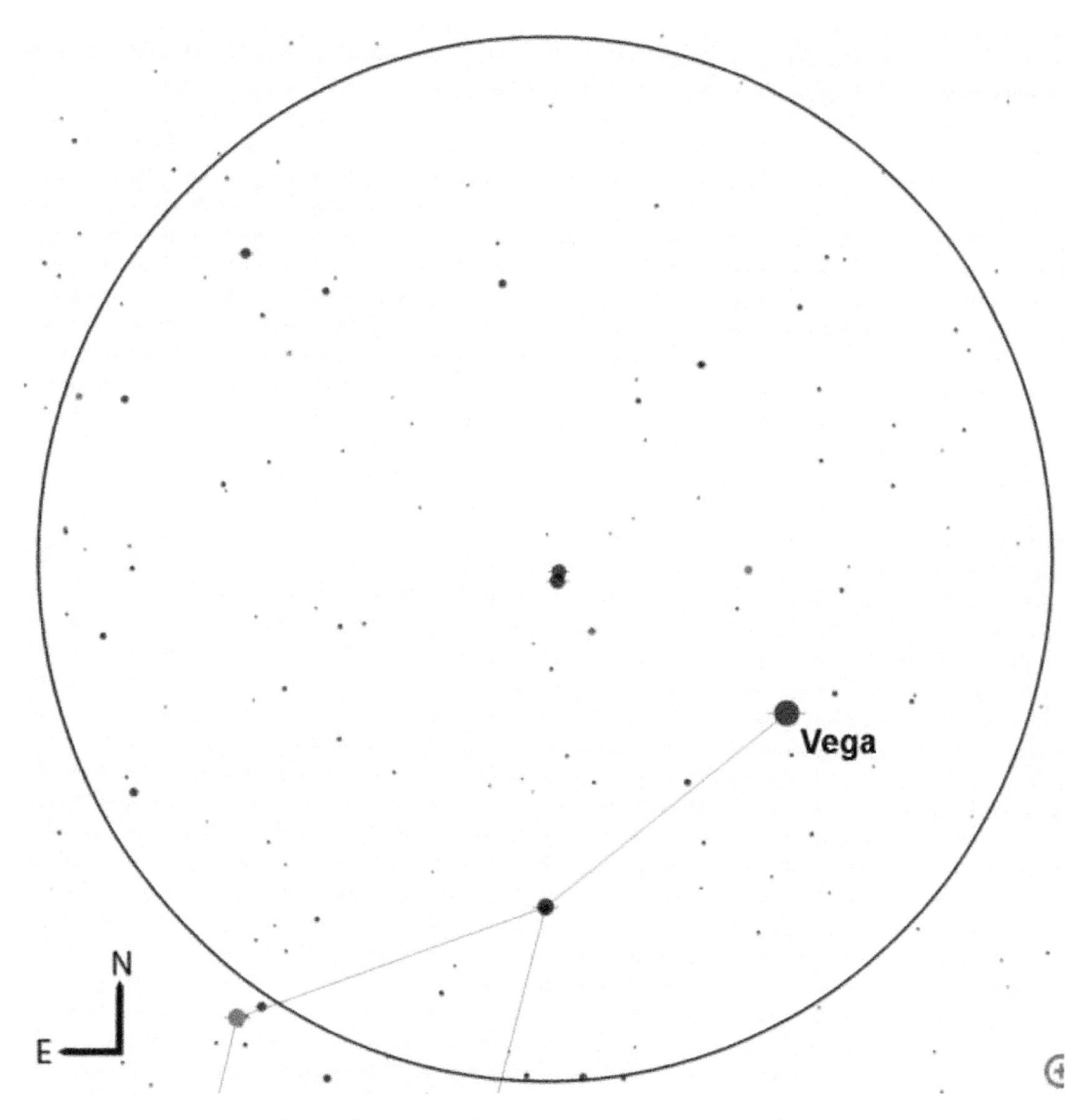

The Double Double, binocular view.

Meanwhile, just a little further east (but still within the same binocular field of view) is Delta Lyrae, another binocular double. In reality, the two stars merely appear close to one another in the sky.

Delta[1], the fainter of the pair, is approximately 1,100 light years away while Delta[2] is about 200 light years closer.

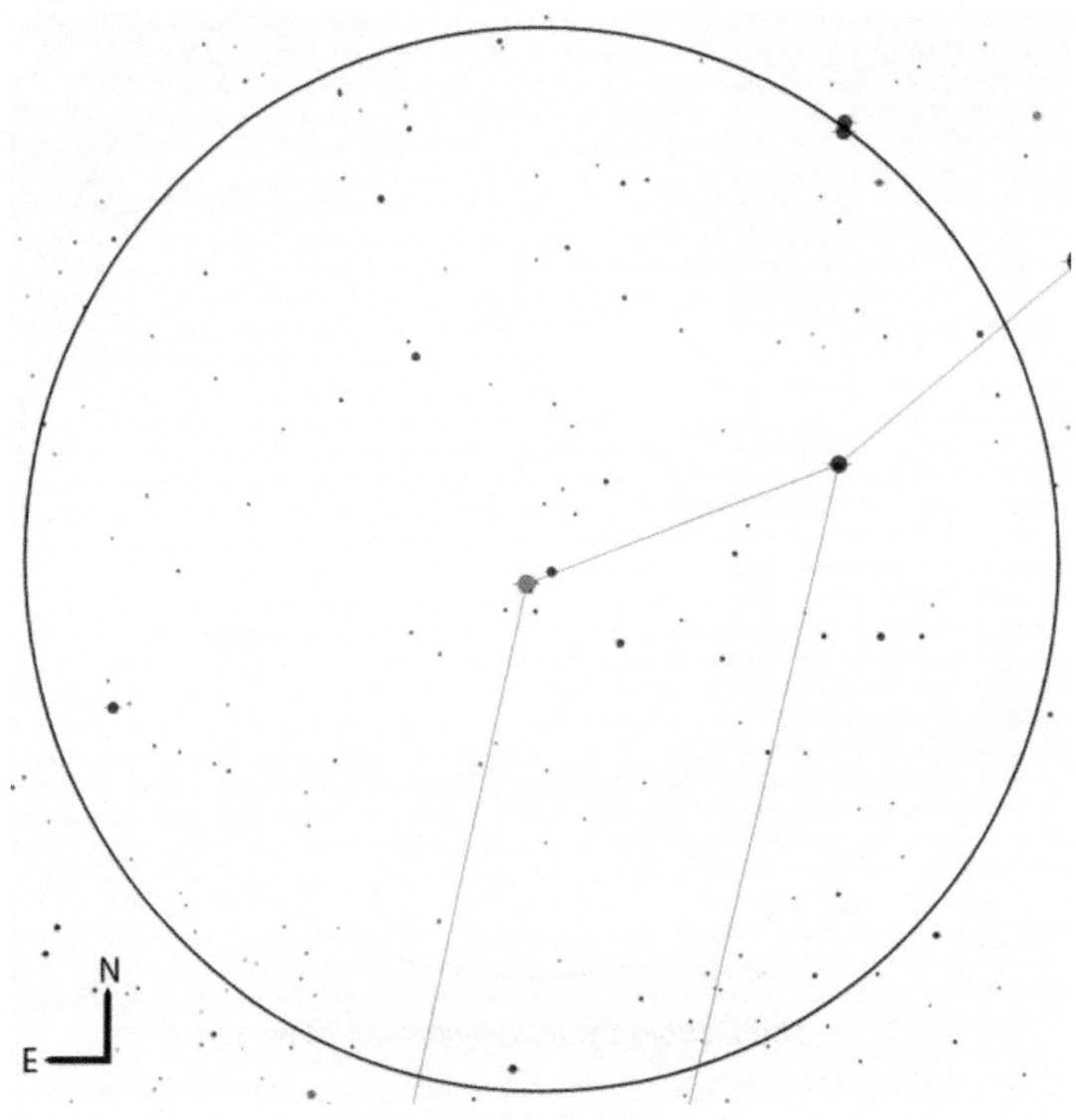

Delta Lyrae, binocular view.

Move to the south-west and look out for Beta Lyrae, known as Sheliak. Like the autumn and winter star Algol in Perseus, Sheliak is an eclipsing binary, which means a fainter star regularly passes in front of the brighter main star. Seen from Earth, the star will fade for a few days before brightening again. Sure enough, Sheliak shines at magnitude 3.25 at its brightest, fades by a full magnitude and then brightens again over a period of 12.9 days.

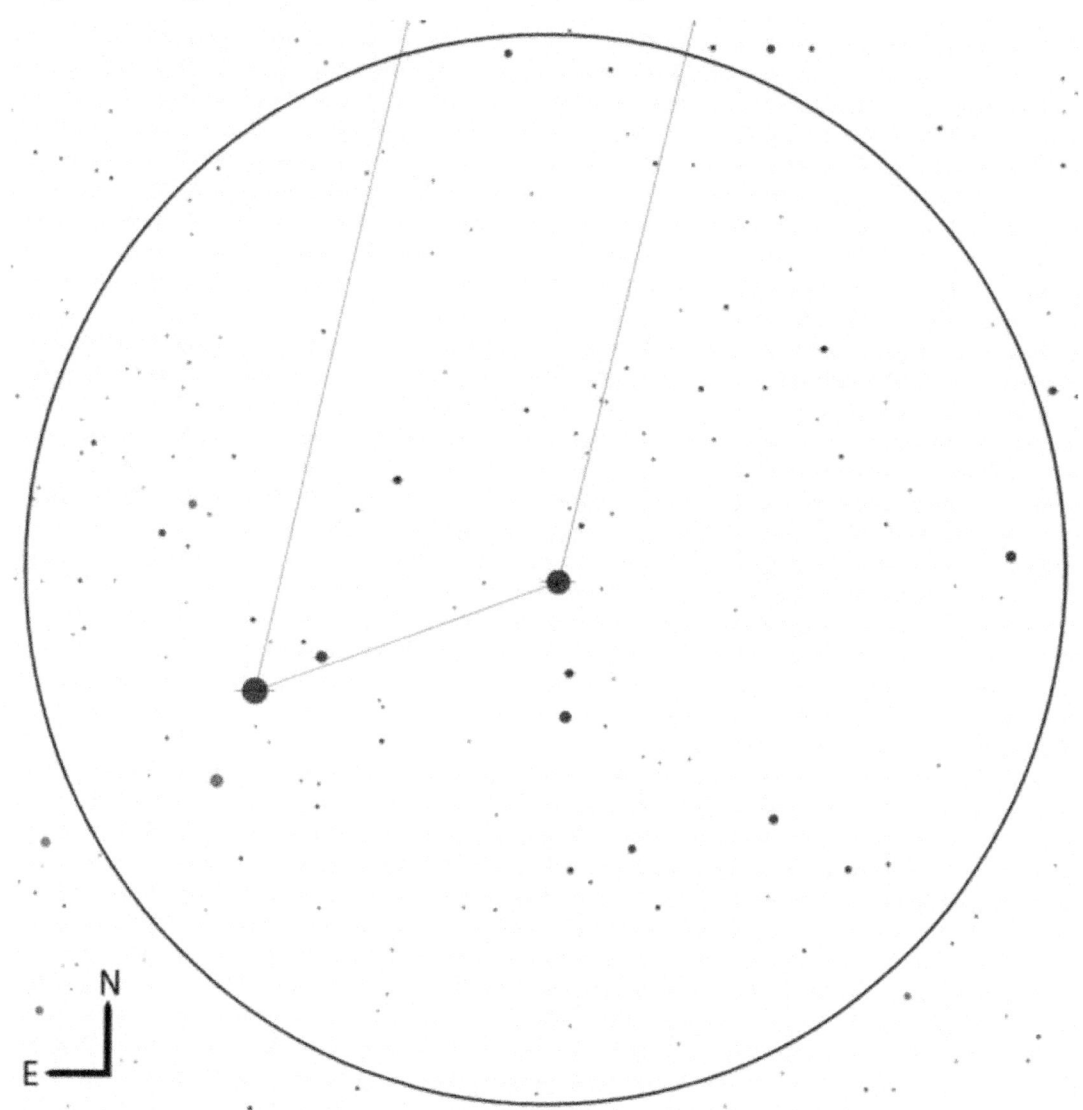

Sheliak, binocular view.

Lyra is home to several other sights, most notably the Ring Nebula and Messier 56 - but both require a small telescope to be fully appreciated.

Ophiuchus

Also known as the Serpent Bearer, Ophiuchus has several associations with the ancient Greek gods and heroes. It's been depicted as the god Apollo wrestling with the snake that guarded the Oracle at Delphi and, alternatively, it's also been identified as Asclepius, a famed healer with a close association with serpents (see also Serpens.)

Covering nearly 950 square degrees, the constellation is the 11th largest in the sky and, with no particularly bright stars, can be tricky to identify, especially from suburban skies. Its brightest star, Alpha, is just under 49 light years away and is also known as Ras Alhague, from the Arabic for "the head of the serpent charmer." A white star of magnitude 2.1, it's a binary system comprising of a giant white primary and a suspected orange companion. The two orbit one another once every 8½ years but the pair are too close to be split with amateur equipment.

If you have binoculars, take a look at the area close to Theta and especially 36 Ophiuchi. Appearing as a modest magnitude 4.3 star to the unaided eye, binoculars will reveal a wide companion. The primary appears golden and about twice as bright as the white-ish secondary. (Look out for a close, faint magnitude 6.4 companion to bright Theta too!)

Just slightly to the west is Messier 19, one of several reasonably bright globular clusters in the constellation. Discovered in 1764 by Charles Messier, it appears as a slightly flattened, faint comet-like star through binoculars. The effect is certainly more noticeable in a small telescope; during one observation, I noted it almost appeared rectangular.

Look a little to the south and you'll encounter Messier 62. If you're using 10x50 binoculars, you should be able to comfortably fit both clusters in the same field of view with both appearing about the same brightness and size. While you're here, look out for a bright pair of stars to the north-west of M19 and a faint, close pair of unrelated stars just to the north of M62.

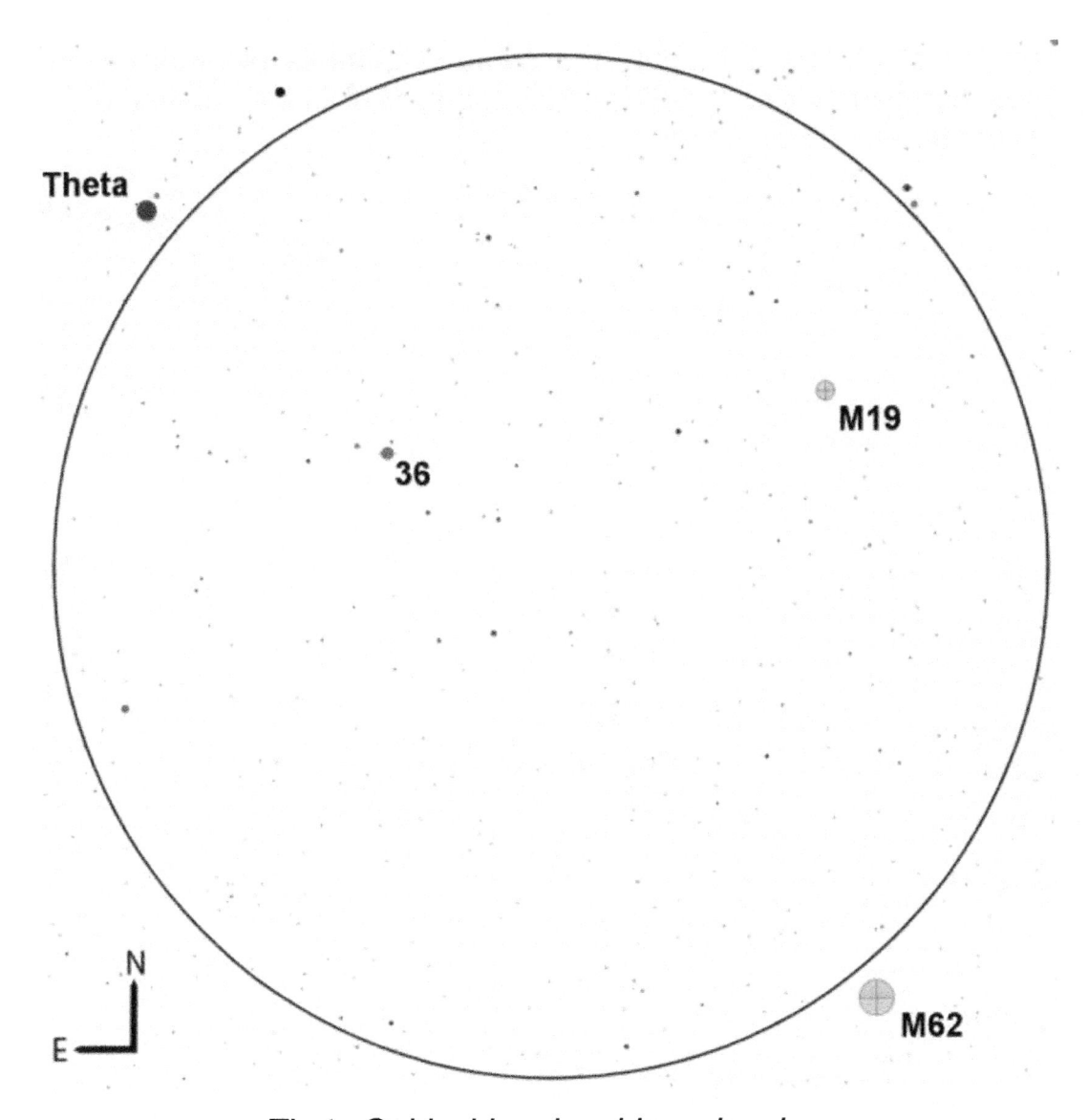

Theta Ophiuchi region, binocular view.

Meanwhile, close to Marfic and near the center of the constellation lie Messier 10 and Messier 12, two other bright globulars easily picked out with binoculars. Again, like M19 and M62, the pair appear within the same field of view, slightly to the south-west of a triangle of three stars of almost equal magnitude.

All four clusters are roughly the same brightness but M62 is the most compact while, at 14,000 light years, M10 is the closest to us. All are about 12 billion years old.

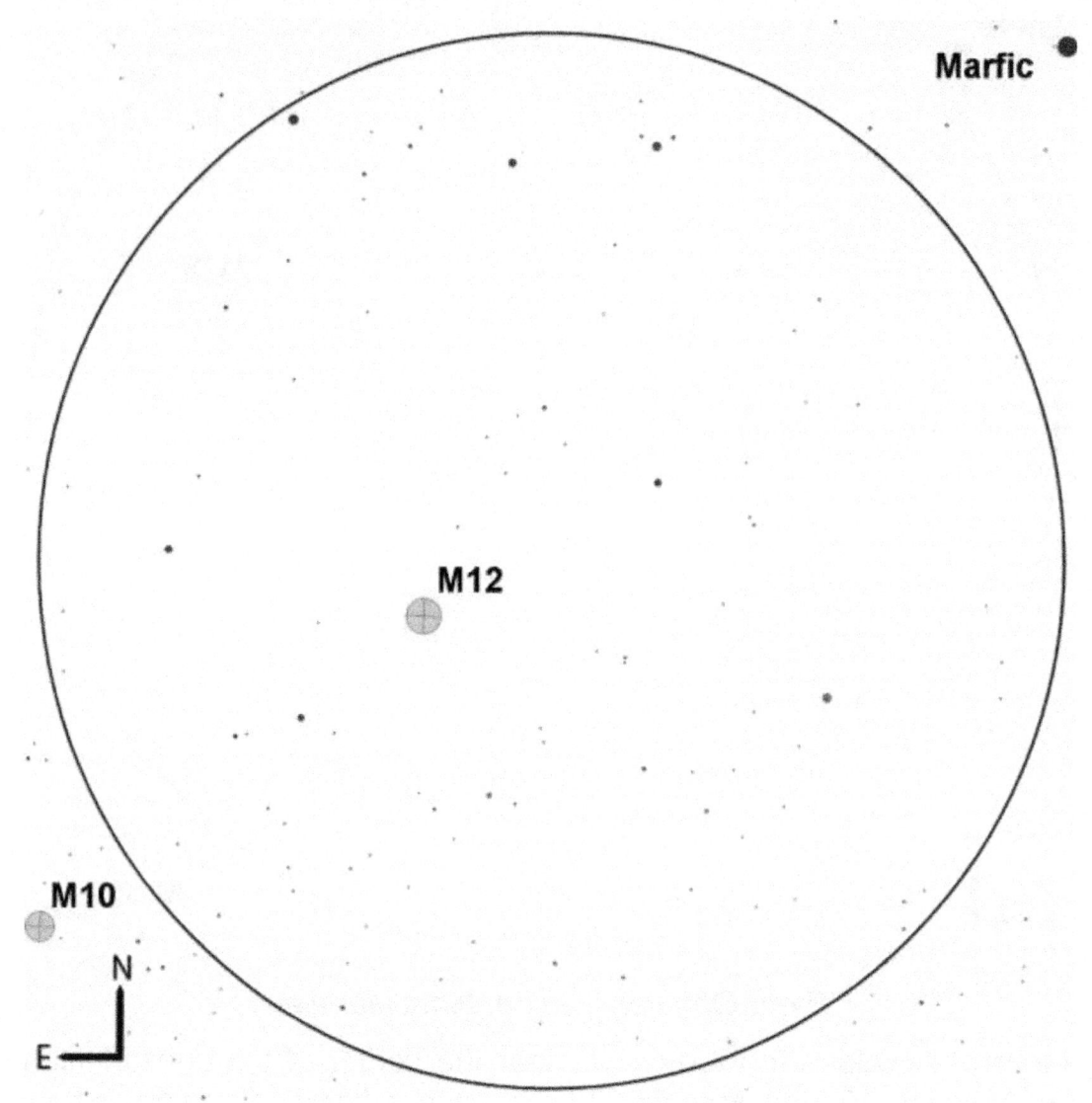

Marfic region, binocular view.

Lastly, head south toward Scorpius and you'll find Rho Ophiuchi, a binocular triple star close to Antares. Together, the three stars form an almost equilateral triangle with the primary appearing at the apex and the two much fainter stars forming the base.

Through a small telescope, the primary appears to have an off-white, creamy colour while the two companions, of equal brightness, both appear blue. In all, there are five stars associated with this system, which lies some 360 light years away.

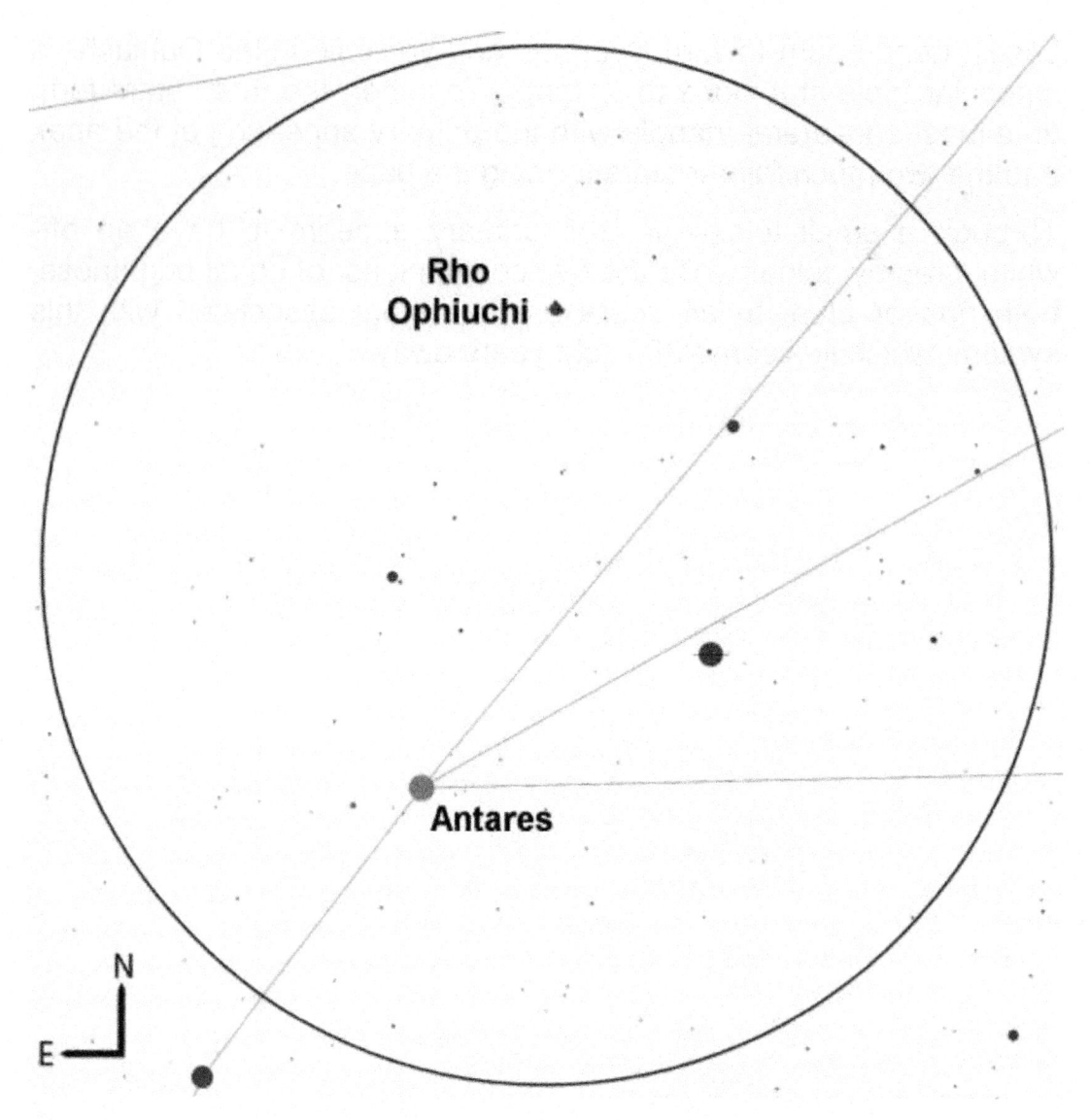

Rho Ophiuchi, binocular view.

Orion

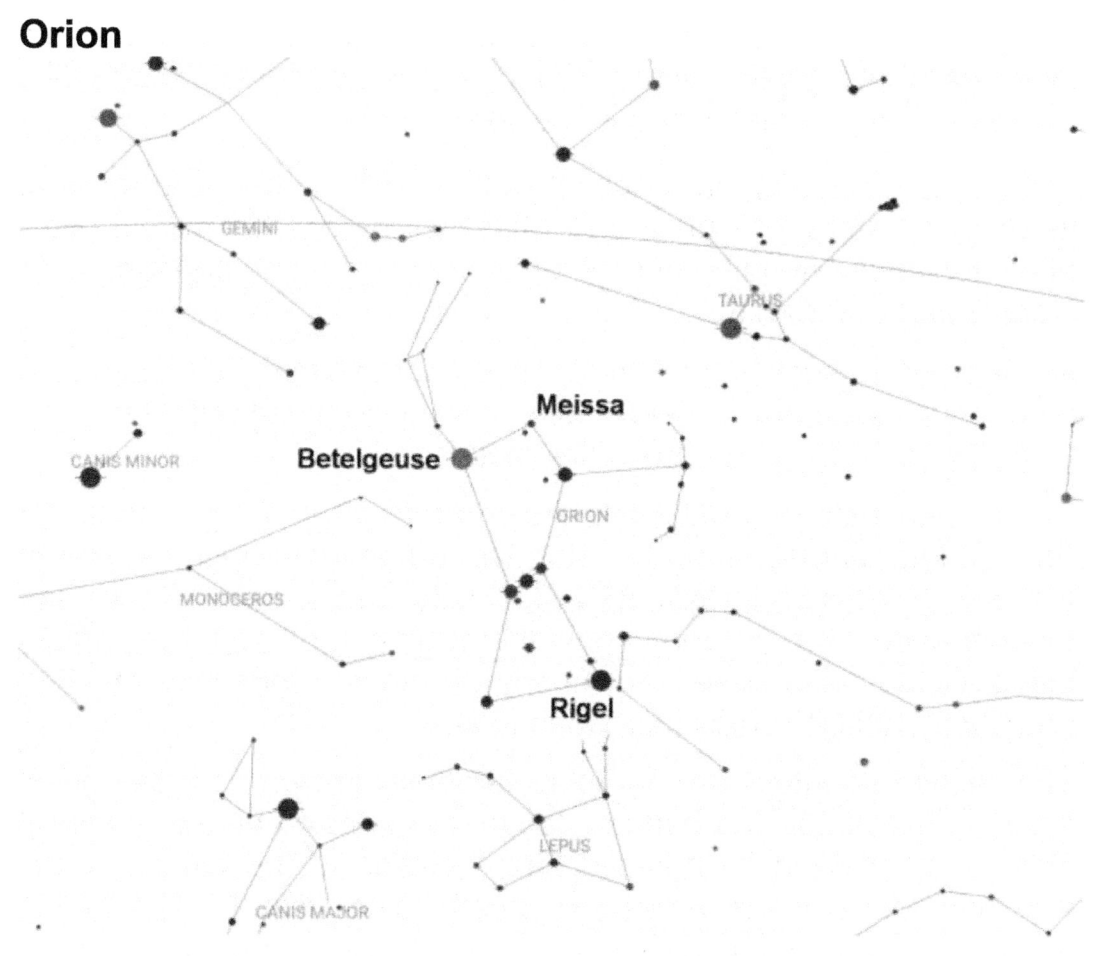

Orion is arguably the most famous constellation in the sky and is certainly one of the brightest. It's been known since antiquity with many myths and legends associated with it from cultures all over the world. To the Greeks, Orion was a skilled hunter, son of Poseidon, god of the sea.

According to one legend, Orion was hunting with the goddess Artemis and boasted he could kill any creature on Earth. This angered the Earth goddess Gaia, who sent a giant scorpion to kill him. Sure enough, the creature succeeded and Zeus placed the hunter amongst the stars. He also immortalized the scorpion,

Scorpius, but placed it opposite Orion in the sky where it would never harm him again. Hence, Orion is a winter constellation while Scorpius rises to prominence in the summer sky.

Orion is a moderately large constellation, 26th in size, with three of its brightest stars forming a distinctive belt across his middle. He's often depicted defending himself against Taurus, who appears to be stampeding toward him.

As Orion is so easily identified, it can be conveniently used to locate other bright stars and constellations (see here), most notably Sirius, Canis Minor, Gemini and the afore-mentioned Taurus.

The brightest star is Beta, also known as Rigel, from the Arabic for "the left leg." A magnitude 0.1 star, it's the seventh brightest star in the sky and lies approximately 850 light years away. There are thought to be three or four stars in the system in all, with the primary being a blue-white supergiant nearly 80 times larger than the Sun and about 120,000 times more luminous.

The second brightest star is Alpha, famously known as Betelgeuse, from the Arabic for "the hand of Jauzā (the Arabic name for Orion.)" There's no officially recognized pronunciation of the name - some say "betel-geez" while others say "beetle-juice", like the Tim Burton film of the same name. The ninth brightest star in the sky, it has a distinctly orange glow and lies about 640 light years away.

Betelgeuse is huge. A red supergiant, if it were placed at the center of the solar system, it would extend well beyond the orbit of Mars and is nearing the end of its life. It could, in theory, explode and appear as a supernova at any time. When it does, it will probably be visible in daylight for months.

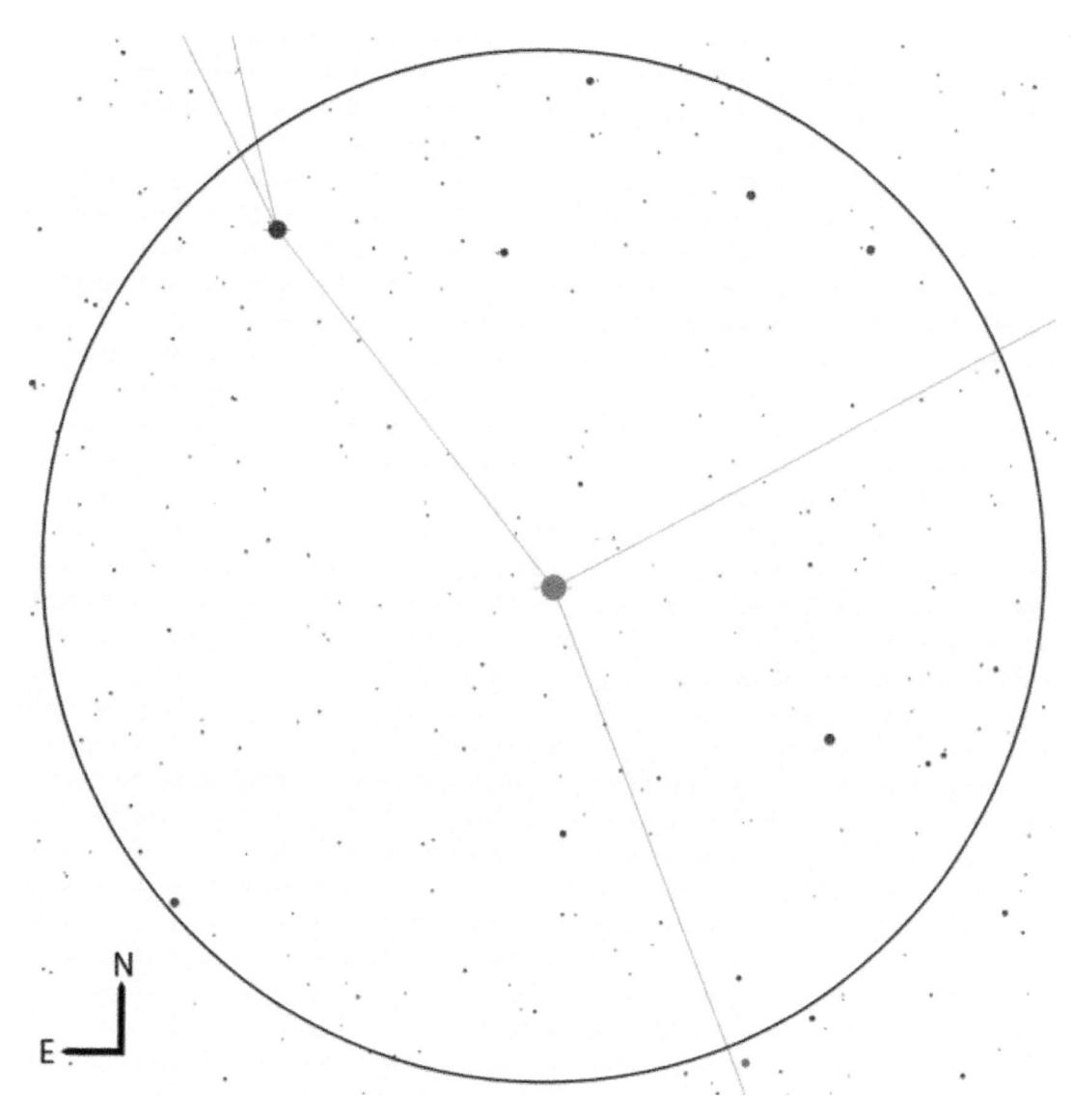

Betelgeuse, binocular view.

Slide over to the north-west to find Lambda, also known as Meissa. This magnitude 3.4 star marks the northernmost corner of a triangle that represents the head of the hunter. Through binoculars you'll also see a tiny trail of three stars that form a slightly curved line to the south.

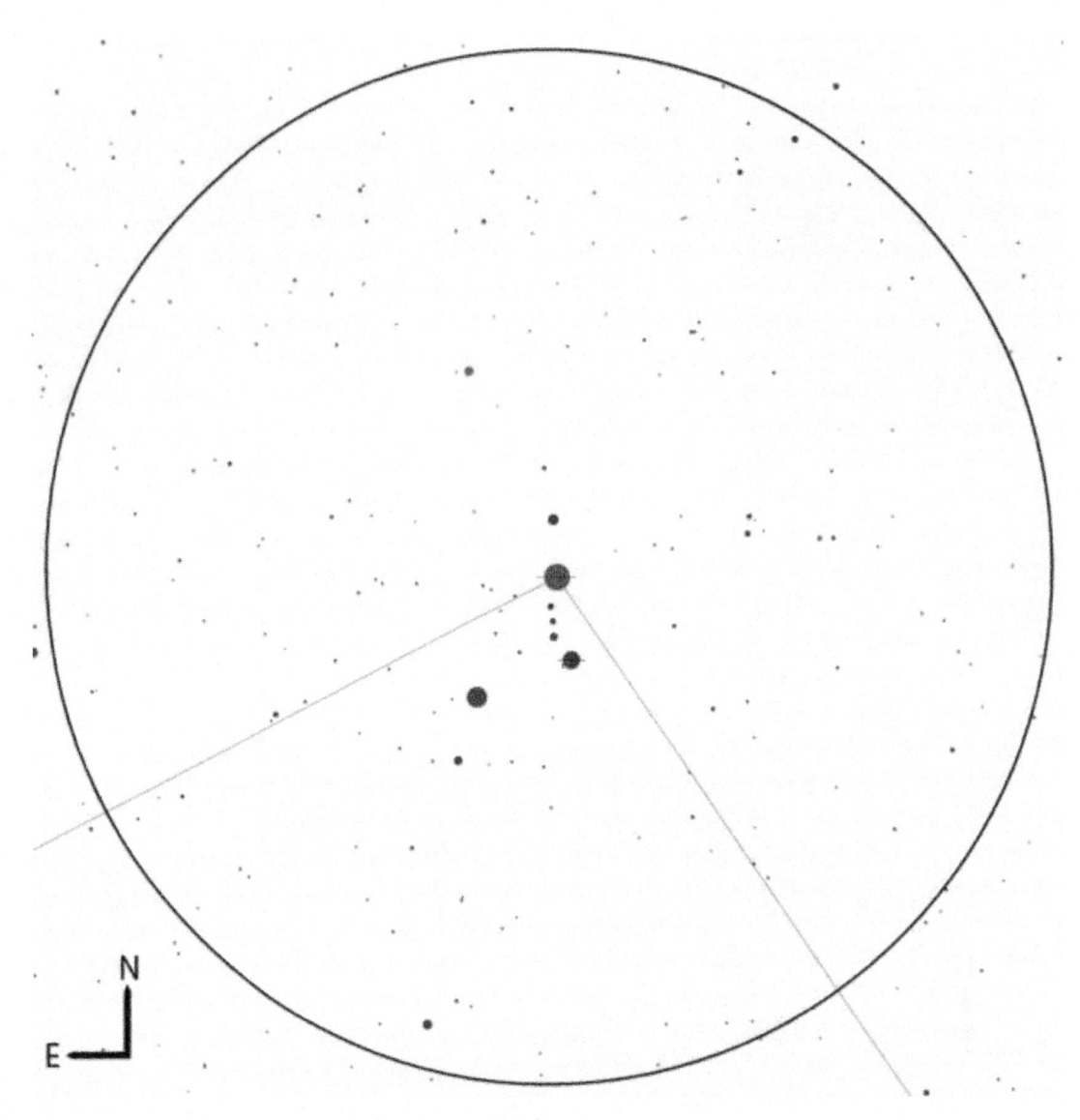

Meissa, binocular view.

The Great Orion Nebula is the only nebula easily visible to the unaided eye from suburban skies and can be found below the starry belt of Orion. Known and observed for thousands of years, it represents the sword of Orion and appears as a bright, misty patch through binoculars. This is the birthplace of stars and even 10x50's will reveal at least two or three tiny points of light – members of the famed Trapezium cluster – young stars in the process of being born.

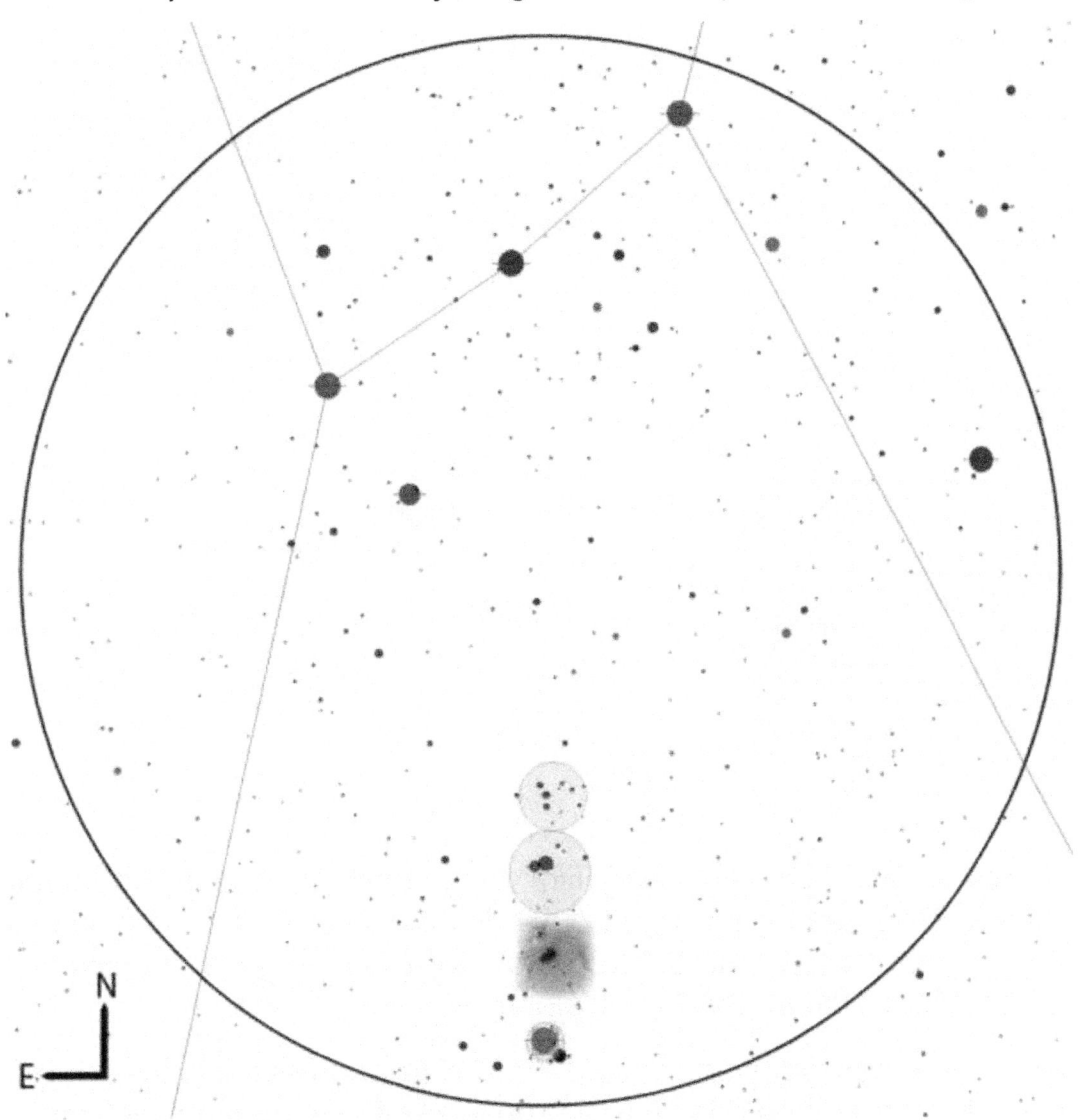

The Orion Nebula and belt, binocular view.

Pegasus & Equuleus

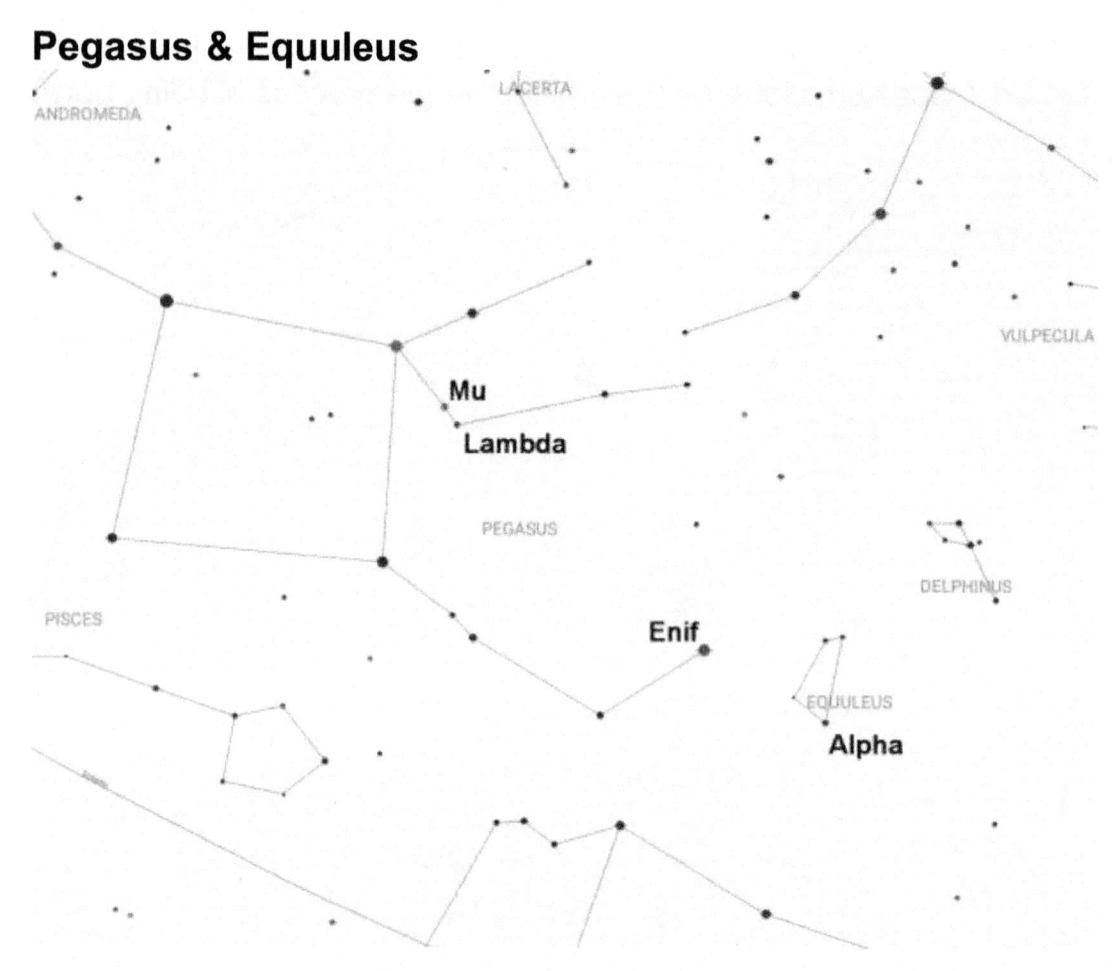

Pegasus, as mythology and film fans know, is the flying horse Perseus rode as he swooped down to rescue the chained princess Andromeda from Cetus the sea monster (see here - or the original *Clash of the* Titans - for the full story.)

It's a large constellation, ranked 7th in size and covering over 1,100 square degrees in a relatively barren area of sky. Its most distinctive feature is the Great Square of Pegasus, a noteworthy asterism for several reasons.

Firstly, Pegasus is one of the few constellations to be directly joined to another, Andromeda. Consequently, the star that marks the north-eastern corner of the square, once known as Delta Pegasi (or Sirrah) now belongs to Andromeda and is more commonly called Alpheratz.

Secondly, by counting the number of stars you see within the square you can get a good idea of the sky conditions from your location.

About five stars can indicate good conditions while ten or more can indicate very clear skies.

Fortunately, you don't need great skies to spot the constellation's brightest star, Epsilon. Also known as Enif (derived from the Arabic for "nose") it's found some way to the west of the great square (which marks the body of the horse.)

Enif is an orange supergiant, some 185 times the size of the Sun with about twelve times its mass and over 12,000 times its luminosity. It's close to 700 light years away and may be nearing the end of its life.

Close to Enif and within the same binocular field of view is Messier 15, a globular cluster discovered by Jean-Dominique Maraldi in 1746. Shining at magnitude 6.3, it has a reasonably bright core and emits X-ray radiation, hinting at a possible black hole within it. M15 is about 33,000 light years away.

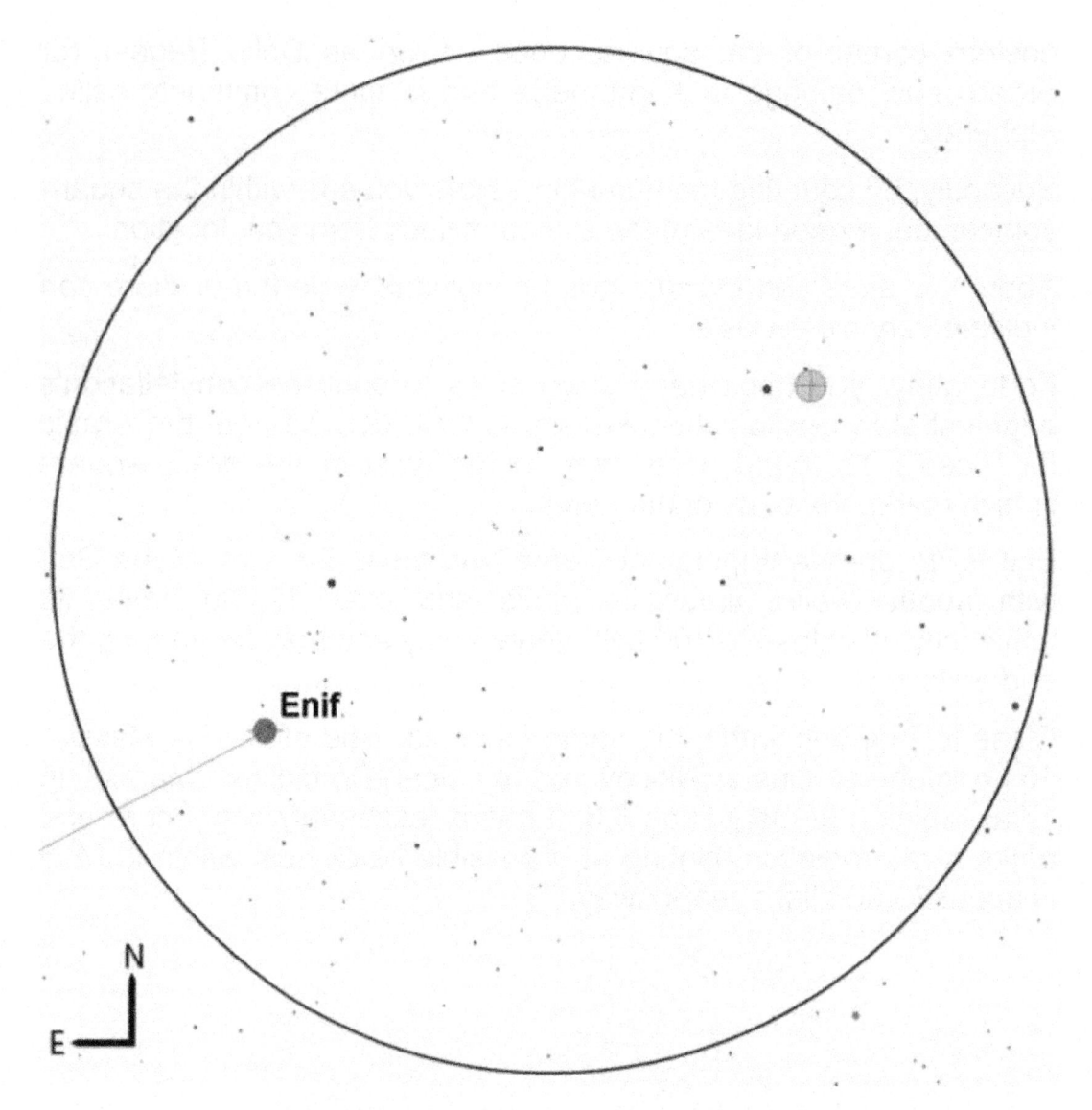

Enif and Messier 15, binocular view.

Just outside the Great Square is another notable object, 51 Pegasi. In 1995, this nearby magnitude 5.5 sun-like star was one of the first found to be orbited by a planet. Thought to be a gas giant half the mass of Jupiter, it orbits its parent star once every four days and has since officially been named Dimidium, from the Latin for "half" – a reference to its mass.

(Incidentally, no planet outside our own solar system can be seen with amateur equipment so binoculars or a telescope will only show the star itself. You can, however, see the star 51 Pegasi within the same field of view as Lambda and Mu Pegasi.)

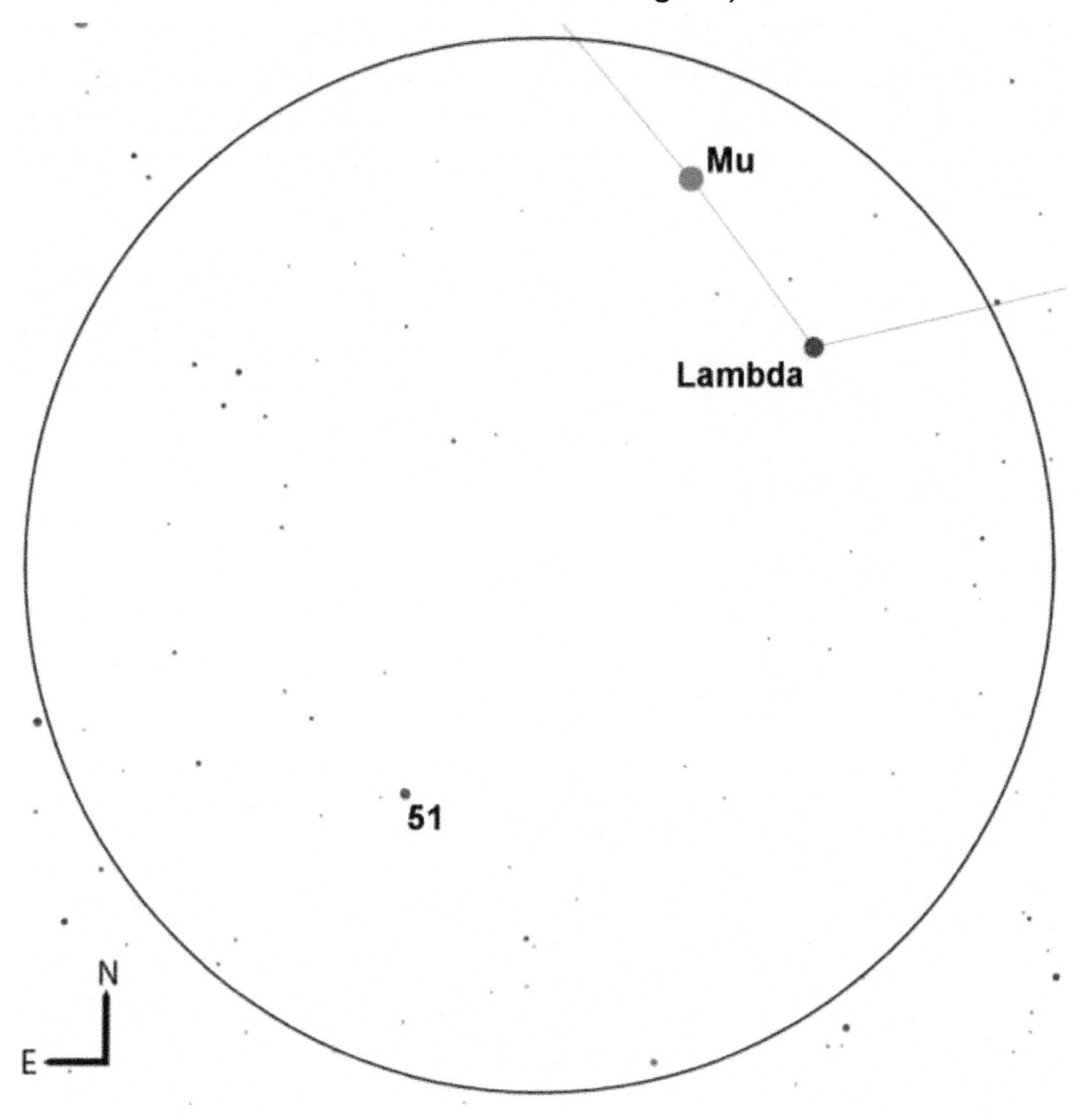

51 Pegasi, binocular view.

Leaving Pegasus behind, we come to Equuleus the Foal to the west. Ranked 87th in size, this is the smallest constellation visible from the northern hemisphere and the second smallest overall. It has no stars brighter than magnitude 3 and even its brightest, Alpha, is only slightly brighter than magnitude 4.

But if you like a challenge, try tracking down Gamma, a wide double star for binoculars or a small telescope at low power. The primary appears white and about 2-3 times brighter than the bluish companion.

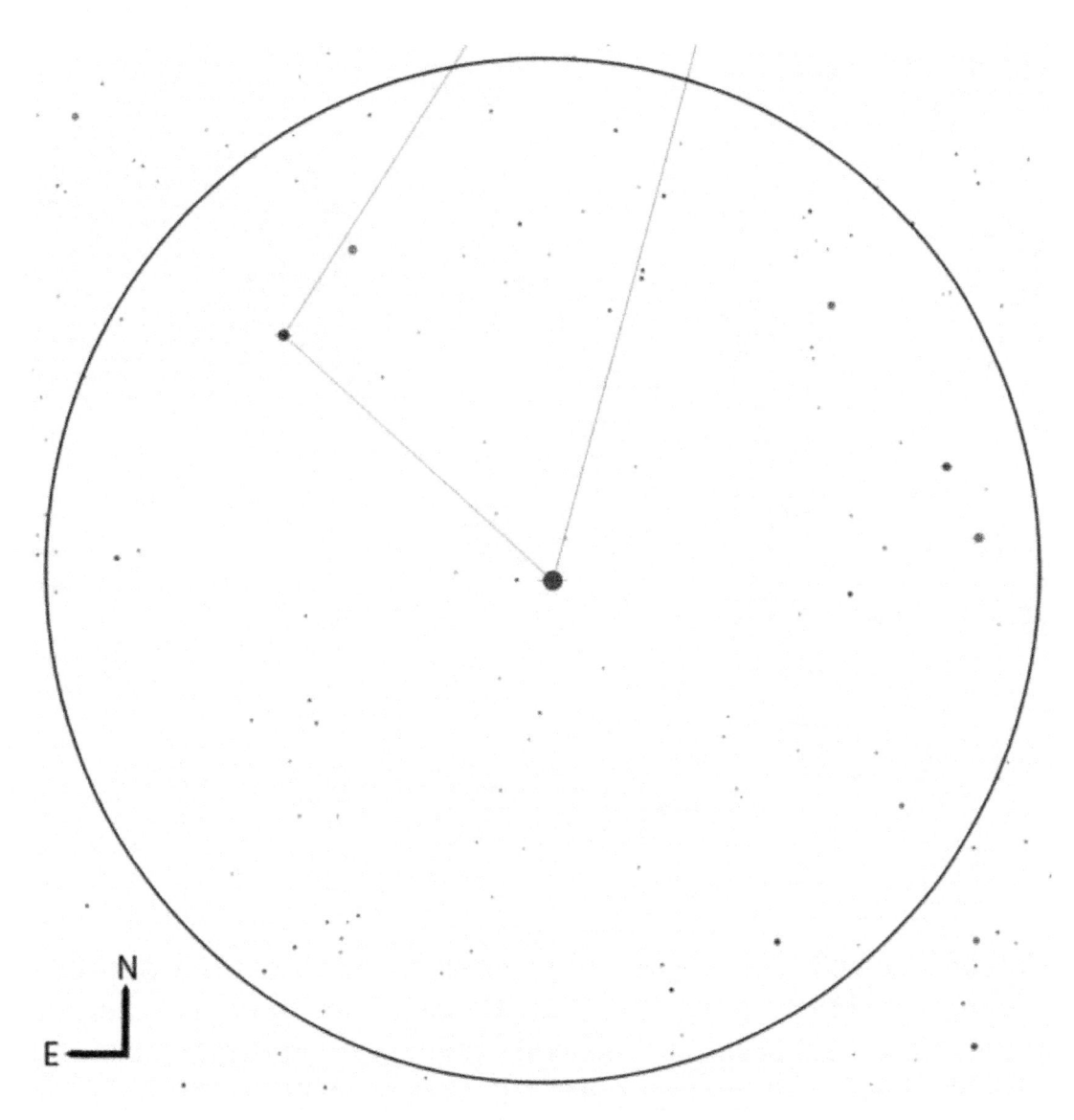

Alpha Equulei, binocular view.

Perseus

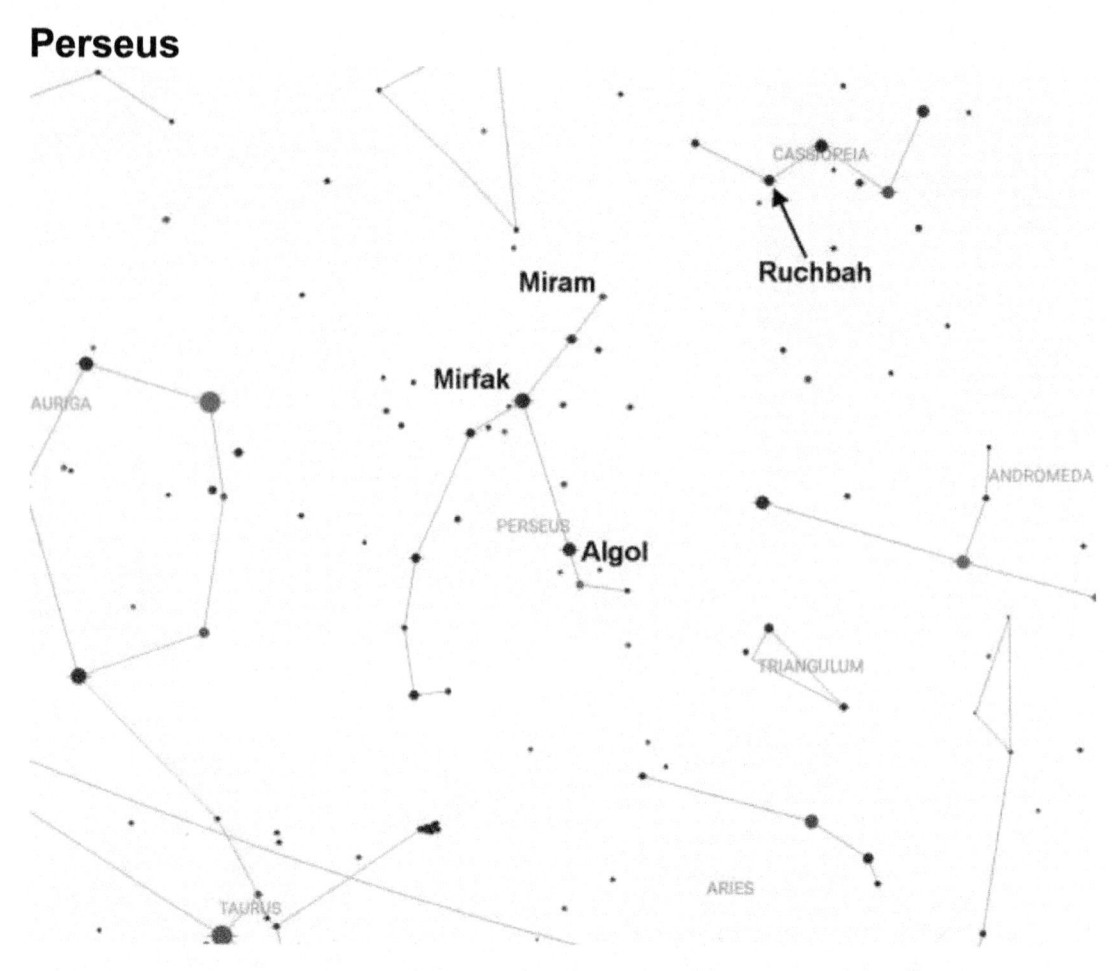

Perseus depicts the Greek hero famed for rescuing the princess Andromeda from Cetus, the Sea Monster (see here for the full story.) It's a mid-sized constellation, ranked 26th in overall size and located close to Andromeda and Cassiopeia in the night sky (see here for more information.) It has a curved shape, almost like a wish-bone, and can be easily seen all the way from early autumn to early spring.

The constellation has a number of bright stars and objects for the casual observer. Its brightest star is Alpha, also known as Mirfak, which is derived from the Arabic word for "elbow." Mirfak is a magnitude 1.8 yellow-white supergiant star, 60 times larger than the Sun with 8 times its mass and about 5,000 times its luminosity. It lies about 600 light years away.

Mirfak itself isn't so remarkable, but the surrounding sky is worth sweeping with binoculars. The Milky Way flows straight through the constellation, leaving a stream of stars in its wake.

In particular, Mirfak swims amongst a large scattering of blue-white stars, appropriately named the Alpha Persei Cluster. It can be seen with just the unaided eye from a dark location but suburban sky observers can still enjoy the view with binoculars. A true cluster, it covers an area of sky six times the size of the full Moon.

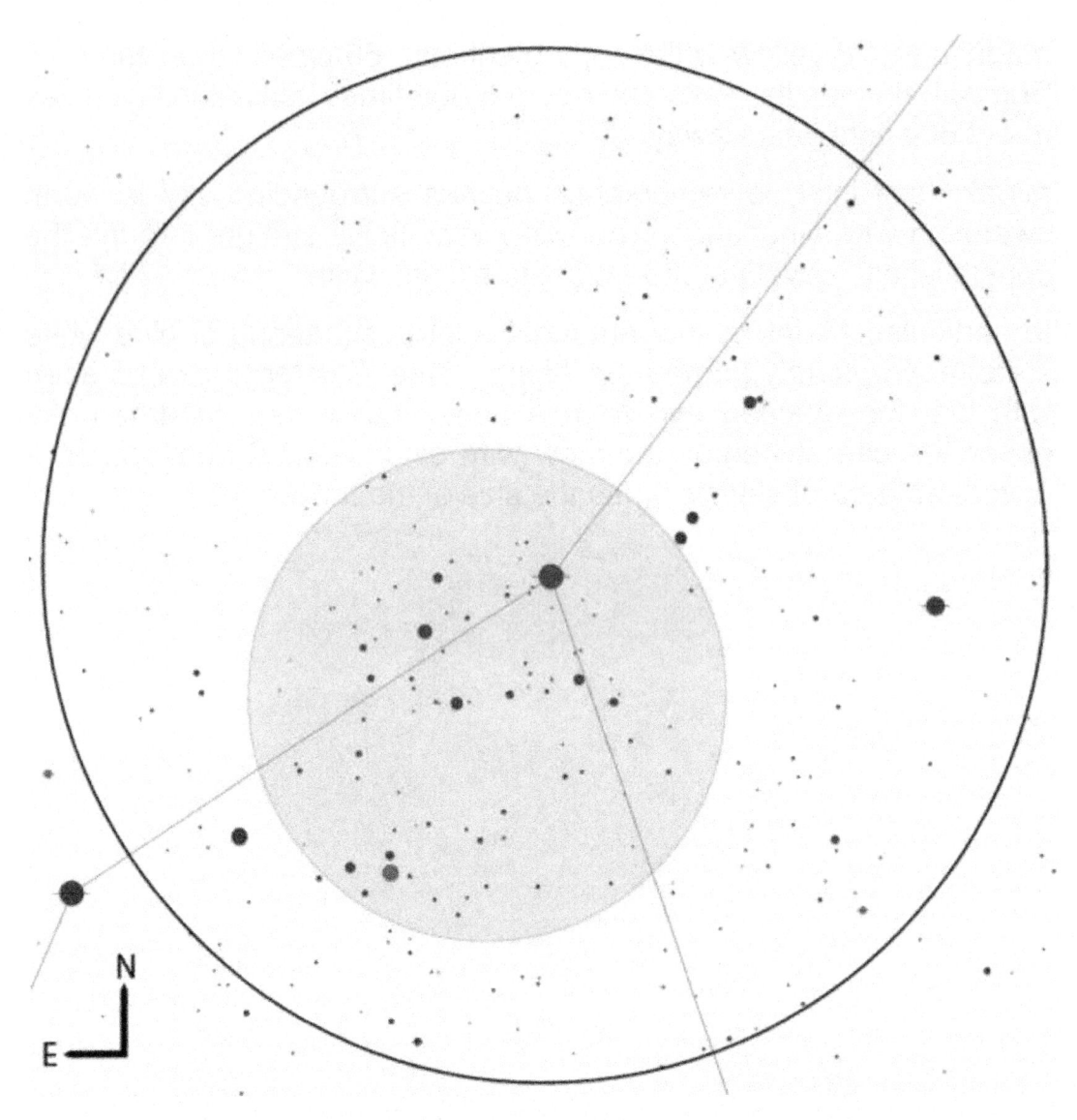

Mirfak and the Alpha Persei Cluster, binocular view.

To the south, we find Beta Persei, arguably the most famous variable star in the entire night sky. It's name is Algol, from the original Arabic, Ras Al Ghul, which means "the head of the demon." In older star charts, Perseus is often depicted as holding the severed head of Medusa, the serpent-haired Gorgon whose gaze could turn all living creatures to stone. Algol marks the eye of Medusa and is still appropriately known as "the demon star."

Algol typically shines at a respectable magnitude 2.1 but will reliably (and predictably) fade to magnitude 3.4 every 2 days, 20 hours and 49 minutes. It remains subdued for about ten hours and then begins to brighten again. A triple star system, this variability is caused by a fainter companion passing in front of the brighter primary, thereby causing the star to apparently dim. Algol was the first of its kind to be discovered.

Close to Algol (and within the same binocular field of view) lies Messier 34, a bright open cluster reminiscent of the Beehive. It can be easily seen as a faint, misty patch through binoculars but is best observed through a small telescope; it appears as an elongated X and a number of double stars are also revealed within it. The cluster spans some 7 light years in space and lies at about 1,500 light years away.

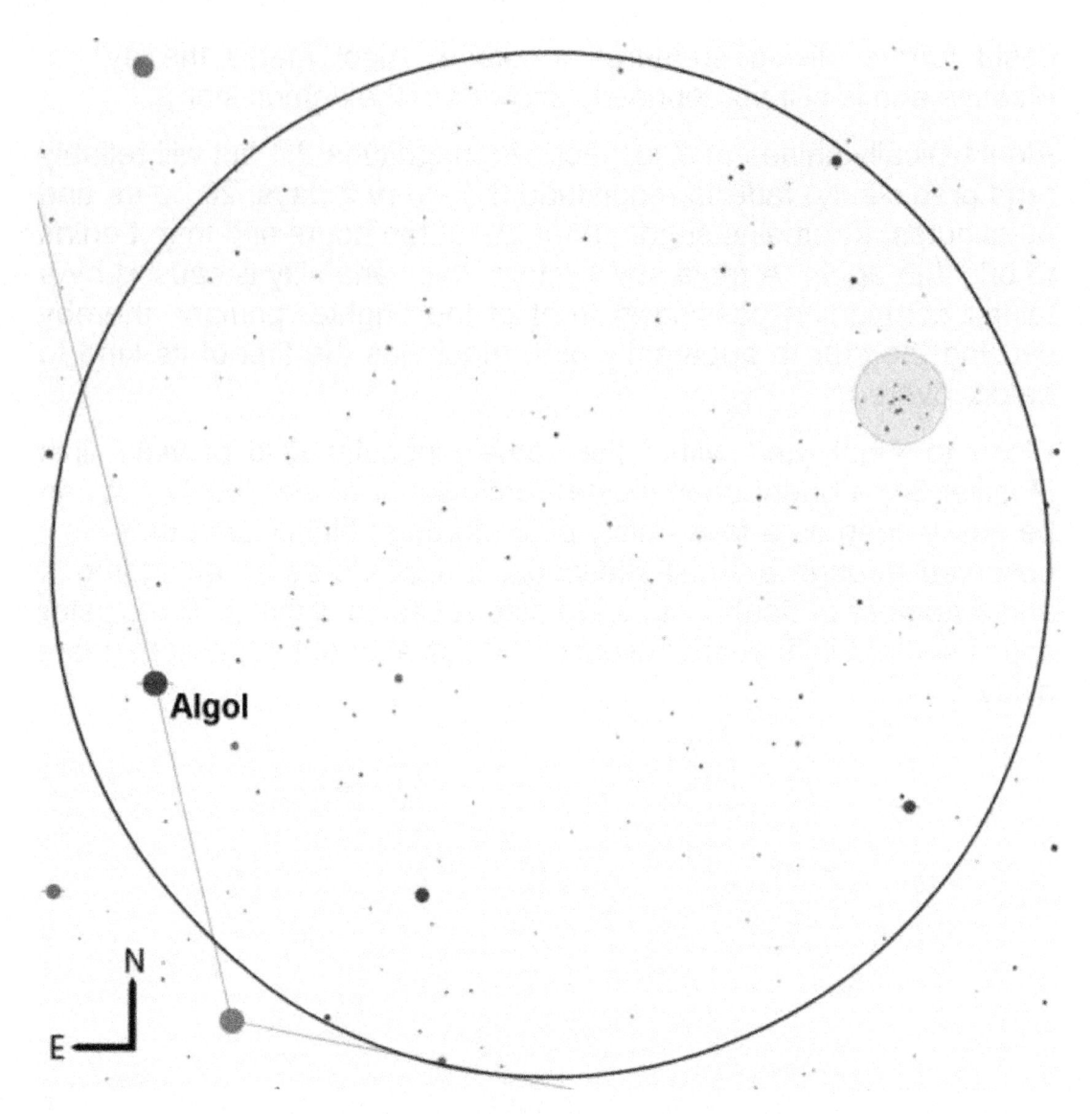

Algol and Messier 34, binocular view.

If you like Messier 34, you'll love the Double Cluster. This isn't a misnomer; found midway between Eta Persei (Miram) and Ruchbah in Cassiopeia, these two clusters can be seen very close together with just your eyes under dark skies and are great in binoculars.

Through 10x50's I've seen curved lines to the north and south, giving the cluster the form of a bow tie or butterfly. A small telescope at low power will provide simply stunning views.

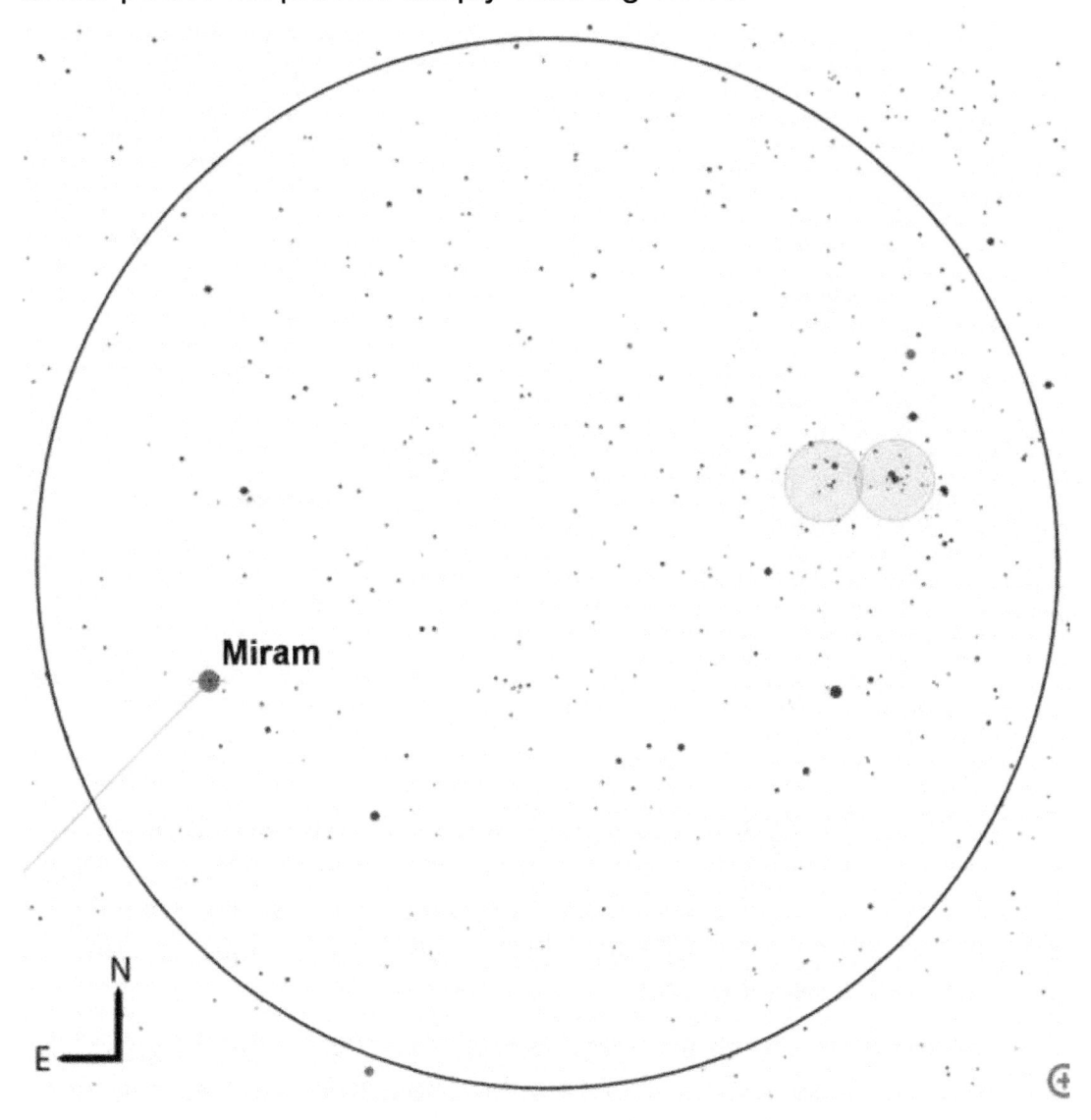

The Double Cluster, binocular view.

Pisces

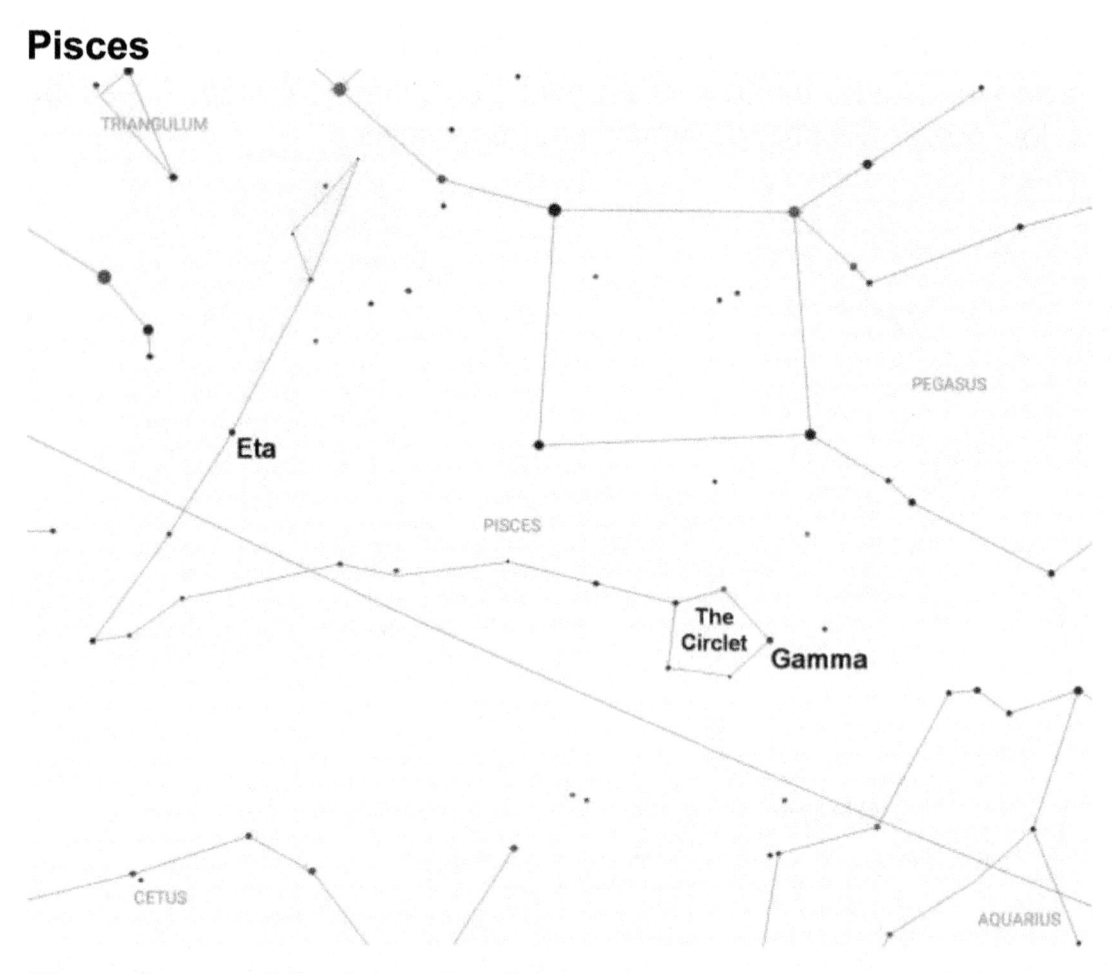

Pisces is one of the large, but faint, watery constellations of autumn and depicts two fishes tied together. In Greek mythology, these fishes were Aphrodite and Eros who, like Pan (see Capricornus, another autumn constellation) threw themselves into a river to escape the monster Typhon.

Transforming themselves into fishes, the two tied themselves together with rope so they could not be separated and become lost.

Pisces is 14th in size, covering nearly 900 square degrees of sky, but contains no stars brighter than magnitude three. Its brightest, Eta, is also known as Kullat Nūnu, an ancient Babylonian name meaning "the cord of the fish." A yellow giant, it's about 26 times more massive than the Sun and is approximately 316 times more luminous. It lies just under 300 light years away.

There are no bright deep sky objects in Pisces but it does have at least one famed feature. Below the Great Square of Pegasus is a circle of stars, giving this asterism the appropriate name "the Circlet."

It's too large to fit within the field of view of 10x50 binoculars and you'll need to be under dark skies to discern the Circlet with just your eyes. At magnitude 3.7, the brightest star in the circle, Gamma, is also the second brightest in Pisces as a whole.

Sagitta and Vulpecula

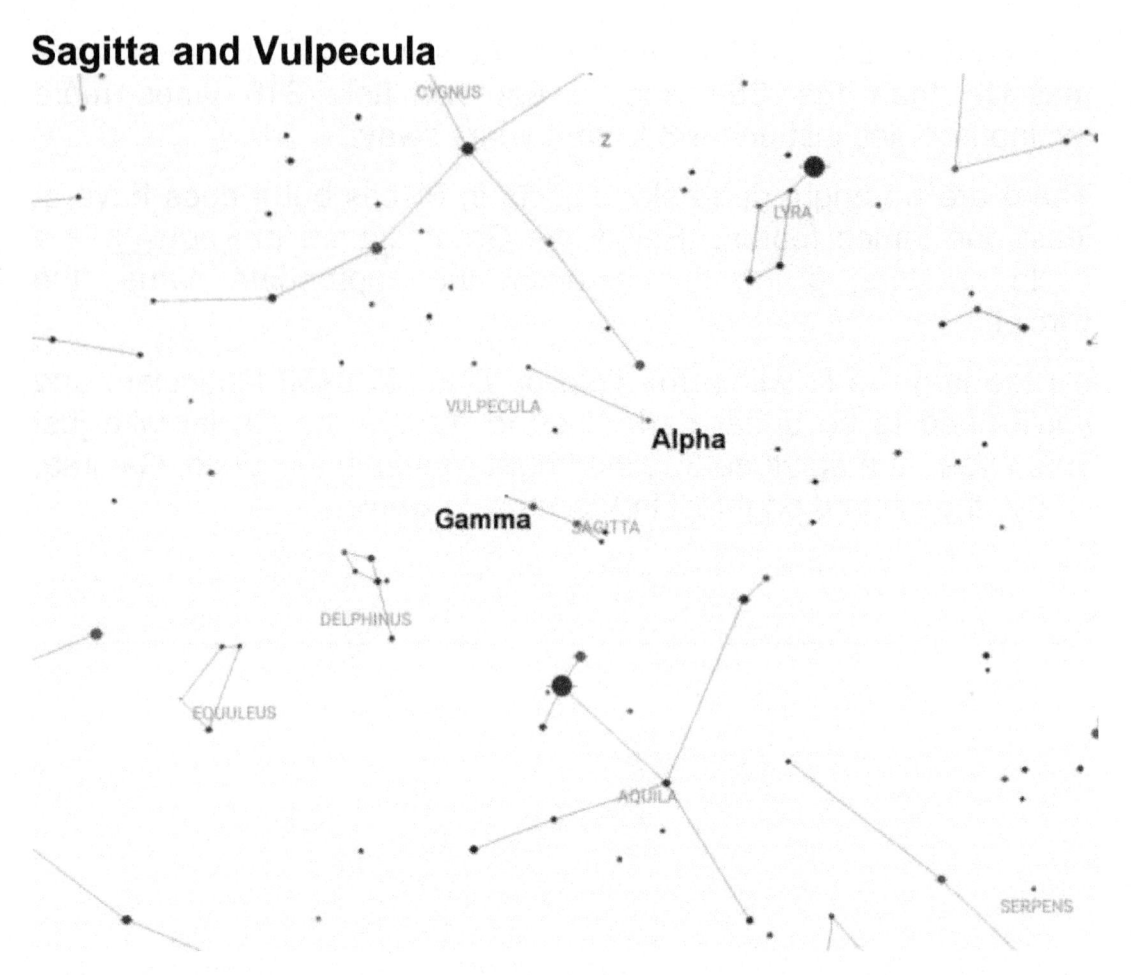

Sagitta, the Arrow, is an ancient Greek constellation and is thought to represent the arrow that Hercules shot to kill the eagle Aquila. Appropriately, both those characters also appear nearby in the sky; Hercules appears to the west and Aquila appears to the south.

Ranked 86th in size, it's the third smallest constellation in the entire night sky with only Delphinus, the dolphin and the bright southern constellation Crux, the Cross, being smaller. Perhaps not surprisingly, it can quite comfortably fit into the field of view of a regular pair of 10x50 binoculars.

Unfortunately, it's not a particularly bright constellation but can still be easily found thanks to its close proximity to both Cygnus and Aquila. Looking midway between Albireo and Altair should help you to locate it.

Its brightest star is Gamma, a magnitude 3.7 red giant star that lies about 250 light years away.

Sagitta might not be a particularly noteworthy constellation by itself, but it can help us to find a number of deep sky objects in the area.

By placing Gamma near the lower left of your binocular field of view and with Delta just to the lower right, you can catch two deep sky objects in the same binocular field of view.

First, look slightly further north for a small, very faint, circular misty patch. This is the Dumbbell Nebula, and like the Helix Nebula it's a shell of gas thrown off by a dying star. It's about 1,400 light years away and is estimated to be roughly 1½ light years in diameter.

If your skies are dark and clear, you might also catch a glimpse of Messier 71, a small magnitude 7.3 globular cluster nestled between Gamma and Delta.

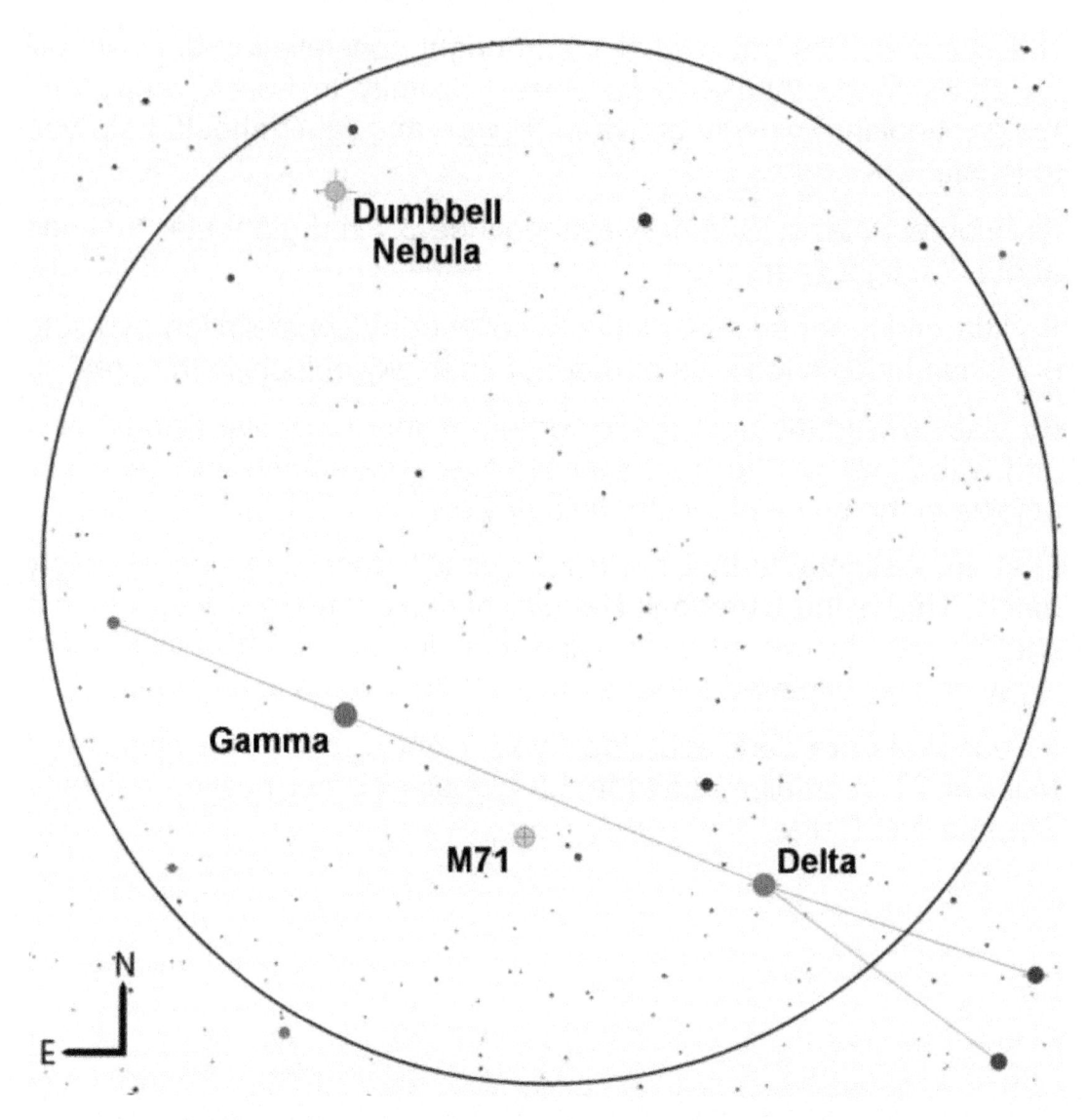

The Dumbbell Nebula and Messier 71, binocular view.

By placing the two end stars of the arrow (Beta and Alpha, also known as Sham) on the left edge of your field of view, you should easily be able to spot the Coathanger Cluster. You can't miss it; it's large, it looks exactly like its name and it looks great in binoculars.

Visible to the unaided eye under dark skies, this is not a true cluster at all, but merely a chance alignment of stars at varying distances across space. It was first noted by the Persian astronomer Al Sufi in 954 A.D. and has proven to be popular ever since.

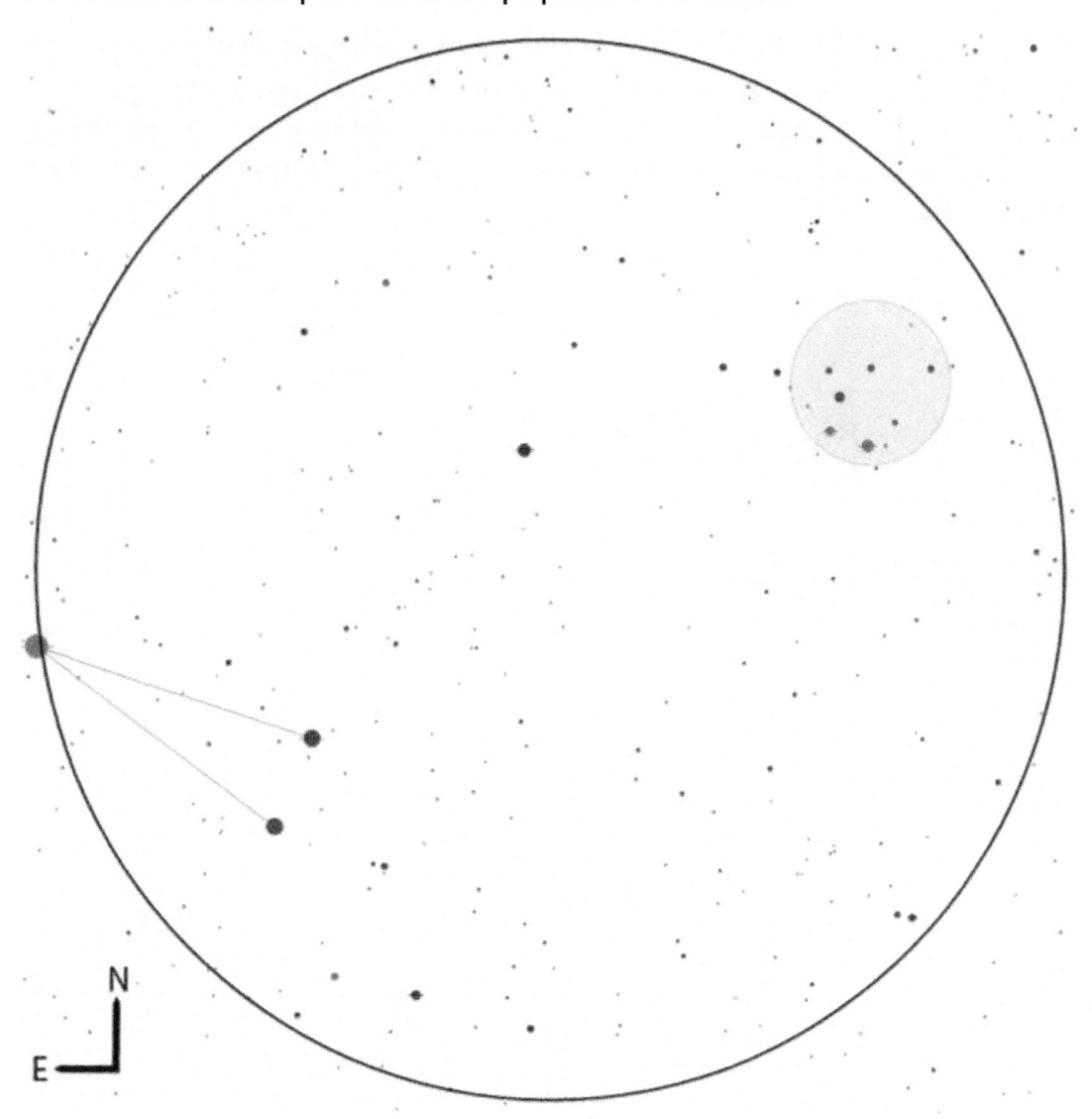

The Coathanger Cluster, binocular view.

Now with the Coathanger at the bottom of our field of view, we can catch a nice double almost due north. This is Alpha Vulpeculae, sometimes known as Anser, the brightest star in the constellation of Vulpecula, the Fox.

A red giant star 300 light years away, it appears as a single magnitude 4.4 star to the unaided eye. But binoculars will show an unrelated star of magnitude 5.8, just to the north-west. To me, Alpha appears a creamy color and about 1½ times brighter than its white companion.

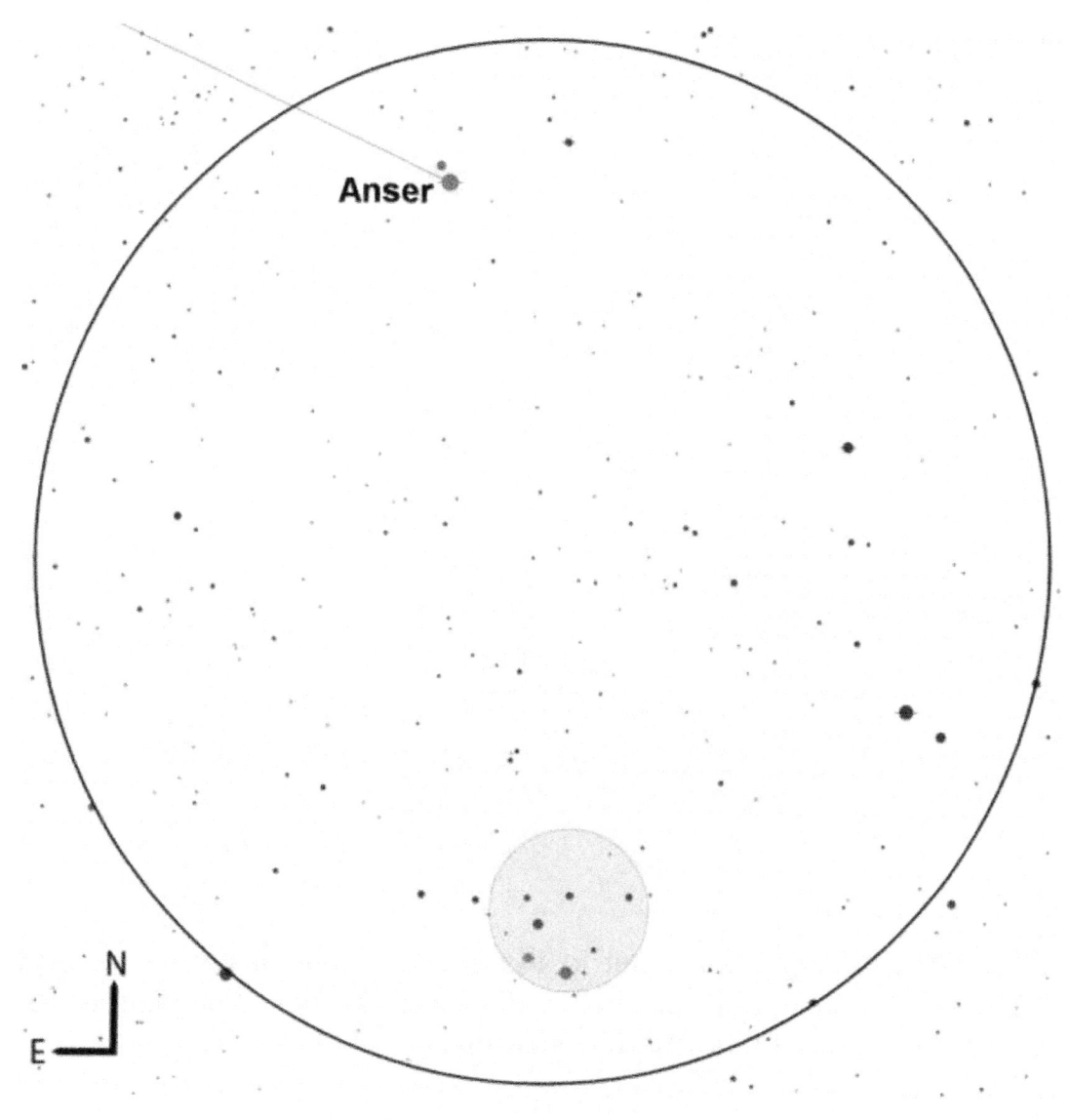

Anser, binocular view.

Vulpecula is a relatively modern constellation, invented by the astronomer Johannes Hevellius in the 17th century. Originally known as the Fox and the Goose, it seems only the fox has survived!

Sagittarius

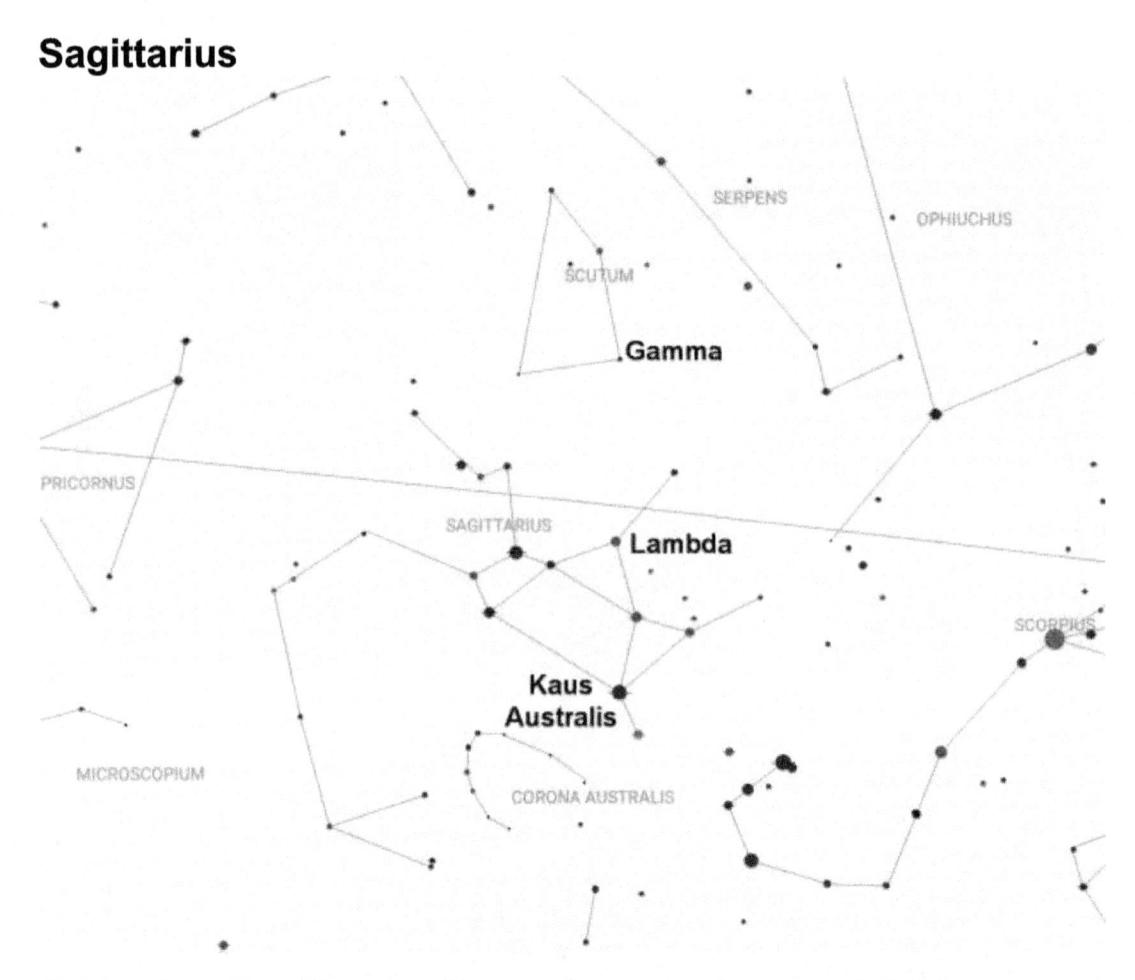

Sagittarius, like Scorpius just to the west, is one of the larger and brighter constellations of the zodiac but is not well-placed for observation from the northern hemisphere.

The constellation is often associated with Chiron, a half-man, half-horse centaur who was the tutor of Jason. Jason, of course, was the hero who embarked on a quest to find the Golden Fleece with his Argonauts. It's said that Chiron invented the constellation to help guide the Argonauts on their quest.

It's a fairly large constellation, 15th in size and covering over 850 square degrees of sky. Its brightest stars form a very distinctive teapot shaped asterism that's easily identified – if the constellation is high enough above the horizon.

Unfortunately, that can be a problem. Sagittarius barely rises over the horizon for much of the northern hemisphere. But for those lucky observers in the southern hemisphere it's a spectacular sight throughout their winter months with the constellation passing directly overhead for many observers.

Its poor visibility is made all the more unfortunate because of one important fact: the Milky Way passes right through the constellation. Its brightest portion appears right above the spout of the teapot and is sometimes compared to steam escaping the brewing pot!

You'll need to get far away from any city lights to appreciate the view, but once you do, it's a truly breathtaking sight. When you look toward this region of the sky, you're actually looking directly into the heart of our galaxy and, not surprisingly, Sagittarius is rich with deep sky objects as a result. Some are easily seen with binoculars.

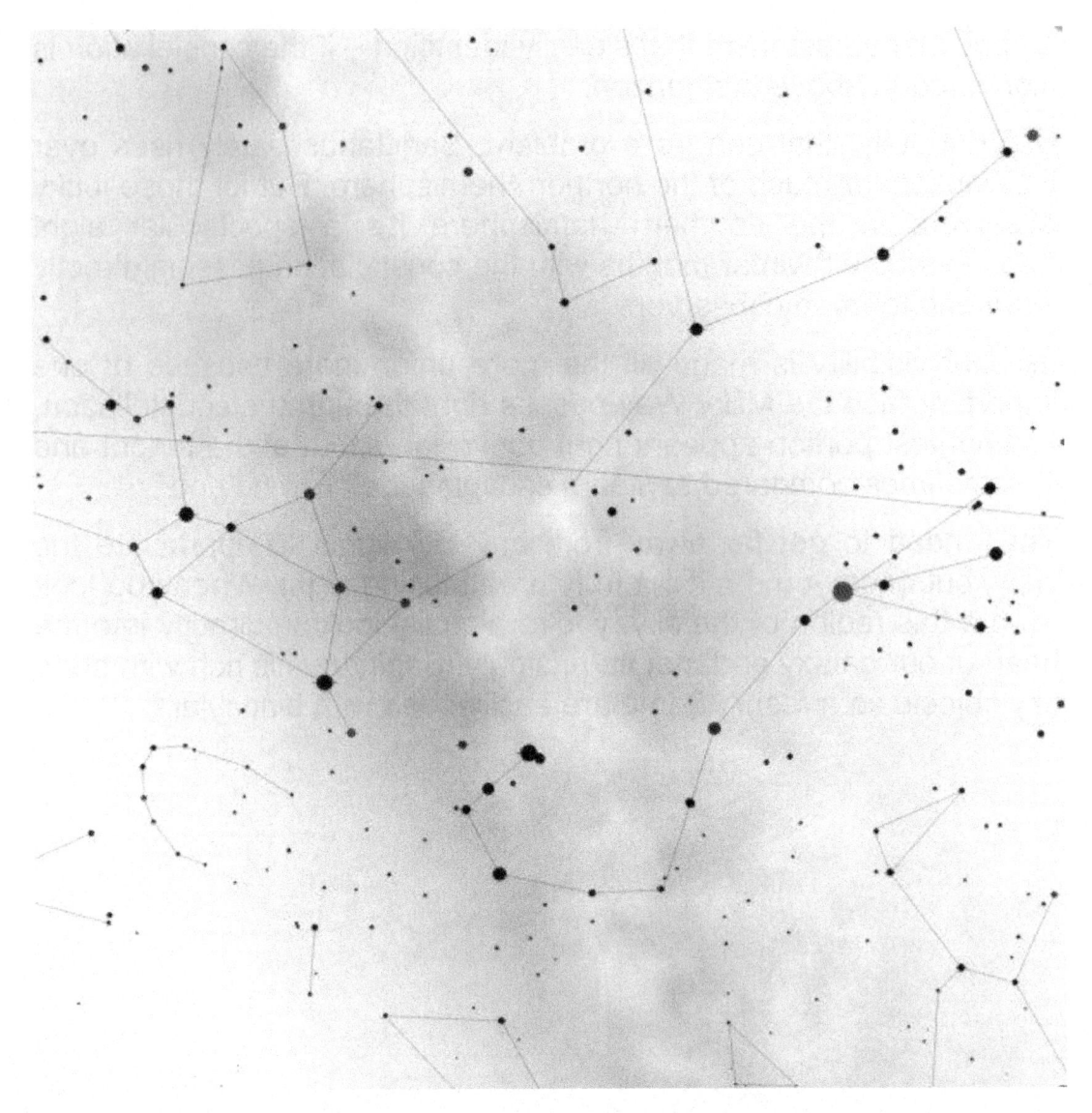

The Milky Way through Sagittarius

Its brightest star is Epsilon, known as Kaus Australis, a name derived from a combination of Arabic and Latin and meaning "southern bow." It's a magnitude 1.9 blue-white star that's over three times more massive than the Sun and about 145 light years away.

To the north-west, just above the spout of the tea-pot, we find several nebulae that are relatively easily seen through binoculars from dark sky locations. With Lambda Sagittarii on the edge of the field of view, look out for Messier 8, the Lagoon Nebula on the opposite side.

The nebula can be faintly seen and appears to run in an east-west direction with a tight line of stars within it.

Messier 20, the Trifid Nebula, also appears within the same field of view but is smaller and fainter. In contrast to the Lagoon, it appears to run in a north-south direction and has a tiny group of stars to the north.

Look carefully at the view; can you see Messier 21, an open cluster to the north-east of the Trifid? And what about Messier 28, the globular cluster close to Lambda Sagitarii?

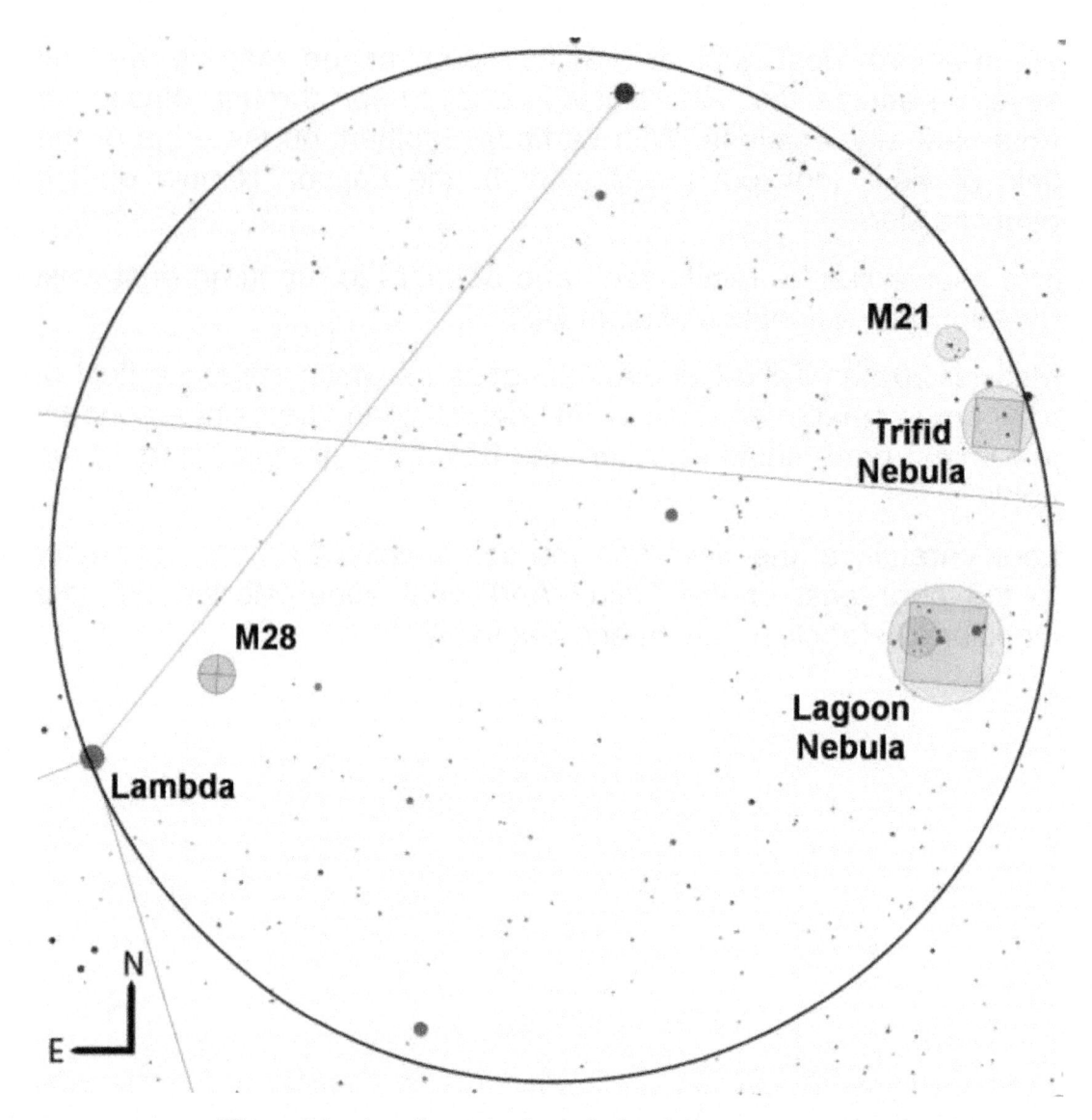

The objects close to Lambda, binocular view.

Lastly, try your hand at Messier 17, the Swan Nebula. It's a little out in the wilderness but can be found in the same binocular field of view as Gamma Scutum, at the bottom of the constellation. Under good conditions, it can appear as an elongated number two and is very nicely seen with a small telescope.

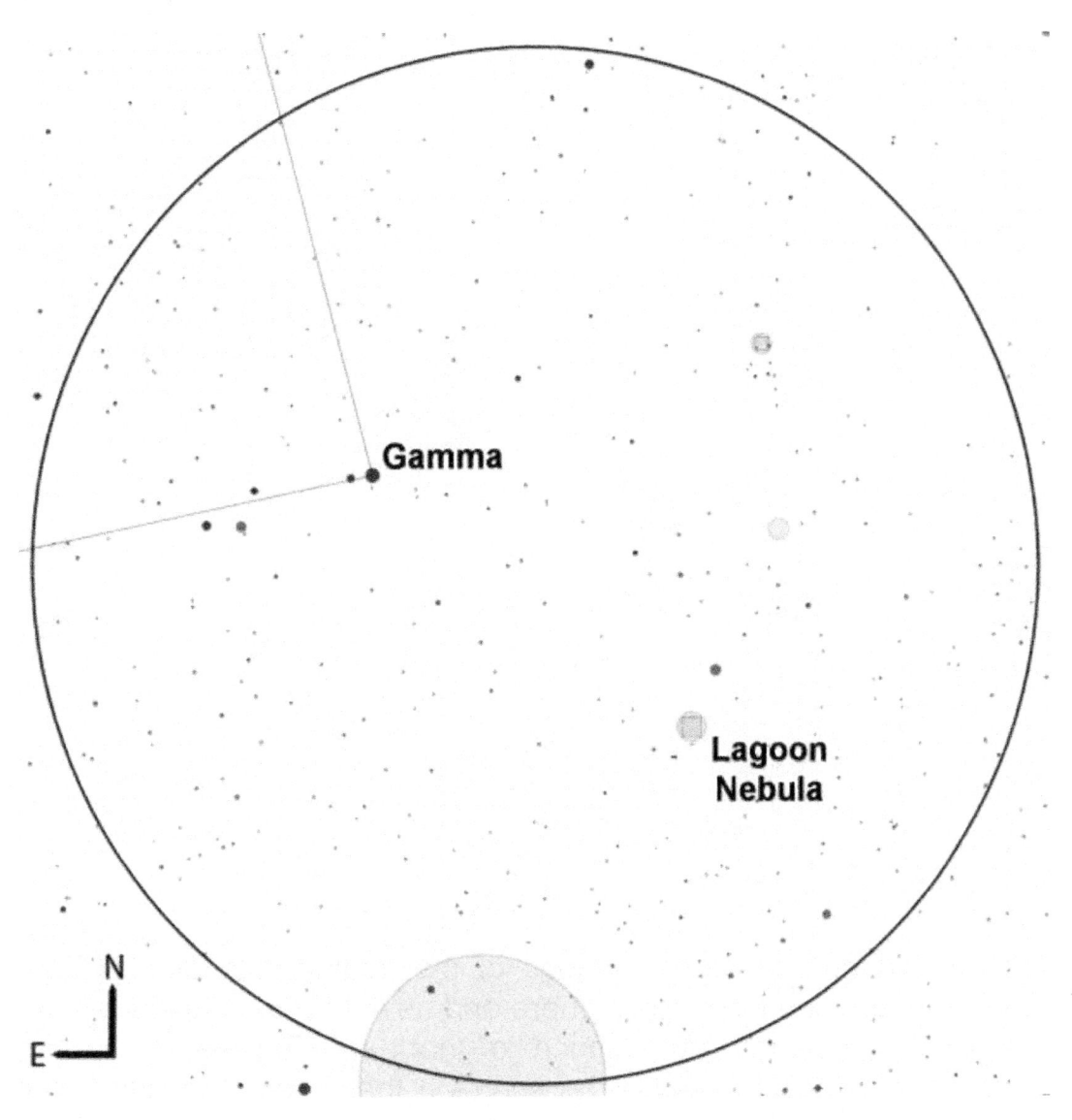

The Swan Nebula, binocular view.

Scorpius

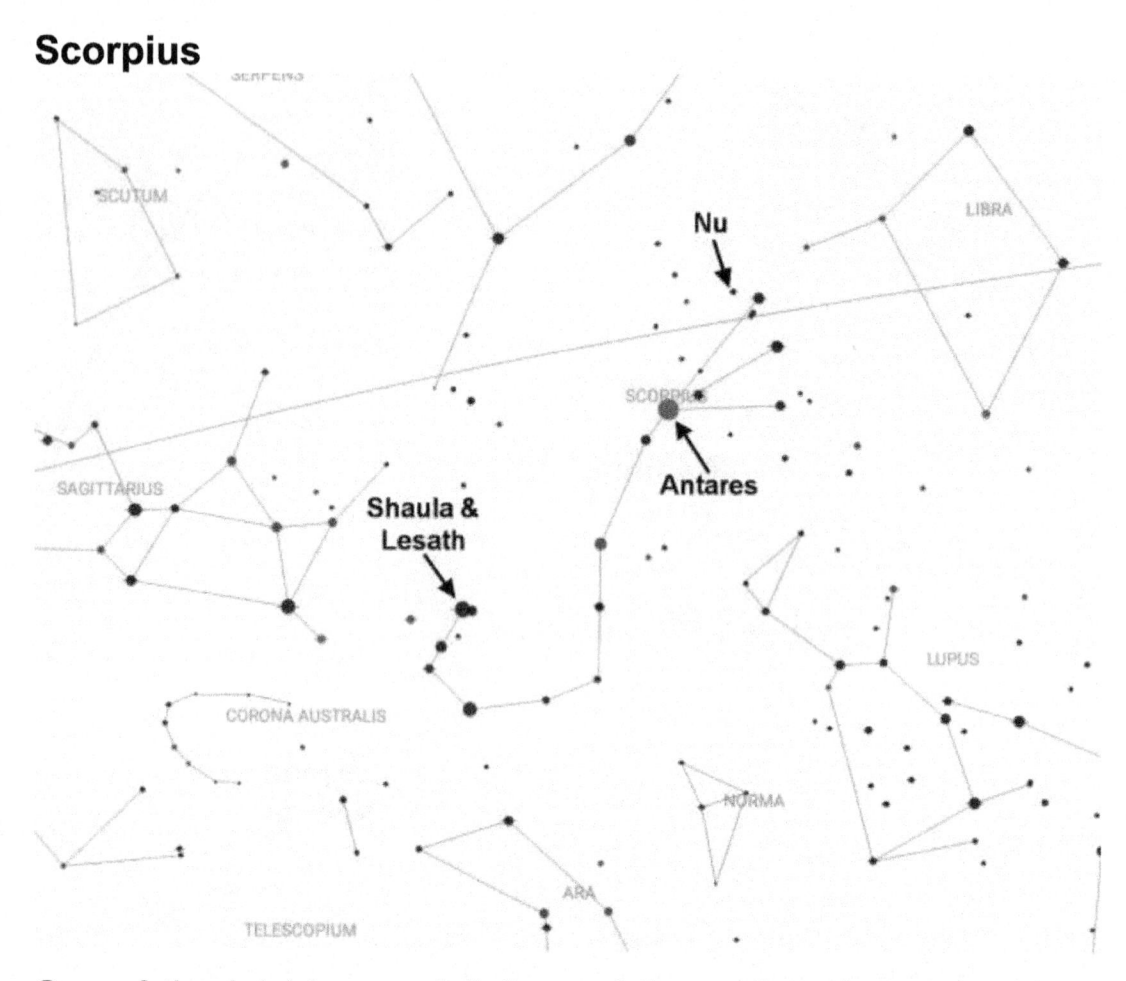

One of the brighter constellations of the zodiac, Scorpius is best seen from the southern hemisphere and never rises completely from the United Kingdom and much of northern Europe. In Greek mythology, Scorpius depicts the scorpion that killed Orion and was consequently placed opposite the hunter in the sky. (There are a number of variations of the story but see here for one version.)

A mid-sized constellation, it ranks 33rd in size and covers nearly 500 square degrees of sky. It has a distinctive S shape, slender and slightly slanted with the claws of the scorpion at the northern end of the constellation and reaching toward the west.

Its brightest star is Alpha, also known as Antares and the 15th brightest star in sky. Unlike most stars, the name is ancient Greek in origin and literally means "rival of Ares" – Ares being the Greek name for Mars - because the star has a strong orange-red hue, similar to our neighboring planet. Its place in the constellation marks the heart of the scorpion.

To say that Antares is a large star would be an incredible understatement. A red supergiant, it's nearly 900 times the size of the Sun and if you were to place it at the center of our solar system it would extend beyond the orbit of Mars. It's also about 15 times more massive and shines with the light of about 10,000 suns.

Antares isn't a solitary star either. It has a blue-white companion that's quite luminous in its own right but its light is overwhelmed by Antares, making it difficult to spot unless you have a larger 'scope. The system lies about 550 light years away.

Scorpius is a summer constellation that has the Milky Way running through it toward the east, between the tail of the scorpion and Sagittarius the Archer. Consequently there are a number of deep sky objects within reach of the binocular observer.

While you're staring at Antares, look out for Messier 4, one of the closest globulars in the sky. You'll need dark skies to properly observe the cluster with binoculars, but you might still catch a glimpse.

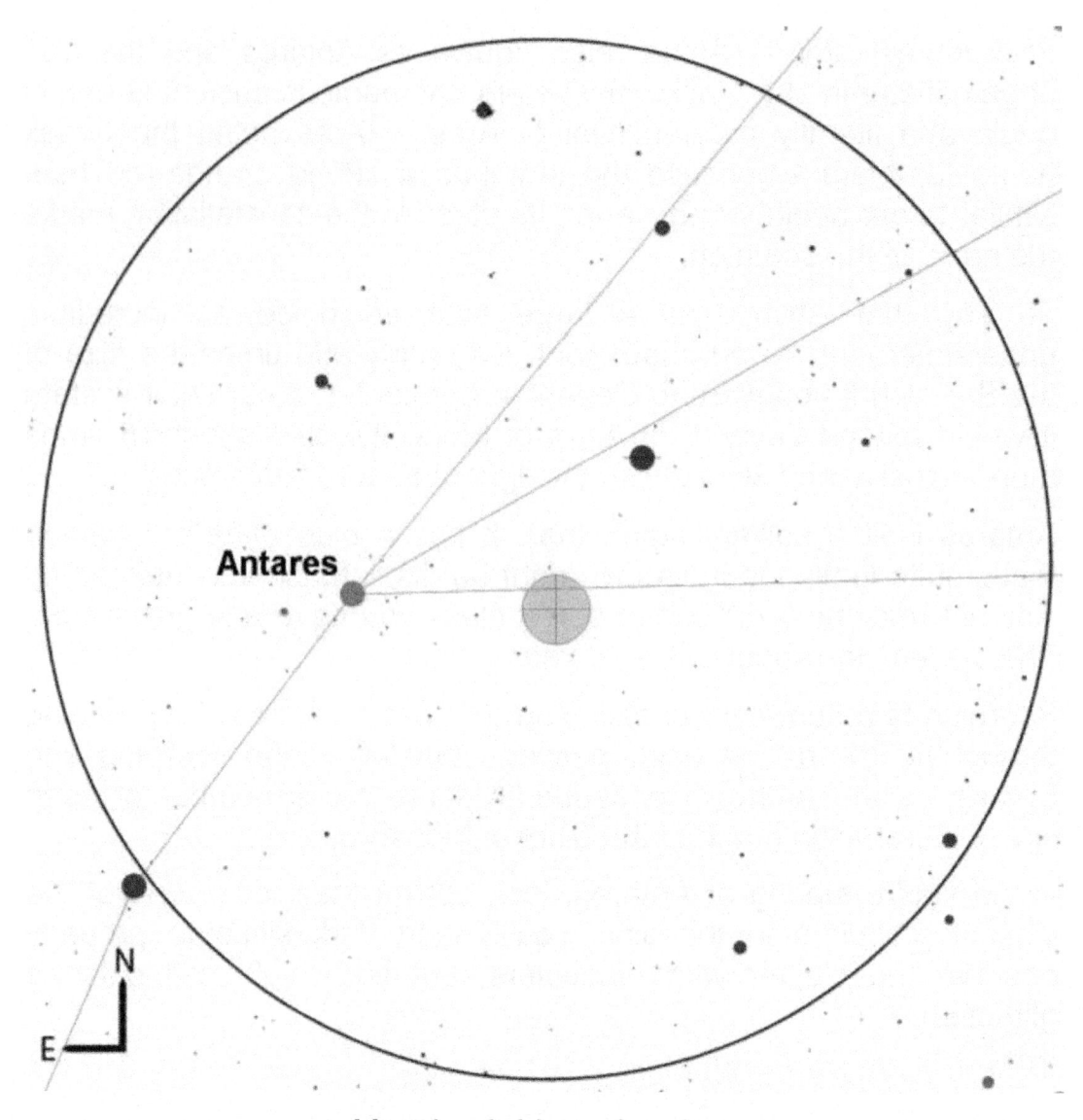

Messier 4, binocular view.

Easier targets lie toward the west; Nu Scopii has two very faint companions to the south-east but Omega[1] and Omega[2] form a nice double pair of white stars just to the south-west.

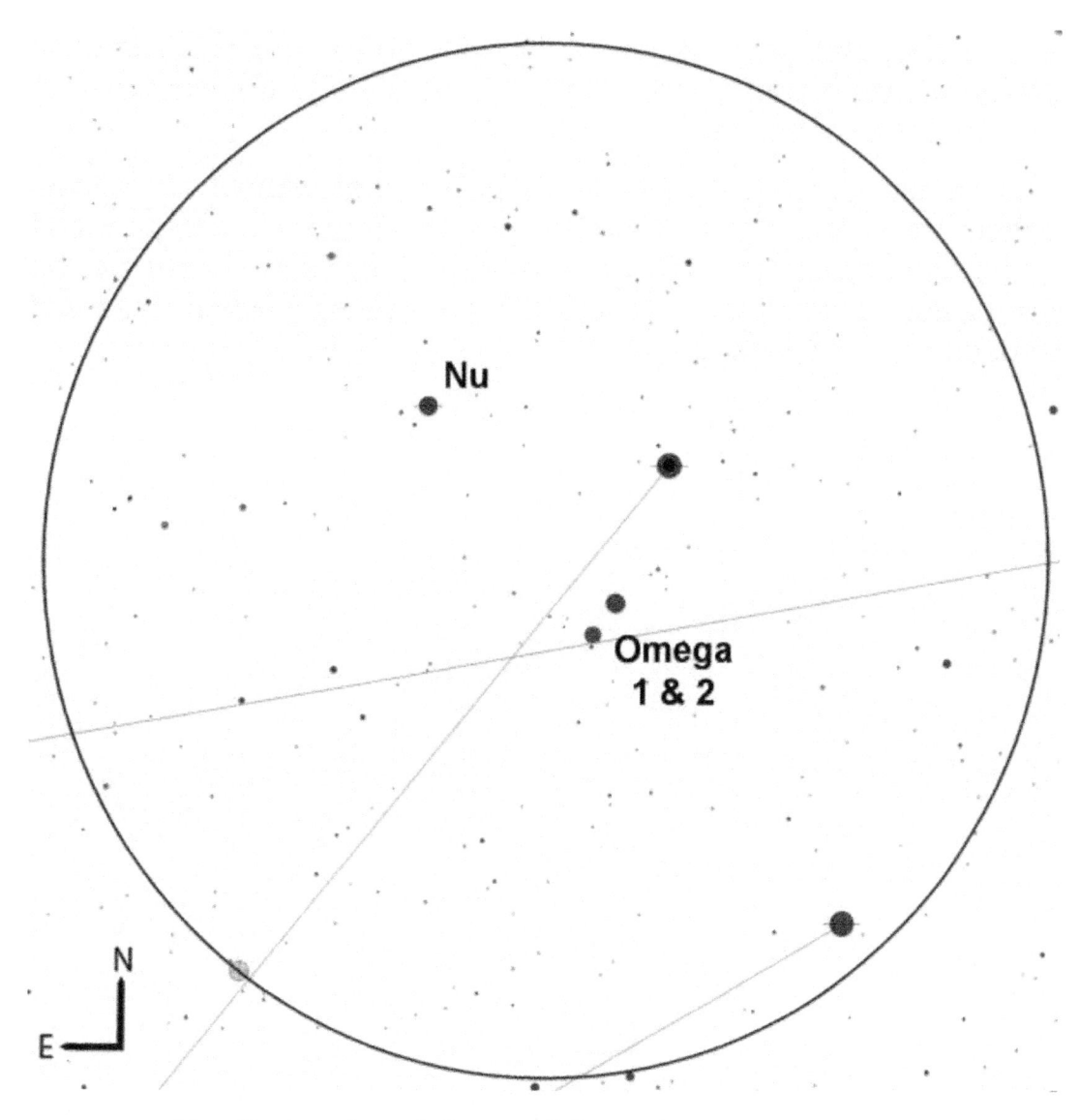

Nu, Omega¹ and Omega² Scorpii, binocular view.

Head east toward the tail of the scorpion for two other fine sights. Messiers 6 (the Butterfly Cluster) and 7 (Ptolemy's Cluster) both appear within the same binocular field of view and are easily found close to Shaula and Lesath, the two stars that form the sting of the scorpion.

Of the two, Messier 7 is larger, brighter and has a close core of possibly hundreds of stars. A line of three stars to the west mimics the head of Scorpius itself.

Despite being half the size, Messier 6 is not without its charms either. Through a pair of 10x50 binoculars it appears compact and forms a triangular shape that points to the east with a bright star on the eastern point. Both M6 and M7 are stunning when observed through a small telescope.

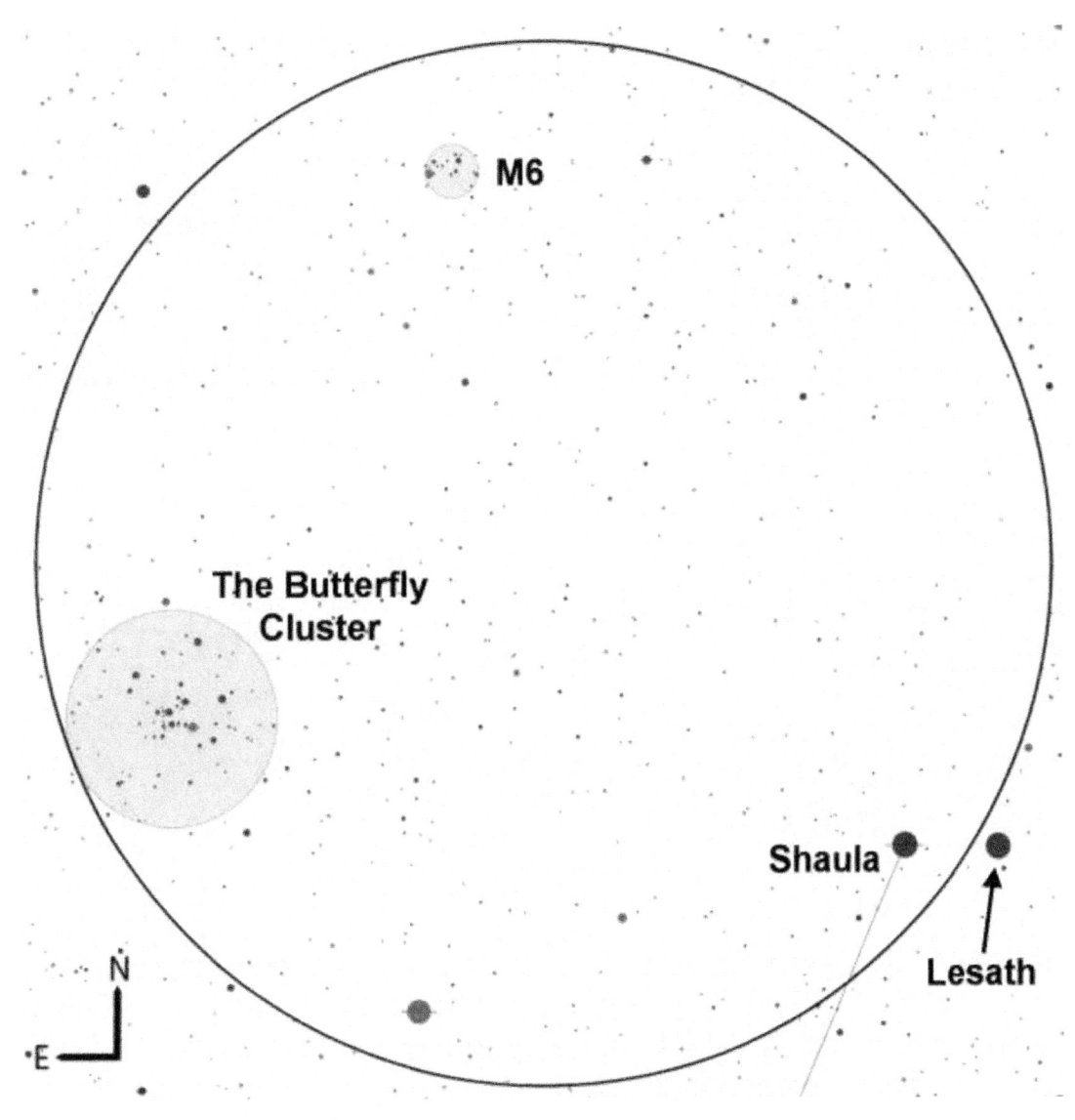

The Butterfly Cluster and Messier 6, binocular view.

Serpens

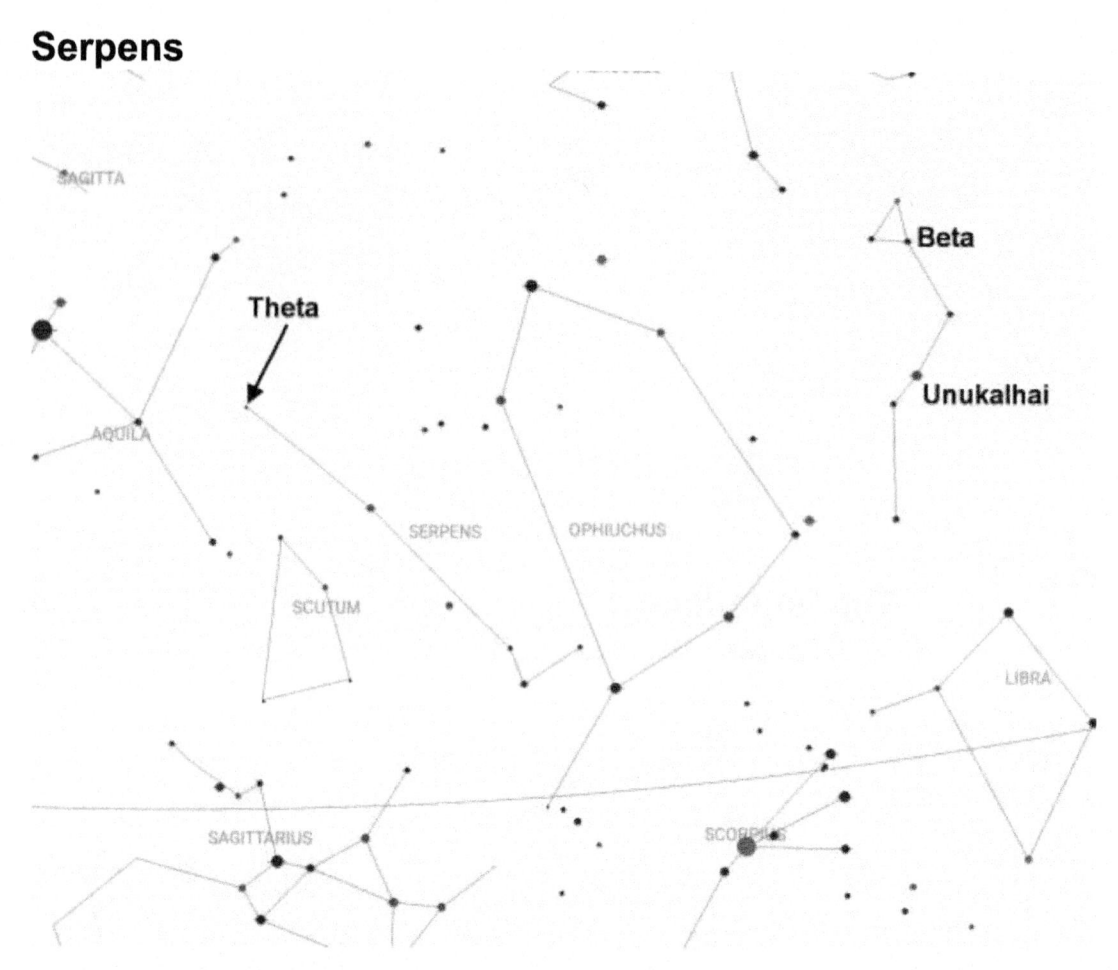

Serpens, the Serpent, is unique in that it's the only constellation that's actually divided in half. To the west is Serpens Caput, representing the head of the serpent, while to east is Serpens Cauda which represents its tail.

Between the two halves is Ophiuchus, the appropriately named Serpent Bearer who is often depicted as carrying the serpent as it curls around him.

Ophiuchus is said to represent Asclepius, a healer who learnt to resurrect the dead after witnessing a snake revive a recently deceased serpent using herbs. Given that snakes habitually shed their skins, it's not surprising that snakes were associated with rebirth in ancient Greece.

For many years Serpens did not officially exist and its stars were counted among those of the Ophiuchus himself. It wasn't until the 1920's that the constellation was finally recognized by the International Astronomical Union as it officially defined the constellations.

If you were to combine both halves of the constellation, it would cover more than 600 square degrees of sky, ranking it 23rd in size. It has several reasonably bright stars, with the brightest, at magnitude 2.6, being Alpha.

This star is a part of Serpens Caput, representing the head of the serpent, and sometimes goes by the name Unukalhai, from the Arabic for "the serpent's neck."

An orange giant star, some 75 light years away, it's nearly five times more massive than the Sun and is roughly 38 times more luminous.

Once you find Unukalhai, you can use it to find Messier 5, the constellation's brightest globular cluster. At magnitude 5.7, it lies at the edge of naked eye visibility but sharp-eyed observers may be able to glimpse it under dark skies.

As with all globulars, it's better observed with a telescope but it may still be glimpsed with binoculars. With Alpha on the edge of your field of view, look for 10 Serpentis, a magnitude 5.2 star, on the opposite edge. Place that star in the middle of your field of view and M5 can be glimpsed to the west with 5 Serpentis just slightly to the south-east.

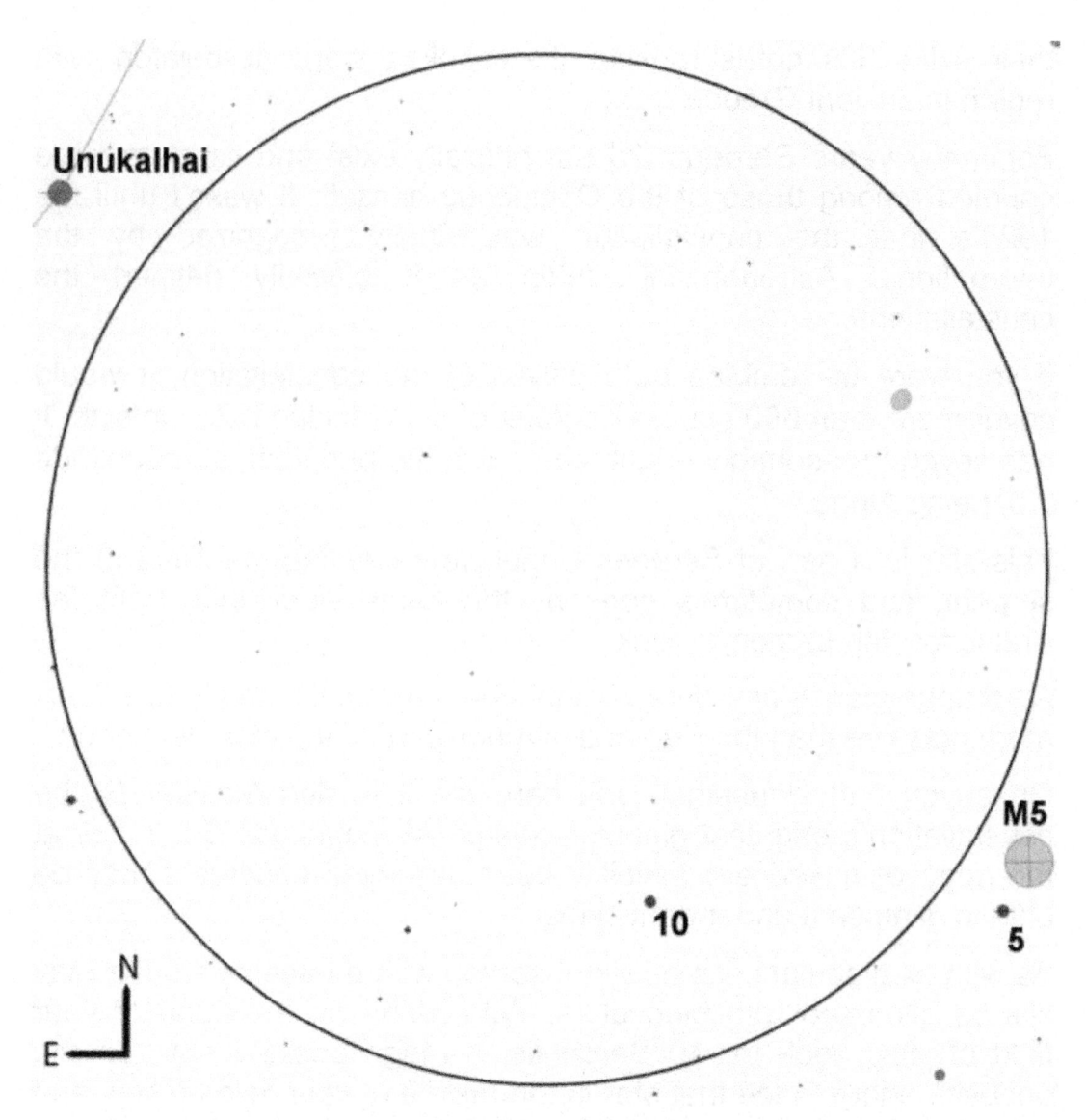

Unukalhai, 10 Serpentis and Messier 5, binocular view.

Meanwhile, further north of Unukalhai is Beta Serpentis, one of the stars that forms an asterism representing the serpent's head. A magnitude 3.7 white star, binoculars will reveal a close, fainter, magnitude 6.7 star just to the north of it.

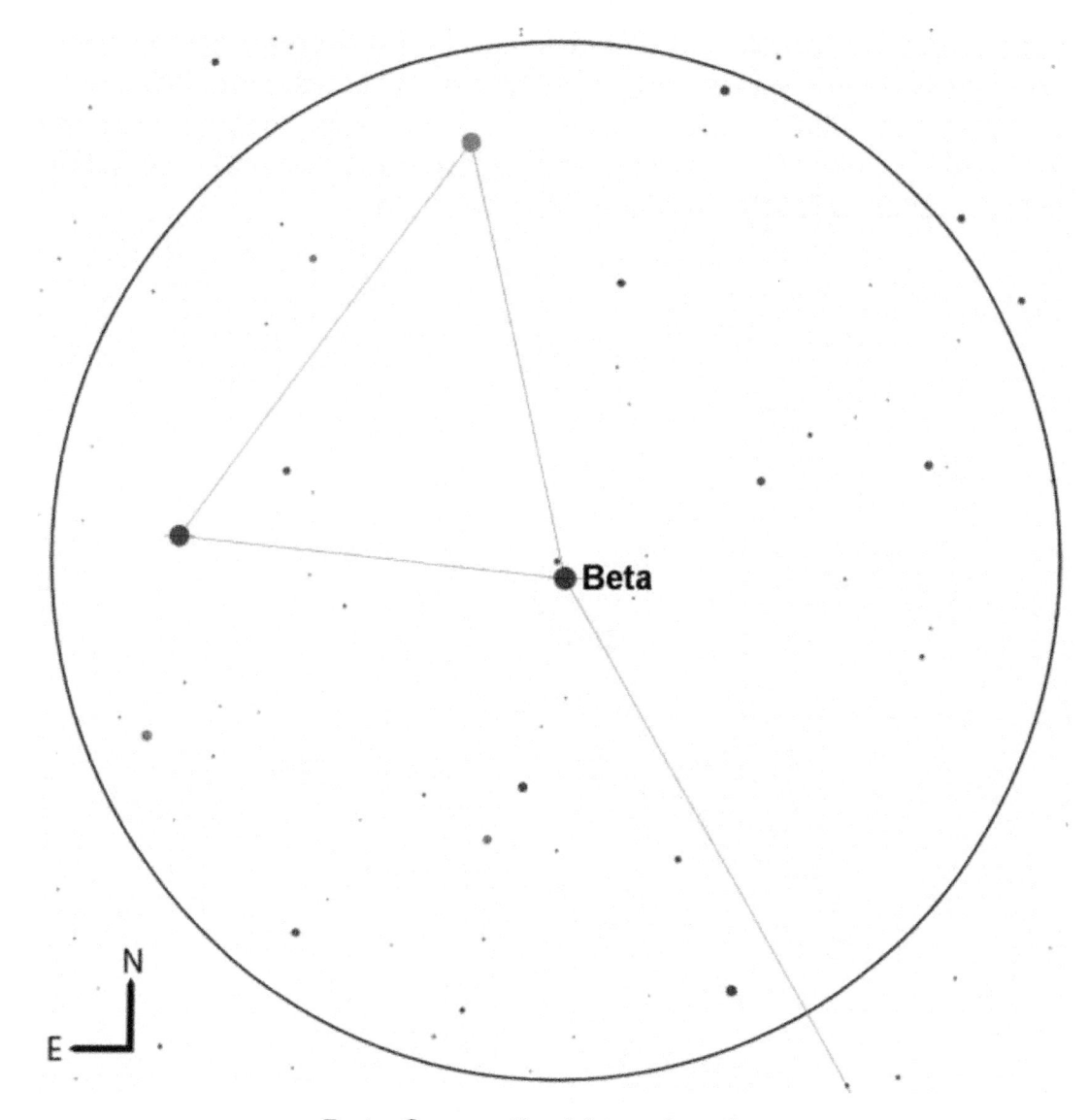

Beta Serpentis, binocular view.

Heading east to Serpens Cauda, we come to Theta Serpentis, a magnitude 4.1 star found just to the west of Aquila, the Eagle. Like Beta, binoculars will also show a close but faint magnitude 6.7 companion just to the north-east.

Lastly, just to the south of Theta and within the same field of view, you'll also see a wider and brighter pair of white stars of slightly unequal magnitude. Can you see a faint star between them? Whether you choose to scan Caput or Cauda with binoculars, either side promises a fascinating and full field of stars.

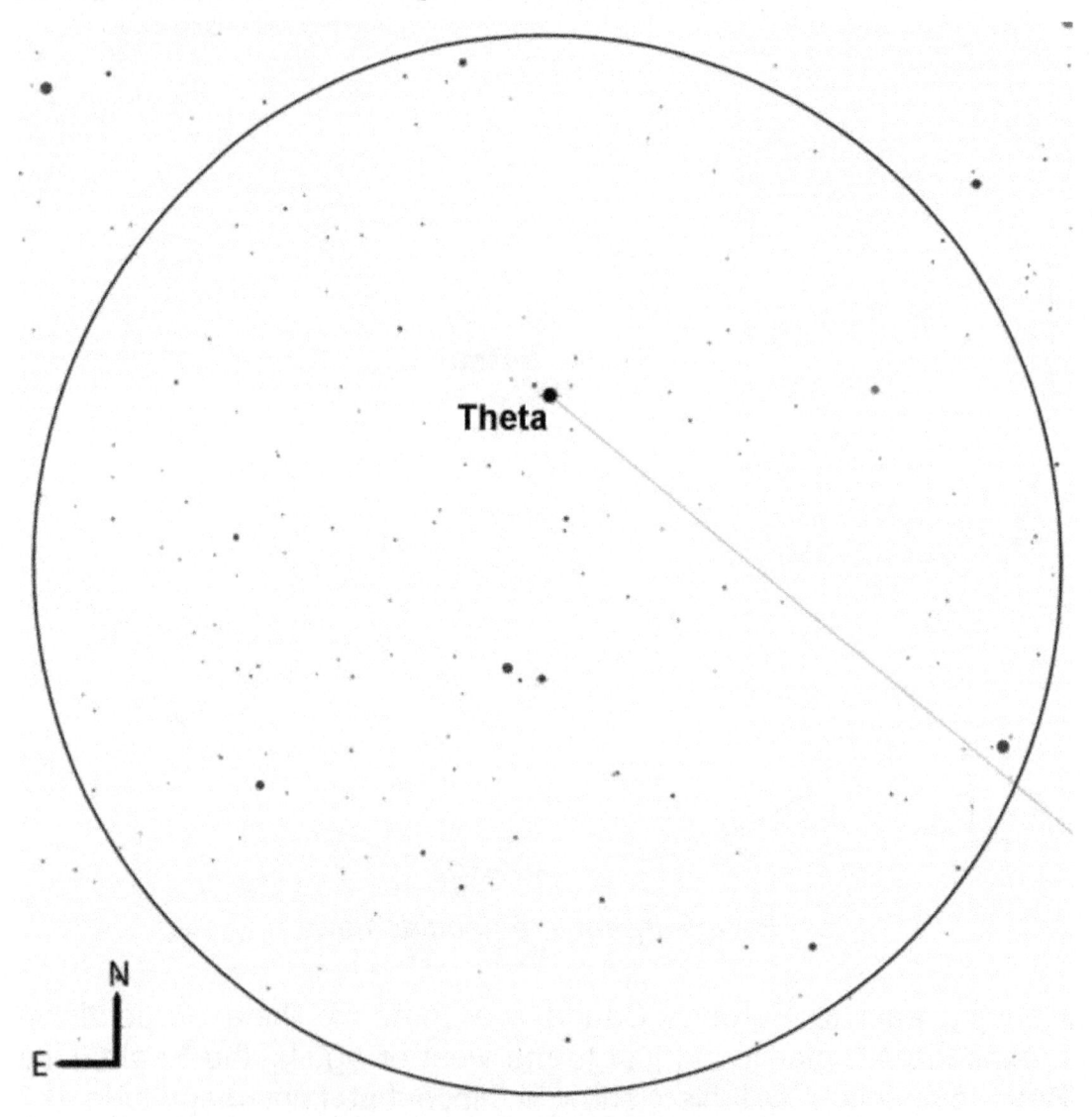

Theta Serpentis, binocular view.

Taurus

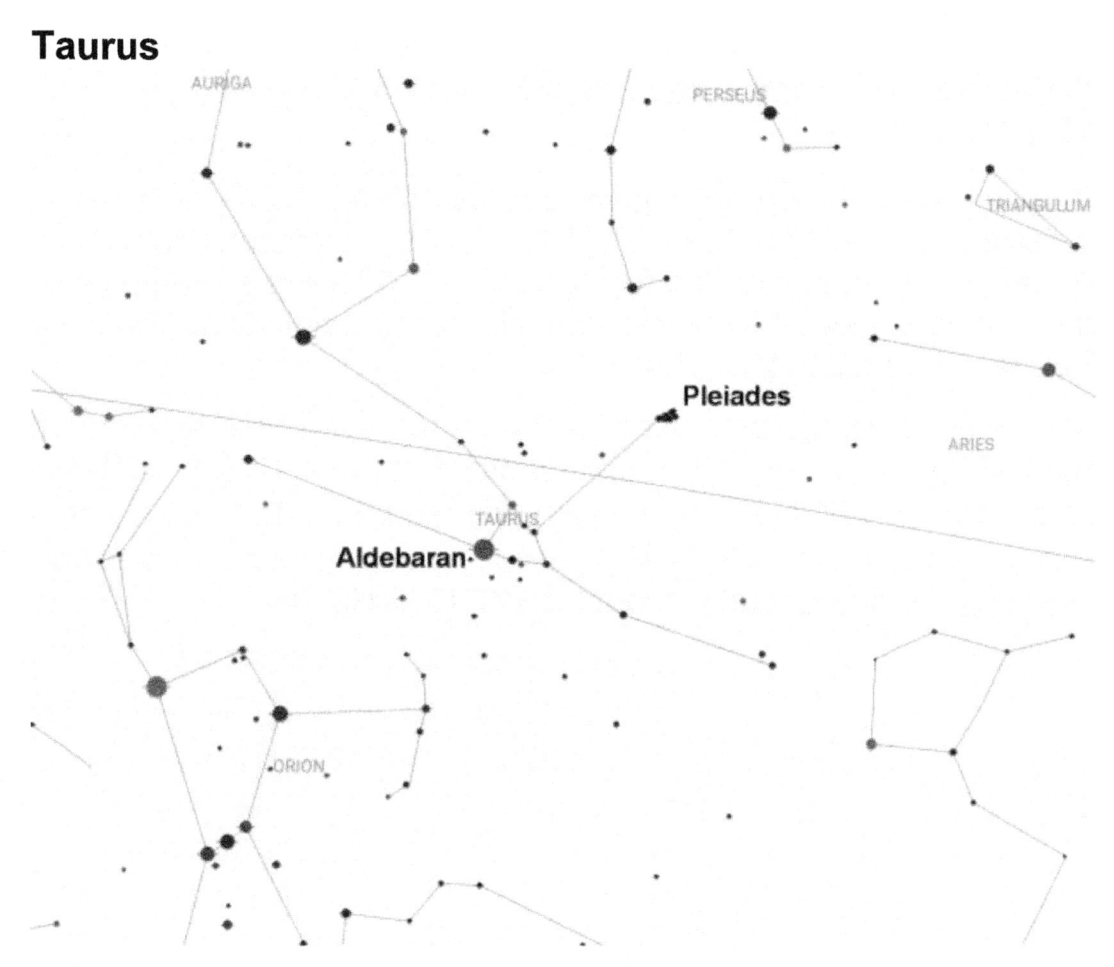

Taurus, one of twelve signs of the zodiac, is one of the largest constellations and certainly one of the brightest. It's been known and associated with a bull for thousands of years and across numerous ancient civilizations, including the Mesopotamians, Egyptians and, of course, the Greeks who linked it to several legends.

In one, Zeus became infatuated with Europa, a beautiful princess from Phoenicia. Turning himself into a bull, he hid himself amongst her father's cattle and after she had climbed upon his back, carried her away.

It's often depicted on older star charts as stampeding toward Orion the hunter, who can be seen raising his club and shield to defend himself against it.

Taurus covers nearly 800 square degrees of sky and is ranked 17th in size. Its brightest star is Alpha, more commonly known as Aldebaran, from the Arabic for "the follower." This is a reference to the Pleaides (see below) as the star rises after (and therefore "follows") that bright star cluster.

This famous orange giant star marks the red eye of the bull and, at magnitude 0.9, is the 14th brightest star in the sky. It's a relatively close star, only 65 light years away, and like many giant stars, could easily swallow the Sun. In fact, despite being about 45 times the radius of the Sun it is only about 50% more luminous.

Aldebaran, binocular view.

You'll notice that Aldebaran appears at the tip of a V shaped cluster of stars, known as the Hyades. This cluster represents the head of the bull and can be easily observed with the unaided eye, but the best way to enjoy them is with a pair of binoculars. It presents a very attractive sight through a pair of 10x50's and nicely fills the view.

Scanning the area will reveal a multitude of blue-white stars, including several doubles and most notably Theta Tauri. As a challenge, try spotting this double with just your eyes.

Although Aldebaran appears at the edge of the Hyades, it's not actually a member of the group as the cluster is about 90 light years further away.

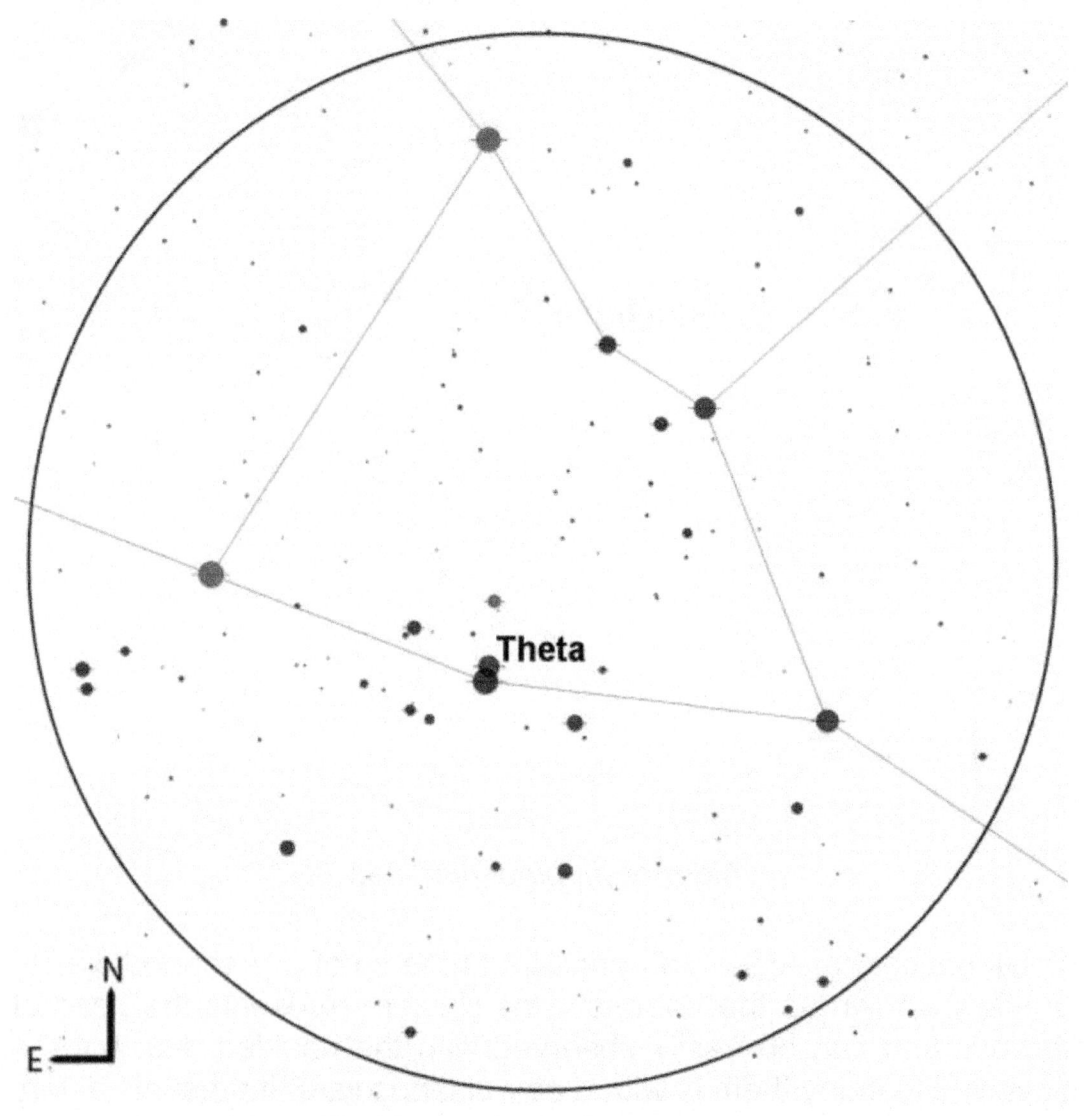

The Hyades, binocular view.

Taurus is home to another well-known open cluster, the Pleiades or Seven Sisters. Easily seen with the naked eye, these stars have been noted and observed by civilizations for thousands of years.

They appear as a tiny group of blue-white stars, like a miniature Delphinus - but how many can you see with only your eyes? Despite being also known as the Seven Sisters, many people will only see six stars, leading astronomers to wonder if one of them has faded over the intervening millennia. (See Ursa Major for a possible answer!)

Like the Hyades, this cluster is best observed with binoculars and a good pair of 10x50's can provide a stunning view – better, in fact, than a telescope, because the entire cluster will easily fit within the field of view. The Pleiades is one of the not-to-be-missed night sky sights and there are very few astronomers who'll go through the night without giving it at least a passing glance!

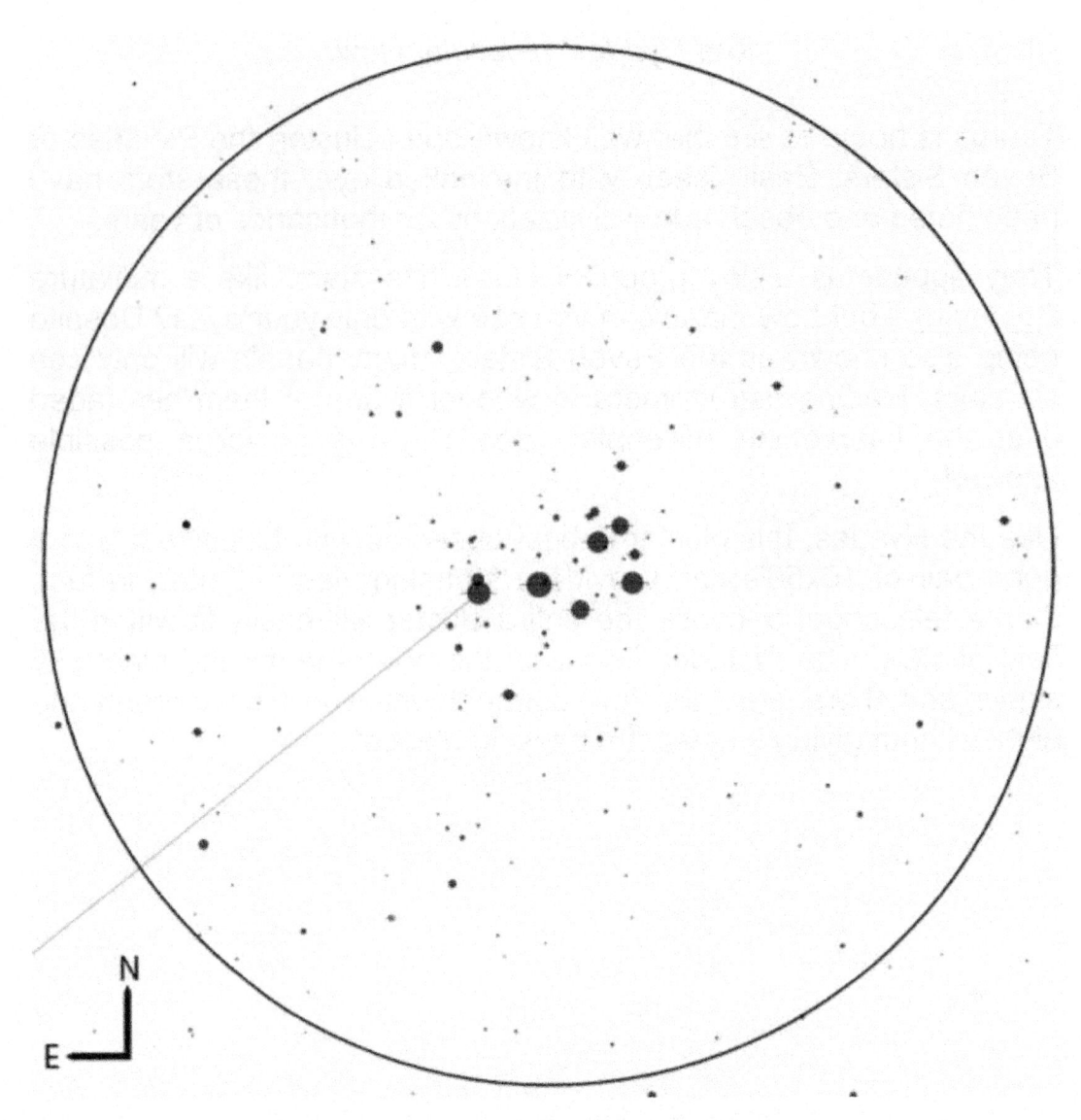

The Pleiades, binocular view.

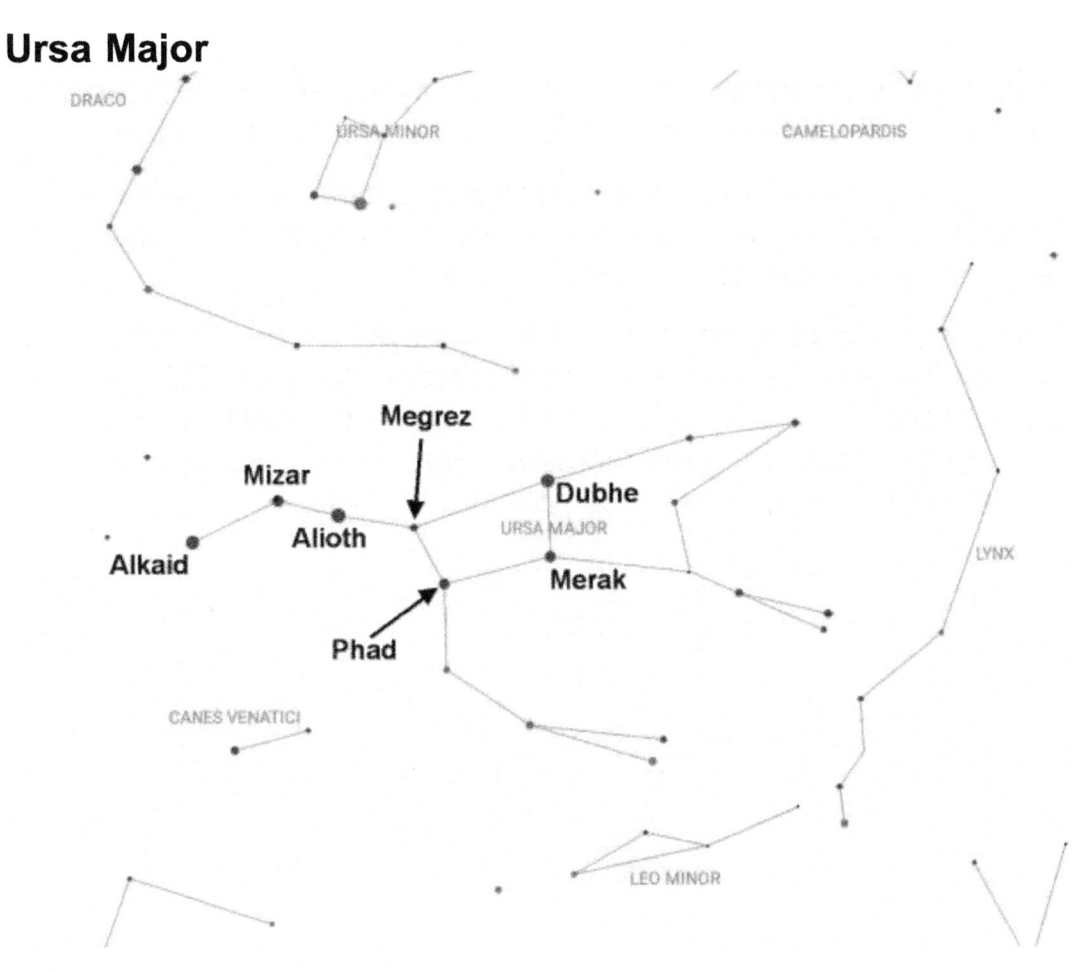

Ursa Major

Ursa Major, the Great Bear, is one of the best known constellations in the entire night sky and is also one of the largest. Third only to Hydra and Virgo, it covers nearly 1,300 square degrees and its stars have been linked to myths and legends across a number of cultures around the world.

To the Greeks, the constellation represents Callisto, a beautiful woman and another of Zeus's potential love interests. Learning of his intentions to seduce the woman, Zeus's wife Hera turned Callisto into a bear. Callisto's son, Arcas, unaware of his mother's fate, sees the bear while hunting and is about to shoot his arrow when Zeus intervenes. Transforming Arcas into a second bear, he immortalized them by placing them among the stars in the sky. Arcas becomes Ursa Minor, the Little Bear while his mother is now Ursa Major.

Its seven brightest stars are circumpolar, meaning they never dip below the horizon for many observers in the northern hemisphere and appear to circle about the pole instead.

These stars form a famous asterism known as the Plough in the United Kingdom and the Big Dipper in North America. This asterism can be used to find other bright stars and constellations (see here) and even many non-astronomers know the westernmost stars (Merak and Dubhe) point to the pole star, Polaris.

The Big Dipper / Plough asterism.

Its brightest star is Epsilon, also known as Alioth, curiously derived from the Arabic for "fat tail of a sheep!" This magnitude 1.8 star is about three times more massive than the Sun, lies at about 82 light years away and may have an undiscovered low mass companion.

However, almost without question, the most interesting sight out of the seven brightest stars is Zeta, also known as Mizar, from the Arabic for "waistband." This magnitude 2.3 star has a close magnitude 4.0 companion, known as Alcor, that should be a relatively easy target for observers without optical aid – even under suburban skies.

A number of ancient cultures have legends and stories associated with them. To the Greeks, Alcor represented the lost Pleiad, Electra (see here), which helps to explain why, despite being known as the Seven Sisters, many observers can only see six stars in the Pleiades star cluster.

The pair make for a nice sight in binoculars with Mizar appearing about twice as bright as Alcor. A small telescope at low power will reveal that Mizar itself can be split into two components. In reality, Mizar and Alcor are unrelated with Alcor being about 82 light years away and Mizar being about five light years further.

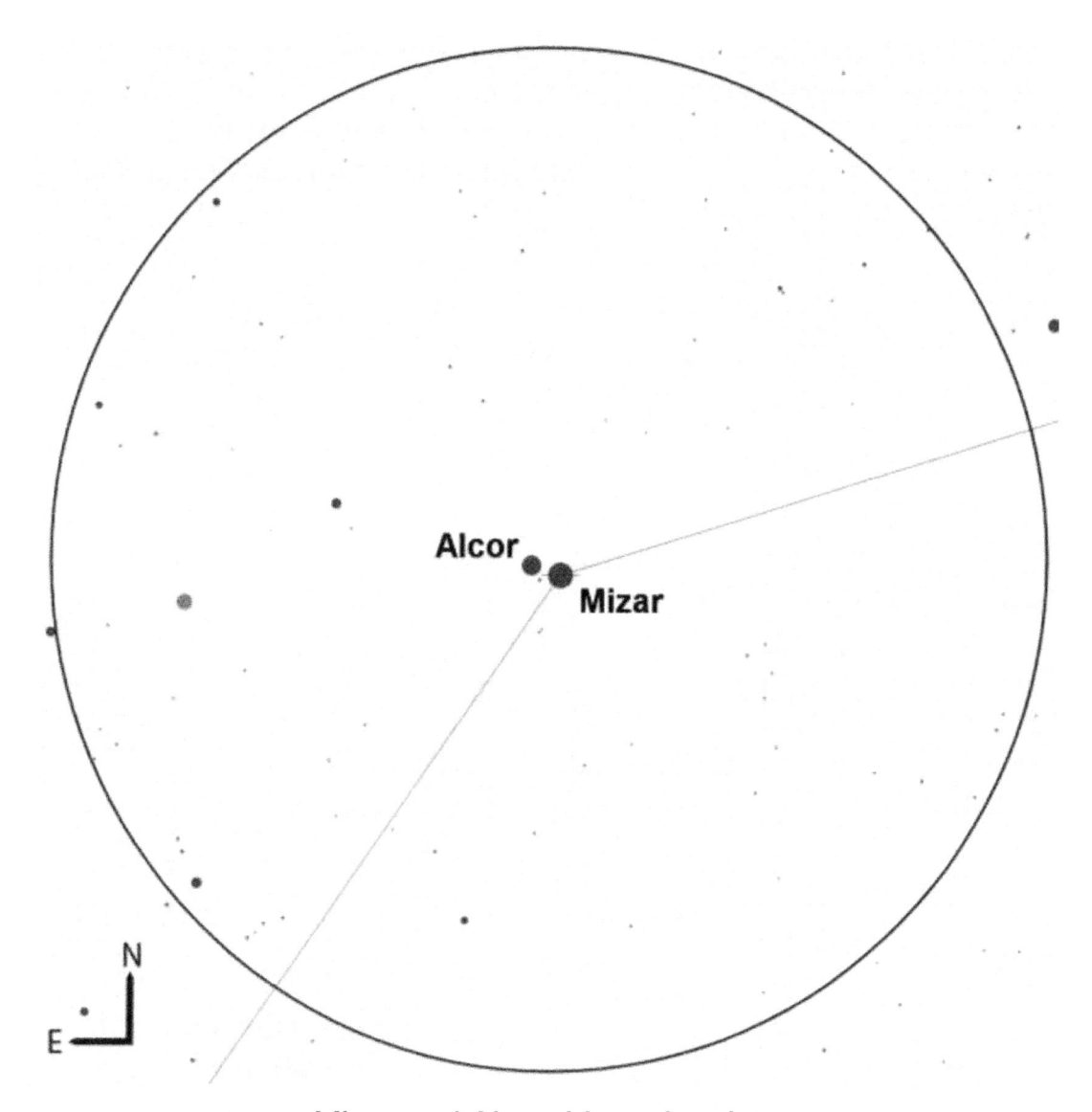

Mizar and Alcor, binocular view.

Now find the end of the great bear's tail, marked by the magnitude 1.9 star, Eta. Better known as Alkaid, this star serves as a useful marker to help you find Messier 51, the Whirlpool Galaxy.

Technically, this belongs in the constellation of Canes Venatici but it's easiest found by starting with Alkaid. Look out for 24 Canum Venaticorum; it forms a triangle with Alkaid and M51, which should appear as a small, faint misty circle within the same binocular field of view.

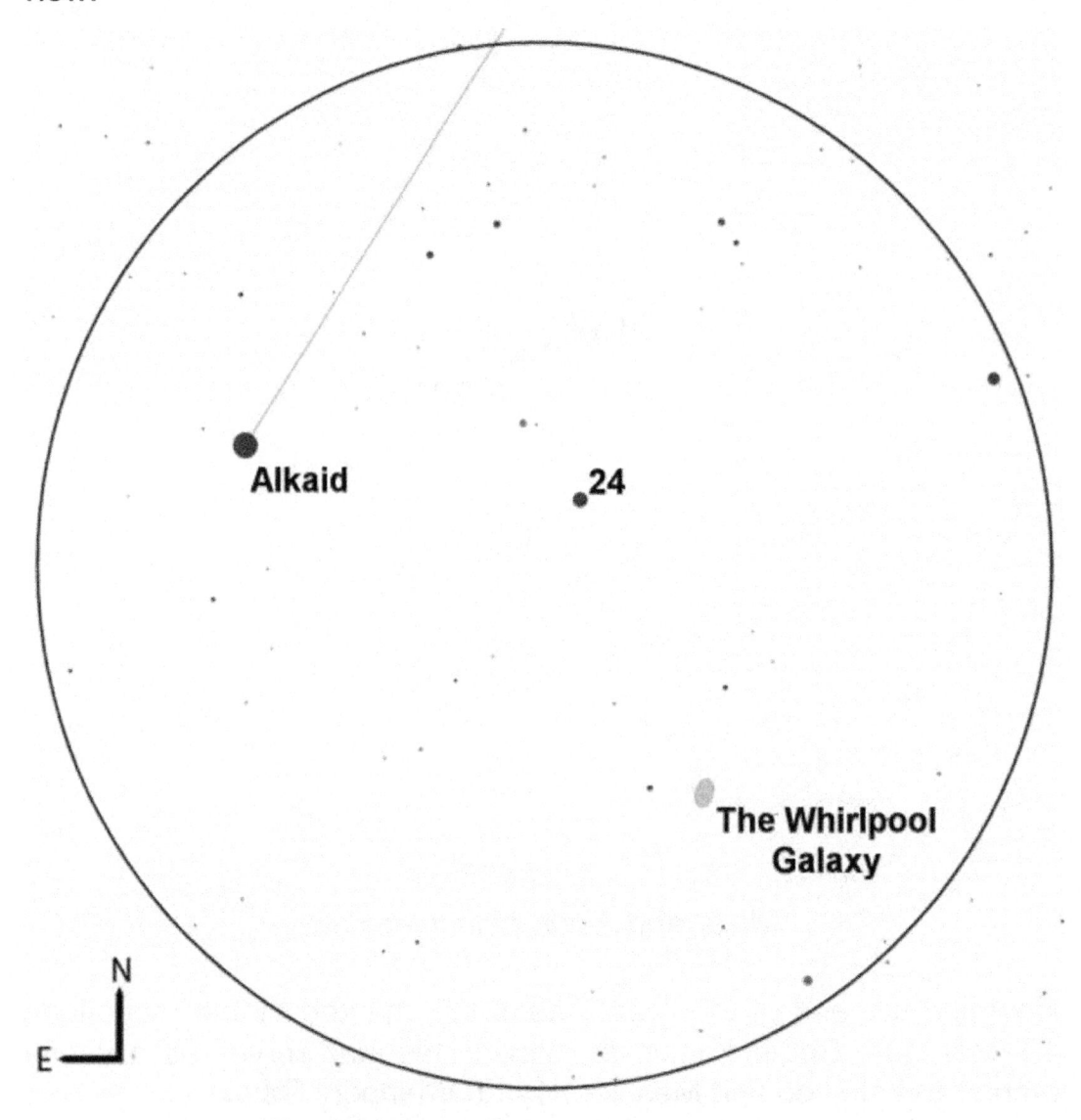

The Whirlpool Galaxy, binocular view.

Ursa Minor

Less well known than Ursa Major is its smaller counterpart, Ursa Minor, the Little Bear. Also known as the Little Dipper in North America, the constellation is most commonly linked to the legend of Callisto and Arcas (see here) but there's an alternate version.

In this story, the two constellations represent the bears that hid the infant god Zeus from his father, Cronus. When Zeus grew older, he rewarded the pair by immortalizing them as stars in the night sky.

This story has the virtue of explaining the long tails of the bears – especially in the case of Ursa Minor – as Zeus was said to have thrown the bears towards the heavens by their tails when he immortalized them.

There's little to see here but, like Pegasus, the constellation can be used to gauge your sky conditions. Of the seven stars that form the constellation, only two (Polaris and Kocab) are brighter than magnitude 3 and four are fainter than magnitude four.

Can you see Eta? At magnitude 4.9, this is the faintest of the group while the other stars range from 4.2 to 4.4.

At the other end of the scale is Alpha, the brightest star in the constellation. As many people know, it's more popularly known as Polaris because it appears almost directly over the Earth's north pole. It never noticeably moves and always marks north (at least in our lifetime and for the foreseeable future) and has been used as a navigation aid for millennia. You can easily find it by drawing a line through Merak and Dubhe in Ursa Major.

Glowing at a modest magnitude 2.0, Polaris is a double star, split with a small telescope, and slightly variable. It lies about 350 light years away.

Take a look with binoculars; you might not see its true companion, but you should still see another, fainter white star close to it. This star should easily be visible, even from suburban skies.

Both Polaris and this companion form part of a faint circle of stars, which will prove harder to spot from suburbia. Polaris is the brightest star in the circle thereby giving the asterism its popular name of "the engagement ring" with Polaris as its diamond.

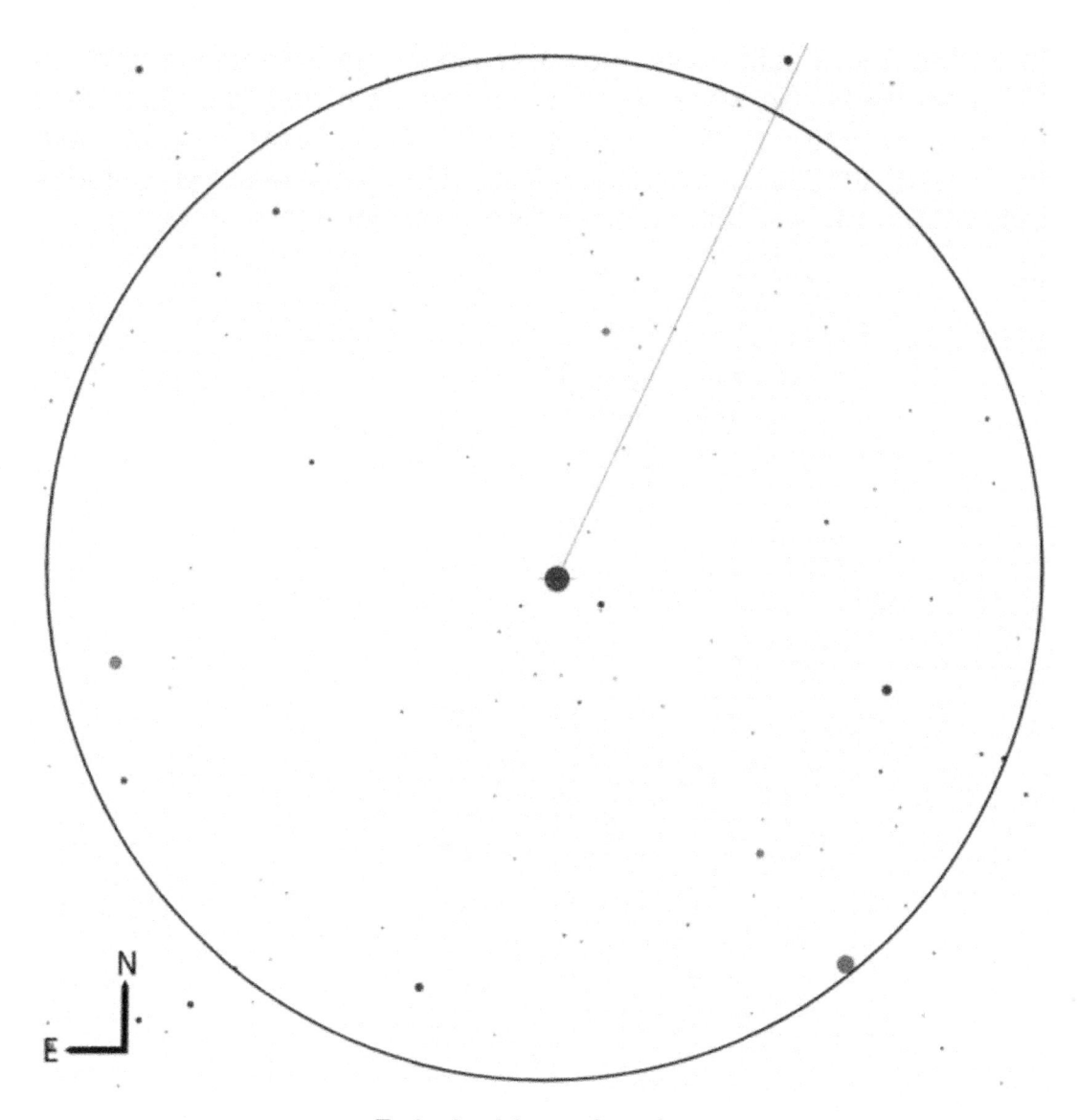

Polaris, binocular view.

After enjoying the view, move down to Beta and Gamma at the bottom of the constellation. Respectively, these are the second and third brightest stars of Ursa Minor and shine at magnitudes 2.1 (Beta) and 3.1 (Gamma.)

With Beta more commonly known as Kocab and Gamma known as Pherkad, these two stars are also sometimes called "the Guardians of the Pole" and can always be seen to circle Polaris from the vast majority of the northern hemisphere. (Only observers at latitudes below 20° north will see the stars disappear below the horizon.)

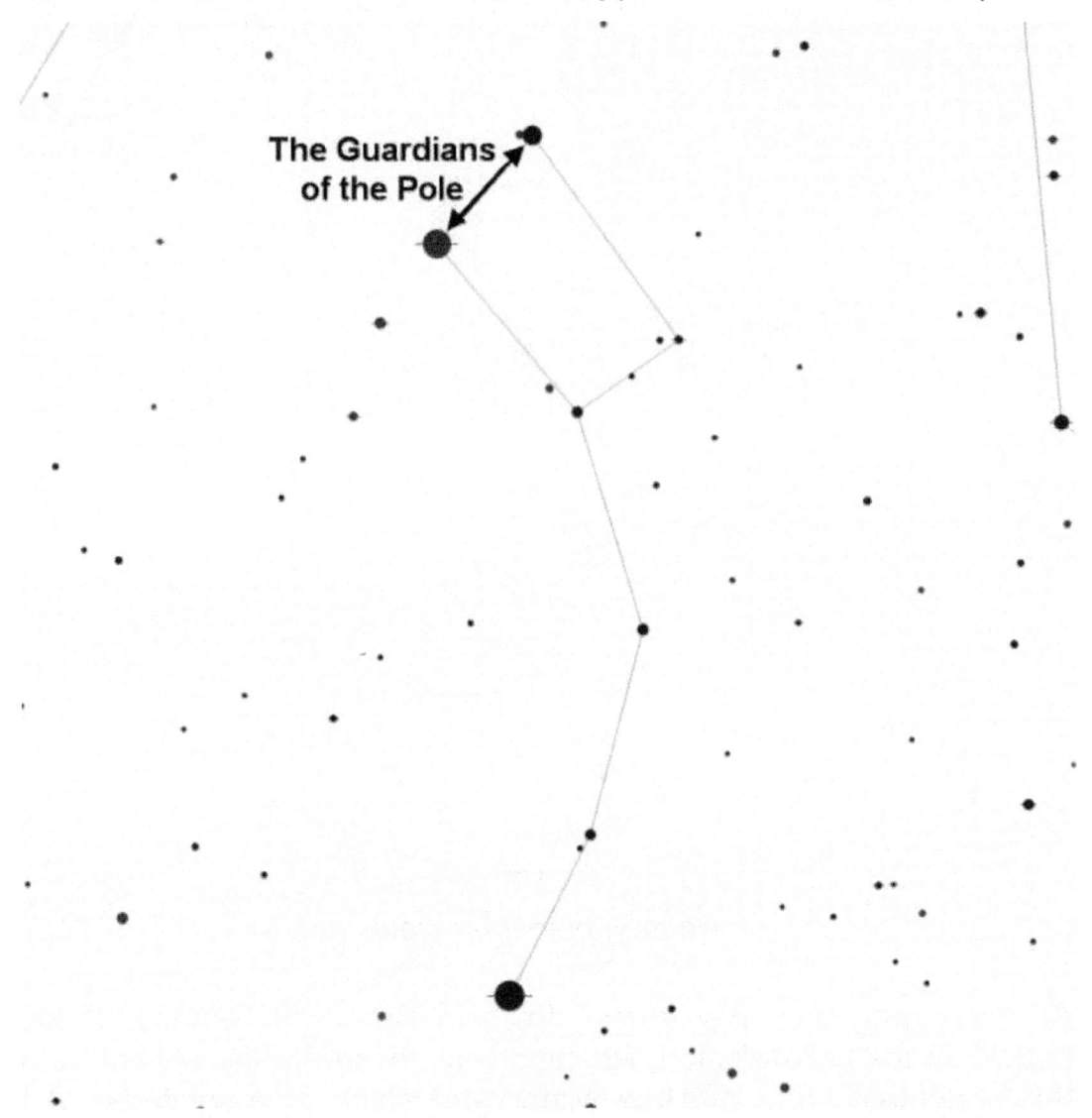

The Guardians of the Pole

Lastly, binoculars will reveal a magnitude 5 companion close to Pherkad while sci-fans might consider Kochab (Beta Ursa Minoris) to be the home of *The Hitchhiker's Guide to the Galaxy.*

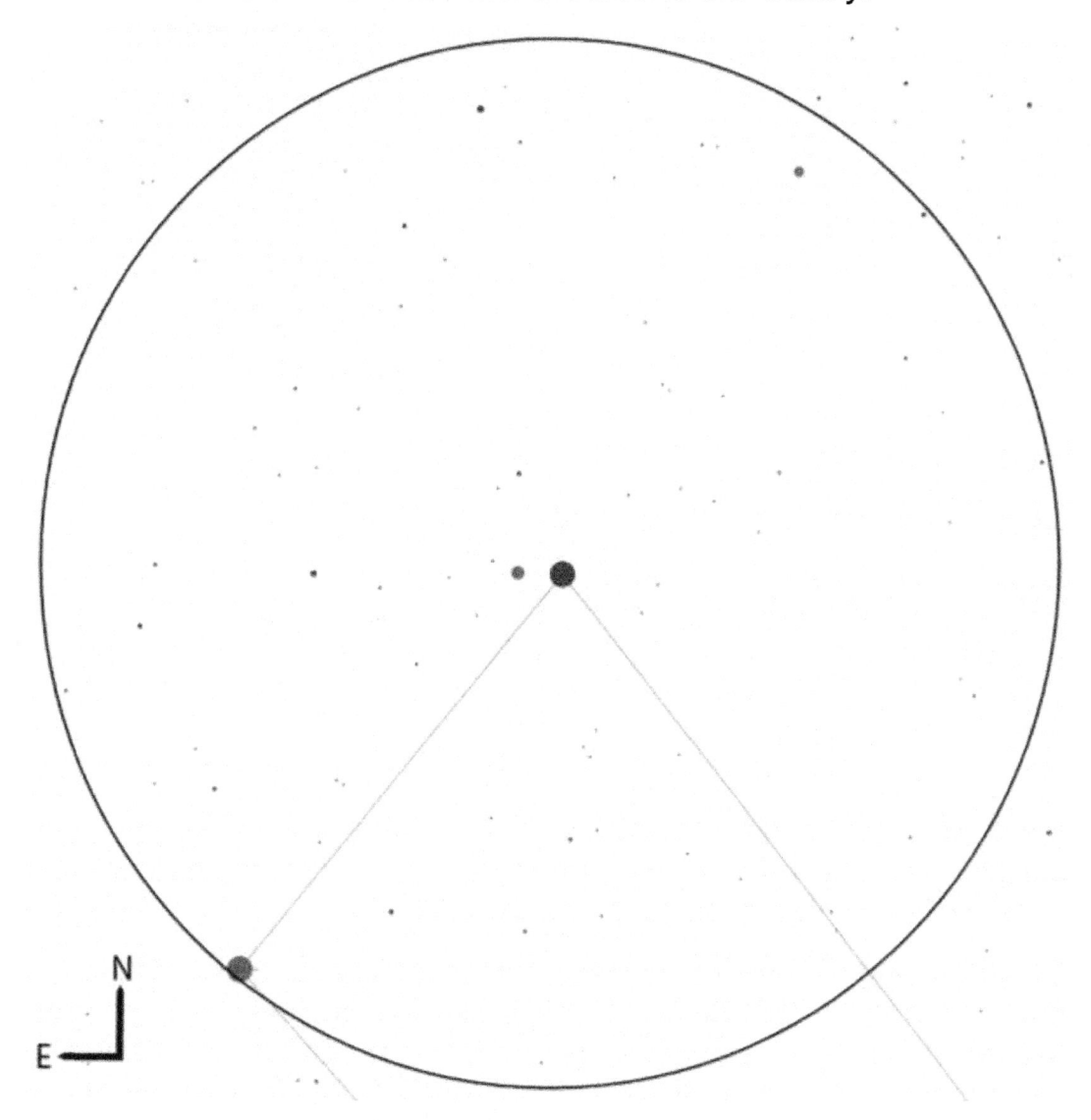

Pherkad, binocular view.

Virgo

Virgo, one of the twelve signs of the zodiac, covers nearly 1,300 square degrees of sky and, after Hydra, is the second largest constellation. (Virgo is only nine degrees smaller.)

Despite being associated with agriculture across different cultures, it has no strong mythological connections. The ancient Greeks linked the constellation to Demeter, the goddess of wheat and harvests, and on older star charts the maiden is depicted as holding an ear of grain.

This depiction is epitomized in the naming of its brightest star, Spica, whose name is derived from the Latin for "ear of grain." The 15th brightest star in the sky, it shines at magnitude 1.0 and is easily found by using the three stars that form the tail of Ursa Major (see here for more details and a graphic.)

Spica is a double star system where the components are so close they're actually egg-shaped (and therefore indivisible with amateur telescopes.) This pair of blue giants orbit one another every four days and lie at a distance of about 250 light years.

Virgo is also home to a number of exoplanet star systems and an entire swarm of galaxies. Unfortunately, the galaxies may be hard for binocular beginners to spot and the exoplanets are beyond every amateur's reach!

Arc Down to Arcturus and Speed On to Spica!

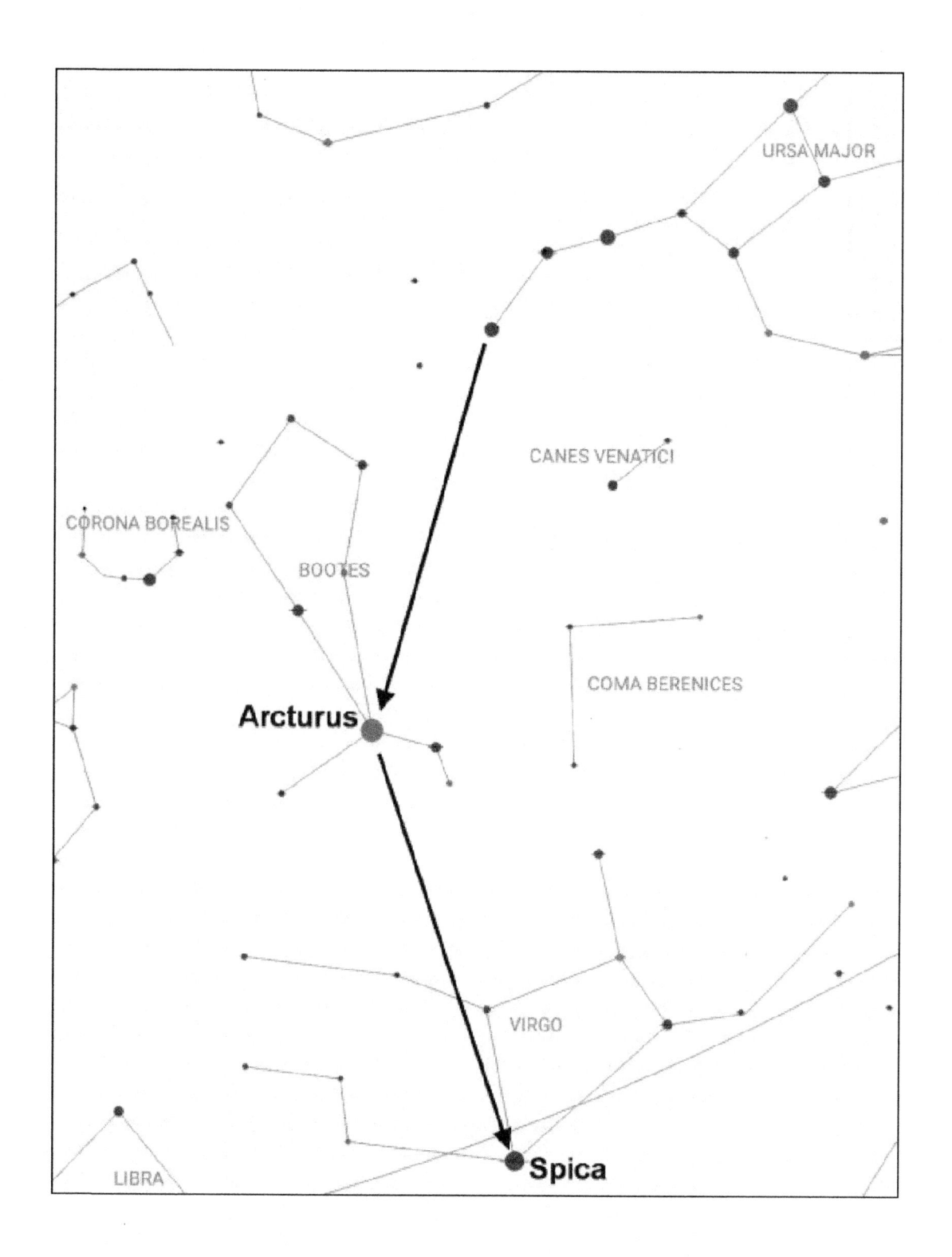

Here's a well-known and handy way to find Spica using the stars of the spring sky. We can follow the tail of Ursa Major, the Great Bear and curve down to ruddy Arcturus, the brightest star in Boötes.

Next, continue the line toward the south until you come to white Spica, the brightest star in constellation of Virgo, the Virgin. Hence the popular phrase "arc down to Arcturus and speed on to Spica!"

The Summer Triangle

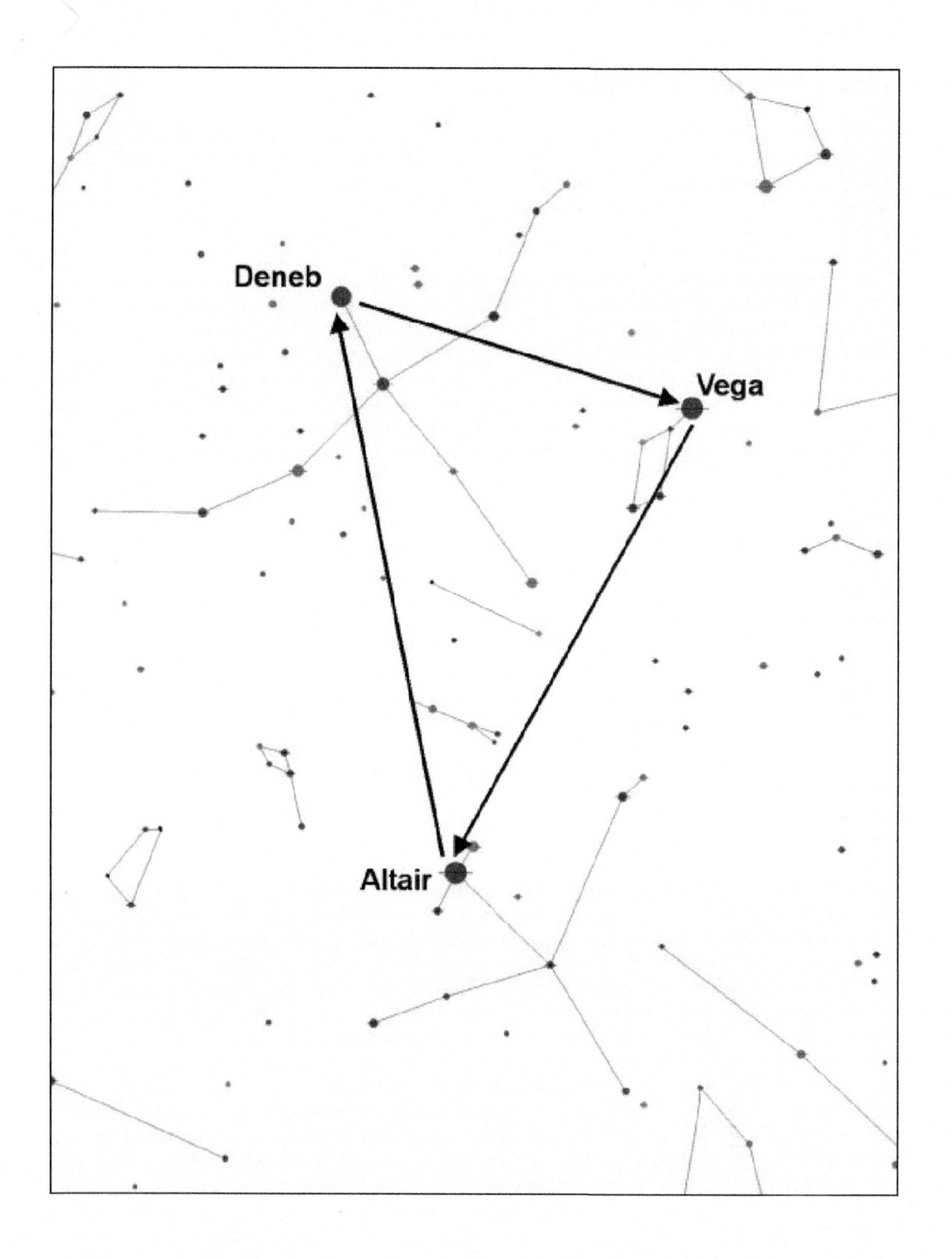

The Summer Triangle is a well known sight for astronomers across the world and features three of the sky's brightest stars. Brilliant Vega in Lyra, the brightest star in the northern celestial hemisphere, shines at magnitude 0.0 and forms the most easterly point of the triangle. Deneb in Cygnus marks it's north-eastern point while Altair in Aquila lies to the south.

Appendix

The Greek Alphabet

Alpha	α
Beta	β
Gamma	γ
Delta	δ
Epsilon	ε
Zeta	ζ
Eta	η
Theta	θ
Iota	ι
Kappa	κ
Lambda	λ
Mu	μ
Nu	ν
Xi	ξ
Omicron	ο
Pi	π
Rho	ρ
Sigma	σ
Tau	τ
Upsilon	υ
Phi	φ
Chi	χ
Psi	ψ
Omega	ω

Recommended Resources

Printed in Great Britain
by Amazon